KEY TO

The Ancient Parish Registers

OF

ENGLAND & WALES

Cristenynges In Januarij a° Henrici
octavi vp a° dm 1538

The ffirst day   Rogardus Conihy
The iij day   Robius Lord
The v day   Alicia Colvns
                        Alicia Clark

The vij day   Thomas Barnet
The viij day   Agnes Norman
The xij day   Carolus Baryngtvon
The vij day   Joanna Lamberty
                        Johannes Gervet
                        Robius Whyat
The xvij day   Joanna Tomsby
The xviij day   Rose Nysk
The xxj day   Suga worsma
The xxij day   Dorathia patonsh

Cristenynges in ffebruary
Anno supradicto

The ij day   Johannes Daves
                        Johannes Phip
The iiij day   Jeromina Ball
The vij day   Robius Symkyns
The ix day   Agnes cory
                        Antgonius Lamberd
The x day   Katherina Vask
The vij day   Rogardus ffarr
The xxij day   Johannes ffarkford bp
The xvij day   Anna Day
The xx day   Johannes Smyth

A.D. 1538-9.
FACSIMILE OF THE FIRST PAGE IN THE REGISTER BOOK
FOR St. MARGARET'S PARISH, WESTMINSTER.

KEY TO

𝕿𝖍𝖊 𝕬𝖓𝖈𝖎𝖊𝖓𝖙
𝕻𝖆𝖗𝖎𝖘𝖍 𝕽𝖊𝖌𝖎𝖘𝖙𝖊𝖗𝖘

OF

ENGLAND & WALES

BY

ARTHUR MEREDYTH BURKE

CLEARFIELD

Originally published:
London, 1908

Reprinted by Genealogical Publishing Co., Inc.
Baltimore, Maryland, 1962, 1971

Library of Congress Catalog Card Number 62-6577

Reprinted for Clearfield Company by
Genealogical Publishing Company
Baltimore, Maryland, 1989, 1996, 2000, 2012

ISBN 978-0-8063-0445-8

Made in the United States of America

PREFACE.

THE object of this work is to provide those who have reason to consult the Parish Registers with an easy and reliable guide as to the accessibility or otherwise of these national records ; and, although the introductory chapter, which treats of the subject from the historical aspect, may possess an interest for the general reader, the book is primarily designed to afford such practical information as is likely to be of service to the intending searcher.

In the performance of my task no available source of information has been unexplored, and it is hoped that the Annotated Index, which shows at a glance the date of the earliest entry in every Parish Register in England and Wales, and in which every transcript that has been printed is noted, will prove by its usefulness that my labours have not been in vain. I am only too conscious of the shortcomings of this publication, but can at least plead that I have honestly endeavoured, at a sacrifice of much time and labour, to compile a work which may be both of some historical interest and of some real value to the genealogist.

I have to express my grateful thanks to the Bishops and Clergy throughout the country for information on various points or for kind permission to inspect the ancient records in their custody. I am particularly indebted to Canon Hensley Henson, Rector of St. Margaret's Church, Westminster, who has not only granted me access to the historical registers of his parish, but has also allowed me to illustrate this volume with extracts from them.

I have only to add that I shall be much obliged to anyone who will point out my omissions, or correct my mistakes, and that it will give me much pleasure to afford any further information in my power to those who consult this work.

A. M. BURKE.

1, Cloisters, Temple.

London, 6th March 1908.

THE
PARISH REGISTERS.

"Every parish must have a history, every parish
has a register, every person has a parish."—*Stubbs.*

N UMEROUS causes, and none more than the Civil War and
the usurpation of Oliver Cromwell, have combined to
render incomplete the series of Parochial Registers ; but still, despite
their many deficiencies, they are invaluable to the family historian
for the clues they afford ; and it is much to be regretted that so
little has been done by the Legislature to secure the safe custody
of these national records, which, it should be pointed out to those
unacquainted with the subject, remain to this day in the hands
of the local clergy.

It may be readily admitted that many incumbents guard and
cherish their Registers with loving care and scrupulous attention,
and many of them, indeed, have been at the pains to restore them
most admirably ; but other Registers have not been so fortunate

in their guardians.   The documents are kept for the most part in
the parish church, and may be daily liable, in spite of "sure
coffers," to the cold and damp which the parishioners not infrequently experience and suffer from perhaps once a week.   Moreover,
they are exposed to the danger of fire, loss, or theft.   In some
cases they are preserved at the parsonage, where, besides liability to
the risks above alluded to, it has unfortunately happened in many
instances that they have been sold to the highest bidder at the death
of the incumbent, and it was stated in evidence before a Select
Committee of the House of Commons that a certain rector "used
to direct his pheasants with the parchment of the old registers."
Another clergyman, in Worcestershire, detected an individual, who
had been given access to the Registers, "with his mouth full of
parchment, nearly chewed to pieces."   Many, indeed, have been the
disasters that have befallen these precious and irreplaceable records.
Even the bare recital of their vicissitudes, the story of hairbreadth
escapes, partial rescues, or total destruction, is enough to turn the
genealogist's hair white "in a single night," and to fill the antiquarian's soul with anguish.

Although the investigator of a pedigree will doubtless regard it
of more importance to know where sources of information may be
found and how to approach them than to busy himself needlessly
as to why those particular sources should happen to be in existence,
there may be some who would wish to extend their knowledge,
and for such inquiring minds it is proposed to adumbrate as
concisely as possible a short outline of the legal history of these
Registers.

In 1535, by virtue of the Act of Supremacy, Henry the Eighth
appointed Thomas, Lord Cromwell,[*] at that time Privy Seal, to

---

[*] Thomas, Baron Cromwell, afterwards Earl of Essex and Knight
of the Garter, was the son of Walter Cromwell, *alias* Smyth, a
blacksmith of Putney, Surrey.   The date of his birth is doubtful,
and little is known of his early life.   Entering the service of Cardinal
Wolsey in about 1518, he was eventually invested by Henry VIII.
with most extensive powers in ecclesiastical affairs, and became a
principal agent in the Reformation.   Having held successively the
offices of Chancellor of Exchequer, Master of the Rolls, Lord Privy
Seal, Vicar-General, and Lord High Chamberlain of England, he
ultimately fell into disfavour, and was beheaded on Tower Hill,
28th July 1540.

be his Vicar-General. Three years after his appointment Cromwell issued Injunctions* that a book and a coffer with two locks should be provided for each parish in England and Wales, and the parson of the parish was ordered to write every Sunday in the presence of the churchwardens, or one of them, and record in the book all the baptisms, marriages, and burials of the immediately preceding week. In case of neglect a fine of three shillings and fourpence was imposed, to be applied to the repair of the church.

---

* "Exhibit quinto die mensis Septebr ano dni (*domini*) Mle Vc XXXVIII.
"In the Name of God Amen. By the authorite and comission of
" the most excellent prince Henry by the grace of god kynge of
" Englonde and of frauce (*France*), defensor of the faithe Lorde of
" Irelonde, and in erthe supme (*supreme*) hedd vndre Christ of the
" church of Englonde I Thomas lorde Crumwell, lorde privie seale
" Vice-gerent to the kynges said highnes for all his Jurisdiction
" eccliasticall within this realme, do for the avancement (*advancement*)
" of the trewe honor of almighty God, encrease of vertu and dis-
" charge of the kynges (*king's*) maiestie geve and exhibite vnto yow
"   theise Iniuctions (*injunctions*) folowing to be kept obsued
" (*observed*) and fulfilled vpon the paynes hereafter declared."
     ✤   ✤   ✤   ✤   ✤   ✤
     ✤   ✤   ✤   ✤   ✤   ✤
     ✤   ✤   ✤   ✤   ✤   ✤
"Item that yow and euy (*every*) pson (*parson*) vicare or curate
" within this dioc (*diocese*) shall for euery churche kepe one boke or
" registre wherin ye shall write the day and yere of every
" weddyng christenyng and buryeng made wtin (*within*) yor pishe for
" yowr tyme, and so euy man succedyng yow lykewise. And shall
" there inserte euy psons (*persons*) name that shalbe so weddid
" christened or buried, And for the sauff keping of the same boke the
" pishe shalbe boude (*bound*) to puide (*provide*) of there comen charges
" one sure coffer with twoo lockes and keys wherof the one to remayn
" wt (*with*) you, and thother with the saide wardons, wherein the
" saide boke shalbe laide vpp. Whiche boke ye shall every sonday
" take furthe and in the psence (*presence*) of the said wardens or one of
" them write and recorde in the same all the weddinges christenynges
" and buryenges made the hole weke before. And that done to lay
" vpp the boke in the said coffer as afore And for euy tyme that the
" same shalbe omytted the partie that shalbe in the faulte therof
" shall forfett to the said churche IIIs IIIId to be emploied on the
" repation (*reparation*) of the same churche."
     ✤   ✤   ✤   ✤   ✤   ✤
     ✤   ✤   ✤   ✤   ✤   ✤
                                        Thomas Crumwell.
Endorsed. "Iniunctions devysed by the Lord Crumwell, Vice-
" gerent to the Kinge for all his Jurisdiction ecclesiasticall."
—"State Papers (Domestic)," Vol. XIII., Part II., No. 281.

From this year date the first original entries in Parish Registers, for, though some few isolated entries, purporting to belong to a prior period, are in existence, it is practically certain that all these will be found on examination to have been actually recorded after 1538.

It was natural enough, however, that this mandate of the avowed enemy of "Popery" and the instigator of innovations in religion, should have met with strong opposition, especially amongst the clergy, and that failure to comply with the order was of constant occurrence. Meetings of protest were held in various parts of the country, and the prevailing idea seems to have been that the real object in view was to levy a tax on all christenings, marriages, and burials.* The following letters addressed to Thomas Cromwell, in 1539, have been preserved amongst the State Papers, and are curious and interesting examples of the alarm that was felt at the time.

"Sir Piers Eggecomb† to Cromwell.‡

"Plesse it ywr goode Lordshyp to be advertyssyd that
"the Kynggs Maiesty hath commandyd me, at my beynge
"in hys gracius presens, that in casse I parceyvyd any
"grugge or myscontentacyon a mongge hys sojectes, I
"shulde ther off advertysse yovr Lordeshyp by my wry-
"tynge. Hyt ys now comme to my knolegge this 20
"daye of Apryll, by a ryght trew honest man, a servant
"off myn, that ther ys moche secrett and severall com-
"munycacyons amongges the Kyngges sojettes, and that many
"off them in sundry places with in the scheres off Cornwall

---

* Almost three centuries later the opposition to the first Act passed for a census of the population (41 Geo. III. c. 15, 1800) was based on the same grounds.

† Sir Piers Edgecomb (or Eggecomb) was the son of Sir Richard Edgecomb, by Joan, his wife, daughter of Thomas Tremayne, of Collacomb, co. Devon. He was one of the twenty Knights of the Bath created "on the eve of St. Andrew," 1489, and served as Sheriff of Devonshire in 1493. "For gallant behaviour," while taking part in the expedition against France in 1513, he was made a Knight Banneret. He married firstly, Jane, daughter and heiress of Stephen Durnford of East Stonehouse, co. Devon, and secondly, Catherine, daughter of Sir John St. John, and widow of Sir Griffith Ryce. He died 14th August 1539 and left issue by his first wife only.

‡ "State Papers (Domestic)," Vol. XIV., Part I., No. 815.

" and Devonsher be in greate feer and mystrust what the
" Kyngges Hyghnes and hys Conseyll schulde meane to
" geve in commaundement to the parsons and vycars off
" every parisse that they schulde make a booke, and surely
" to be kept, wher in to be specyfyyd the namys off as
" many as be weddyd, and the namys off them that be
" buryyd, and of all thoes that be crystynyd.

" Now ye maye perceyve the myndes off many what ys
" to be don, to avoyde ther unserteyn coniecturys, and to
" contynue and stablysse ther hartes in trew naturall loff
" accordynge ther dewties I refferre to yovr wyssdom. Ther
" mystrust ys that somme charges more than hath byn in
" tymys past schall growe to theym by this occacyon off
" regesstrynge of thes thyngges; wher in yff hyt schall
" please the Kyngges Maieste to put them yowte off dowte
" in my poor mynde schall encresse moche harty loff. And
" I besseche our Lorde preserve yow ever to his pleasser.

" 20th daye off Apryll. Scrybelyd in hast.

(Signed)   " P. EGGECOMB.

(Superscribed)—

" To my Lorde Privy Seall ys goode
Lordesshyp be this gevyn."

" Richard Covert and John Michell to the Lord Privy Seal
" and the Council.[*]

" To the Right honorable lorde pryvye Seale and other
" the lordes of the kynges most honorable counsell
" thys letter to be red fyrste."

" Plesyth yt your good lordeshyppes to be adveysed that
" thys daye the XIIth day of Marche an informacon wasse
" gevyn to us of certen Artycles towching the kynges highe
" maieste of wordes that shuld be spokyn by one Wyllyam
" Hole of Horsham Smyth the saide Wyllyam before some
" substancyall psons by us examyned spake and sayde these
" wordes folowyng — ther wasse come downe comyssion
" or comandement that a certen trybute or some of monye

---

[*] "State Papers (Domestic)," Vol. XIV., Part I, No. 507.

" shuld by payde to the kynges highnes for weddynges
" crystenyngs and buryalls, and that ther shuld be payde
" to the kyng for evy one of these XVd or more and to the
" lorde of the ffranches asmoch. Wheruppon we imme-
" dyatly sent for the same pson and examyned hym apon the
" saide Artycles wyche seid that he remembred not he
" spake eny suche wordes but saide that a man of Okewood
" spake suche wordes, but what he wasse he knowyth not.
" Wherefore according to the kynges highe comandement we
" have sent uppe the same Wyllyam to your lordeshyppes
" remytting thys matter to your ordre and highe dyscression
" and that these foure psons shall be at all tymes redy at
" your plesuer to recorde and testyfye evy thyng as ys
" before spoken. And Jhu psve your good lordshippes."
                                        " RICHARD COVERT."
                                        " JOHN MICHELL."

" John Marshall to Cromwell.*
        " To the Right Honerable and my synguler good lawrde
        . " my lawrde prevy seall, thys be delyvered.
        " Ryght honerable and my synguler good lawrde in my
" moste dew and humble manr soe thys ys to assure yor
" good lawrdshyp that at my laste beyng wyth my lawrde
" of Cantoburye at Lambythe hee comandyd me to wryte to
" yor lawrdshyp some letts of the mannrs and ffassyons
" of the comes and people of thes ptes as nere as I coulde
" pceve. In consederatyon where of yt maye plese yor good
" lawrdship to know thes ptes of notts shyre and lyncolns nere
" adioyneng to Newerke appon Trentte ys of these ffassyons
" as nere as I cane pceyve and moche ruled and poletykeley
" enterteyned and orderyd by the worshypfulls of thes ptes
" and in espetyall by on Sr John Marchaam knyght, and
" here ys nather beryng nor mayteyneng of no querrells nor
" revengyng of no owle matts nor males but as the law
" wyll, for men bene gladde to leve in quyetnes sferde to

---

* " State Papers (Domestic)," Vol. XIV., Part I., No. 295.

" ruffele in oulde broken matts but leve now in good
" and sober manr and charely wt wythoute pdyn glete and
" excez but under dew and moste humble obedyens ffor
" the Comens saye yt ys a good worlede ffor ye power men
" maye nowe leve in pese by the grete men, ffor now thanke
" God ther grette ruffelings ys well sowbyd and power men
" may leve in pese by them. And at suche tyme as the
" people unlernyd here of any papysts enormytes to be re-
" dressed then they alynell wysper and rounde on to another
" and blesse them therat but lyttell they saye and sowne that
" ys sonken oute of ther heddes and fforgotten and then
" they ffall to better jugements but the last acte of redresse
" ys moste in memory and when they here of another and
" new thyng to be reformyd a lyttell they wyll talke therof
" and then the owlde is clerely fforgotten. And the people
" come resonable well well forwardes in the englysh pater-
" noster and sence the unyfourme translatyon came downe
" howbeyt affore that they lyghtly estemed and regardyd yt
" nor the lernyng therof. And abbes be now nothyng
" estemed or peteyed ffor the comens saye they nowe pceyve
" more commen welthe to grow to them by theyr sup-
" pressyng then wasse affore ffor they saye many good
" ffermes and other benyfyttes come therby deyle abrode
" whych they here to ffore kepete and hadde accoumy-
" lated in grette nowmber to ther awne synguler pffetts
" and advantage sayng they where but the bellymonds and
" glottons of the world and the most xystyons psons of
" the world savyng they thynke ther ys mooste and grette
" losses of ther preers. Alsoo they moche mvell ffor what
" cosederatyon and intente the buryalls weddyngs and
" crystenyngs shuld be thus and in evy pyche churche
" recordyd and regesteryd thynkyng and fferyng that some
" paymentes schuld or myght grawe uppon them at lengthe
" to the kyngs hyghnes thereby in some ffassyon. And
" also by reson of the tresons of the lawrde Montakew
" they suspec the Bysshope Powle hys brother shulde
" make besenes on daye to all the power he maye. And
" here wasse a glasse wyndow in the Churche of Newerke
" of Thomas Bekket, but at the laste affore Crystenmes yt

" was taken downe. And some kepes the days abrogated
" workedays as men of reputatyon but many of the power
" wyll not labowr of thos days as yet. And owre valyant
" beggers be gone and all unlawffull games wyth them
" except yt be in some all alehowses that suffers men to
" playe at shuffeabourd in defaulte of the constables that
" loketh not therto as the Justes comandyth. And here ys
" nowadays noo new ffounde tales ne tydyngs amonste hus
" here but the hygh ways be here moche cryed out ppon
" and nothyng amendyd as they shulde be by the acts and
" spetyally here aboute Newerke appon Trent soo that at
" eny small fflowde no man canne passe in a myle space
" nawther by ffowte nor ppon horsbake as they myght in
" tymes not long paste wythout mrvelous grete danger
" bothe of horse and man.

    " Thus the blessed Trenyte presve yor good lawrdshypp
" in moche honor and good lyve long to endewre."

        " ffrome Sowthe Carleton the XVth deye of ffebruary
            " Yowr good lawrdshyppe's
                " humble and dayley bedeman
                    " JOHN MARSHALL."

Endorsed—
" Ao XXX JOHN MARSHALL."

Little change was made for the next sixty years. In 1547
(I Edward VI.) a similar Injunction directed that the fines should
go to the poor-box of the parish, and in 1559 (I Elizabeth) it
was enjoined that the penalty should be divided equally, one half
to the poor and the other half to the repair of the church.

In 1563 Parliament for the first time intervened, and a Bill
was read in the House of Commons " to erect an office of registership
of all the church books to be kept in every diocese," but the clergy,
ever jealous of their privileges, interposed, and the Bill was dropped,
while in 1590, the influence of the Archbishop of Canterbury* was

---

   * John Whitgift, Archbishop of Canterbury, was born at Great
Grimsby, Lincolnshire, in 1530. He was sent to Queen's College,
Cambridge, in 1548, but soon after removed to Pembroke, where he

sufficient to defeat a proposal of Lord Treasurer Burghley that there should be an annual summary of the registrations of all baptisms, marriages, and burials, in England and Wales, arranged according to counties.

The next change of any importance was made in 1597 (39 Elizabeth), when a constitution, issued by the Archbishop, bishops, and the clergy of the province of Canterbury, approved by the Queen, under the seal of Great Britain, directed the more careful preservation of parochial Registers *(quorum permagnus usus est)*, and enjoined that a copy of the records should be sent annually within a month after Easter to the Register of each diocese without fee. Certain penalties were threatened against those who disobeyed the precept.

Those copies are known as "Bishops' Transcripts," but, owing to want of arrangement, they are very difficult and laborious to consult. Moreover, not only were the clergy lax in obeying the precept, but in many cases the diocesan authorities were careless to preserve them. In some dioceses, although subsequent ordinances have directed their punctual transmission, no attention whatever has been paid to the subject, and in no single diocese are they perfect.

Nevertheless, these transcripts are of immense value in the elucidation of a genealogy, providing, as they do, not infrequently copies of entries of which the originals are no longer in existence, and thus yielding information of an earlier date than the parish books afford. It should be borne in mind, however, that during the Civil War and at the time of the Commonwealth, when to some extent the registration had passed out of the hands of the clergy, the sequence is particularly imperfect, and that for some counties there appear to be no returns whatever.

A somewhat similar mandate to that of 1597 was issued in the first year of James the First's reign with the laudable object of

---

graduated in 1554, becoming Master of the Hall in 1567. In 1573 he was appointed Dean of Lincoln, and in 1576 Bishop of Worcester. On the death of Archbishop Grindall, in 1583, he was translated to the See of Canterbury. He died 29th February, 1604, and was interred in the parish church of Croydon, where a monument was erected to him.

securing greater accuracy as to the entries and more care in the preservation of the Registers themselves. It was directed that :—

"In every Parish Church and Chapel within this Realm
" shall be provided one Parchment Book at the charge of
" the Parish, wherein shall be written the day and year of
" every Christening, Wedding, and Burial which have been
" in that Parish since the time that the Law was first made
" in that behalf, so far as the ancient Books thereof can
" be procured, but especially since the beginning of the
" Reign of the late Queen. And for the safe keeping of the
" said Book the Churchwardens at the charge of the Parish
" shall provide one sure Coffer with three Locks and Keys
" whereof the one to remain with the Minister and the other
" two with the Churchwardens severally so that neither the
" Minister without the two Churchwardens, nor the Church-
" wardens without the Minister shall at any time take that
" Book out of the said Coffer. And henceforth upon every
" Sabbath Day immediately after Morning or Evening
" Prayer the Minister and Churchwardens shall take the
" said Parchment Book out of the said Coffer, and the
" Minister in the presence of the Churchwardens shall write
" and record in the said Book the names of all persons
" christened together with the names and surnames of their
" parents, and also the names of all Persons married and
" buried in that Parish, in the week before, and the day
" and year of every such Christening, Marriage and Burial.
" And that done they shall lay up that Book in the Coffer
" as before ; and the Minister and Churchwardens unto every
" page of that Book when it shall be filled with such inscrip-
" tions shall subscribe their names. And the Churchwardens
" shall once every year within one month after the five and
" twentieth day of March, transmit unto the Bishop of the
" Diocese or his Chancellor a true copy of the names of all
" persons Christened, Married or Buried in the Parish in
" the year before (ended the said five and twentieth day of
" March) and the certain days and months in which such
" Christening, Marriage and Burial was had, to be subscribed
" with the hands of the said Minister and Churchwardens
" to the end the same may faithfully be preserved in the

" Registry of the said Bishop, which certificate shall be
" received without fee. And if the Minister and Church-
" wardens shall be negligent in performance of anything
" herein contained it shall be lawful for the Bishop or his
" Chancellor to convent them and proceed against every of
" them as Contemnors of this our Constitution."

But in spite of these regulations it was found necessary during
the Commonwealth to issue further ones. By an Act of 1653,
" How Marriages shall be Solemnized and Registered, as also a
Register for Births and Burials," the registration duties were taken
out of the hands of the clergy, births (not baptisms) were required
to be registered, and Marriage was to be treated as a civil contract.
" An able and honest person, to be called The Parish Register,"
was to be elected triennially by the inhabitants of each parish, and
a fee of 12d. was to be paid for each entry of marriage, and 4d.
for every birth or death. But, admirable as these provisions were,
at the Restoration the registration reverted to the clergy.*

Although it has but an indirect connection with the history
of Parish Registers, it may not perhaps be uninteresting to recall at
this point the curious Act for burial in woollen.† This was ordained
" for the encouragement of the woollen manufacturers, and pre-
" venting of the exportation of money for the importing of linen,"
and thereby "no corpse shall be buried but in woollen after the
" first of August, and not in any shirt, sheet, shift, or shroud, or
" anything whatsoever made or mingled with flax, hemp, hair, gold,
" or silver, or any stuff or thing other than what is made of sheep's
" wool only, under a penalty of £5."

An affidavit was required within eight days of burial that the
corpse had been duly clad according to law, and the Act was to
be read in church on the first Sunday after St. Bartholomew's
Day every year for seven years after the passing of the Act.

Many references are made in entries of burials to this whim-
sical piece of legislation. Interference with the liberty of the

---

* Where the requisition of this Act was complied with at all,
both the date of birth and baptism will usually be found recorded,
although in some instances a separate Register book was kept during
the Cromwellian period.

† 32 Charles II., c. 1. (1680); repealed 54 Geo. III., c. 108 (1814).

subject, even when dead, is always resented, and this post-mortem Sumptuary Law was very unpopular, and had become a dead letter long before its repeal in 1814.

In the reign of William the Third several Registration Acts were passed, but these, like the one we have just noticed, had more the object of increasing the State revenue than of obtaining proper entries and the better preservation of the records.

Thus it was enacted (6 & 7 William III., cap. 6) that the penalty of £100 was to be exacted from clergy who neglected to register marriages, burials, births, or baptisms; and in the following year (7 & 8 William III., cap. 35) a fine of forty shillings was imposed on parents who should have omitted to give notice within five days of the birth of a child, and the vicar was enjoined under a like penalty "to take an exact and true account of, and keep a distinct register of, such so born and not christened," for doing which the parents were to pay sixpence to the vicar.

As an example of its fiscal purpose it may be mentioned that this Act also "granted his Majesty certain rates and duties upon " bachelors and widowers for the term of five years, for carrying " on the war against France with vigour." Ordinary persons, being over twenty-five years of age and bachelors, or widowers of any age, were liable to the fine of one shilling yearly, while a duke or marquess, being celibate or widowed, were mulcted in the sums of £12 10s. or £10 respectively.

"An Act for the preventing of Clandestine Marriages" (known generally as Lord Hardwicke's* Act—26 Geo. II. cap. 33), passed in 1753, prescribed a special form of entry for banns and marriages, somewhat similar to that now in use. It directed all marriages to be by license or banns and to be solemnized in some church or

---

* Sir Philip Yorke, first Earl of Hardwicke, was born 1st December 1690; called to the bar 6th May 1715; and appointed Solicitor General and knighted, 22nd March 1720. On the 31st January 1724 he succeeded to the office of Attorney-General, and thus within nine years after his call to the bar, and before he had attained the age of thirty-four years he had become leader in Westminster Hall. Upon the death of Lord Raymond, in 1733, he was appointed Lord Chief Justice of England, and raised to the peerage as Baron Hardwicke of Hardwicke, County Gloucester, in the same year. He was constituted Lord Chancellor of England 21st February 1737, and advanced, the 2nd April 1754, to a viscountcy and earldom by the titles of Viscount Royston and Earl of Hardwicke. His lordship was appointed, in 1746

chapel where banns had been theretofore usually published, and consequently a stop was put to marriages being performed in the chapels in and about London, as at these chapels it had not been usual to publish banns, and it was even found that St. Paul's Cathedral and Westminster Abbey were included in the prohibition, as banns had never been published in them.

Lord Hardwicke's Act had for its principal object the suppression of the Fleet and May Fair Chapel marriages.* The former were performed without license or certificate of banns, by regularly ordained clergymen, residing within the Fleet Prison or its rules, and usually confined for debt. A score or more couples were joined in one day and if they chose to pay an extra fee their names were concealed by private marks. That the measure was a timely one may be evidenced by the following letter which appeared on 27th February 1734–5 in *The Grub Street Journal :* —

" SIR,

" There is a very great evil in this town, and of dangerous
" consequence to our sex, that has never been suppressed,
" to the great prejudice and ruin of many hundreds of
" young people every year ; which I beg some of your learned
" heads to consider of, and consult of proper ways and
" means to prevent for the future ; I mean the ruinous
" marriages that are practised in the liberty of the Fleet and
" thereabouts, by a sett of drunken swearing parsons, with
" their Myrmidons that wear black coats, and pretend to be
" clerks and registers to the Fleet. These ministers of
" wickedness ply about Ludgate-hill ; pulling and forcing
" people to some peddling ale-house or brandy-shop to be

Lord High Steward of England for the trials of the Earls of Kilmarnock and Cromartie and the Lords Balmerino and Lovat. By his marriage with Margaret, daughter of Charles Cocks, M.P. for the city of Worcester, he had five sons and two daughters. His second son, Charles, the eminent lawyer, held the office of Lord High Chancellor of England, and died suddenly 22nd January 1770, at the moment when the patent conferring the title of Baron Morden upon him was in progress of completion.

* The Registers of baptisms and marriages performed at the Fleet and King's Bench prisons, at May Fair, at the Mint in Southwark, and in certain other places are inadmissible as evidence on the ground that they were not compiled under public authority.—*Taylor on Evidence.*

" married, even on a Sunday stopping them as they go to
" church, and almost tearing their cloaths off their backs.
" To confirm the truth of these facts, I will give you a case
" or two which lately happened.

　　" Since midsummer last, a young lady of birth and fortune
" was deluded and forced from her friends, and by the assist-
" ance of a wry-necked swearing parson, married to an
" atheistical wretch, whose life is a continual practice of all
" manner of vice and debauchery. And since the ruin of my
" relation, another lady of my acquaintance had like to have
" been trepanned in the following manner. This lady had
" appointed to meet a gentlewoman at the Old Play-house in
" Drury Lane, but extraordinary business prevented her coming.
" Being alone when the play was done, she bade a boy call a
" coach for the city. One drest like a gentleman helps her
" into it, and jumps in after her. 'Madam,' says he, ' this
" ' coach was called for me ; and since the weather is so bad,
" ' and there is no other, I beg leave to bear you company ; I
" ' am going into the city, and will set you down wherever you
" ' please.' The lady begged to be excused ; but he bade the
" coachman drive on. Being come to Ludgate-hill, he told
" her his sister who waited for his coming, but five doors up
" the court, would go with her in two minutes. He went,
" and returned with his pretended sister, who asked her to
" step in one minute and she would wait upon her in the
" coach. Deluded with the assurance of having his sister's
" company, the poor lady foolishly followed her into the
" house ; when instantly the sister vanished, and a tawny
" fellow in a black coat, and a black wig, appeared. 'Madam,
" you are come in good time, the doctor was just a-going.'
" 'The doctor,' says she, horridly frighted, fearing it was a
" madhouse. 'What has the doctor to do with me ?' 'To
" ' marry you to that gentleman ; the doctor has waited for
" ' you these three hours, and will be payed by you or by
" ' that gentleman before you go.' 'That gentleman,' says she,
" recovering herself, ' is worthy a better fortune than mine,'
" and begged hard to be gone. But Doctor Wryneck swore
" she should be married, or if she would not, he would still
" have his fee, and register the marriage from that night. The

" lady, finding she could not escape without money or a
" pledge, told them she liked the gentleman so well, she would
" certainly meet him to-morrow night, and gave them a ring as
" a pledge ; 'which,' says she, 'was my mother's gift on her
" 'death-bed, injoining, that if ever I married, it should be my
" 'wedding ring.' By which cunning contrivance she was
" delivered from the black doctor, and his tawny crew. Some
" time after this, I went with this lady and her brother in a
" coach to Ludgate-hill, in the day-time, to see the manner
" of their picking-up people to be married. As soon as our
" coach stops near Fleet-bridge, up comes one of the myr-
" midons. 'Madam,' says he, 'you want a parson.' 'Who
" are you ?' says I. 'I am the clerk and register of the Fleet.'
" 'Show me the chapel.' At which comes a second, desiring
" me to go along with him. Says he, 'That fellow will carry
" you to a pedling ale-house.' Says a third, 'Go with me, he
" will carry you to a brandy-shop.' In the interim comes
" the doctor: 'Madam,' says he, ' I will do your jobb for you
" presently.' 'Well, gentlemen,' says I, 'since you can't agree,
" 'and I can't be married quietly, I'll put it off till another
" 'time,' so drove away. Learned Sirs, I wrote this in regard
" to the honour and safety of my own sex ; and if, for our
" sakes, you will be so good as to publish it, correcting the
" errors of a woman's pen, you will oblige our whole sex,
" and none more than,

" Sir,

" your constant reader and admirer,

Jan. 15, 1734.   " VIRTUOUS."

The marriages at May Fair Chapel* were almost as notorious as
those of the Fleet, and as many as 6,000 are said to have been solemnized in one year. The registers,† consisting of nine volumes, are
now at the General Register Office, Somerset House.‡

---

* On the site of this famous chapel in Curzon Street now stands the
recently erected Sunderland House.
† These have been printed by the Harleian Society, Vol. 15, Register
section.
‡ The three folio volumes relating to May Fair Chapel, preserved
with the parish books of St. George's, Hanover Square, are apparently
transcripts.

In 1783 a stamp duty of threepence was imposed* (23 Geo. III. c. 67) on each entry of births or baptisms, marriages, and burials, and later (25 Geo. III. c. 75) this Act was extended to Dissenters, but was repealed within ten years.

Rose's† Act, "An Act for the better regulating and preserving " Parish and other Registers of Births, Baptisms, Marriages, and " Burials in England" (52 Geo. III. c. 146), was an endeavour, but a curiously slipshod and careless one, to improve the existing state of things. In spite of its title, for instance, it omits provision for registration of births, and it has no power of enforcing any of its enactments, except that respecting forgery. The only penalty imposed is that of transportation for fourteen years; and by a sub sequent clause it is enacted that one-half of all penalties shall go to the informer, and the remainder to the poor of the parish, or to charitable purposes ! Even the most relentless and malicious of informers was hardly likely to demand his share in the delights of Botany Bay.

Its chief provisions were :—

(1) After the 31st December 1812, registers of public and private baptisms, marriages, and burials were to be made and kept by the rector, &c., in books provided by the King's

---

* On the 26th May 1783, Lord John Cavendish, in moving on behalf of the Government "that towards raising the supply granted " to His Majesty, a stamp duty of threepence be charged upon the " entry of any burial, marriage, birth or christening, in any parish " register in Great Britain," observed that "he proposed a register " of births, marriages, and deaths, and the amount of this regulation " he stated at the sum of fifteen thousand pounds " (*Annual Register*, 1783). The proposal was vehemently condemned by Pitt and others in the House, and the imposition of the tax met with strong opposition in the country.

† The Right Hon. George Rose (1744–1818) was educated at Westminster School. After serving in the Navy for some years, he was appointed, in 1762, Clerk in the Register Office of the Exchequer. In 1777 he became Secretary to the Board of Taxes, and served as Secretary to the Treasury during Shelburne's ministry, 1782-3, and again during Pitt's ministry, 1784-1801. He was elected M.P. for Launceston, 1784; appointed for life Master of the Pleas in the Court of the Exchequer; elected M.P. for Lymington, 1788, and for Christchurch, 1790; made a Privy Councillor, 1802; served as Vice-President of the Board of Trade and joint Paymaster-General during Pitt's second administration, 1804-6; Vice-President of the Board of Trade and Treasurer of the Navy, 1807-12; Deputy Warden of the New Forest, 1808; and subsequently again Treasurer of the Navy.

printer at the expense of respective parishes, according to the forms contained in certain annexed schedules.

(2) Registers of baptisms, marriages, and burials to be made in separate books.

(3) The rector, etc., as soon as possible after the solemnization of the rite, to enter in the proper Register Book the several particulars described in the schedules and to sign the same ; and in no case (unless prevented by sickness or other unavoidable impediment) later than within seven days after the ceremony.

(4) The Register Books to be kept in a dry, well-painted iron chest, in some dry, safe and secure place within the usual residence of such rector, etc. (if resident within the parish), or in the parish church.

(5) Within two months after the end of every year, fair copies of all the entries of the preceding year to be made by the rector, etc., on parchment, verified and signed by him and to be sent before the 1st June in each year to the registrar of the diocese.

(6) The registrars to cause such copies to be securely deposited and preserved from damage by fire or otherwise, and to be carefully arranged with correct alphabetical lists of all persons and places mentioned.

(7) Any persons making any false entry in any Register, or altering, defacing, or injuring any such Register Book, Transcript, or List, to be liable to transportation for fourteen years.

(8) The rector, etc., of every parish, before the 1st of June, 1813, to transmit to the registrar of the diocese a list of all Registers then in the parish, stating the periods at which they respectively began and ended, the periods (if any) for which they were deficient, and the places where they were deposited.

This Act with all its defects remained in force and unamended for upwards of twenty-five years. During that time the whole system of parish registration depended on it, two attempts to amend it (in 1824 and 1830 respectively) failing to get beyond the first reading in the House of Commons.

c

The matter was, however, at length definitely grappled with in 1833, and a Select Committee was appointed to consider and report on Parochial Registers in England and Wales and on a General Registration of Births, Baptisms, Marriages, Deaths and Burials. The Report of the Committee was printed and issued in the same year, and, as a consequence of their labours, an Act (6 & 7 William IV. c. 86—later amended and explained by an Act of 1837) was passed " for Registering Births, Deaths, and Marriages in England," and establishing a civil registration. It repealed so much of the Acts of 1812 and 1823 as related to the registration of marriages, and provided a Registrar-General, Superintendent Registrars, etc., for registering births, deaths, and marriages. Register books in dupli- cate to be furnished to every church and chapel where marriages may be solemnized. Section 35 provides that rectors, &c., are to allow searches in any register book after certain fees have been paid, but no provision (and this omission is certainly much to be regretted) was made by the legislators for the safe custody of the Parish Registers then in existence. No one can deny that it is imperative that the strictest of stringent regulations should be made for this purpose.

Since the 1st of July 1837 all births, marriages, and deaths in England and Wales are to be found in perfectly indexed volumes at Somerset House. As all may have access to these records, and procure copies, obtainable for a small fee, it becomes unnecessary to trace the history of Parish Registers beyond this date. But there is still work for the Legislature to do. It is time that the ancient Registers were collected under one central roof where they could be properly arranged, carefully indexed, and securely guarded. This, besides safeguarding what has been called " the title deeds of the middle classes," would greatly facilitate the work of searching them.

Lord Romilly,* who as Master of the Rolls rendered the public records—political, domestic and legal—accessible to all, had doubtless

---

* The Right Honourable Sir John Romilly, first Baron Romilly, was the second surviving son of the eminent jurisconsult and statesman Sir Samuel Romilly, by Anne, his wife, daughter of Francis Garbett of Knill Court, co. Hereford. He was born in 1802; called to the bar in 1827; and appointed Solicitor-General in March 1848, receiving

in view some Parliamentary measure dealing with the subject of the parochial records when, on the 19th March 1872, he moved in the House of Lords, "That an humble Address be presented to " Her Majesty, to request that Her Majesty will be graciously " pleased to order that there be laid before this House, Return " from the Rector, Vicar, Curate, Officiating Minister, or Incumbent " in charge of each Parish, Chapelry, or Ecclesiastical District in " England and Wales, of all Registers, Records, Books, Documents " or other Instruments relating to Baptisms, Marriages, and Burials, " in their possession on 31st December 1871, stating their nature, " the dates from which and to which they extend, their state and " condition, and how and where they are preserved :

"Also, a Return from each of the same Persons, to the 31st " December 1871, whether the Parchment Copies of Baptisms, " Marriages or Burials required by the Act 52 Geo. III. cap. 146, " have been annually sent to the Diocesan Registrars, the number " of times when such Copies have not been sent, and the reasons " for not sending them."

Although "the same was agreed to," no further reference to this Motion can be found in the records of the House of Lords, and it is probable that the matter lapsed, so far as the House was concerned, through the neglect of some official, and that it escaped the notice of Lord Romilly and the other Lords. This seems to be the only possible explanation, as there is no doubt that there should have been both a formal reply as well as a return.*

Ten years later, a Bill was read in the House of Commons to make provision for the better preservation of the ancient Parochial Registers of England and Wales, but the proposed measure unfor-

---

at the same time the honour of knighthood. In July 1850 he became Attorney-General, from which office, in eight months he was raised to that of Master of the Rolls, to which he was appointed 28th March 1851. On the 19th December 1865 he was raised to the Peerage as Baron Romilly of Barry, co. Glamorgan. He married, in 1833, Caroline, daughter of the Right Reverend William Otter, D.D., Bishop of Chichester, by whom he had issue. His death took place 22nd December 1874.

* To some small extent the order was complied with by the parochial clergy, although no return was presented to the House.

tunately never reached a second reading and was withdrawn on 5th July 1882.

A certain number of Parish Registers have already been printed and published, and it could be wished that this process should be made obligatory and applied to the remainder, the necessary work to be undertaken by experts* and carried out at the cost of the State and under its supervision.

In treating the subject of Parish Registers from the historical aspect it may not be out of place to mention that until 1752 the civil year began on Lady Day (March 25) and ended on the eve of the following Lady Lady. In 1751 an Act † was passed whereby the legal year was to be reckoned in 1752 and onwards from the 1st of January; and this explains what often looks like the discrepancy of a whole year's difference in date.

It may also be pointed out that in very few of the old Register books were the entries made at the time of the performance of the ceremonies to which they refer; they were generally transcripts‡ made in pursuance of the Injunction of 1597 or that of 1603, and compiled not unlikely from the memoranda made in the private journals or diaries of the parochial clergy, as many of these early records contain references to the appointment of churchwardens and overseers, notices as to titles, moduses, and so forth.

The following extracts, from the well-preserved and deeply interesting Register books of St. Margaret's Church, Westminster,§ which commence in 1538 and are almost complete from that date, will serve to illustrate in what manner the baptisms, marriages, and burials were registered at the different periods, and also to show

---

* A special knowledge is necessary to decipher accurately the early entries, and the extracts of unqualified searchers are seldom to be relied upon. Indeed, some of the printed registers are not above suspicion in this respect, and reference to the original is often most advisable.

† 25 Geo. II. c. 30.

‡ Whether this is so or not may be generally discovered by the title of the book or by the similarity of the handwriting up to the year 1598, or thereabouts, and by the signatures at the bottom of each page.

§ In the Churchwardens' accounts of 1538, for this parish, is the following entry:—"Paid for a Book to registre in the names of buryals, weddings, and Christenings, 2d."

AN EXAMPLE OF MISCELLANEOUS PARTICULARS RECORDED
IN PARISH REGISTERS.

the miscellaneous particulars* which have from time to time been recorded in Parish Registers :—

1539. April 30. *Willms Shakspere.* [Buried.]

[From this date until 1553 occur many entries of

---

* The Licenses to eat meat during Lent are recorded on the fly-leaf as follows :—

License given and made of whom and to whom for eating } None to eat flesh without of flesh in the time of sickness on the 6th day of February 1568. } license.

1. William Stanton, Headborough, the 26th day of February.
2. William Worlye, Yeoman of the Guard, the 2nd day of March.
3. Thomas Lyghton, gentleman, the 3rd day of March.
4. Lawrence Griffyn, the 6th day of March.
5. To Thomas Payne, one of the Guard, the 12th day of March.
6. To Margerie Spencer, wife to William Spencer, the 2nd day of March.
7. To Richard Jordon, the 20th day of March.

License given for eating flesh in the time of Sickness the 7th day of February 1569.

First, Ralph Cannocke a license to kill from "my Lord Keeper," the 7th day of February.

Richard Hodges, licensed by "my Lord of Canterbury," the 9th day of February.

William Moore and Elizabeth his wife, 17th day of February.

Robert Bowmont and Agnes his wife, the 15th day of February.

William Smethe, the 17th day of February.

William Clerke, the 20th day of February.

Margaret Stynte, the 22nd day of February.

John Thrushe, the 5th day of March.

William Maddocke, the 7th day of March. { No butcher to Barnes, a license to kill from "my Lord of Leicester," } kill flesh with-the last day of January 1569. { out license.

William Lyngard, the 13th day of March.

Richard Preiste, the 20th day of March.

License given to eat flesh in time of sickness for this Lent time 1570.

Mistress Margaret Staunton, licensed by the physician and the Curate, the 22nd day of February.

Mr. Richard Preist and his wife are licensed to eat flesh by "my Lord of Canterbury," the 4th day of March 1570.

Richard Jordayne, licensed by the Curate, the 2nd day of March.

Ralph Cannock, licensed by "my Lord Keeper," the 4th day of March.

John Barnes, licensed to kill flesh by the Earl of Leicester, the 4th day of March.

Beatrice Hutton, licensed by the Curate, the 13th day of March.

Elizabeth Bacheler, licensed by the Curate, the 15th day of March.

William Hudson and Agnes his wife, licensed the 16th day of March.

Bartholomew Sylva, physician, licensed the 16th day of March.

the burials of Clergymen, with the prefix of "Syr,"* and the addition of "Presbyter" to their names.]

1549.　Feb 1.　*Mr. Doctor Henry Egylsby, Presbuter, to Tamasyne Darke.* [Married].

1553.　July 19.　*Was my Lady Marye her Grace proclamed Quene in London, and the 21st day in Westmynster.*

Feb. 8.　Edmond Pyrry,
John Sympson,　} *Souldyars with Wyat.†*
Anthony Adason,　　[Buried.]

1554.　May 9.　M. *That Jone Wylson, the heretyk, was buryed without ye Churchyarde.*

[Many Spaniards are recorded as having been buried in this year and the next.]

Dec. 27.　*John de Mendoza, Knyght, Spaynearde.* [Buried.]

1557.　[The words "very povertye"; "famyne"; "with a surfeit"; "pynynge syckness"; "bloody fluxe"; or "burnynge ague"; are added to no less than twenty entries in this year.]

1563.　June 23.　[The first record of the Plague appears. Fourteen who had died of it were on the 27th September buried. It continued until the end of November.]

1566.　[Several entries in this and the following years have the addition of "convicte person," "ye blacke garde," "the pantry," "the laundrye," or "the kytchin."]

Nov. 28.　*Edwd. Courtney, gent. of Deveshire.* [Buried.]

1574.　In May occurs again the affix of "Plague," which lasted till August. In April 1575, until January 1. In July 1576, it re-appears until December; again in June 1577 until June 1579; in July 1581, until January 1583; from August 1592, until May 1594.]

---

* "Syr" was attached to the names of such Priests as had not graduated at either of the Universities. In ancient times there were only three "Syrs"—"Syr Kynge," "Syr Knyghte," and "Syr Prieste."

† Sir Thomas Wyatt (1520-1554) was the son of Sir Thomas Wyatt, the poet. Indignant at the marriage of Queen Mary with Philip II. of Spain, he raised a rebellion in Kent, took Rochester Castle, and marched on London, where he was defeated and taken prisoner. He was executed for high treason in 1554.

October 1618

November 1618

November 1618

December 1618

A.D. 1618.

FACSIMILE OF THE PAGE ON WHICH THE BURIAL OF
SIR WALTER RALEIGH IS RECORDED.

1586. Aug. 12. *The Rt. Hon. Sr. Edw. Dudleye, Knt., Baron of Dudley, ye Lord Dudleye.** [Buried.]

1587. Aug. 26. *Davy Duke, Bishopp of Kerry in Ireland.* [Buried.]

1594. March 3. *This daie came in one Willm. Drap, alais ffarmer, Petti-Cannon of St. Peter's, Westminster, to be Vicar of St. Margarets in Westminster.*

[The Plague-mark re-appears in June 1603, until September 1604. On September 11, twenty persons died. On October 20, twenty-one persons were buried. Again, in September 1605, until November 1607; in June 1608, until October 1611.]

1609. Dec. 24. *Philipe Warwick, son to Thomas. This Philip was knighted by K. Chas.: he wrote Warwick's Memoires.*

1613. May 11. *Paule, sonne to Richard Neale, Bishopp of Coventry and Lychfeilde.* [Baptized.]

1615. April 18. *Thomas, son to Sir Christopher Hatton, Knight.* [Baptized.]

July 20. *Sir Henery Portman, Knt. Bart., of Orchard, Somerset, to Lady Anne, daughter to Rt. Hon. Wm. Stanley, Earle of Derby.* [Married.]

1616. June 4. *Christopher, son to Francis Winnybancke, Secrety. of State to King Ch. I.* [Baptized.]

1618. Oct. . *Sir Walter Rawleigh, Knight.†* [Buried.]

1620. Sept. 18. *Roger Johnson buried; the first when the Churchyarde was inlareged.*

1623. May 9. *Theodernus, a noble Gretian.* [Buried.]

1624. Aug. 23. *John, son of Sir Jno. Trevor, Knt., Master of the Rolls.* [Baptized.]

---

* The 8th Lord Dudley. He married firstly, Catherine, daughter of John, 1st Baron Chandos of Sudeley, who died in 1566; secondly, Jane, daughter of Edward, 3rd Earl of Derby, who died in 1569; and thirdly, Mary, sister of Charles, 1st Earl of Nottingham. By his second wife, he left a son and heir, Edward, 9th Lord Dudley.

† The illustrious Englishman who was beheaded in Old Palace Yard, 29th October 1618.

1625. May 1. *Thomas, son to Henry Cornish, Sheriff of London. Beheaded in the reign of Ch. II.* [Baptized.]

> [In June the Plague broke out again. On August 15th thirty-eight persons were buried. In September, no less that 557 victims to it were interred.]

1627. May 9. *Dennis Nowell; the first buried in the New Chapell Yard.*

1627. June 11. *Richard Barrow, slaine in the Churchyard.* [Buried.]

1629. May 28. *Margarett Boyle,* daughter of William Earl of Corke.* [Baptized.]

1630. March 9. *Anne Pyerport, daughter to Henry Lord Newarke.* [Baptized.]

1634. April 5. *Robert Montague, son to the Rt. Hon. Edward Lord Mandeville.†* [Baptized.]

1635. June 16. *The Lady Eliz. Broughton.* [Buried.]

> *The Quire attendants and boys had* - £2 10 0
> *The Almsmen* - - - - 0 12 0

> Oct. 2. *Mrs. Ann Allan.* [Buried.]

> *The Quire had* - - - £3 16 8
> *And for Breakfaste* - - - 0 5 0

> Dec. 19. *Dorothy Smith, daughter to Lord Strangford.* [Baptized.]

1636. May 3. *At the funeral of Mrs. Edw. Carne—*

> *The Quire had* - - - - £3 16 5
> *The Quiristers* - - - 0 10 0

> May 26. *Mrs. Alice, daughter to Sir Robt. Eaton, Secretary to King Charles I.* [Baptized.]

> *The Quire attended; the boys had* - £3 16 8

---

* This daughter of the great Lord Cork died unmarried.

† The eldest son of Sir Henry Montagu, Earl of Manchester, whom he succeeded, as 2nd Earl, in 1642. He was a prominent and successful general of the Parliamentary army during the civil wars, and particularly distinguished by his celebrated victory over Prince Rupert at Marston Moor, in which engagement Cromwell acted as his Lieutenant-General. Refusing however to sanction the murder of the King, he retired from Parliament, and in 1660 he took an active part in the restoration of Charles II. Robert Montagu, whose baptism is here recorded, was his eldest son, and eventually succeeded to the earldom of Manchester.

1636. Aug. [The Plague-mark re-appears, and continues till Oct. 1638.]

1638. Oct. 15. *Thomas Shirley, sonne to Sr Thomas.* [Baptized.]

Dec. 8. *Mr. Richard James,* that most famous Antiquary.* [Buried.]

1639. Oct. 31. *Wm. Villars, Vice Count Grandison, to Mary Banning, daughter to Lord Banning, Vice Count Sudbury.†* [Married.]

1640. Dec. 7. *Philip, son to Philip Warwick, Esq., by Dorothy his wife.* [Baptized.] *This Philip, the father, was an excellent scholar, and a great sufferer in the Rebellion ; was asked and wrote in the King's defence.*

1641. Mar. 15. *Lawrence Hyde, son to Lawrence, now Earle of Rochester.* [Baptised.]

1642. May 31. *Robert Uvdall,‡ son to Robert by Margaret his wife.* [Baptized.]

1647. Jan. 22. *Henry Aldridg,§ son to Henry by Judith.* [Baptized].

1650. Nov. 13. *Col. Jno. ffox lies buried within the Communion Rails North and South not East and West.*

Dec. 19. *Mr. Jesper Collins executed for his loyalty.* [Buried.]

1653. Nov. 25. *Gilbert Wimberly, D.D., once Minister of this Church, and Prebendary, was outed, sequestered, imprisoned, and plundered by the Rebells.*

[At this period many marriages are entered as performed by Justices of the Peace.]

1654. Dec. 3. *Robt. Ld. Willoughbye of Earsby, sonne of ye Hon. Earle of Lindsey, to Mrs. Margaret Massingberd, ye daughter of Mrs. Cecillia Massingberd.* [Banns published.]

1655. July 7. *Baptist Ld. Visc. Campden of Kinsington, co. Middx., to the Lady Elizabeth Bertie, daughter of Montagu, Earle of Lindsay.* [Banns published.]

---

* Imprisoned by order of the House of Lords, in 1629.

† The famous Barbara, Duchess of Cleveland, mistress of Charles II., was a child of this marriage.

‡ The noted botanist.

§ Henry Aldrich, Dean of Christ Church, Oxford, who is said to have designed Trinity College Chapel and All Saints Church, Oxford.

1655.   Feb. 5. *Godfrey Goodman, Lord Bp. of Gloucester. He
dyd the 19th of January last ; and because Bishops were
hateful to the Saints of '48 they omitted his qualitie. He
being a pious man would not yield to the Parliament's
unreasonable designs ; for which they outed, sequestered,
plundered, and imprisoned him.* [Buried.]

1656.   June 16. *Alexander Stuart, Earle of Murrye, to Emila,
daughter of Sir William Balfour.*   [Banns published.]

Sept. 30. *Mr. Henry Elsinge, Esq. the famous. See the
Schollars of Westminster. He dyed at or near Cotton
House, and not at Hounslow, as Ath. Oxon. p. 105,
Vol. II., where he is said to be buried. His attchievement
at large on the East Pillar in the North Galery.* [Buried.]

Oct. 20. *Richard Barry, Earle of Barrymore, or Barry
the Great, to Mrs. Martha, daughter of the Rt. Hon. the
Lord President Lawrence.* [Banns published.]

Nov. 7. *John Milton of this parish and Mrs. Katherin
Woodcocke of the parish of Aldermanbury, Spinster.*
[Banns published.]

1657.   Oct. 19. *Katherin Milton D. (daughter) to John, Esq.,
by Katherin.   This is Milton, Oliver's Secretary.**
[Baptized.]

Feb. 10. *Mrs. Katherin Milton.*†   [Buried.]

March 20. *Mrs. Katherin Milton's child.* [Buried.]

1660.   June 30. *Mr. Edward Martin. He was Churchwarden
when the Vestry was built ; at which time the King lost
the Batel of Worcester, and for joy he gave drink to the
workmen.* [Buried.]

Sept. 18. *Robert Meldrum, Esqr., the Scotch Rebell.*
[Buried.]

---

* The poet was appointed Latin Secretary to the Council of State,
and was retained in the same capacity by Cromwell when he assumed
the Protectorate.

† Daughter of a Captain Woodcock of Hackney, and the second
wife of Milton, by whom she has been immortalized in his beautiful
sonnet : "Methought I saw my late espousèd saint." The entry, however, proves the generally accepted tradition that Katherine Milton died
in giving birth to a child to be without foundation. It will be observed
that in point of fact her death did not take place until almost four
months after her confinement.

October 1657

18	John	Wabanks	S to Richard by Elizabeth
18	John	York	S to William by Mary
18	Dorothy	Spoard	D to Robert by Dorothy
18	Garthwrite	Keniggston	D to John by Ann
18	Susanna	Garrett	D to John by Susanna
19	Francis	Derington	S to Francis by Ann
19	John	Reynolds	S to John by Mary
19	Kathrin	Milton	D to John by Kathrin

this is milton olivers Secretary

20	Edward	Woodford	S to Edward by Hester
20	Thomas	Shipman	S to John by Abigail
20	Priscilla	Shirword	D to Thomas by Mary
21	Phillip	Watkins	S to Phillip by Elizabeth
21	Thomas	Purras	S to William by Frances
22	Elizabeth	Johnson	D to William by Anne
22	Sarah	Wilkins	D to Henry by Mary
22	Elizabeth	Lerkor	D to Nathaniell by Eliza:
25	William	Bridgod	S to William by Elizabeth
25	Geory	Robinson	S to George by Joane
25	James	Baudwins	S to John by Sarah
25	Ann	Spyer	D to John by Margrett
25	Margarett	Evans	D to John by Anne
26	Edward	Barnes	S to William by Susanna
27	Thomas	Francis	S to William by Alice
28	John	Binnett	S to John by Jane
28	Henry	Sawder	S to Thomas by Martha
28	Sarah	Bouth	D to John by Ann
29	Mary	English	D to Anthony by Rose
30	Anne	Charlton	D to Edward by Susanna

A.D. 1657.

FACSIMILE OF ENTRIES MADE AT THE TIME OF THE COMMONWEALTH.

Note reference to Milton, the Poet, on this page.

1662. June 19. *Charles Palmer, Lord Limbricke, son to the Right Honourable Roger Earle of Castlemaine.* [Baptized.]

1665. [From June 14, until the end of August, over 200 persons died of the Plague.]

[During September, 263. In this month occur several gaps without Plague-mark or name affixed, severally 7, 9, 15, 4, 12, 6, 8 ; in all 61.]

[During October, 147. In October there are also similar gaps of 2, 2, 4, 3, 4, 4, 1, 2, 3, 6 ; in all 31.]

[During November, 77.] [In December, 39.]

1666. [In January, 13, During the Plague, in all 759.]

Jan. 1. *Carey Rawleigh,*[*] *Esq. Killed.* [Buried.]

1667. April 24. *Sir Wm. Throgmorton.* [Buried.]

1670. Dec. 6. *James Levingston, Earl of Newburghe.*† [Buried.]

1671. Aug. 14. *Meriso Margreta, Dowager Countice of Belcarris.* [Buried.]

1680. Aug. 27. *Thomas Blood.*‡ [Buried.]

1683. Dec. 28. *Mrs. Elizabeth Thompson.* [Buried.]

1684. Jan. 20. *Ralph, son to Sir Ralph Dutton, Knt. Bart. by Dame Mary.* [Baptized.]

March 8. *Mary Wollins, daughter to William by Alice the first child carryed from ye Font through ye East new door.* [Baptized.]

1688. April 11. *Robt. Moore, son to Rt. Hon. Hy. Earle of Droheda, by Dame Mary.* [Baptized.]

---

* A son of Sir Walter Raleigh.

† A staunch cavalier and gentleman of bedchamber to Charles II. He was created Viscount Newburgh, 13 September 1647, and at the Restoration, Earl of Newburgh, Viscount Kynnaird, and Lord Levingstone.

‡ The notorious adventurer, usually styled Colonel Blood. For his services to Cromwell he was rewarded with estates in Ireland, which he lost at the Restoration, but received again from Charles II. In 1663, he took part in a plot to surprise Dublin Castle and seize the Lord Lieutenant; and in 1670 attempted to kill the Duke of Ormonde. He was imprisoned in 1671 for the theft of the Crown Jewels, but was shortly afterwards released by the King, and was eventually the recipient of many Royal favours.

1690. Feb. 11. *Wm. Fred. de Danckelman, son to Thos. Earnst by Hendrina Gardrudt, Elector of Brandinburg's Envoy to King William.* [Baptized.]

1693. March 14. *Thos., son to Gilbert Burnett, Ld. Bishop of Sarum, by Mary his wife.* [Baptized.]

1700. Oct. 3. *Rebecca Crisp Oates, daughter to Dr. Titus* by Rebecca.* [Baptized.]

1702. July 18. *Lettice Holdsworth. She rid in the great bell called Great Tom, when it was carried from the Tower in the Palace Yard to St. Paul's in London.* [Buried.]

Dec. 27. *Lady Henrietta Finch, daughter to the Rt. Hon. Daniel, Earle of Nottingham, Principall Secretary of State, by Anne his Countess, baptized, in white habit att his house facing the parrade.*

1702. Jan. 14. *Hon. James Scott, son to the Rt. Hon. James, Earle of Dalkeith,† by Henrietta his Countess, borne and baptized in the Cock-pit in Whitehall at the Earle of Rochester's house.*

Oct. 1. *Christopher Wilson, M.A., Lecturer of this Church.*

1704. May 11. *Helen, daughter to Christr Schneider, Organist to Her Majesty.* [Baptized.]

1705. Feb. 5. *Phillip Raleigh, Esqr.; grandson of Sir Walter Raleghe who was beheaded in the temp. of King James I.* [Buried.]

1708. June 25. *Charles Grahame, son to Very Rev. Wm., D.D., Dean of Wells, by Alice, baptized by Jno. Ld. Arch Bishop of York. Her Majestie being godmother, and the Dukes of Somerset, Queensberry, and Dover, godfathers. Born ye 6th.*

---

* The infamous informer and perjurer.

† Eldest surviving son of the unhappy James, Duke of Monmouth, K.G. (natural son of Charles II., by Lucy Walters) and the famous Anne, his wife, Countess Buccleuch, who on their marriage in 1663 were created Duke and Duchess of Buccleuch. Lord Dalkeith was born in 1674 and died in the lifetime of his mother, having married in 1693, Lady Henrietta Hyde, second daughter of Laurence, Earl of Rochester, by whom he had issue four sons: Francis, who on the death of his grandmother became 2nd Duke of Buccleuch; Charles; James, whose baptism is here recorded; and Henry.

Christnings

2 Ann Smedley D. to William by Ann.
2 Mary Atherton D. to Daniel by Mary.
Jane Kips D. to Jacob by Jane.
Godolphin Edwards S. to Sam: by Rebecca.
Thomas Lloyd S. to John by Ann.
Ann Brocuall D. to George by Susana.
Charles Toll S. to Bartholomew by Ann.
Frances Withers to Charles by Kather.
Edwin S. to Sam: Esq. by Lady Kather.
Lovell S. to Joseph by Sarah.
Blackshaw D. to Wm. by Jane.
Elizabeth Scrath D. to Paul by Mary.
Griffith D. to John by Mary.
Winthrop S. to Edm: by Bridm.
Elizabeth Kirby D. to Edw. by Euphenia.

15 Anthony Heymans S. to Jacobus by Sarah.
16 James a foundling.
18 Edward Troop S. to Edward by Elizabeth.
19 John Wale S. to Charles by Mary.
19 Mary Lorenz D. to William Esq. by Rebecca.
20 Thomas Booth S. to William by Margaret.
20 Elizabeth Durfrott D. to Henry by Elizabeth.
20 Nathaniel Davis S. to Rice by Joice.
20 Jane Edwards D. to David by Jane.
24 William Potts S. to Roger by Margaret.
24 Sarah Read D. to Joseph by Elizabeth.
24 Charles Aland S. to John by Ann.
27 Steven Stewart S. to Richard by Mary.
27 Nathaniel Blunt S. to Nathan: by Mary.
27 William Carr S. to James by Elizabeth.
27 Henry Summers S. to Tho: by Jane.
27 Elizabeth Lutfin D. to Will: by Hester.
27 Phillis Norris D. to Roger by Phillis.
27 Ruben Bennett S. to Ruben by Elizabeth.
27 William Meredith S. to Will: by Barbara.
27 Mary Quinton D. to Edward by Joanna.
28 Lewis Garrett S. to Tho: by Bridgett.
30 Edward Edmunds S. to John by Susana.
30 Richard Wright S. to Charles by Grace.

October.

Thomas Ripp Oates S. to Dr. Titus by Rebecca.
Dolieus S. to John by Hannah.
Rhetts D. to Joseph by Mary.
Phillip Pott S. to Phillip by Jane.
John Soak S. to John by Alice.
Barbara Whithurst D. to July by Lidia.
Catherine Mills D. to Joseph by Elizabeth.

A.D. 1700

FACSIMILE OF A RECORD OF BAPTISMS.

Note reference to Dr. Titus Oates.

1711. May 30. *Thom. Lawrence,* son to Thomas by Elizabeth.* [Baptized.]

1714. May 13. *Be it remembered that upon the death of Mr. John Clayton, late Parish Clerk, the Rt. Rev. Father in God Francis,† Lord Bishopp of Rochester and Dean of Westminster, put in one Roger Gethin to be Clerk; but the Vestry refused to admit him, alledging the right of electing the Clerk of the Parish, Clerk of the Vestry, Organist, and Sexton, &c., was in them by ancient custom. After eleven Hearings in the Ecclesiastical Courts, and Seven Motions in the Queens Bench, for a Prohibition, this Day was appointed for the Tryall before my Ld. Chief Justice Parker, and a Speciall Jury of Gentlemen of Middlesex, who found for the Vestry; so that Mr. Gethin was put out, and Henry Turner established in the Vestry's choice.*

June 25. *Capt. Patrick Drew killed with a sword in St. James' Park.* [Buried.]

1715. August 31. *His Excellency Don Bentura de Zara, Ambassadour from the Emperor of Fez and Morrocco.* [Buried.]

Dec. 18. *The Rev. (or Rt. Rev.) George Hickes, D.D.,‡ Dean of Worcester; which Deanary he lost by refusing to take the Oaths at the Revolution. He was consecrated Bishop Suffragan of Thetford, by Dr. Lloyd, the deprived Bishop of Norwich.* [Buried.]

1716. April 27. *Col. Thos. Becker. He was famous for walking under water; he proposed to go from Manchester Court Stairs to Black Fryers, and had done, but the guard of his head hit against the keel of a lighter or barge. He after, for the King's satisfaction, walked across the Thames, for which he had a good reward.* [Buried.]

---

* Afterwards President of the College of Physicians.

† The well-known Francis Atterbury.

‡ As a non-juror Hickes held out to the last, and occupied his enforced leisure in writing theological treatises of great ability. His "*Institutiones Grammaticæ Anglo-Saxonicæ*" is considered one of the best antiquarian works in our literature.

1718. March 31. *Mary Mountague, daughter to Rt. Hon. Geo. Earl of Halifax, by Mary his Countess.* [Baptised.]

1720. June 22. *Lord George Johnstone, son to the Most Honourable William Lord Marquess of Annundale, by Lady Charlotte, his Marchioness. His godfathers, His Majestie King George (by proxy the Earl of Orkney), the Lord Viscount Allington the other ; and Her Grace the Dutches of Hamilton his godmother.* [Baptized.]

1732. May 18. *Wm. Hamilton, son to the Rt. Hon. Ld. Visc. Limerick, by the Lady Harriot, baptized in the Privy Garden.*

1736. Feb. 19. *Anthony Sugg, who roasted the Ox upon the Thames in the Great Frost,* 1683. [Buried.]

1740. April 25. *John, son of Dr. Tenison, Chancellour of Oxford, by Mary his wife.* [Baptized.]

1743. April 1. *Dr. Lancelot Blackburn, Ld. Archbishop of York.* [Buried.]

1746. April 3. *The Hon. Peter, Marquis of Contri Gravina of the Kingdom of Sicily, to Elizabeth Watson.* [Married.]

1758. Dec. 23. *Earl of Arran.* [Buried.]

1759. Dec. 10. *Sir William Musgrave, Bart., to Rt. Hon. Isabel Countess Dowager of Carlisle.*❋ [Married].

1766. Oct. 14. *Jeremiah Bentham*† *married to Sarah Abbott.*

1769. February 23. *Rt. Hon. Max. Eman. Gabriel, Visc. de Mauldé, to Mary Francoise Victoire Preudhomme de Barry.* [Married.]

1773. April 15. *Rev. Reginald Heber, bachelor, married to Sarah Baylie Spinster.*

❋ Only daughter of William, 4th Baron Byron, and widow of Henry, 4th Earl of Carlisle, K.G.

† The father, by a previous marriage, of Jeremy Bentham, the well-known writer, and of Sir Samuel Bentham, the Naval architect and inventor. Sarah Abbot, Jeremiah Bentham's second wife, was the daughter of Jonathan Farr, and widow of the Rev. John Abbot, D.D., Rector of All Saints, Colchester, by whom she had Charles Abbot, Speaker of the House of Commons from 1802 to 1817 and subsequently created Baron Colchester.

1786. March 20. *Frances Temple,* daughter to Henry Visc. Palmerstone, by Mary his wife.* [Baptized.]

1795. June 1. *William Leonard, son to Rt. Hon. Hy. Addington,† by Ursula his wife.* [Baptized.]

---

* A sister of Henry John Temple, Viscount Palmerston, the Prime Minister. She married Captain Bowles, R.N.

† Henry Addington, 1st Viscount Sidmouth, Speaker of the House of Commons and afterwards First Lord of the Treasury and Chancellor of Exchequer, married firstly, Mary, daughter and co-heiress of Leonard Hammond of Cheam, in Surrey, and by her, who died in 1811, he had an only son, William Leonard, whose baptism is here recorded. In 1823 he married secondly, the Hon. Marianne Townsend, widow of Thomas Townsend of Honington, co. Warwick, and only daughter and eventual heiress of William, Lord Stowell.

ANNOTATED INDEX

TO

THE PARISH REGISTERS

OF

ENGLAND AND WALES.

D

ANNOTATED INDEX

TO

THE PARISH REGISTERS

OF

ENGLAND AND WALES.

Only those Parishes having Registers of an earlier date than 1813 are included in this List.
P *signifies that the particular Register has been printed in its entirety (as distinguished from extracts) for the period specified. Where the printed copy is stated to contain entries of an earlier date than the existing Parish Register, it should be understood that the former has been supplemented by the Bishop's Transcripts.*

Parish.	County.	Date of Earliest Entry.	Parish.	County.	Date of Earliest Entry.
			Aberyskir - -	Brecon - -	1721
A.			Aberystruth - -	Monmouth -	1736
			Aberystwyth - -	Cardigan -	1788
Abbas Combe -	Somerset -	1563	Abingdon St. Helen -	Berks - -	1538
Abberley- -	Worcester -	1559	„ St. Nicholas	- -	1538
Abberton - -	Essex - -	1703	Abinger - - -	Surrey - -	1559
Abberton - -	Worcester -	¹1661	Abington - -	Northampton -	1637
Abbey-cwm-hir -	Radnor - -	² —	Abington, Great -	Cambridge -	1664
Abbey-Dore -	Hereford -	1634	Abington, Little -	Cambridge -	1687
Abbots-Ann -	Hants - -	1561	Abington Pigotts -	Cambridge -	⁴1653
Abbots-Bickington	Devon - -	1717	Ab-Kettleby - -	Leicester -	1580
Abbots-Bromley -	Stafford -	1558	Abson - - -	Gloucester -	⁵ —
Abbotsbury -	Dorset - -	1574	Abthorpe - -	Northampton- -	⁶1737
Abbotsham -	Devon - -	1653	Aby - - -	Lincoln - -	⁷ —
Abbots-Kerswell -	Devon - -	1607	Acaster-Malbis -	York - -	1693
Abbots Langley -	Hertford -	1538	Accrington - -	Lancaster -	1766
Abbots Leigh -	Somerset -	1656	Acklam, East -	York - -	1716
Abbotsley -	Huntingdon -	1754	Acklam, West -	York - -	1732
Abbots-Morton -	Worcester -	³1728	Ackworth - -	York - -	1558
Abdon - -	Salop - -	1554	Acle - - -	Norfolk - -	⁸1664
Abenhall - -	Gloucester -	1596	Acomb - -	York - -	1635
Aber - -	Carnarvon -	1682	Acrise - -	Kent - -	⁹1561
Aberavon -	Glamorgan -	1597	Acton - -	Chester -	1653
Aberdare -	Glamorgan -	1734	Acton - - -	Middlesex -	1539
Aberdaron -	Carnarvon -	1753	Acton - - -	Suffolk - -	1564
Aber-edw -	Radnor - -	1690	Acton Beauchamp -	Worcester -	1539
Abererch -	Carnarvon -	1614	Acton Burnell -	Salop - -	1568
Aberffraw -	Anglesey -	1720	Acton Round -	Salop - -	1651
Aberford -	York - -	1540	Acton Scott -	Salop - -	1690
Abergavenny -	Monmouth -	1653	Acton Trussell -	Stafford -	1571
Abergele - -	Denbigh -	1647	Acton Turville -	Gloucester -	¹⁰1665
Abergwili -	Carmarthen -	1661	Adbaston - -	Stafford -	1600
Aberhafesp -	Montgomery -	1578	Adderbury - -	Oxford - -	1598
Abernant -	Carmarthen -	1754	Adderley - -	Salop - -	¹¹1692
Aberporth -	Cardigan -	1663	Addingham - -	Cumberland -	1604

¹ Bishop's Transcripts commence 1608.
² Included with Registers of Llanbister (*q.v.*).
³ Bishop's Transcripts commence 1611.
⁴ **P** 1653–1812. Edited by the Rev. W. G. F. Pigott, rector, 1890.
⁵ Included with the Registers of Wick (*q.v.*).
⁶ Abthorpe was not constituted as a separate parish until 1737, but there are entries from a very early date concerning this parish in the Towcester Registers.
⁷ Included with Registers of Belleau (*q.v.*).
⁸ **P** (Marriages only) 1664–1812. Norfolk Parish Registers, vol. 1, 1899.
⁹ There is a note on the outside of the Register Book, " from the year 1541 to 1698," but the first date is evidently an error.
¹⁰ **P** (Marriages only) 1671–1812. Gloucestershire Parish Registers, vol. 13, 1908.
¹¹ **P** 1692–1812. Shropshire Parish Register Society, vol. 4, 1903.

Parish.	County.	Date of Earliest Entry.	Parish.	County.	Date of Earliest Entry.
Addingham	York	1612	Aldbourne	Wilts	1637
Addington	Buckingham	1558	Aldburgh	York	1653
Addington	Kent	1562	Aldbury	Hertford	[3] 1693
Addington	Surrey	1559	Aldeburgh	Suffolk	1558
Addington, Great	Northampton	1692	Aldeby	Norfolk	1558
Addington, Little	Northampton	1588	Aldenham	Hertford	[9] 1559
Addlethorpe	Lincoln	1564	Alderbury	Wilts	1673
Adel	York	[1] 1606	Alderford	Norfolk	1723
Adisham	Kent	1539	Alderley	Chester	1629
Adelstrop	Gloucester	1538	Alderley	Gloucester	[10] 1559
Adlingfleet	York	1684	Aldermaston	Berks	1558
Adstock	Buckingham	1538	Alderminster	Worcester	[11] 1628
Adstone	Northampton	1671	Aldershot	Hants	[12] 1571
Advent	Cornwall	[2] 1709	Alderton	Gloucester	1596
Adwell	Oxford	1539	Alderton	Northampton	1597
Adwick-le-Street	York	1547	Alderton	Suffolk	1676
Adwick-on-Dearne	York	1690	Alderton	Wilts	[13] 1603
Affpuddle	Dorset	1722	Aldford	Chester	1639
Agnes, St.	Cornwall	1653	Aldham	Essex	1559
Aikton	Cumberland	1694	Aldham	Suffolk	1666
Ainderby-Steeple	York	1668	Aldingbourne	Sussex	1558
Ainstable	Cumberland	1664	Aldingham	Lancaster	1539
Ainsworth	Lancaster	1727	Aldington	Kent	1558
Airmyn	York	1726	Aldridge	Stafford	1660
Aisholt	Somerset	[3] 1645	Aldringham	Suffolk	1538
Aisthorpe	Lincoln	1594	Aldsworth	Gloucester	1683
Akeley	Buckingham	1682	Aldwincle All Saints	Northampton	1653
Akenham	Suffolk	1538	St. Peter's		1563
Albans, St. Abbey	Hertford	[4] 1558	Aldworth	Berks	1556
St. Michael		1649	Alexton	Leicester	1638
St. Peter		1558	Alfold	Surrey	1658
Alberbury	Salop	[5] 1564	Alford	Lincoln	1538
Albourne	Sussex	1553	Alford	Somerset	1763
Albrighton, near Shrewsbury.	Salop	[6] 1555	Alfreton	Derby	1706
			Alfrick	Worcester	[14] 1656
Albrighton, near Wolverhampton.	Salop	[7] 1649	Alfriston	Sussex	1538
			Algarkirk	Lincoln	1678
Alburgh	Norfolk	1541	Alkborough	Lincoln	1538
Albury	Hertford	1558	Alkerton	Oxford	1545
Albury	Oxford	1653	Alkham	Kent	1558
Albury	Surrey	1559	All Cannings	Wilts	1579
Alby	Norfolk	1558	Allen, St.	Cornwall	1680
Alcester	Warwick	1560	Allen, West, or Ninebanks.	Northumberland	1767
Alciston	Sussex	1701			
Alconbury	Huntingdon	1559	Allendale	Northumberland	1662
Aldborough	Norfolk	1539	Allenheads	Northumberland	1807
Aldborough	York	1538	Allensmore	Hereford	1698

[1] **P** 1606–1812. Thoresby Society, vol. 5, 1895.
[2] **P** (Marriages only) 1676–1801. Cornwall Parish Registers, vol. 1, 1900.
[3] **P** (Marriages only) 1654–1812. Somersetshire Parish Registers, vol. 6, 1905.
[4] **P** 1558–1689. Edited by W. Brigg, 1897.
[5] **P** 1564–1812. Shropshire Parish Register Society, vol. 6.
[6] **P** 1555–1812. Shropshire Parish Register Society, vol. 3, 1901.
[7] **P** 1649–1812. Shropshire Parish Register Society, vol. 1, 1900.
[8] **P** (Marriages only) 1694–1812. Hertfordshire Parish Registers, vol. 1, 1907.
[9] **P** 1559–1659. Edited by Rev. and Hon. K. F. Gibbs, 1902.
[10] **P** (Marriages only), 1559–1812. Gloucestershire Parish Registers, vol. 10, 1905.
[11] **P** (Marriages only) 1641–1812. Worcestershire Parish Registers, vol. 1, 1900. Bishop's Transcripts commence 1611.
[12] **P** (Marriages only) 1590–1812. Hampshire Parish Registers, vol. 2, 1900.
[13] **P** (Marriages only) 1606–1812. Wiltshire Parish Registers, vol. 1, 1905.
[14] Bishop's Transcripts commence 1622.

Parish.	County.	Date of Earliest Entry.	Parish.	County.	Date of Earliest Entry.
Aller -	Somerset	[1] 1560	Althorpe	Lincoln	[13] 1670
Allerston	York	1680	Alton -	Hants	1615
Allerthorpe	York	1620	Alton	Stafford	1660
Allerton, Chapel	Somerset	1692	Alton Barnes	Wilts	1592
Allerton, Chapel	York	1789	Alton Pancras	Dorset	1674
Allerton, Mauleverer -	York	1562	Alton Priors	Wilts	1664
Allesley	Warwick	1562	Altrincham	Chester	1799
Allestree	Derby	[2] 1595	Alvanley	Chester	1791
Allhallows	Cumberland	1666	Alvaston	Derby	1614
Allington	Dorset	[3] 1570	Alvechurch	Worcester	1545
Allington	Kent	1630	Alvediston	Wilts	1592
Allington	Wilts	[4] 1623	Aveley	Salop	1561
Allington, East	Devon	1554	Alverdiscott	Devon	1602
Allington, East -	Lincoln	1559	Alverstoke	Hants	[14] 1559
Allington, West	Lincoln	[5] 1559	Alvescott	Oxford	1663
Allonby -	Cumberland	1759	Alveston	Gloucester	1742
Alltmawr	Brecon	[6] —	Alveston	Warwick -	1539
Almeley	Hereford	1595	Alvingham	Lincoln	1579
Almer -	Dorset	[7] 1538	Alvington	Gloucester	1688
Almondbury -	York	1557	Alvington, West	Devon -	1558
Almondsbury	Gloucester	1696	Alwalton	Huntingdon	1572
Almsford. See Ansford.	—	—	Alwington	Devon	1555
			Alwinton	Northumberland	1719
Alne	York	1561	Amberley -	Sussex	1560
Alne, Great -	Warwick	1605	Ambleside	Westmorland	1642
Alnham	Northumberland	[8] 1688	Ambleston	Pembroke	1755
Alnwick	Northumberland	1646	Ambrosden	Oxford	1611
Alphamstone	Essex	1705	Amersham	Buckingham	1561
Alpheton	Suffolk	1571	Amesbury	Wilts	1579
Alphington	Devon	1602	Amlwch	Anglesey	1633
Alpington	Norfolk	[9] —	Amotherby	York -	[15] —
Alresford	Essex	1742	Ampleforth	York	1646
Alresford, Old	Hants	1556	Ampney St. Mary	Gloucester	1602
Alresford, New -	Hants	1698	Ampney St. Peter	Gloucester	1620
Alrewas	Stafford	1547	Ampney Crucis	Gloucester	1566
Alsager -	Chester	1789	Ampney Down	Gloucester	1603
Alsop-le-Dale	Derby	1640	Amport	Hants	[16] 1665
Alston	Worcester	[10] 1550	Ampthill	Bedford	1605
Alstonfield	Stafford	[11] 1538	Ampton -	Suffolk -	1559
Alston Moor -	Cumberland	[12] 1700	Amroth -	Pembroke	1759
Altarnon	Cornwall	1688	Amwell, Great -	Hertford	1558
Altcar -	Lancaster	1664	Ancaster	Lincoln	1722
Altham	Lancaster	1518	Ancroft -	Durham	1742
Althorne	Essex	1734	Anderby	Lincoln	1565

[1] **P** (Marriages only) 1560-1812. Somersetshire Parish Registers, vol. 1, 1898.
[2] **P** (Marriages only) 1595-1812. Derbyshire Parish Registers, vol. 1, 1906.
[3] **P** (Marriages only) 1570-1812. Dorset Parish Registers, vol. 2, 1907.
[4] **P** (Marriages only) 1623-1812. Wiltshire Parish Registers, vol. 3, 1906.
[5] **P** (Marriages only) 1559-1812. Lincolnshire Parish Registers, vol. 2, 1907.
[6] Included with Registers of Llanafawfawr (q.v.).
[7] **P** 1538-1812. Parish Register Society, vol. 56, 1907.
[8] **P** 1688-1812. Durham and Northumberland Parish Register Society, vol. 14, 1907.
[9] Included with Yelverton Registers (q.v.).
[10] **P** (Marriages only) 1550-1805. Worcestershire Parish Registers, vol. 1, 1901.
[11] **P** 1538-1812. Staffordshire Parish Register Society, vol. 1, 1902.
[12] **P** "North Country Parish Registers" by Robert Blair.
[13] The Parliamentary Return, printed in 1833, states that "there are two register books of earlier date (supposed to commence in 1483) which were taken away by the Archdeacon in 1824"; but neither the Rector of Althorpe nor the Diocesan authorities appear to know anything of the books referred to. The date at which they are supposed to begin is obviously erroneous, and the Transcripts, for this parish, preserved at Lincoln, do not commence until about 1600.
[14] **P** Index to Church Inscriptions and Parish Register, 1559-79, Geo. Parker, 1885.
[15] Included with Registers of Appleton-le-Street (q.v.).
[16] **P** (Marriages only) 1665-1812. Hampshire Parish Registers, vol. 2, 1900.

Parish.	County.	Date of Earliest Entry.	Parish.	County.	Date of Earliest Entry.
Anderstone Winterbourne.	Dorset - -	1763	Arkengarth-Dale -	York - -	1659
			Arkesden - -	Essex - -	1690
Andover - - -	Hants - -	1587	Arkholme - -	Lancaster -	1626
Andrew, St. - -	Glamorgan -	1744	Arksey - -	York - -	1557
Angersleigh - -	Somerset -	¹ 1678	Arlecdon - -	Cumberland -	1730
Angle - - -	Pembroke -	1763	Arlesey - -	Bedford - -	1538
Angmering - -	Sussex - -	1562	Arley, Upper - -	Stafford -	1564
Anmer - - -	Norfolk -	1678	Arley - -	Warwick -	1557
Annesley - -	Nottingham -	² 1599	Arlingham - -	Gloucester -	1539
Ansford - - -	Somerset -	1554	Arlington - -	Devon - -	1598
Ansley - - -	Warwick -	1639	Arlington - -	Sussex - -	1607
Anstey - - -	Hertford - -	1541	Armathwaite -	Cumberland -	1759
Anstey - - -	Leicester -	1556	Arminghall - -	Norfolk - -	1571
Anstey - - -	Warwick -	³ 1589	Armitage - -	Stafford -	1673
Anstey - - -	Wilts - -	1686	Armley - -	York - -	1722
Anstey, East - -	Devon - -	1596	Armthorpe - -	York - -	1653
Anstey, West - -	Devon - -	1653	Arncliffe - -	York - -	1669
Anston - - -	York - -	1550	Arncliffe, Ingleby -	York - -	1654
Anthony,St.,in Meneage	Cornwall -	1602	Arne - - -	Dorset - -	1762
Anthony, St., in Roseland.	Cornwall -	1660	Arnesby - - -	Leicester - -	1602
			Arnold - -	Nottingham -	1544
Antingham - -	Norfolk -	1679	Arreton, Isle of Wight	Hants - -	1656
Antony, East - -	Cornwall -	1569	Arrington - -	Cambridge -	1538
Anwick - - -	Lincoln -	1573	Arrow - - -	Warwick - -	1588
Apesthorpe - -	Nottingham -	⁴ 1707	Arthingworth - -	Northampton -	1650
Apethorpe - -	Northampton -	1676	Arthuret - -	Cumberland -	1610
Apley - - -	Lincoln -	1561	Arundel - -	Sussex - -	1560
Appleby - - -	Leicester -	1572	Arvans, St. - -	Monmouth -	1686
Appleby - -	Lincoln - -	1576	Asaph, St. - -	Flint - -	1613
Appleby St. Lawrence	Westmorland -	1694	Asby - - -	Westmorland -	⁸ 1657
Appleby St.Michael (or Bongate).	Westmorland -	1582	Ascot - under - Wych - wood.	Oxford - -	1569
Appledore - -	Kent - -	1700	Asfordby - -	Leicester - -	1564
Appledram. See Apuldram.			Asgarby (Sleaford) -	Lincoln -	1676
			Asgarby (Spilsby) -	Lincoln -	1595
Appleford - -	Berks - -	1563	Ash (Sevenoaks) -	Kent - -	1553
Appleshaw - -	Hants -	⁵ 1744	Ash (Sandwich) - -	Kent - -	1558
Appleton - -	Berks - -	1569	Ash - - -	Surrey - -	1549
Appleton-le-Street -	York - -	1715	Ashampstead - -	Berks - -	1686
Appleton-on-Wisk -	York - -	1629	Ash-Bocking - -	Suffolk - -	1555
Apuldram - -	Sussex - -	1661	Ashbourne - -	Derby - -	1547
Arborfield - -	Berks - -	⁶ 1705	Ashbrittle - -	Somerset -	1563
Ardeley - - -	Herts - -	1546	Ashburnham - -	Sussex - -	1656
Ardingly - -	Sussex - -	1558	Ashburton - -	Devon - -	1603
Ardington - -	Berks - -	1674	Ashbury - -	Berks - -	1653
Ardleigh - -	Essex - -	1555	Ashbury - - -	Devon - -	1615
Ardley - - -	Oxford -	1758	Ashby - - -	Lincoln -	1723
Ardsley, East - -	York - -	1654	Ashby-by-Partney -	Lincoln -	1552
Ardsley, West (or Woodkirk).	York - -	1652	Ashby - -	Norfolk -	1559
			Ashby - - -	Norfolk -	1620
Ardwick - - -	Lancaster -	1740	Ashby - - -	Suffolk -	1553
Areley-Kings - -	Worcester -	1539	Ashby, Canons -	Northampton -	1708
Argam - - -	York - -	⁷ —	Ashby Castle -	Northampton -	1564
Arkendale - -	York - -	1780	Ashby Cold -	Northampton -	1560

¹ **P** (Marriages only) 1693–1812. Somersetshire Parish Registers, vol. 7, 1906.
² **P** (Marriages only) 1599–1812. Nottinghamshire Parish Registers, vol. 9, 1906.
³ **P** (Marriages only) 1591–1812. Warwickshire Parish Registers, vol. 1, 1904.
⁴ Included with North Leverton Registers (q.v.).
⁵ Earlier entries at Amport (q.v.).
⁶ According to the Parliamentary Return of 1831, the first volume of registers contained entries for 1558, 1599, 1619–1706. This register has, it appears, been lost or destroyed since the date of the Return.
⁷ Included with the Registers of Bridlington (q.v.).
⁸ **P** 1657–1798, London, 1894.

Parish.	County.	Date of Earliest Entry.	Parish.	County.	Date of Earliest Entry.
Ashby-de-la-Launde -	Lincoln - -	1695	Ashton on Mersey -	Chester - -	1636
Ashby-de-la-Zouch -	Leicester -	1561	Ashton Steeple - -	Wilts - -	1538
Ashby Folville -	Leicester - -	1653	Ashton-under-Hill -	Gloucester -	1586
Ashby Magna - -	Leicester -	1586	Ashton-under-Lyne -	Lancaster -	1594
Ashby Mears - -	Northampton -	1670	Ashurst - - -	Sussex - -	1560
Ashby Parva - -	Leicester - -	1585	Ashurst - - -	Kent - -	1692
Ashby Puerorum -	Lincoln -	1657	Ashwater - - -	Devon - -	1558
Ashby St. Leger's -	Northampton -	1554	Ashwell - -	Hertford -	1678
Ashby West - -	Lincoln - -	1561	Ashwell - - -	Rutland -	1595
Ashchurch - -	Gloucester -	1556	Ashwellthorpe -	Norfolk - -	1558
Ashcombe - -	Devon - -	1583	Ashwick - - -	Somerset - -	1701
Ashcott - -	Somerset -	1678	Ashwicken - -	Norfolk - -	1717
Ashdon - -	Essex - -	1553	Ashworth - -	Lancaster -	1741
Ashe - - -	Hants - -	¹ 1606	Askerswell - -	Dorset - -	1558
Asheldam - -	Essex - -	1721	Askham - - -	Nottingham -	1538
Ashelworth - -	Gloucester -	1566	Askham - -	Westmorland -	⁶1568
Ashen - - -	Essex - -	1558	Askham Bryan - -	York - -	1695
Ashendon - -	Buckingham -	1670	Askham Richard -	York - -	1579
Ashfield - -	Suffolk -	1693	Askrigg - - -	York - -	1701
Ashfield, Great -	Suffolk - -	1678	Aslackby - - -	Lincoln - -	1558
Ashford - -	Devon - -	1700	Aslacton - - -	Norfolk - -	1556
Ashford - -	Kent - -	1570	Aspall - - -	Suffolk - -	1558
Ashford - - -	Middlesex -	1699	Aspall Stonham. See		
Ashford Bowdler -	Salop - -	1609	Stonham Aspall.		
Ashford Carbonell -	Salop - -	1721	Aspatria - - -	Cumberland -	1660
Ashford in the Water -	Derby - -	1687	Aspenden - - -	Hertford -	1559
Ashill - - -	Norfolk - -	1538	Aspley-Guise - -	Bedford -	1563
Ashill - - -	Somerset -	² 1558	Assington - - -	Suffolk - -	1598
Ashingdon - -	Essex - -	1564	Astbury - - -	Chester -	1572
Ashington - -	Somerset -	1567	Asterby - - -	Lincoln -	1698
Ashington - -	Sussex - -	1736	Asthall - - -	Oxford -	1684
Ashley - - -	Cambridge -	1746	Astley - - -	Lancaster -	1760
Ashley - -	Hants - -	1725	Astley - - -	Salop - -	⁷1579
Ashley - - -	Northampton -	1588	Astley - - -	Warwick -	1670
Ashley - -	Stafford - -	1551	Astley - - -	Worcester -	1539
Ashley - - -	Wilts - -	⁵1658	Astley Abbots -	Salop - -	1561
Ashmanhaugh -	Norfolk - -	1562	Aston - - -	Salop - -	1558
Ashmansworth -	Hants - -	1811	Aston - - -	Hereford -	1685
Ashmore - -	Dorset -	⁴1651	Aston - - -	Hertford -	1558
Ashover - - -	Derby - -	1622	Aston - - -	York - -	1567
Ashow - - -	Warwick -	1733	Aston Abbots - -	Buckingham -	1559
Ashperton - -	Hereford -	1538	Aston Blank - -	Gloucester -	1724
Ashprington - -	Devon - -	1607	Aston Botterell -	Salop - -	1559
Ash Priors - -	Somerset -	⁵1700	Aston by Birming-	Warwick -	⁸1544
Ashreigney - -	Devon - -	1653	ham.		
Ashtead - - -	Surrey - -	1662	Aston by Sutton -	Chester -	1635
Ashton - - -	Devon - -	1541	Aston Cantlow - -	Warwick -	1578
Ashton - - -	Northampton -	1778	Aston Church - -	Salop - -	1621
Ashton, Cold -	Gloucester -	1734	Aston Clinton - -	Buckingham -	⁹1560
Ashton - -	Lancaster -	1698	Aston Flamville -	Leicester -	1579
Ashton in Makerfield -	Lancaster -	1698	Aston Ingham - -	Hereford -	1633
Ashton, Keynes -	Wilts - -	1582	Aston-le-Walls - -	Northampton -	1540
Ashton, Long -	Somerset -	1691	Aston, North - -	Oxford - -	1598

¹ **P** " History of Ashe, Hants, including Parish Registers, 1606–1887," by F. W.Thoyts, London, 1888.
² **P** (Marriages only) 1558–1815. Somersetshire Parish Registers, vol. 4, 1902.
³ **P** (Marriages only) 1658–1812. Wiltshire Parish Registers, vol. 3, 1906.
⁴ **P** Index to Registers, 1651–1820. E. W. Watson, 1890.
⁵ **P** (Marriages only) 1700–1812. Somersetshire Parish Registers, vol. 8, 1907.
⁶ **P** 1568–1812. By M. A. Noble, 1904.
⁷ **P** 1692–1812. Shropshire Parish Register Society, vol. 5.
⁸ **P** 1544–1640. By W. F. Carter, 1900.
⁹ **P** (Marriages only) 1560–1812. Buckinghamshire Parish Registers, vol. 2, 1904. Also vol. 3, 1907.

Parish.	County.	Date of Earliest Entry.	Parish.	County.	Date of Earliest Entry.
Aston-on-Trent -	Derby - -	1667	Avon-Dassett - -	Warwick -	1559
Aston, Rowant -	Oxford -	1554	Awliscombe - -	Devon - -	1559
Aston, Sandford -	Buckingham -	1615	Awre - - -	Gloucester -	1538
Aston, Somerville -	Gloucester -	[1] 1668	Awsworth - -	Nottingham -	[9] 1756
Aston, Steeple -	Oxford - -	1538	Axbridge - -	Somerset - -	1562
Aston-sub-Edge -	Gloucester -	[2] 1539	Axminster - -	Devon - -	1559
Aston, Tirrold - -	Berks - -	1726	Axmouth - -	Devon - -	1603
Aston, White Ladies -	Worcester -	1558	Aycliffe - -	Durham - -	1560
Astwick - -	Bedford - -	1718	Aylburton - -	Gloucester -	[10] —
Astwood - -	Buckingham -	1666	Aylesbeare - -	Devon - -	1580
Aswarby - -	Lincoln - -	[3] 1754	Aylesbury - -	Buckingham -	1564
Aswardby - -	Lincoln - -	1713	Aylesby - -	Lincoln - -	1561
Atcham - - -	Salop - -	1619	Aylesford - -	Kent - -	1653
Athan, St. - -	Glamorgan -	1663	Aylestone - -	Leicester - -	1561
Athelhampton -	Dorset - -	1692	Aylmerton - -	Norfolk - -	1696
Athelington - -	Suffolk - -	1694	Aylsham - -	Norfolk - -	1653
Atherington - -	Devon - -	1538	Aylton - - -	Hereford - -	1748
Atherstone-upon-Stour	Warwick -	[4] 1611	Aymestrey - -	Hereford - -	1568
Atherton - -	Lancaster -	[5] —	Aynhoe - - -	Northampton -	1562
Atlow - - -	Derby - -	1685	Ayott, St. Lawrence -	Hertford - -	1566
Attenborough -	Nottingham -	[6] 1560	Ayott, St. Peter -	Hertford - -	1686
Attercliffe - -	York - -	1719	Aysgarth - -	York - -	1709
Attleborough -	Norfolk - -	1552	Ayston - - -	Rutland - -	1656
Attlebridge - -	Norfolk - -	1714	Ayton, Great - -	York - -	1666
Atwick - - -	York - -	1538			
Atworth - -	Wilts - -	1658			
Aubourn - -	Lincoln - -	1749			
Auckland, St. Andrew	Durham -	1558			
St. Ann -	- -	1558			
St. Helen -	- -	1593			
Audlem - -	Chester - -	1557	**B.**		
Audley - - -	Stafford -	1538			
Aughton - -	Lancaster -	1541			
Aughton - -	York - -	1611	Babcary - - -	Somerset -	1704
Aukborough. *See* Alk-			Babingley - -	Norfolk -	[11] 1662
borough.			Babington - -	Somerset -	1725
Ault Hucknall -	Derby - -	[7] 1660	Babraham - -	Cambridge -	1561
Aunsby - - -	Lincoln -	1681	Babworth - -	Nottingham -	1622
Aust - - -	Gloucester -	1538	Backford - -	Chester - -	1562
Austell, St. - -	Cornwall -	1565	Backwell - -	Somerset -	1693
Austerfield - -	Nottingham -	1559	Baconsthorpe -	Norfolk -	1692
Austrey - - -	Warwick -	1558	Bacton - - -	Hereford -	1724
Authorpe - -	Lincoln -	1561	Bacton - - -	Norfolk -	1558
Avebury - - -	Wilts - -	1696	Bacton - - -	Suffolk -	1558
Aveley - - -	Essex - -	1563	Bacup - - -	Lancaster -	[12] 1788
Avenbury - -	Hereford -	1661	Badby - - -	Northampton -	1559
Avening - - -	Gloucester -	[8] 1557	Baddesley Clinton -	Warwick -	1747
Averham - -	Nottingham -	1538	Baddesley Ensor -	Warwick - -	1688
Aveton Gifford -	Devon - -	1603	Baddesley, North -	Hants - -	1682
Avington - -	Berks - -	1725	Baddiley - -	Chester - -	1579
Avington - -	Hants - -	1609	Baddow, Great -	Essex - -	1538

[1] **P** (Marriages only) 1661–1812. Gloucestershire Parish Registers, vol. 4, 1898.
[2] **P** (Marriages only) 1539–1812. Gloucestershire Parish Registers, vol. 3, 1898.
[3] The old Register books were, it is stated, destroyed by rats.
[4] **P** (Marriages only) 1611–1812. Warwickshire Parish Registers, vol. 1, 1904.
[5] Included in Registers of Leigh (*q.v.*).
[6] **P** (Marriages only) 1560–1812. Nottinghamshire Parish Registers, vol. 6, 1904.
[7] **P** (Marriages only) 1660–1812. Derbyshire Parish Registers, vol. 1, 1906.
[8] **P** (Marriages only) 1557–1812. Gloucestershire Parish Registers, vol. 10, 1905.
[9] **P** (Marriages only) 1756–1812. Nottinghamshire Parish Registers, vol. 8, 1905.
[10] Included with Lydney Registers (*q.v.*).
[11] **P** (Marriages only) 1662–1812. Norfolk Parish Registers, vol. 2, 1900.
[12] Baptisms and burials only.

Parish.	County.	Date of Earliest Entry.	Parish.	County.	Date of Earliest Entry.
Baddow, Little -	Essex - -	1561	Bardfield, Great -	Essex - -	1662
Badger - - -	Salop - -	1662	Bardfield, Little -	Essex - -	1539
Badgeworth - -	Gloucester ⸿	1559	Bardfield, Saling -	Essex - -	1561
Badgington - -	Gloucester -	1630	Bardney - - -	Lincoln -	1653
Badgworth - -	Somerset - -	1671	Bardsey - -	York - -	1538
Badingham - -	Suffolk - -	1538	Bardwell - -	Suffolk -	²1538
Badlesmere - -	Kent - -	1558	Barford - -	Norfolk -	1700
Badley - - -	Suffolk - -	1593	Barford St. Michael -	Oxford -	1643
Badminton - -	Gloucester -	¹1538	Barford St. John -	Oxford - -	1598
Badsey - - -	Worcester -	1538	Barford - -	Warwick -	1538
Badsworth - -	York - -	1680	Barford - - -	Wilts - -	1653
Badwell-Ash - -	Suffolk - -	1559	Barford, Great -	Bedford -	1564
Bagborough, West -	Somerset -	1558	Barford, Little -	Bedford -	1653
Bagby - - -	York - -	1556	Barfreston - -	Kent - -	1572
Bagendon - -	Gloucester -	1630	Barham - - -	Huntingdon -	1688
Baginton - -	Warwick - -	1628	Barham - - -	Kent - -	1558
Baglan - - -	Glamorgan -	1626	Barham - - -	Suffolk -	1563
Bagnall - - -	Stafford - -	² —	Barholm - -	Lincoln -	1726
Bagthorpe - -	Norfolk - -	1562	Barkby - - -	Leicester -	1586
Bagworth - -	Leicester -	1559	Barkestone - -	Leicester -	1569
Baildon - - -	York - -	1621	Barkham - -	Berks - -	1538
Bainton - - -	York - -	1561	Barking - -	Essex - -	1558
Bainton - - -	Northampton -	1713	Barking - -	Suffolk -	1538
Bakewell - - -	Derby - -	1614	Barkstone - -	Lincoln - -	1561
Balcombe - - -	Sussex - -	1539	Barkway - -	Hertford -	1538
Balderstone - -	Lancaster -	1767	Barkwith, East -	Lincoln - -	1695
Balderton - - -	Nottingham -	³1538	Barkwith, West -	Lincoln - -	1685
Baldock - - -	Hertford - -	1558	Barlaston - - -	Stafford - -	⁹1573
Baldon-Marsh - -	Oxford - -	1559	Barlavington - -	Sussex - -	1656
Baldon-Toot - -	Oxford - -	1579	Barlborough - -	Derby - -	1648
Bale - - - -	Norfolk - -	1538	Barlby - - -	York - -	¹⁰1780
Ballingdon - -	Essex - -	⁴1564	Barleston - -	Leicester -	1655
Ballingham - -	Hereford - -	1588	Barley - - -	Hertford - -	¹¹1559
Balsall, Temple -	Warwick - -	1679	Barling - - -	Essex - -	1555
Balscott - - -	Oxford - -	1548	Barlings - - -	Lincoln -	1627
Balsham - - -	Cambridge -	1558	Barlow, Great -	Derby - -	1573
Balstonborough -	Somerset - -	1538	Barlow with Brayton.		
Bamburgh - -	Northumberland	1638	Barmby-Moor -	York - -	1683
Bampton - - -	Devon - -	1653	Barmby-on-the-Marsh	York - -	1783
Bampton - - -	Oxford - -	1538	Barming - -	Kent - -	1540
Bampton - - -	Westmorland -	⁵1637	Barming, West, with		
Banbury - - -	Oxford - -	1558	Nettlestead.		
Bangor - - -	Carnarvon -	1727	Barmouth with Llan-		
Bangor-Monachorum -	Denbigh and	1675	aber.		
	Flint.		Barmston - - -	York - -	1571
Banhaglog - -	Montgomery -	⁶ —	Barnack - - -	Northampton -	1696
Banham - - -	Norfolk - -	1558	Barnard-Castle -	Durham -	1609
Banningham - -	Norfolk - -	1709	Barnardiston - -	Suffolk -	1540
Banstead - - -	Surrey - -	⁷1547	Barnburgh - -	York - -	1558
Banwell - - -	Somerset - -	1570	Barnby - - -	Suffolk - -	1701
Bapchild - - -	Kent - -	1562	Barnby-in-the-Willows	Nottingham -	¹²1593
Barby - - -	Northampton -	1748	Barnby-on-Don -	York - -	1600
Barcheston - -	Warwick - -	1559	Barnes - - -	Surrey - -	1538
Barcombe - - -	Sussex - -	1580	Barnet, Chipping -	Hertford - -	1678

¹ **P** (Marriages only) 1538–1812. Gloucestershire Parish Registers, vol. 13, 1908.
² With Bucknall. ³ **P** (Marriages only) 1538–1812. Nottinghamshire Parish Registers, vol. 3, 1900.
⁴ No Church. Registers at All Saints, Sudbury.
⁵ **P** 1637–1812. Edited by Mary E. Noble, Kendall, 1897. ⁶ With Llandinam (q.v.).
⁷ **P** 1547–1789. Parish Register Society, vol. 1, 1896.
⁸ **P** 1538–1650. Edited by F. E. Warren, 1893.
⁹ **P** 1573–1812. Staffordshire Parish Register Society, 1905.
¹⁰ Previously included in the Registers of Hemingbrough (q.v.).
¹¹ **P** (Marriages only) 1560–1812. Hertfordshire Parish Registers, vol. 1, 1907.
¹² **P** (Marriages only) 1593–1812. Nottinghamshire Parish Registers, vol. 3, 1900.

Parish.	County.	Date of Earliest Entry.	Parish.	County.	Date of Earliest Entry.
Barnet, East -	Hertford -	1553	Barton - - -	York -	1581
Barnet, Friern	Middlesex	1674	Barton Bendish	Norfolk -	1726
Barnetby-le-Wold	Lincoln -	[1] 1753	Barton St. Andrews -	Norfolk -	1695
Barney	Norfolk -	1538	Barton Blount -	Derby -	1763
Barnham	Suffolk -	1775	Barton, Great	Suffolk	1563
Barnham	Sussex -	1675	Barton Hartshorn	Buckingham -	1582
Barnham-Broom	Norfolk	1630	Barton-le-Clay -	Bedford -	1558
Barningham -	Suffolk -	1538	Barton-le-Street	York -	[6] 1751
Barningham	York -	1581	Barton Mills -	Suffolk -	1663
Barningham, Little -	Norfolk -	1538	Barton on the Heath -	Warwick -	[7] 1575
Barningham-Norwood	Norfolk	1538	Barton on Dunsmore -	- -	
Barningham Winter -	Norfolk -	1703	Barton Seagrave	Northampton -	1609
Barnoldby-le-Beck	Lincoln	1572	Barton Stacey -	Hants -	1713
Barnoldswick -	York -	1587	Barton Steeple -	Oxford -	1678
Barnsley	Gloucester	1574	Barton Turf -	Norfolk -	1558
Barnsley -	York -	1568	Barton under Need-	Stafford -	[8] 1571
Barnstaple -	Devon -	[2] 1538	wood.		
Barnston -	Essex -	1539	Barton on Humber -	Lincoln	1566
Barnston	Nottingham -	1596	Barton Westcott	Oxford -	1559
Barnwell -	Northampton -	1558	Barwell	Leicester	1652
Barnwood	Gloucester	1651	Barwick	Somerset -	1560
Barr, Great	Stafford -	1654	Barwick-in-Elmett	York -	1653
Barrington -	Cambridge -	1699	Baschurch - -	Salop -	1600
Barrington	Somerset -	[3] 1653	Basford	Nottingham -	[9] 1561
Barrington, Great	Gloucester	1547	Basildon -	Essex -	1653
Barrington, Little	Gloucester	1640	Basildon	Berks -	1540
Barrow	Chester -	1571	Basing -	Hants -	[10] 1655
Barrow-on-Trent	Derby -	1662	Basingstoke -	Hants -	[11] 1638
Barrow	Salop -	1727	Baslow	Derby -	1569
Barrow -	Suffolk -	1542	Bassaleg	Monmouth -	1754
Barrow Gurney	Somerset -	[4] 1590	Bassenthwaite	Cumberland -	1573
Barrow, North -	Somerset -	1568	Bassingbourne -	Cambridge -	1558
Barrow, South	Somerset -	1679	Bassingham -	Lincoln -	1572
Barrow on Humber -	Lincoln	1561	Bassingthorpe -	Lincoln	1542
Barrow on Soar	Leicester -	1563	Baston -	Lincoln -	1558
Barrowby -	Lincoln	1538	Baswich	Stafford -	[12] 1601
Barrowden	Rutland -	1603	Batcombe -	Dorset -	1783
Barry - -	Glamorgan -	1724	Batcombe	Somerset	1642
Barsham -	Suffolk -	1558	Bath Abbey -	Somerset	[13] 1569
Barsham, East	Norfolk	1646	St. Michael	- -	1569
Barsham, North	Norfolk .	1557	St. James	- -	1569
Barsham, West -	Norfolk	1756	Bathampton -	Somerset -	1754
Barston -	Warwick -	1598	Bathealton -	Somerset	1712
Barthomley -	Chester -	1563	Batheaston -	Somerset -	1634
Bartlow -	Cambridge -	1573	Bathford	Somerset	1727
Barton - -	Cambridge -	1688	Bathwick	Somerset -	1668
Barton in Fabis	Nottingham -	[5] 1558	Batley	York -	1559
Barton St. David	Somerset -	1714	Batsford	Gloucester	[14] 1562
Barton	Westmorland -	1676	Battersea . -	Surrey -	1539

[1] There are a few crumbling scraps of a Register book from 1678 to 1718. The transcripts at Lincoln contain entries for this parish from 1562 down to 1809, but with considerable lacunæ.

[2] **P** 1538–1812. Edited by Thos. Wainwright, 1903.

[3] **P** (Marriages only) 1654–1812. Somersetshire Parish Registers, vol. 4, 1902.

[4] **P** (Marriages only) 1593–1811. Somersetshire Parish Registers, vol. 1, 1898.

[5] **P** (Marriages only) 1558–1812. Nottinghamshire Parish Registers, vol. 7, 1905.

[6] Bishop's Transcripts for this parish commence about 1600.

[7] **P** (Marriages only) 1577–1812. Warwickshire Parish Registers, vol. 3, 1906.

[8] **P** 1571–1812. Staffordshire Parish Register Society, 1902–1903.

[9] **P** (Marriages only) 1568–1812. Nottinghamshire Parish Registers, vol. 6, 1902.

[10] **P** (Marriages only) 1655–1812. Hampshire Parish Registers, vol. 3, 1902.

[11] **P** (Marriages only) 1638–1812. Hampshire Parish Registers, vol. 5, 1903.

[12] **P** 1601–1812. Staffordshire Parish Register Society, 1903.

[13] **P** 1659–1800. Harleian Society Registers, 1900–1901, vols. 27 and 28.

[14] **P** (Marriages only) 1565–1812. Gloucestershire Parish Registers, vol. 6, 1900.

Parish.	County.	Date of Earliest Entry.	Parish.	County.	Date of Earliest Entry.
Battisford - -	Suffolk - -	1711	Beckingham - -	Lincoln -	1573
Battle - -	Sussex - -	1610	Beckingham - -	Nottingham -	[10] 1619
Battle - -	Brecon -	1720	Beckington - -	Somerset - -	1559
Battlefield - -	Salop - -	[1] 1663	Beckley - - -	Oxford -	1703
Battlesden - -	Bedford -	1807	Beckley - - -	Sussex - -	1597
Baughurst - -	Hants - -	[2] 1678	Bedale - - -	York - -	1560
Baulking - -	Berks - -	[3] 1550	Beddgelert - -	Carnarvon -	1734
Baumber - -	Lincoln - -	[4] 1691	Beddingham - -	Sussex - -	1685
Baunton- - -	Gloucester -	1625	Beddington - -	Surrey - -	1538
Baverstock - -	Wilts - -	1559	Bedfield - - -	Suffolk - -	1538
Bawburgh - -	Norfolk - -	1555	Bedfont, East - -	Middlesex -	1678
Bawdeswell - -	Norfolk -	1557	Bedford, St. Cuthbert -	Bedford -	1607
Bawdrip - -	Somerset - -	1748	St. John - -	- - -	1669
Bawdsey - -	Suffolk -	1744	St. Mary -	- - -	1544
Bawsey - -	Norfolk -	1540	St. Paul -	- - -	1565
Bawtry - -	Nottingham -	1653	St. Peter -	- - -	1572
Baxterley - -	Warwick -	1654	Bedhampton - -	Hants - -	1688
Bayton - -	Wilts - -	1695	Bedingfield - -	Suffolk -	1538
Bayford - - -	Hertford -	1538	Bedingham - -	Norfolk - -	1555
Baylham - -	Suffolk -	1661	Bedlington - -	Durham -	1654
Baydon - - -	Worcester -	1564	Bedminster - -	Somerset - -	1690
Beachampton -	Buckingham -	1628	Bednall - - -	Stafford -	1571
Beaconsfield - -	Buckingham -	1631	Bedstone - -	Salop - -	[11] 1719
Beadnell - -	Northumberland	1766	Bedwardine, St. John -	Worcester -	1558
Beaford - -	Devon - -	1653	Bedwardine, St. Michael.	Worcester -	1546
Bealings, Great -	Suffolk - -	1539			
Bealings, Little - -	Suffolk - -	1558	Bedwas - - -	Monmouth -	1653
Beaminster - -	Dorset - -	[5] 1684	Bedwelty - -	Monmouth -	1624
Bearley - - -	Warwick -	1546	Bedwin, Great - -	Wilts - -	1538
Bearsted - -	Kent - -	1659	Bedwin, Little - -	Wilts - -	1722
Beauchamp-Roding -	Essex - -	1688	Bedworth - -	Warwick -	1653
Beauchief Abbey -	Derby - -	1768	Beeby - - -	Leicester -	1538
Beaudesert - -	Warwick -	[6] 1661	Beechamwell - -	Norfolk -	1558
Beaulieu - -	Hants - -	1654	Beeching Stoke - -	Wilts - -	1566
Beaumaris - -	Anglesea -	1655	Beeding, Upper - -	Sussex - -	1544
Beaumont - -	Cumberland -	1692	Beedon - - -	Berks - -	[12] 1732
Beaumont - -	Essex - -	[7] 1565	Beeford - - -	York - -	1564
Beaworthy - -	Devon - -	1758	Beeley - - -	Derby - -	1651
Bebington - -	Chester - -	[8] 1558	Beelsby - - -	Lincoln -	1560
Beckbury - -	Salop - -	1738	Beenham-Valence -	Berks - -	1561
Beccles - -	Suffolk - -	1586	Beer-Crocombe - -	Somerset -	[13] 1542
Becconsall - -	Lancaster -	1745	Beer-Ferrers - -	Devon - -	1539
Beckenham - -	Kent - -	1538	Beer-Hacket - -	Dorset - -	[14] 1549
Beckermet, St.Bridget's	Cumberland -	1675	Bees, St. - -	Cumberland -	1538
Beckermet, St. John's -	Cumberland -	1680	Beesby-in-the-Marsh -	Lincoln -	1561
Beckford - -	Gloucester -	1549	Beeston - -	Norfolk -	1538
Beckham, West - -	Norfolk - -	[9] 1689	Beeston, St. Lawrence	Norfolk - -	1558

[1] **P** 1663–1812. Parish Register Society, vol. 19, 1899.
[2] **P** (Marriages only) 1678–1812. Hampshire Parish Registers, vol. 5, 1903.
[3] Included in the Registers of Uffington (q.v.).
[4] Includes entries for the parishes of Minting, Gaulby, Sotby, Waddingworth and Hatton, 1695–1779.
[5] **P** (Marriages only) 1686–1812. Dorsetshire Parish Registers, vol. 1, 1906. The diocesan transcripts contain entries for this parish from 1585, and are fairly complete.
[6] Bishop's Transcripts commence 1607.
[7] **P** 1565–1678. Edited by F. A. Crisp, 1897.
[8] **P** 1558–1701. Edited by F. Saunders and W. F. Twine, 1897.
[9] **P.** (Marriages only) 1689–1836. Norfolk Parish Registers, vol. 3, 1907.
[10] For several years the leaves of the Register are in a very dilapidated condition.
[11] **P** 1719–1812. Shropshire Parish Register Society, vol. 5.
[12] The earlier registers were destroyed by fire.
[13] **P** (Marriages only) 1542–1812. Somersetshire Parish Registers, vol. 4, 1902.
[14] **P** 1549–1812. Parish Register Society, vol. 3, 1896.

Parish.	County.	Date of Earliest Entry.	Parish.	County.	Date of Earliest Entry.
Beeston - - -	Nottingham -	[1] 1558	Bentworth - -	Hants - -	1604
Beeston - -	York - -	1720	Beoley - - -	Worcester -	1558
Beeston-Regis -	Norfolk -	1743	Bepton - - -	Sussex - -	1723
Beetham - -	Westmorland -	1608	Berden - - -	Essex - -	1715
Beetley - -	Norfolk -	1539	Berechurch - -	Essex - -	1664
Begbroke - -	Oxford -	1664	Bere-Regis - -	Dorset - -	[6] 1592
Begelly - - -	Pembroke -	1771	Bergholt, East -	Suffolk -	1653
Beguildy - -	Radnor -	1703	Bergholt, West - -	Essex -	1598
Beighton - -	Norfolk -	1589	Berkeley - -	Gloucester -	[7] 1653
Beighton - -	Derby - -	1653	Berkeswell - -	Warwick -	1653
Bekesborne -	Kent - -	[2] 1558	Berkhamsted St. Mary	Hertford -	1655
Belaugh - -	Norfolk -	1538	Berkhamsted, Great -	Hertford -	[8] 1538
Belbroughton -	Worcester -	1539	Berkhamsted, Little -	Hertford -	1646
Belchamp Otten -	Essex - -	1578	Berkley - - -	Somerset -	1546
Belchamp, St. Paul -	Essex - -	1538	Bermondsey - -	Surrey - -	[9] 1548
Belchamp-Walter -	Essex - -	1559	Berners-Roding -	Essex - -	1538
Belford - - -	Northumberland	1661	Berriew - -	Montgomery -	1596
Belgrave - -	Leicester - -	1653	Berrington - -	Salop - -	1559
Belleau - - -	Lincoln -	1650	Berrow - -	Somerset -	[10] 1699
Bellingham -	Northumberland	1684	Berrow - - -	Worcester -	1698
Belper - - -	Derby - -	1783	Berrynarbor - -	Devon - -	1540
Belshford - -	Lincoln -	1698	Berry-Pomeroy - -	Devon - -	1602
Belstead - -	Suffolk -	1539	Bersted, South -	Sussex - -	1564
Belstone - -	Devon - -	1552	Berwick - -	Sussex - -	1609
Belton - - -	Leicester - -	1538	Berwick St. James -	Wilts - -	1731
Belton, All Saints -	Lincoln -	1568	Berwick St. John -	Wilts - -	1556
Belton - - -	Lincoln -	1538	Berwick St. Leonard -	Wilts - -	1759
Belton - - -	Rutland -	1577	Berwick-Bassett -	Wilts - -	1674
Belton - - -	Suffolk -	1560	Berwick Salome -	Oxford -	1609
Bemerton - -	Wilts - -	[3] —	Berwick-on-Tweed -	Northumberland	[11] 1572
Bempton - -	York - -	1597	Besford - -	Worcester -	1539
Benacre - -	Suffolk -	[4] 1727	Besselsleigh - -	Berks - -	1689
Benefield - -	Northampton -	1570	Bessingby - -	York - -	1690
Benenden - -	Kent - -	1653	Bessingham - -	Norfolk -	1538
Benfleet, North -	Essex - -	1647	Besthorpe - -	Norfolk -	1558
Benfleet, South -	Essex - -	1582	Beswick - -	York - -	1657
Bengeo - - -	Hertford -	1539	Betchworth - -	Surrey - -	1558
Bengworth - -	Worcester -	1538	Bethersden - -	Kent - -	1556
Benhall - - -	Suffolk -	1562	Betley - - -	Stafford -	1538
Benington - -	Lincoln -	1560	Betteshanger - -	Kent - -	1562
Bennington - -	Hertford -	1538	Bettiscombe - -	Dorset - -	1746
Bennington, Long -	Lincoln -	1560	Bettws - -	Carmarthen -	1706
Benniworth - -	Lincoln -	1691	Bettws - - -	Glamorgan -	1721
Benson - - -	Oxford -	1566	Bettws - - -	Monmouth -	1696
Benthall - -	Salop - -	1558	Bettws - - -	Montgomery -	1655
Bentham - -	York - -	1662	Bettws-Disserth -	Radnor - -	1731
Bentley - - -	Hants - -	[5] 1539	Bettws-Evan - -	Cardigan -	1795
Bentley - - -	Suffolk -	1539	Bettws-Garmon -	Carnarvon -	1778
Bentley, Fenny -	Derby - -	1604	Bettws-Gwerfil-Goch -	Merioneth -	1661
Bentley, Great -	Essex - -	1558	Bettws-Newydd -	Monmouth -	1734
Bentley, Little -	Essex - -	1558	Bettws-y-Coed -	Carnarvon -	1731
Benton, Long -	Northumberland	1669	Bettws-y-Cruen -	Salop - -	1624

[1] **P** (Marriages only) 1559–1812. Nottinghamshire Parish Registers, vol. 6, 1904.
[2] **P** 1558–1812. Edited by Rev. C. H. Wilkie, 1896.
[3] Included with the Registers of Fugglestone (q.v.).
[4] The previous Registers of this parish were destroyed by fire, 27th August, 1727.
[5] **P** (Marriages only) 1541–1812. Hampshire Parish Registers, vol. 9, 1907.
[6] The earlier Registers were burnt with the Vicarage in the year 1788.
[7] **P** 1653–1677. Edited by F. A. Crisp, 1897.
[8] **P** (Marriages only) 1538–1812. Hertfordshire Parish Registers, vol. 1, 1907.
[9] **P** 1548–1608. *The Genealogist*, vols. 6, 7, 8, 9.
[10] Bishop's Transcripts commence 1611.
[11] **P** 1574–1699. Durham and Northumberland Parish Register Society, vol. 2, 1905.

Parish.	County.	Date of Earliest Entry.	Parish.	County.	Date of Earliest Entry.
Bettws-yn-Rhos	Denbigh	1705	Billingshurst	Sussex	1630
Beverley-Minster	York	1558	Billingsley	Salop	[7] 1625
Beverley	York	1561	Billington	Bedford	1651
Beverstone	Gloucester	[1] 1563	Billockby	Norfolk	1560
Bewcastle	Cumberland	1737	Bilney, East	Norfolk	1713
Bewdley	Worcester	[2] —	Bilney, West	Norfolk	1562
Bexhill	Sussex	1558	Bilsby	Lincoln	1679
Bexley	Kent	1565	Bilsdale	York	1588
Bexwell	Norfolk	1558	Bilsington	Kent	1562
Beyton	Suffolk	1539	Bilsthorpe	Nottingham	1654
Bibury	Gloucester	1551	Bilston	Stafford	1684
Bicester	Oxford	1558	Bilton	Warwick	1650
Bickenhall	Somerset	1682	Bilton	York	1571
Bickenhill	Warwick	1558	Binbrooke, St. Gabriel	Lincoln	1688
Bicker	Lincoln	1561	St. Mary	-	1694
Bickington	Devon	1603	Bincombe	Dorset	1657
Bickington, High	Devon	1707	Binegar	Somerset	1717
Bickleigh	Devon	1538	Binfield	Berks	1538
Bickleigh, West	Devon	1694	Bingham	Nottingham	[8] 1598
Bicknoller	Somerset	1558	Bingley	York	[9] 1577
Bicknor	Kent	1571	Binham	Norfolk	1702
Bicknor, English	Gloucester	1561	Binley	Warwick	1660
Bicknor, Welsh	Monmouth	1699	Binsey	Oxford	1591
Bicton	Devon	1557	Binstead, Isle of Wight	Hants	1710
Bidborough	Kent	1632	Binsted	Hants	1590
Biddenden	Kent	1538	Binsted	Sussex	1638
Biddenham	Bedford	1663	Binton	Warwick	1539
Biddestone	Wilts	1688	Bintree	Norfolk	1686
Biddisham	Somerset	1621	Birch	Lancaster	1752
Biddlesden	Buckingham	1686	Birch, Great	Essex	1560
Biddulph	Stafford	1558	Birch, Little	Hereford	1560
Bideford	Devon	1561	Birch, Much	Hereford	1599
Bidford	Warwick	[3] 1664	Bircham, Great	Norfolk	1668
Bidston	Chester	[4] 1581	Bircham, Newton	Norfolk	[10] 1562
Bielby	York	—	Bircham, Tofts	Norfolk	1715
Bierton	Buckingham	1560	Birchanger	Essex	1688
Bigbury	Devon	1678	Birchington	Kent	[11] 1539
Bigby	Lincoln	1696	Birdbrook	Essex	1633
Biggleswade	Bedford	1697	Birdforth	York	1616
Bighton	Hants	1573	Birdham	Sussex	1538
Bignor	Sussex	1556	Birdingbury	Warwick	1559
Bilborough	Nottingham	[5] 1569	Birdsall	York	1593
Bilbrough	York	1695	Birkby	York	1721
Bildeston	Suffolk	1558	Birkenhead	Chester	1719
Billesdon	Leicester	1599	Birkin	York	1684
Billing, Great	Northampton	1662	Birley	Hereford	1754
Billing, Little	Northampton	1635	Birling	Kent	1558
Billingborough	Lincoln	1561	Birlingham	Worcester	1566
Billinge	Lancaster	1696	Birmingham	Warwick	— —
Billingford (Scole)	Norfolk	1640	St. Martin	-	[12] 1554
Billingford	Norfolk	1744	St. Philip	-	1715
Billingham	Durham	1570	St. Mary's Chapel	-	1774
Billinghay	Lincoln	1627	St. Paul's Chapel	-	1779

[1] **P** (Marriages only) 1563-1812. Gloucestershire Parish Registers, vol. 6, 1900.
[2] Included in Registers of Ribbesford (q.v.).　　　[3] Bishop's Transcripts commence 1612.
[4] **P** 1581-1700. Edited by W. F. Twine, 1893.
[5] Included in Registers of Hayton (q.v.).
[6] **P** (Marriages only) 1569-1812. Nottinghamshire Parish Registers, vol. 6, 1904.
[7] **P** 1625-1812. Shropshire Parish Register Society, vol. 3.
[8] **P** (Marriages only) 1598-1812. Nottinghamshire Parish Registers, vol. 1, 1898.
[9] **P** 1577-1686. Yorkshire Parish Register Society, vol. 9, 1901.
[10] **P** 1562-1743. Edited by Richard Howlett, 1888.
[11] **P** 1539-1675. Edited by F. A. Crisp.
[12] **P** 1554-1708. Edited by J. Hill and W. B. Bickley, 2 vols., 1889.

Parish.	County.	Date of Earliest Entry.	Parish.	County.	Date of Earliest Entry.
Birstall - -	York - -	1558	Bisley - -	Gloucester -	1547
Birstall - -	Leicester - -	1574	Bisley - -	Surrey - -	1561
Birtley - -	Northumberland	1728	Bispham - -	Lancaster -	1599
Birtley - -	Durham -	[1] —	Bisterne - -	Hants - -	[7] 1561
Birts-Morton - -	Worcester -	1539	Bitchfield - -	Lincoln - -	1674
Bisbrooke - -	Rutland - -	1665	Bittadon - -	Devon - -	1712
Biscathorpe - -	Lincoln -	1700	Bittering, Little -	Norfolk - -	1733
Bisham - - -	Berks - -	[2] 1560	Bitterley - -	Salop - -	[8] 1658
Bishampton - -	Worcester -	1599	Bitteswell - -	Leicester - -	1558
Bishop-Auckland. See Auckland.			Bitton - -	Gloucester -	[9] 1572
			Bix - - -	Oxford - -	1577
Bishop-Burton - -	York - -	1562	Bixley - -	Norfolk - -	1561
Bishop-Cropwell. See Cropwell, Bishop.			Blaby - - -	Leicester -	1560
			Blackawton - -	Devon - -	1538
Bishop-Middleham -	Durham -	[3] 1559	Blackborough - -	Devon - -	1695
Bishop-Norton. See Norton, Bishop-.			Black Bourton -	Oxford - -	1542
			Blackburn, St. Mary -	Lancaster -	1568
Bishopsbourne -	Kent - -	1558	St. John -	- -	1789
Bishops-Cannings -	Wilts - -	1591	Black Burton - -	York - -	[10] —
Bishops-Castle - -	Salop - -	1559	Blackford - -	Somerset -	1606
Bishops-Caundle. See Caundle, Bishops-.			Blackland - -	Wilts - -	1757
			Blackley - -	Lancaster -	1655
Bishops-Cleeve -	Gloucester -	[4] 1563	Blackmore - -	Essex - -	1602
Bishops-Fonthill. See Fonthill, Bishops-.			Blackrod - -	Lancaster -	1607
			Blacktoft - -	York - -	[11] 1700
Bishops-Frome. See Frome, Bishops-.			Black Torrington -	Devon - -	1547
			Blackwell - -	Derby - -	1685
Bishops-Hull - -	Somerset - -	[5] 1562	Bladon - -	Oxford - -	1545
Bishops-Itchington -	Warwick - -	1559	Blaenavon - -	Monmouth -	1804
Bishops-Lavington -	Wilts - -	1598	Blaengwrach - -	Glamorgan -	1702
Bishops Lydeard -	Somerset -	1674	Blaenpenal - -	Cardigan -	1797
Bishops-Nympton -	Devon - -	1556	Blaen-Porth - -	Cardigan -	1716
Bishops-Stortford -	Hertford - -	1561	Blagdon - -	Somerset - -	[12] 1555
Bishops-Sutton - -	Hants - -	1711	Blaisdon - -	Gloucester -	1635
Bishops-Tachbrook -	Warwick - -	[6] 1538	Blakemere - -	Hereford -	1662
Bishops-Tawton - -	Devon - -	1558	Blakeney - -	Gloucester -	[13] —
Bishops-Teignton -	Devon - -	1558	Blakeney - -	Norfolk - -	1538
Bishopstoke - -	Hants - -	1658	Blakenham, Great -	Norfolk - -	1549
Bishopston - -	Wilts - -	1636	Blakenham, Little -	Norfolk - -	1728
Bishopston - -	Glamorgan -	1754	Blakesley - -	Northampton -	1538
Bishopstone - -	Hereford -	1727	Blanchland - -	Northumberland	1753
Bishopstone - -	Sussex - -	1561	Blandford St. Mary -	Dorset - -	1581
Bishopstone - -	Wilts - -	1573	Blandford Forum -	Dorset - -	1732
Bishopstrow - -	Wilts - -	1686	Blankney - -	Lincoln - -	1558
Bishops-Wickham -	Essex - -	1662	Blaston - -	Leicester -	1676
Bishopthorpe - -	York - -	1692	Blatchington, East -	Sussex - -	1563
Bishopton - -	Durham -	1649	Blatherwycke - -	Northampton -	1621
Bishopton - - -	Warwick - -	1590	Blawith - -	Lancaster -	1728
Bishopswearmouth -	Durham - -	1567	Blaxhall - -	Suffolk - -	[14] 1673
Bishop-Wilton - -	York - -	1603	Blazey, St. - -	Cornwall -	1710

[1] Included with Chester-le-Street (q.v.).
[2] **P** 1560–1812. Parish Register Society, vol. 15, 1898.
[3] **P** 1559–1812. Durham and Northumberland Parish Register Society, vol. 13, 1906.
[4] **P** (Marriages only) 1563–1812. Gloucestershire Parish Registers, vol. 3, 1898.
[5] **P** (Marriages only) 1562–1812. Somersetshire Parish Registers, vol. 10, 1907.
[6] **P** (Marriages only) 1538–1812. Warwickshire Parish Registers, vol. 3, 1906.
[7] Included with the Registers of Ringwood (q.v.).
[8] **P** 1658–1812. Shropshire Parish Register Society, vol. 4.
[9] **P** 1572–1674. Parish Register Society, vol. 32, 1900.
[10] Included with the Registers of Thornton-in-Lonsdale (q.v.).
[11] **P** 1700–1812. Yorkshire Parish Register Society, vol. 8, 1901.
[12] Almost illegible until 1600.   [13] Included in the Registers of Awre (q.v.).
[14] One volume (containing burials 1663-1709, marriages 1663-1700, and baptisms 1675-1710), lost since date of Parliamentary Return of 1831.

Parish.	County.	Date of Earliest Entry.	Parish.	County.	Date of Earliest Entry.
Bleadon - -	Somerset - -	1713	Bodenham - -	Hereford -	1584
Blean - - -	Kent - -	1558	Bodewryd - -	Anglesea - -	1763
Bleasby - -	Nottingham -	1573	Bodham - - -	Norfolk -	1708
Blechingdon - -	Oxford - -	1559	Bodiam - -	Sussex -	1557
Bledington - -	Gloucester -	1700	Bodicote - -	Oxford - -	1563
Bledlow - -	Buckingham -	1592	Bodfaen - -	Carnarvon -	1679
Blendworth - -	Hants - -	1586	Bodfari - - -	Flint - -	1571
Bletchingley - -	Surrey - -	1538	Bodmin - -	Cornwall -	[3] 1558
Bletchley - -	Buckingham -	1665	Bodney - - -	Norfolk -	1754
Bletherston - -	Pembroke -	1654	Bognor *with South*		
Blethvaugh (or Bledfa)	Radnor - -	1616	*Bersted.*		
Bletsoe - -	Bedford - -	1582	Bolam - - -	Northumberland	1661
Blewbury - -	Berks - -	1588	Bolas, Great - -	Salop - -	1582
Blickling - -	Norfolk - -	1559	Boldre - -	Durham -	1571
Blidworth - -	Nottingham -	1566	Boldon - - -	Hants - -	1596
Blisland - -	Cornwall -	[1] 1539	Bole - - -	Nottingham -	[6] 1755
Blisworth - - -	Northampton -	1551	Bolingbroke - -	Lincoln - -	1538
Blithfield - -	Stafford - -	1538	Bollingham - -	Hereford -	1630
Blockley - -	Worcester -	1538	Bolney - - -	Sussex - -	1541
Blofield - -	Norfolk - -	1545	Bolnhurst - -	Bedford - -	1685
Blo-Norton - -	Norfolk -	1562	Bolsover - -	Derby - -	1604
Blore-Ray - -	Stafford -	1558	Bolsterstone - -	York - -	[7] 1736
Bloxham - -	Oxford - -	1630	Bolton - - -	Cumberland -	[8] 1619
Bloxholm - -	Lincoln - -	1708	Bolton - - -	Westmorland -	1665
Bloxwich - -	Stafford - -	1733	Bolton Abbey - -	York - -	[9] 1689
Bloxworth - -	Dorset - -	1759	Bolton (by Bolland) -	York - -	[10] 1558
Blubberhouses -	York - -	1593	Bolton Castle - -	York - -	1684
Blundeston - -	Suffolk - -	[2] 1558	Bolton-le-Moors -	Lancaster -	1587
Blunham - -	Bedford - -	1571	St. George	- - -	1796
Blundsdon St. An-	Wilts - -	1650	Bolton-le-Sands -	Lancaster -	1653
drew.			Bolton-Percy - -	York - -	1571
Blunsdon, Broad -	Wilts - -	1679	Bolton-on-Dearne -	York - -	1560
Bluntisham - -	Huntingdon -	1538	Bolton-on-Swale -	York - -	1653
Blyborough - -	Lincoln - -	1691	Bonby - - -	Lincoln - -	1649
Blyford - -	Suffolk - -	1695	Bonchurch, Isle of Wight	Hants - -	1734
Blymhill - -	Stafford -	1561	Bondleigh - -	Devon - -	1734
Blyth - -	Nottingham -	1556	Bongate. *See Ap-*		
Blythurgh - -	Suffolk - -	1690	*pleby.*		
Blyton - -	Lincoln - -	1571	Boningale - -	Salop - -	[11] 1698
Boarhunt - -	Hants - -	1653	Bonnington - -	Kent - -	1679
Boarstall - -	Buckingham -	1640	Bonsall - -	Derby - -	1634
Bobbing - -	Kent - -	1738	Bonvilstone - -	Glamorgan -	1758
Bobbington - -	Stafford - -	1571	Bookham, Great -	Surrey - -	1632
Bobbingworth (or	Essex - -	[3] 1558	Bookham, Little -	Surrey - -	1642
Bovinger).			Boothby-Graffoe -	Lincoln -	1720
Bocking - -	Essex - -	[4] 1558	Boothby-Pagnell -	Lincoln - -	1566
Bockleton - -	Worcester -	1574	Bootle - - -	Cumberland -	1655
Boconnoc - -	Cornwall -	1709	Booton - -	Norfolk -	[12] 1558
Boddington - -	Gloucester -	1656	Borden - - -	Kent - -	1555
Boddington - -	Northampton -	1558	Bordesley Chapel -	Warwick -	[13] 1704
Bodedern - -	Anglesea -	1722	Boreham : -	Essex - -	1559

[1] **P** (Marriages only) 1539-1812.   Cornwall Parish Registers, vol. 4, 1903.
[2] Included with the Registers of Fewston (*q.v.*).
[3] **P** 1558-1785.   Edited by F. A. Crisp, 1888.
[4] **P** 1558-1639.   Edited by J. J. Godwin, Hartford, Connecticut, 1903.
[5] **P** (Marriages only) 1559-1812.   Cornwall Parish Registers, vol. 11, 1907.
[6] Very fragmentary until 1800.
[7] Before this date included in the Registers of Bradford (*q.v.*).
[8] The early Registers are considerably the worse for wear and damp, and very imperfect in parts.
[9] **P** 1689-1812.   Edited by A. P. Howes, 1895.
[10] **P** 1558-1724.   Yorkshire Parish Register Society, vol. 19, 1904.
[11] **P** 1698-1812.   Shropshire Parish Register Society, vol. 3, 1901.
[12] **P** (Marriages only) 1560-1812.   Norfolk Parish Registers, vol. 3, 1907.
[13] Earlier entries in the Registers of Tardebigge (*q.v.*).

Parish.	County.	Date of Earliest Entry.	Parish.	County.	Date of Earliest Entry.
Borley - - -	Essex - - -	1652	Bovey Tracey - -	Devon - -	1675
Borrowdale - -	Cumberland -	[1] 1775	Bovingdon - -	Hertford - -	1674
Bosbury - -	Hereford - -	1559	Bovinger. *See* Bob-		
Boscombe - -	Wilts - -	[2] 1695	bingworth.		
Bosham - - -	Sussex - -	1557	Bow (or Nymet Tracey)	Devon - -	1604
Bosherston - -	Pembroke -	1670	Bow - - -	Middlesex -	1539
Bosley - - -	Chester - -	1720	Bowden, Great -	Leicester - -	1559
Bossall - -	York - -	1613	Bowden, Little - -	Northampton -	1653
Bossington - -	Hants - -	1763	Bowdon - -	Chester - -	1628
Boston - -	Lincoln - -	1557	Bowerchalke - -	Wilts - -	1653
Bosworth, Husband's -	Leicester - -	1557	Bowers-Gifford -	Essex - -	1558
Bosworth Market -	Leicester - -	1570	Bowes - -	York - -	1670
Botesdale - -	Suffolk - -	[3] —	Bowness - -	Cumberland -	1642
Bothal - - -	Northumberland	[4] 1678	Box - - -	Wilts - -	1587
Bothamsall - -	Nottingham -	1538	Boxford - - -	Berks - -	1558
Bothenhampton -	Dorset - -	[5] 1725	Boxford - -	Suffolk - -	1557
Botley - -	Hants - -	1679	Boxgrove - -	Sussex - -	1561
Botolph - -	Sussex - -	1607	Boxley - -	Kent - -	1558
Botolph Bridge -	Huntingdon -	1556	Boxted - - -	Essex - -	1559
Bottesford - -	Leicester - -	1563	Boxted - -	Suffolk - -	1538
Bottesford - -	Lincoln - -	1603	Boxwell - -	Gloucester -	[13] 1548
Bottisham - -	Cambridge -	1561	Boxworth - -	Cambridge -	1588
Bottwnog - -	Carnarvon -	1741	Boylestone - -	Derby - -	1734
Botus-Fleming -	Cornwall - -	1548	Boynton - -	York - -	1563
Boughrood - -	Radnor - -	1689	Boyton - -	Cornwall -	1568
Boughton - -	Norfolk - -	1729	Boyton - -	Suffolk - -	1539
Boughton - -	Northampton -	1549	Boyton - -	Wilts - -	1560
Boughton - -	Nottingham -	1686	Bozeat - -	Northampton -	1729
Boughton-Aluph -	Kent - -	1558	Brabourne - -	Kent - -	1558
Boughton-Malherbe -	Kent - -	1671	Braceborough -	Lincoln - -	1593
Boughton-Monchelsea	Kent - -	1560	Bracebridge - -	Lincoln - -	1663
Boughton-under-Blean	Kent - -	[6] 1558	Braceby - -	Lincoln - -	1759
Boulge - -	Suffolk - -	1539	Brace Meole - -	Salop - -	1681
Boulston - -	Pembroke -	1799	Bracewell - -	York - -	1587
Boulstone - -	Hereford - -	[7] —	Brackley - -	Northampton -	1560
Boultham - -	Lincoln - -	1716	Bracon-Ash - -	Norfolk - -	1563
Boulton - -	Derby - -	[8] 1614	Bradbourne - -	Derby - -	1713
Bourn - -	Cambridge -	1564	Bradden - -	Northampton -	1559
Bourne - -	Lincoln - -	1562	Braddock - -	Cornwall -	1555
Bourne, St. Mary -	Hants - -	[9] 1661	Bradeley - -	Stafford - -	1538
Bourne, West - -	Sussex - -	1550	Bradenham - -	Buckingham -	1627
Bourton - - -	Dorset - -	[10] 1810	Bradenham, East -	Norfolk - -	1695
Bourton Black -	Oxford - -	1542	Bradenham, West -	Norfolk - -	1538
Bourton Flax -	Somerset - -	1702	Bradeston - -	Norfolk - -	[14] 1731
Bourton-on-the-Hill -	Gloucester -	1568	Bradfield - -	Berks - -	1539
Bourton-on-the-Water	Gloucester -	1654	Bradfield - -	Essex - -	1695
Bourton-on-Dunsmore	Warwick - -	[11] 1560	Bradfield - -	Norfolk - -	1725
Boveney - -	Buckingham -	[12] —	Bradfield - -	York - -	1559
Bovey, North - -	Devon - -	1572	Bradfield, St. Clare -	Suffolk - -	1538

[1] Previous to 1775 included in the Registers of Crosthwaite (*q.v.*).
[2] **P** (Marriages only) 1696–1812. Wiltshire Parish Registers, vol. 3, 1906.
[3] Included with Redgrave (*q.v.*).
[4] **P** 1678–1812. Durham and Northumberland Parish Register Society, vol. 5, 1901.
[5] **P** (Marriages only) 1636–1812. Dorset Parish Registers, vol. 1, 1906.
[6] **P** 1558–1626. Parish Register Society, vol. 48, 1903.
[7] Included with the Registers of Holme Lacy (*q.v.*).
[8] **P** (Marriages only) 1756–1812. Derbyshire Parish Registers, vol. 1, 1906.
[9] **P** (Marriages only) 1662–1812. Hampshire Parish Registers, vol. 1, 1899.
[10] Included in the Registers of Gillingham (*q.v.*)
[11] **P** (Marriages only) 1560–1812. Warwickshire Parish Registers, vol. 1, 1904.
[12] Included with Burnham (*q.v.*).
[13] **P** (Marriages only) 1572–1810. Gloucestershire Parish Registers, vol. 13, 1908.
[14] **P** (Marriages only) 1623–1812. Norfolk Parish Registers, vol. 1, 1892.

Parish.	County.	Date of Earliest Entry.	Parish.	County.	Date of Earliest Entry.
Bradfield St. George -	Suffolk - -	1555	Brampford-Speke -	Devon - -	1739
Bradfield-Combust -	Suffolk - -	1538	Brampton - -	Cumberland -	1663
Bradford - -	Devon - -	1538	Brampton - -	Derby - -	1658
Bradford - - -	Somerset - -	¹ 1558	Brampton - -	Huntingdon -	1653
Bradford - -	York - -	² 1596	Brampton - - -	Norfolk - -	⁸ 1600
Bradford-Abbas -	Dorset - -	1579	Brampton - - -	Suffolk - -	1755
Bradford-on-Avon -	Wilts - -	1579	Brampton-Abbots -	Hereford - -	1556
Bradford-Peverell -	Dorset - -	1653	Brampton-Ash -	Northampton -	1580
Brading, Isle of Wight	Hants - -	1547	Brampton-Bryan -	Hereford - -	1598
Bradley - -	Derby - -	1579	Brampton Church -	Northampton -	1561
Bradley - - -	Lincoln - -	1664	Bramshall - -	Stafford - -	1578
Bradley - -	Hants - -	1725	Bramshaw - -	Wilts - -	1598
Bradley - - -	Worcester -	⁸ 1562	Bramshott - -	Hants - -	1560
Bradley, Great -	Suffolk - -	1702	Bramwith-Kirk. See		
Bradley-in-the-Moors	Stafford -	1708	Kirk-Bramwith.		
Bradley, Little - -	Suffolk - -	1561	Brancaster - -	Norfolk - -	1538
Bradley, Maiden -	Wilts - -	1753	Brancepeth - -	Durham - -	1599
Bradley, North -	Wilts - -	1641	Brandesburton -	York - -	1558
Bradley, West - -	Somerset -	1633	Brandeston - -	Suffolk - -	1559
Bradninch - -	Devon - -	1559	Brandiston - -	Norfolk - -	1610
Bradpole - - -	Dorset - -	⁴ 1695	Brandon-Ferry -	Suffolk - -	1653
Bradstone - -	Devon - -	1656	Brandon, Little -	Norfolk - -	1694
Bradwell - - -	Buckingham -	1577	Brandsby - -	York - -	1575
Bradwell - -	Oxford - -	1601	Branscombe - -	Devon - -	1539
Bradwell - - -	Suffolk - -	1556	Bransford - -	Worcester -	1767
Bradwell, near Brain-	Essex - -	1704	Branston - - -	Lincoln - -	1626
tree.			Branstone - -	Leicester - -	1591
Bradwell-on-Sea -	Essex - -	1558	Brant Broughton -	Lincoln - -	1710
Bradworthy - -	Devon - -	1548	Brantham - -	Suffolk - -	1634
Brafferton - - -	York - -	1798	Brantingham - -	York - -	⁹ 1653
Brafield-on-the-Green	Northampton -	1540	Branxton - -	Northumberland	1739
Brailes - - -	Warwick -	1570	Brassington - -	Derby - -	1716
Brailsford - -	Derby - -	1647	Brasted - - -	Kent - -	1557
Braintfield - -	Hertford - -	1559	Bratoft - - -	Lincoln - -	1685
Braintree - -	Essex - -	1660	Brattleby - -	Lincoln - -	1686
Braiseworth. See			Bratton - - -	Wilts - -	1795
Brayesworth.			Bratton-Clovelly -	Devon - -	1555
Braithwell - -	York - -	1559	Bratton-Fleming -	Devon - -	¹⁰ 1673
Bramber - - -	Sussex - -	1601	Bratton St. Maur -	Somerset -	¹¹ 1754
Bramcote - -	Nottingham -	⁵ 1562	Braughing - -	Hertford - -	1563
Bramdean - -	Hants - -	1573	Brauncewell - -	Lincoln - -	1760
Bramerton - -	Norfolk - -	1561	Braunston - -	Northampton -	1538
Bramfield. See Braint-			Braunston - -	Rutland - -	1553
field.			Braunstone - -	Leicester - -	1561
Bramfield - -	Suffolk - -	⁶ 1539	Braunton - -	Devon - -	1538
Bramford - - -	Suffolk - -	1553	Brawdy - - -	Pembroke -	1754
Bramham - -	York - -	1586	Braxted, Great -	Essex - -	1558
Bramhope with Otley -	York - -	—	Braxted, Little - -	Essex - -	1730
Bramley - -	Hants - -	⁷ 1580	Bray - - - -	Berks - -	1652
Bramley - - -	Surrey - -	1566	Bray, High. See High		
Bramley - - -	York - -	1717	Bray.		

¹ **P** (Marriages only) 1558–1812. Somersetshire Parish Registers, vol. 7, 1906.
² **P** (Burials only) 1596–1680. The Bradford Antiquary, vol. 1, 2, &c.
³ **P** (Marriages only) 1630–1812. Worcestershire Parish Registers, vol. 1, 1901.
⁴ **P** (Marriages only) 1695–1812. Dorset Parish Registers, vol. 1, 1906.
⁵ **P** (Marriages only) 1576–1812. Nottinghamshire Parish Registers, vol. 6, 1904.
⁶ **P** 1539–1596, &c. Edited by T. S. Hill, 1894.
⁷ **P** (Marriages only) 1580–1812. Hampshire Parish Registers, vol. 1, 1899.
⁸ **P** 1600–1812. Edited by A. T. Michell, 1897.
⁹ **P** 1653–1812. Yorkshire Parish Register Society, vol. 12, 1902.
¹⁰ Volume 1 (1559–1670) lost or destroyed since Parliamentary Returns of 1831.
¹¹ Earlier Registers are known to have been in existence in the early part of last century, but there is now no trace of them.

Parish.	County.	Date of Earliest Entry.	Parish.	County.	Date of Earliest Entry.
Braybrooke - -	Northampton -	1653	Bretton-Monk - -	York -	1750
Bravesworth - -	Suffolk -	1709	Breward, St. - -	Cornwall -	⁷1558
Brayfield, Cold -	Buckingham -	1693	Brewham - - -	Somerset -	1660
Braytoft. See Bratoft.			Brewood - -	Stafford -	⁸1562
Brayton - - -	York - -	1615	Briavells, St. - -	Gloucester -	1665
Breadsall - -	Derby -	1573	Bricet, Great -	Suffolk -	1680
Breage, St. - -	Cornwall -	¹1559	Brickhill, Bow -	Buckingham -	1687
Breamore - -	Hants -	1675	Brickhill, Great -	Buckingham -	1558
Breane - -	Somerset -	1730	Brickhill, Little -	Buckingham -	1559
Breaston - -	Derby -	²1719	Bricklehampton -	Worcester -	⁹1756
Breccles - -	Norfolk -	1540	Bridekirk - -	Cumberland -	1585
Brechfa - -	Carmarthen -	1780	Bridell - -	Pembroke -	1705
Brecknock St. David (or Llanfaes).	Brecon -	1730	Bride, St. See Wentloog.		
Brecon, St. John -	Brecon -	1727	Bride, St. - -	Pembroke -	1724
Brecon, St. Mary -	Brecon -	1685	Bridenbury. See Bredenbury.		
Brede - - -	Sussex -	1559	Bride's, St. - -	Monmouth -	1754
Bredenbury - -	Hereford -	1607	Bride's, St., Major -	Glamorgan -	1732
Bredfield - -	Suffolk -	1711	Bride's, St., Minor -	Glamorgan -	1723
Bredgar - - -	Kent -	1559	Bride's, St., super Ely	Glamorgan -	1747
Bredhurst - -	Kent -	1545	Bridestow - -	Devon -	1696
Bredicot - -	Worcester -	³1702	Bridford - -	Devon -	1538
Bredon - -	Worcester -	1559	Bridge - - -	Kent -	1579
Bredon's Norton -	Worcester -	⁴1754	Bridgerule - -	Devon -	1561
Bredwardine - -	Hereford -	1723	Bridge Sollars -	Hereford -	1615
Bredy, Long - -	Dorset -	1649	Bridgford, East -	Nottingham -	¹⁰1557
Bredy, Little - -	Dorset -	1717	Bridgford, West -	Nottingham -	¹¹1559
Breedon-on-the-Hill -	Leicester -	1562	Bridgham - -	Norfolk -	1558
Breinton - -	Hereford -	1662	Bridgnorth, St. Mary Magdalene.	Salop -	1610
Bremhill - -	Wilts -	1590	Bridgnorth, St. Leonard.	Salop -	1556
Bremilham - -	Wilts -	1699	Bridgwater - -	Somerset -	1558
Brenchley - -	Kent -	1560	Bridlington - -	York -	1564
Brendon - -	Devon -	1620	Bridport - -	Dorset -	1600
Brent, East - -	Somerset	1556	Bridstow - -	Hereford -	1560
Brent-Eleigh - -	Suffolk -	1580	Brierley-Hill - -	Stafford -	1766
Brent, Pelham. See Pelham-Brent.			Briers - -	York -	1800
Brent, Knoll - -	Somerset -	1679	Brigg with Wrawby -	- -	—
Brent, South - -	Devon -	1677	Brigham - -	Cumberland -	1563
Brentford, New -	Middlesex -	1570	Brightling - -	Sussex -	1560
Brentingby - -	Leicester -	⁵—	Brightlingsea -	Essex -	1697
Brent, Tor - -	Devon -	1720	Brighton - -	Sussex -	1558
Brentwood - -	Essex -	1695	Brightstone (Isle of Wight).	Hants -	¹²1644
Brenzett - -	Kent -	1538	Brightwaltham -	Berks -	¹³1559
Breock, St. - -	Cornwall -	1561	Brightwell - -	Berks -	1564
Brereton - -	Chester -	1538	Brightwell -	Suffolk -	1653
Bressingham - -	Norfolk -	1559	Brightwell-Baldwin -	Oxford -	1545
Bretby - -	Derby -	⁶1766	Brignall - -	York -	1588
Bretforton - -	Worcester -	1538			
Brettenham - -	Norfolk -	1777			
Brettenham - -	Suffolk -	1584			

¹ **P** (Marriages only) 1559-1812. Cornwall Parish Registers, vol. 5, 1903.
² **P** (Marriages only) 1719-1810. Derbyshire Parish Registers, vol. 1, 1906.
³ Bishop's Transcripts commence 1609. ⁴ Bishop's Transcripts commence 1612.
⁵ Included with Thorpe Arnold (q.v.).
⁶ Baptisms only. Burials and marriages included with the Registers of Repton.
⁷ **P** (Marriages only) 1558-1812. Cornwall Parish Registers, vol. 1, 1900. Also **P** 1558-1900. Edited by T. Taylor, Beverley, 1900.
⁸ **P** 1562-1812. Staffordshire Parish Register Society, 1906. ⁹ Bishop's Transcripts commence 1611.
¹⁰ **P** (Marriages only) 1614-1812. Nottinghamshire Parish Registers, vol. 1, 1898.
¹¹ **P** (Marriages only) 1559-1812. Nottinghamshire Parish Registers, vol. 7, 1905.
¹² The parish account books begin 1566.
¹³ The churchwarden account book of this parish dates from 1481.

Parish.	County.	Date of Earliest Entry.	Parish.	County.	Date of Earliest Entry.
Brigsley - - -	Lincoln -	1558	Broad-Blunsdon. *See* Blunsdon, Broad-.		
Brigstock - -	Northampton -	1641			
Brill - - -	Buckingham -	1588	Broad-Chalke -	Wilts - -	[2] 1538
Brilley - -	Hereford -	1581	Broad-Clyst - -	Devon - -	1653
Brimfield - -	Hereford -	1566	Broadfield *with* Cottered.	Hertford - -	—
Brimington - -	Derby - -	1759			
Brimpsfield - -	Gloucester -	1588	Broadhembury - -	Devon - -	1538
Brimpton - -	Berks - -	1564	Broadhempston -	Devon - -	1678
Brimpton - -	Somerset - -	1699	Broad Hinton. *See* Hinton, Broad.		
Brindle - - -	Lancaster -	[1] 1558			
Bringhurst - -	Leicester -	1640	Broadmayne - -	Dorset - -	1693
Brington - -	Huntingdon -	1685	Broadoak - -	Cornwall -	1555
Brington - -	Northampton -	1558	Broadwas - - -	Worcester -	[4] 1676
Briningham - -	Norfolk - -	1709	Broadwater - -	Sussex - -	1558
Brinkhill - -	Lincoln - -	1562	Broadway - -	Dorset - -	1673
Brinkley - -	Cambridge -	1684	Broadway - -	Somerset -	1678
Brinklow - -	Warwick - -	1558	Broadway - - -	Worcester -	1539
Brinkworth - -	Wilts - -	1653	Broadwell - -	Gloucester -	1697
Brinsop - -	Hereford - -	1695	Broadwell. *See* Bradwell (Oxon).		
Brinton - -	Norfolk - -	1547			
Brisley - -	Norfolk - -	1698	Broadwinsor - -	Dorset - -	1562
Brislington - -	Somerset -	1566	Broadwood-Kelly -	Devon - -	1654
Bristol, All Saints' -	Gloucester -	1560	Broadwood-Widger -	Devon - -	1654
St. Augustine -	- - -	1577	Brobury - -	Hereford -	1786
Christ Church -	- - -	1538	Brockdish - - -	Norfolk - -	1558
St. John - -	- - -	1558	Brockenhurst - -	Hants - -	1629
Cathedral Church (Holy Trinity).	- - -	1669	Brockford *with* Wetheringsett.	Suffolk - -	—
St. Leonard -	- - -	1689	Brockhall - -	Northampton -	1561
St. Nicholas -	- - -	1538	Brockhampton - -	Hereford - -	[3] 1578
St. Mary-le-Port -	- - -	1560	Brocklesby - -	Lincoln - -	1672
St. Mary Redcliffe	- - -	1559	Brockley - -	Somerset - -	1696
St. Thomas -	- - -	1552	Brockley - -	Suffolk - -	1560
St. Michael - -	- - -	1653	Brockworth - -	Gloucester -	1559
St. Peter - -	- - -	1653	Brodsworth - -	York - -	1538
St. Stephen - -	- - -	1559	Brokenborough -	Wilts - -	[6] —
Temple, or Holy Cross.	- - -	1588	Brome. *See* Broome.		
St. Werburgh -	- - -	1559	Bromborough -	Chester -	1621
St. James -	- - -	1559	Bromeswell -	Suffolk - -	1638
St. Paul - -	- - -	1794	Bromfield - - -	Cumberland -	1654
St. Philip and St. Jacob.	- - -	1575	Bromfield - -	Salop - -	[7] 1559
			Bromham - -	Bedford - -	1570
St. George - -	- - -	1756	Bromham - -	Wilts - -	1560
Briston - -	Norfolk -	1689	Bromley - -	Kent - -	1558
Britford - -	Wilts - -	[2] 1573	Bromley Abbots. *See* Abbots-Bromley.		
Briton-Ferry - -	Glamorgan -	1667			
Britwell-Salome -	Oxford - -	1574	Bromley, Great -	Essex - -	1559
Brixham - -	Devon - -	1556	Bromley, King's -	Stafford -	1673
Brixton - -	Devon - -	1668	Bromley St. Leonard -	Middlesex -	1622
Brixton. *See* Brightstone.			Bromley, Little - -	Essex - -	1538
			Brompton (Northallerton).	York - -	1594
Brixton-Deverill -	Wilts - -	1653	Brompton (Scarborough).	York - -	1584
Brixworth - - -	Northampton -	1546			
Brize-Norton. *See* Norton, Brize-.			Brompton-Patrick -	York - -	1558

[1] **P** 1558–1714. Lancashire Parish Register Society, vol. 9, 1901.
[2] **P** (Marriages only) 1573–1812. Wiltshire Parish Registers, vol. 3, 1906.
[3] **P** 1538–1780. Edited by the Rev. C. G. Moore, 1880.
[4] Bishop's Transcripts commence 1612.
[5] The early entries are very indistinct and in some cases impossible to decipher.
[6] Included with Westport (*q.v.*).
[7] **P** 1559–1812. Shropshire Parish Register Society, vol. 5.

Parish.	County.	Date of Earliest Entry.	Parish.	County.	Date of Earliest Entry.
Brompton-Ralph	Somerset	1557	Brown-Candover	Hants	1611
Brompton-Regis	Somerset	1690	Brownsover	Warwick	1593
Bromsberrow	Gloucester	1558	Broxbourne	Hertford	1688
Bromsgrove	Worcester	1590	Broxholme	Lincoln	1643
Bromwich, Castle	Warwick	1619	Broxted	Essex	1654
Bromwich, West	Stafford	[1] 1608	Bruera	Chester	1657
Bromyard	Hereford	1538	Bruisyard	Suffolk	1565
Brongwyn	Cardigan	1559	Brundall	Norfolk	[10] 1563
Brynllws	Brecon	1755	Brundish	Suffolk	[11] 1562
Brook	Kent	1695	Brunstead	Norfolk	1560
Brook, Isle of Wight	Hants	1653	Bruntingthorpe	Leicester	1550
Brooke	Norfolk	1558	Brushford	Devon	1694
Brooke	Rutland	1576	Brushford	Somerset	1558
Brookland	Kent	1558	Bruton	Somerset	[12] 1554
Brooksby	Leicester	1767	Bryanston	Dorset	1598
Brookthorpe	Gloucester	[2] 1730	Bryncroes	Carnarvon	1730
Broome	Norfolk	1538	Bryn-Eglwys	Denbigh	1687
Broome	Suffolk	1559	Bryngwyn	Monmouth	1643
Broome	Worcester	[3] 1664	Bryngwyn	Radnor	1725
Broomfield	Essex	1546	Brynllws	Brecon	1755
Broomfield	Kent	1579	Bubbenhall	Warwick	1698
Broomfield	Somerset	[4] 1630	Bubwith	York	1623
Broseley	Salop	[5] 1570	Buckby, Long	Northampton	1583
Brothertoft	Lincoln	1708	Buckden	Huntingdon	1559
Brotherton	York	1562	Buckenham	Norfolk	1714
Brotton	York	1653	Buckenham, New	Norfolk	1538
Brough-under-Stainmore.	Westmorland	1556	Buckenham, Old	Norfolk	[13] 1560
			Buckerell	Devon	1653
Brougham	Westmorland	1681	Buckfastleigh	Devon	1602
Broughton	Buckingham	1720	Buckhorn-Weston	Dorset	1678
Broughton	Hants	1639	Buckingham	Buckingham	1559
Broughton	Huntington	1572	Buckland	Berks	1691
Broughton	Lancaster	1653	Buckland	Buckingham	1657
Broughton	Lincoln	1538	Buckland	Gloucester	[14] 1539
Broughton	Northampton	1560	Buckland	Hertford	1659
Broughton	Oxford	1683	Buckland (in Dover)	Kent	1580
Broughton	Salop	[6] 1705	Buckland St. Mary	Somerset	[15] 1538
Broughton-Astley	Leicester	1581	Buckland	Surrey	1560
Broughton Brant-	Lincoln	1710	Buckland-Brewer	Devon	1603
Broughton Church	Derby	[7] 1538	Buckland Dinham	Somerset	1569
Broughton-Gifford	Wilts	1665	Buckland, East	Devon	1684
Broughton-Hackett	Worcester	[8] 1761	Buckland, Egg	Devon	1653
Broughton-in-Craven-	York	1689	Buckland, Filleigh	Devon	1622
Broughton-in-Furness	Lancaster	1634	Buckland-in-the-Moor.	Devon	1693
Broughton Nether	Leicester	1572			
Broughton-Pogis	Oxford	1557	Buckland, Monachorum.	Devon	1538
Broughton-Sulney	Nottingham	[9] 1571			

[1] **P** 1608–1616. West Bromwich Parish Magazine, 1879 (*et seq.*).
[2] **P** (Marriages only) 1617–1812 (including Bishop's Transcripts). Gloucestershire Parish Registers, vol. 13, 1908.
[3] Bishop's Transcripts commence about 1613.
[4] **P** (Marriages only) 1630–1812. Somersetshire Parish Registers, vol. 6, 1905.
[5] **P** 1570–1750. Edited by A. F. C. Langley, 1889–90.
[6] **P** 1705–1812. Shropshire Parish Register Society, vol. 1, 1900.
[7] **P** (Marriages only) 1538–1812. Derbyshire Parish Registers, vol. 1, 1906.
[8] Bishop's Transcripts commence 1609.
[9] **P** (Marriages only) 1572–1812. Nottinghamshire Parish Registers, vol. 2, 1899.
[10] **P** (Marriages only) 1563–1812. Norfolk Parish Registers, vol. 1, 1899.
[11] **P** 1562–1785. Edited by F. A. Crisp, 1885.
[12] **P** 1554–1680. Parish Register Society, vol. 60, 1907.
[13] **P** 1565–1649. Edited by Walter Rye, 1902.
[14] **P** (Marriages only) 1539–1812. Gloucestershire Parish Registers, vol. 6, 1898.
[15] **P** (Marriages only) 1538–1812. Somersetshire Parish Registers, vol. 4, 1902.

Parish	County.	Date of Earliest Entry.	Parish.	County.	Date of Earliest Entry.
Buckland, Newton -	Dorset - -	1568	Bures - - -	Suffolk - -	1538
Buckland, Ripers -	Dorset - -	1695	Bures-Mount - -	Essex - -	1540
Buckland, Tout Saints	Devon - -	[1] —	Burford - -	Oxford - -	1612
Buckland, West -	Devon - -	1625	Burford - - -	Salop - -	1558
Buckland, West -	Somerset -	[2] 1538	Burgate - -	Suffolk - -	1560
Bucklebury - -	Berks - -	1538	Burgh next Aylsham -	Norfolk - -	[9] 1563
Bucklesham - -	Suffolk -	1678	Burgh St. Margaret -	Norfolk -	1739
Buckminster - -	Leicester -	1538	Burgh, St. Peter. See		
Bucknall - - -	Lincoln -	1708	Wheatacre-Burgh.		
Bucknall with Bag-	Stafford -	1758	Burgh - - -	Suffolk - -	1547
nall.			Burgh-Apton - -	Norfolk - -	1556
Bucknell - -	Salop - -	1598	Burgh-Castle - -	Suffolk - -	1694
Bucknell - - -	Oxford -	1700	Burgh-in-the-Marsh -	Lincoln -	1538
Buckthorpe - -	York - -	1661	Burgh, Little - -	Norfolk - -	1594
Buckworth - -	Huntingdon -	1664	Burgh, Mattishall -	Norfolk -	1653
Budbrooke - -	Warwick -	1539	Burgh, South - -	Norfolk - -	1558
Budeaux, St. - -	Devon - -	1538	Burgh-on-Bain -	Lincoln -	1735
Budleigh, East -	Devon - -	1555	Burgh-by-Sands -	Cumberland -	1695
Budock - -	Cornwall -	1603	Burgh-Wallis - -	York - -	1597
Budworth, Great -	Chester -	1558	Burghclere - -	Hants - -	[10] 1559
Budworth, Little -	Chester -	1561	Burghfield - -	Berks - -	1559
Bugbrooke - -	Northampton -	1657	Burghill - -	Hereford -	1655
Bugthorpe. See Buck-			Burham - - -	Kent - -	1626
thorpe.			Buriton - - -	Hants - -	1678
Buildwas - -	Salop - -	1659	Burlescombe - -	Devon - -	1579
Builth - - -	Brecon - -	1687	Burlestone - - -	Dorset - -	1692
Bulcote - - -	Nottingham -	[3] —	Burley-on-the-Hill -	Rutland -	1577
Bulford - - -	Wilts - -	[4] 1762	Burley-in-Wharfedale	York - -	1774
Bulkington - -	Warwick -	1606	Burleydam - -	Chester -	1770
Bulkworthy - -	Devon - -	1714	Burlingham, St. An-	Norfolk - -	[11] 1538
Bulley - - -	Gloucester -	1673	drew.		
Bullingham - -	Hereford -	1682	Burlingham, St. Ed-	Norfolk -	1554
Bullington - -	Hants - -	[5] 1725	mund.		
Bulmer - - -	Essex - -	1559	Burlingham, St. Peter	Norfolk - -	[12] 1560
Bulmer - - -	York - -	1571	Burmarsh - - -	Kent - -	1572
Bulphan - - -	Essex - -	1722	Burmington - -	Warwick -	1582
Bulwell - - -	Nottingham -	[6] 1621	Burnby - - -	York - -	1584
Bulwick - - -	Northampton -	1568	Burneside - -	Westmorland -	1717
Bumpstead-Helions -	Essex and Cam-	1558	Burneston - - -	York - -	1566
	bridge.		Burnett - - -	Somerset -	1749
Bumpstead-Steeple -	Essex - -	1676	Burnham - - -	Buckingham -	1561
Bunbury - - -	Chester -	1559	Burnham - - -	Essex - -	1559
Bungay, St. Mary -	Suffolk -	1538	Burnham - - -	Somerset -	1638
Bungay, Holy Trinity	Suffolk -	1557	Burnham-Deepdale -	Norfolk - -	1539
Bunney - - -	Nottingham -	[7] 1556	Burnham-Westgate -	Norfolk -	1538
Buntingford - -	Hertford -	[8] —	Burnham-Norton -	Norfolk - -	1559
Bunwell - - -	Norfolk - -	1551	Burnham-Ulph -	Norfolk - -	[13]
Burbage - - -	Leicester -	1562	Burnham-Sutton -	Norfolk -	1653
Burbage - - -	Wilts - -	1561	Burnham-Overy -	Norfolk -	1653
Burcombe - - -	Wilts - -	1682	Burnham-Thorpe -	Norfolk - -	1559

[1] Included in the Registers of Loddiswell (q.v.).
[2] **P** (Marriages only) 1558–1812. Somersetshire Parish Registers, vol. 8, 1907.
[3] Included with Burton-Joyce (q.v.).
[4] **P** (Marriages only) 1608–1812. Wiltshire Parish Registers, vol. 3, 1906.
[5] **P** (Marriages only) 1755–1812. Hampshire Parish Registers, vol. 1, 1899.
[6] **P** (Marriages only) 1635–1812. Nottinghamshire Parish Registers, vol. 9, 1906.
[7] **P** (Marriages only) 1556–1818. Nottinghamshire Parish Registers, vol. 9, 1906.
[8] Included with Register of Layston (q.v.).   [9] **P** 1563–1810. Edited by Rev. E. T. Yates.
[10] **P** (Marriages only) 1559–1812. Hampshire Parish Registers, vol. 8, 1906.
[11] **P** (Marriages only) 1540–1812. Norfolk Parish Registers, vol. 1, 1899.
[12] **P** (Marriages only) 1560–1812. Norfolk Parish Registers, vol. 1, 1899.
[13] Included with Registers of Burnham-Sutton (q.v.).

Parish.	County.	Date of Earliest Entry.	Parish.	County.	Date of Earliest Entry
Burnley - - -	Lancaster -	[1] 1562	Bury - - -	Sussex - -	1560
Burnsall - -	York - -	[2] 1559	Bury St. Edmunds -	Suffolk - -	1538
Burpham - - -	Sussex - -	1653	St. James - -	- - -	1558
Burrington - -	Devon - -	1592	Buryan, St. - -	Cornwall -	[10] 1653
Burrington - -	Hereford - -	1541	Burythorpe - -	York - -	1720
Burrington - -	Somerset -	1687	Buscot - - -	Berks - -	1676
Burrough-on-the-Hill	Leicester - -	1612	Bushbury - -	Stafford - -	1747
Burrough-Green -	Cambridge -	1571	Bushey - - -	Hertford -	1684
Bursledon - -	Hants - -	1660	Bushley - - -	Worcester -	1538
Burslem - - -	Stafford - -	1639	Buslingthorpe -	Lincoln -	1762
Burstall - - -	Suffolk - -	1542	Butcombe - -	Somerset - -	1692
Burstead, Great -	Essex - -	1558	Butleigh - -	Somerset -	1578
Burstead, Little -	Essex - -	1681	Butlers-Marston. See		
Burstock - -	Dorset - -	1688	Marston-Butlers.		
Burston - - -	Norfolk - -	1653	Butley - - -	Suffolk - -	1785
Burstow - - -	Surrey - -	1547	Buttercrambe - -	York - -	1635
Burstwick - - -	York - -	[3] 1747	Butterleigh - -	Devon - -	1698
Burton - - -	Chester - -	1538	Buttermere - -	Cumberland -	[11] 1801
Burton - - -	Pembroke -	1716	Buttermere - -	Wilts - -	1727
Burton - - -	Sussex - -	1559	Butterton - -	Stafford -	1686
Burton-Agnes - -	York - -	1700	Butterwick - -	Lincoln - -	1658
Burton, Bishop. See			Butterwick - -	York - -	1796
Bishop-Burton.			Butterwick, West -	Lincoln - -	[12] —
Burton-Bradstock -	Dorset - -	1614	Buttington - -	Montgomery -	1723
Burton-by-Lincoln -	Lincoln - -	1558	Buttolphs - -	Sussex - -	1607
Burton-Cherry. See			Buttsbury - -	Essex - -	1657
Cherry-Burton.			Buxhall. - -	Suffolk - -	1558
Burton-Coggles -	Lincoln - -	1565	Buxted - - -	Sussex - -	1568
Burton-Dassett -	Warwick - -	1660	Buxton - - -	Derby - -	1718
Burton-Fleming -	York - -	[4] 1538	Buxton - - -	Norfolk - -	1665
Burton-Gate - -	Lincoln - -	1575	Byfield - - -	Northampton -	1636
Burton-Hastings -	Warwick - -	1574	Byfleet - - -	Surrey - -	1698
Burton-in-Kendal -	Westmorland -	1653	Byford - - -	Hereford -	1660
Burton-Joyce - -	Nottingham -	[5] 1559	Bygrave - - -	Hertford -	1765
Burton-Kirk - -	York - -	[6] 1540	Byland, Old - -	York - -	1653
Burton-Latimer - -	Northampton -	1538	Bylaugh - - -	Norfolk - -	1557
Burton-Lazars - -	Leicester - -	[7] 1718	Byrness - - -	Northumberland -	1786
Burton-Leonard -	York - -	1672	Bytham, Little - -	Lincoln - -	1681
Burton, Long - -	Dorset- -	[8] 1590	Bytham-Castle -	Lincoln - -	1597
Burton-Overy - -	Leicester - -	1575	Bythorn - - -	Huntingdon -	1571
Burton-Pedwardine -	Lincoln - -	1736	Byton - - -	Hereford -	1763
Burton-Pidsea - -	York - -	1708	Bywell, St. Andrew -	Northumberland	1668
Burton-on-Stather -	Lincoln - -	1567	Bywell, St. Peter -	Northumberland	1663
Burton-on-Trent -	Stafford - -	1539			
Burton, West - -	Nottingham -	1602			
Burton-Wood - -	Lancaster -	1668			
Burwarton - -	Salop - -	1575			
Burwash - - -	Sussex - -	1558			
Burwell - - -	Cambridge -	1562			
Burwell - - -	Lincoln - -	1586			
Bury - - -	Huntingdon -	1561			
Bury - - -	Lancaster -	[9] 1590			

[1] **P** 1562-1653. Lancashire Parish Register Society, vol. 2, 1899.
[2] **P** 1559-1812. Edited by Rev. W. J. Stavert, 1893.   [3] Including Skeckling.
[4] **P** 1538-1812. Yorkshire Parish Register Society, vol. 2, 1899.
[5] **P** (Marriages only) 1559-1812. Nottinghamshire Parish Registers, vol. 10, 1907.
[6] **P** 1541-1711. Edited by F. A. Collins, 2 vols., 1887 and 1902.
[7] See also Registers of Melton Mowbray.
[8] **P** 1580-1812. Edited by Rev. C. H. Mayo, 1894.
[9] **P** 1590-1646. Lancashire Parish Register Society, vol. 1, 1898.
[10] **P** (Marriages only) 1654-1812. Cornwall Parish Registers, vol. 3, 1903.
[11] Previous to 1801 included in the Registers at Lorton (q.v.).
[12] Included with Owston Registers (q.v.).

Parish.	County.	Date of Earliest Entry.	Parish.	County.	Date of Earliest Entry.
			Camberwell	Surrey -	1558
C.			Camborne	Cornwall	1538
			Cambridge, All Saints	Cambridge	1548
Cabourn	Lincoln -	1559	St. Andrew the Great.	- -	1635
Cadbury	Devon -	1756			
Cadbury, North	Somerset -	1558	St Andrew the Less, or Barnwell.	- -	1753
Cadbury, South	Somerset	1559			
Caddington -	Bedford -	1558	St. Benedict	- -	1539
Cadeby	Lincoln	[1] 1695	St. Botolph	- -	1564
Cadeby	Leicester -	1574	St. Clement	- -	[4] 1567
Cadeleigh	Devon -	1665	St. Edward	- -	1558
Cadney	Lincoln -	1564	St. Giles' -	- -	1596
Cadoxton juxta Barry	Glamorgan	1753	St. Peter -	- -	1586
Cadoxton juxta Neath	Glamorgan	1754	St. Mary the Great	- -	1559
			St. Mary the Less	- -	1557
Caenby	Lincoln	1713	St. Michael	- -	[7] 1538
Caerau -	Glamorgan	1741	St. Sepulchre	- -	1567
Caerhun	Carnarvon	1662	Holy Trinity	- -	1566
Caerphilly	Glamorgan	1754	Camel, Queen	Somerset	1639
Caerwent	Monmouth	1752	Camel, West -	Somerset -	1678
Caerwys	Flint	1673	Cameley -	Somerset	1561
Cainham (or Caynham)	Salop -	1558	Cameringham	Lincoln -	1662
Caistor -	Lincoln -	1583	Camerton	Cumberland -	1599
Caistor	Norfolk	1557	Camerton	Somerset	1684
Caistor-by-Yarmouth	Norfolk -	1563	Campden, Chipping -	Gloucester	1616
Calbourne, Isle of Wight.	Hants -	1562	Campsall	York -	1563
			Campsea-Ashe -	Suffolk -	1559
Calceby -	Lincoln -	1622	Campton	Bedford -	1568
Calcethorpe -	Lincoln	1651	Camrose	Pembroke -	1716
Caldbeck	Cumberland -	1640	Candlesby	Lincoln -	1753
Caldecot	Cambridge	1662	Candover, Brown	Hants -	1611
Caldecote	Warwick	1725	Candover, Chilton -	Hants -	1612
Caldecote	Hertford -	1726	Candover, Preston -	Hants -	[8] 1688
Caldecote	Huntingdon -	1739	Canewdon -	Essex -	1636
Caldecote	Rutland -	1605	Canfield, Great -	Essex -	1538
Calderbridge -	Cumberland -	1687	Canfield, Little	Essex -	1560
Caldicot -	Monmouth	1716	Canford, Magna	Dorset -	1656
Callington	Cornwall	1558	Cann -	Dorset -	1563
Callow	Hereford -	1576	Cannings, Bishop's -	Wilts -	1591
Callwen	Brecon -	1778	Cannington	Somerset	[9] 1559
Calne	Wilts -	1538	Cannock	Stafford -	1744
Calstock	Cornwall	[2] 1654	Canonby, Cross	Cumberland -	1663
Calstone-Wellington -	Wilts -	1716	Canon-Frome -	Hereford -	[10] 1680
Calthorpe	Norfolk -	[3] 1539	Canon-Pyon -	Hereford -	1707
Calton -	Stafford	1762	Canterbury, All Saints	Kent -	1559
Calverhall	Salop -	1668	St. Mary in the Castle.	- -	1558
Calverleigh	Devon -	1679			
Calverley	York -	[4] 1574	St. Mildred -	- -	1558
Calverton	Buckingham -	1559	St. Alphege	- -	[11] 1558
Calverton	Nottingham -	1568	St. Mary	- -	1640
Cam -	Gloucester -	[5] 1569	St. Andrew	- -	1563

[1] Included in the Registers of Wyham.

[2] "Calstock Registers from 1560 to 1715" is printed on the cover of the oldest Register book, but the entries for the first 94 years were cut out at some time, and 1654 is now the date of the first entry in the Register.

[3] **P** (Marriages only) 1558-1812. Norfolk Parish Registers, vol. 1, 1899.

[4] **P** 1574-1720. Edited by S. Margerison, 3 vols, 1880-7.

[5] **P** (Marriages only) 1569-1812. Gloucestershire Parish Registers, vol. 8, 1902.

[6] **P** (Marriages only) 1559-1812. Cambridgeshire Parish Registers, vol. 1, 1907.

[7] **P** 1538-1837. Cambridge Antiquarian Society, vol. 25, 1891.

[8] **P** (Marriages only) 1584-1812. Hampshire Parish Registers, vol. 9, 1907.

[9] **P** (Marriages only) 1559-1812. Somersetshire Parish Registers, vol. 6, 1905.

[10] **P** 1680-1812. Parish Register Society, vol. 45, 1905.

[11] **P** 1558-1800. Edited by J. M. Cowper, 1889.

Parish.	County.	Date of Earliest Entry.	Parish.	County.	Date of Earliest Entry.
Canterbury—*continued.*			Carleton St. Peter -	Norfolk - -	1544
St. Mary Bredman	- - -	1558	Carleton-in-Cleveland	York - -	1700
Cathedral (Christ	- - -	[1] 1564	Carleton-in-Craven -	York - -	1538
Church).			Carleton - -	Cambridge -	[11] 1725
St. Dunstan -	- - -	[2] 1559	Carleton-Forehoe -	Norfolk -	1699
St. George the	- - -	[3] 1538	Carleton-Rode - -	Norfolk - -	1560
Martyr.			Carlisle, St. Mary -	Cumberland -	1648
St. Mary Mag-	- - -	[4] 1634	St. Cuthbert -	- - -	1693
dalen.			Carlton-by-Snaith -	York - -	1618
St. Margaret -	- - -	1653	Carlton - -	Bedford - -	1554
St. Martin -	- - -	1662	Carlton - -	Leicester -	1714
St. Paul -	- - -	[5] 1562	Carlton - - -	Suffolk - -	[12] 1538
St. Mary Bredin -	- - -	1633	Carlton Castle -	Lincoln - -	1570
St. Peter -	- - -	[6] 1560	Carlton Colville -	Suffolk - -	1710
Holy Cross -	- - -	1568	Carlton Curlieu -	Leicester -	1749
Cantley - -	Norfolk -	1559	Carlton, East -	Norfolk - -	1544
Cantley - -	York -	1538	Carlton, East -	Northampton -	1625
Cantreff - -	Brecon -	1754	Carlton, Great -	Lincoln - -	1561
Canwick - -	Lincoln -	1681	Carlton-in-Lindrick -	Nottingham -	1559
Capel - -	Kent -	[7] 1754	Carlton, Little -	Lincoln -	1726
Capel - -	Suffolk -	1785	Carlton Miniott -	York -	1706
Capel, St. Mary -	Suffolk -	1538	Carlton-le-Moorland -	Lincoln -	1562
Capel - - -	Surrey -	1653	Carlton, North -	Lincoln -	1653
Capel Bettws *with*	Brecon -	—	Carlton-Scroop -	Lincoln -	1558
Llanspythid.			Carlton, South -	Lincoln -	1653
Capel-Calwen -	Brecon -	1778	Carmarthen -	Carmarthen -	1671
Capel-Colman -	Pembroke -	1777	Carnaby - -	York -	1596
Capel-Curig -	Carnarvon -	1730	Carnarvon -	Carnarvon -	[13] —
Capel Garmon *with*	Denbigh -	—	Carngiwch -	Carnarvon -	[14] —
Llanrwst.			Carno - -	Montgomery -	1638
Capel Kings -	Hereford -	1683	Caron-Uwch-Elawdd-	Cardigan -	1750
Capel-le-Ferne -	Kent -	1592	Carrington -	Chester -	1759
Capesthorne -	Chester -	1722	Carshalton -	Surrey -	1538
Carbrooke -	Norfolk -	1539	Carsington -	Derby -	1592
Carburton - -	Nottingham -	[8] 1538	Cartmel - -	Lancaster -	1559
Car-Colston -	Nottingham -	[9] 1570	Cartmel-Fell -	Lancaster -	1754
Cardeston -	Salop -	1706	Cascob - -	Radnor -	1624
Cardiff -	Glamorgan -	1669	Cassington -	Oxford -	1653
Cardigan -	Cardigan -	1653	Casterton, Great -	Rutland -	1665
Cardington -	Bedford -	1574	Casterton, Little -	Rutland -	1559
Cardington -	Salop -	1598	Castle Acre -	Norfolk -	[15] 1695
Cardynham -	Cornwall-	[10] 1701	Castle Ashby. *See*		
Careby - -	Lincoln -	1562	Ashby Castle.		
Carew - -	Pembroke -	1718	Castle-Bigh -	Pembroke -	1760
Carham - -	Northumberland	1684	Castle Bromwich. *See*		
Carhampton -	Somerset -	1634	Bromwich Castle.		
Carisbrooke (Isle of	Hants -	1695	Castle Caereinion -	Montgomery -	1689
Wight).			Castle Camps -	Cambridge -	1565
Carlby - -	Lincoln	1660	Castle Carrock -	Cumberland -	1679

[1] **P** 1564–1878. Harleian Society Registers, vol. 2, 1878.
[2] **P** 1559–1800. Edited by J. M. Cowper, 1887.
[3] **P** 1538–1800. Edited by J. M. Cowper, 1891.
[4] **P** 1559–1800. Edited by J. M. Cowper, 1890.
[5] **P** 1562–1800. Edited by J. M. Cowper, 1893.
[6] **P** 1560–1800. Edited by J. M. Cowper, 1888.
[7] Previous to 1754 included in the Registers of Tudeley (*q.v.*).
[8] **P** 1538–1812. Edited by G. W. Marshall, 1888.
[9] **P** (Marriages only) 1570–1812. Nottinghamshire Parish Registers, vol. 1, 1898.
[10] **P** (Marriages only) 1675–1812. Cornwall Parish Registers, vol. 4, 1903.
[11] There are a few worm-eaten pages of a Register dated 1588.
[12] **P** 1538–1885. Edited by F. A. Crisp, 1886.
[13] Included in the Registers of Llanbeblig (*q.v.*).   [14] Included in the Registers of Edeyrn (*q v.*).
[15] **P** (Marriages only) 1710–1812. Norfolk Parish Registers, vol, 1, 1899.

Parish.	County.	Date of Earliest Entry.	Parish.	County.	Date of Earliest Entry.
Castle Cary - -	Somerset -	1564	Cawthorne - -	York - -	1653
Castle Church -	Stafford - -	[1] 1567	Cawthorpe, Little -	Lincoln -	1679
Castle Combe - -	Wilts - -	1653	Caxton - -	Cambridge -	1741
Castle Donington. See			Caythorpe - -	Lincoln -	1663
Donington, Castle.			Cayton - -	York - -	1684
Castle-Eaton - -	Wilts - -	1549	Cefnllys - -	Radnor -	1679
Castle Eden. See Eden,			Ceirchiog - -	Anglesea - -	1754
Castle.			Cellan - -	Cardigan -	1780
Castle Frome. See			Cemmaes - -	Montgomery -	1711
Frome Castle.			Cerne Abbas - -	Dorset - -	1653
Castle Hedingham. See			Cerne Nether - -	Dorset - -	1694
Hedingham Castle.			Cerne Upper - -	Dorset - -	1650
Castle-Morton - -	Worcester -	1558	Cerney, North - -	Gloucester -	1568
Castle-Rising - -	Norfolk - -	1573	Cerney, South - -	Gloucester -	1583
Castle Sowerby. See			Cerregceinwen - -	Anglesea - -	1720
Sowerby Castle.		—	Cerrig-y-Druidion -	Denbigh -	1590
Castleford - -	York - -	1653	Chaceley - -	Worcester -	1538
Castlemartin - -	Pembroke -	1783	Chacombe. See Chal-		
Castlethorpe - -	Buckingham -	1562	combe.		
Castleton - -	Derby - -	1645	Chaddesden - -	Derby - -	1718
Castleton - -	Dorset - -	1715	Chaddesley-Corbett -	Worcester -	1538
Caston - -	Norfolk - -	1539	Chaddleworth - -	Berks - -	1538
Castor - - -	Northampton -	1538	Chadkirk - -	Chester -	1747
Catcott - -	Somerset -	1733	Chadlington - -	Oxford -	1561
Caterham - -	Surrey - -	1543	Chadsunt - -	Warwick -	1701
Catesby - -	Northampton -	1705	Chadwell - -	Essex -	1539
Catfield - -	Norfolk - -	1723	Chaffcombe - -	Somerset -	1678
Cathedine - -	Brecon -	1732	Chagford - -	Devon -	1598
Catherine, Saint -	Somerset -	[2] 1752	Chailey - -	Sussex -	1538
Catherington -	Hants - -	1602	Chalbury - -	Dorset -	1629
Catmere - -	Berks - -	1724	Chalcombe - -	Northampton -	1566
Caton - - -	Lancaster -	1585	Chaldon - -	Surrey -	1564
Catsfield - -	Sussex - -	1611	Chaldon-Herring -	Dorset -	1622
Catterick - -	York - -	1653	Chale (Isle of Wight) -	Hants - -	1679
Catthorpe - -	Leicester -	1573	Chalfield, Magna -	Wilts - -	1545
Cattistock - -	Dorset - -	[3] 1558	Chalfont St. Giles -	Buckingham -	1584
Catton - -	Norfolk -	1688	Chalfont St. Peter -	Buckingham -	1539
Catton - -	York - -	1592	Chalgrave - -	Bedford -	1539
Catwick - -	York - -	1583	Chalgrove - -	Oxford -	1538
Catworth - -	Huntingdon -	1561	Chalk - - -	Kent -	1661
Cauldon - -	Stafford -	1580	Challacombe - -	Devon -	1676
Cauldwell - -	Derby - -	1679	Challock - -	Kent -	1558
Caulk St. Giles -	Derby - -	1699	Challow, East -	Berks -	1711
Caundle, Bishops -	Dorset - -	[4] 1570	Challow, West -	Berks -	1653
Caundle-Marsh -	Dorset - -	1704	Chalton - -	Hants -	1538
Caundle-Purse -	Dorset - -	1730	Chalvington - -	Sussex -	1538
Caundle-Stourton -	Dorset - -	1670	Chapel-en-le-Frith -	Derby -	1620
Caunton - -	Nottingham -	1709	Chapel-Hill - -	Monmouth -	1695
Cave, North -	York - -	1678	Chapel-le-Dale -	York -	1754
Cave, South - -	York - -	1558	Chard - - -	Somerset -	1649
Cavendish - -	Suffolk -	1594	Chardstock - -	Dorset -	1597
Cavenham - -	Suffolk -	1539	Charfield - -	Gloucester -	1587
Caversfield - -	Buckingham -	1640	Charing - -	Kent -	1590
Caversham - -	Oxford -	1597	Charlbury - -	Oxford -	1559
Caverswall - -	Stafford -	1559	Charlcombe - -	Somerset -	1709
Cawkwell - -	Lincoln -	1683	Charlecote - -	Warwick - -	[5] 1539
Cawood - -	York - -	1591	Charles - -	Devon -	1538
Cawston - -	Norfolk -	1538	Charleton - -	Devon - -	1562

[1] P 1567-1812. Staffordshire Parish Register Society, 1903.
[2] Previously included in the Registers of Batheaston (q.v.).
[3] P (Marriages only) 1558-1812. Dorsetshire Parish Registers, vol. 1, 1906.
[4] P 1570-1814. Edited by Rev. C. H. Mayo, 1895.
[5] P (Marriages only) 1543-1812. Warwickshire Parish Registers, vol. 3, 1906.

Parish.	County.	Date of Earliest Entry.	Parish.	County.	Date of Earliest Entry.
Charlinch - -	Somerset -	[1] 1744	Chedington - -	Dorset - -	1756
Charlton (in Dover) -	Kent - -	1564	Chediston - -	Suffolk -	1653
Charlton - -	Kent - -	1562	Chedworth - -	Gloucester -	[9] 1653
Charlton (near Marl- borough.	Wilts - -	1695	Chedzoy - -	Somerset -	1558
			Cheetham - -	Lancaster -	1794
Charlton (near Mal- mesbury).	Wilts - -	1661	Chelborough, East -	Dorset - -	1682
			Chelborough, West -	Dorset - -	1660
Charlton-Abbots -	Gloucester -	1727	Cheldon - -	Devon - -	1708
Charlton-Adam -	Somerset -	[2] 1704	Chelford - -	Chester -	1674
Charlton-Horethorne	Somerset -	1739	Chellaston - -	Derby - -	1570
Charlton-Kings -	Gloucester -	[3] 1538	Chellesworth - -	Suffolk -	1559
Charlton-Mackrell -	Somerset -	[4] 1575	Chellington - -	Bedford -	1567
Charlton-Marshall -	Dorset - -	1575	Chelmarsh - -	Salop -	[10] 1556
Charlton-Musgrove -	Somerset - -	1534	Chelmorton - -	Derby - -	1580
Charlton-on-Otmoor -	Oxford - -	1577	Chelmondiston - -	Suffolk -	1727
Charlton-Queen -	Somerset -	1562	Chelmsford - -	Essex - -	1538
Charlwood - -	Surrey - -	1595	Chelsea - -	Middlesex -	1559
Charminster - -	Dorset - -	[5] 1561	Chelsfield - -	Kent - -	1538
Charmouth - -	Dorset - -	1653	Chelsham - -	Surrey -	1669
Charney - -	Berks - -	1700	Cheltenham - -	Gloucester -	[11] 1558
Charsfield - -	Suffolk - -	1727	Chelveston - -	Northampton -	1579
Chart, Great -	Kent - -	1558	Chelvey - -	Somerset -	1735
Chart, Little - -	Kent - -	1562	Chelwood - -	Somerset -	1783
Chart, Sutton -	Kent - -	1558	Chenies - -	Buckingham -	1592
Chartham - -	Kent - -	1558	Chepstow - -	Monmouth -	1596
Charwelton - -	Northampton -	1697	Cherhill - -	Wilts - -	[12] 1690
Chastleton - -	Oxford - -	1586	Cherington - -	Warwick -	1538
Chatham - -	Kent - -	1568	Cheriton - - -	Hants - -	1557
Chatteris - -	Cambridge -	1613	Cheriton - -	Kent - -	1562
Chattisham - -	Suffolk - -	1559	Cheriton Bishop -	Devon - -	1538
Chatton - -	Northumberland	1715	Cheriton-Fitzpaine -	Devon - -	1660
Chawleigh - -	Devon - -	1544	Cheriton North -	Somerset -	1558
Chawton - -	Hants - -	1596	Cherrington - -	Gloucester -	[13] 1568
Cheadle - -	Chester -	1558	Cherry-Burton -	York - -	[14] 1561
Cheadle - -	Stafford - -	1569	Cherry - Hinton. See		
Cheam - -	Surrey - -	1538	Hinton Cherry.		
Chearsley - -	Buckingham -	1570	Cherry-Willingham. See		
Chebsey - -	Stafford - -	1713	Willingham Cherry.		
Checkendon - -	Oxford - -	1719	Chertsey - - -	Surrey - -	1606
Checkley - -	Stafford - -	1625	Cheselborne - -	Dorset - -	[15] 1644
Chedburgh - -	Suffolk - -	1538	Chesham - -	Buckingham -	[16] 1538
Cheddar - -	Somerset -	1678	Chesham-Bois -	Buckingham -	1562
Cheddington - -	Buckingham -	[6] 1558	Cheshunt - -	Hertford -	1559
Cheddleton - -	Stafford - -	1696	Chessington - -	Surrey - -	1656
Cheddon-Fitzpaine -	Somerset -	[7] 1558	Chester Cathedral -	Chester -	[17] 1687
Chedgrave - -	Norfolk -	[8] 1550	St. Bridget - -	- - -	1649

[1] **P** (Marriages only) 1607–1779. Somersetshire Parish Registers, vol. 6, 1905.
[2] **P** (Marriages only) 1707–1812. Somersetshire Parish Registers, vol. 1, 1898.
[3] **P** (Marriages only) 1538–1812. Gloucestershire Parish Registers, vol. 3, 1908.
[4] **P** (Marriages only) 1575–1812. Somersetshire Parish Registers, vol. 1, 1898.
[5] **P** (Marriages only) 1561–1812. Dorsetshire Parish Registers, vol. 2, 1907.
[6] **P** (Marriages only) 1552–1812. Buckinghamshire Parish Registers, vol. 1, 1902.
[7] **P** (Marriages only) 1559–1812. Somersetshire Parish Registers, vol. 8, 1907.
[8] **P** (Marriages only) 1550–1812. Norfolk Parish Registers, vol. 2, 1900.
[9] **P** (Marriages only) 1653–1812. Gloucestershire Parish Registers, vol. 2, 1897.
[10] **P** 1556–1812. Shropshire Parish Register Society, vol. 3.
[11] **P** (Marriages only) 1558–1812. Gloucestershire Parish Registers, vol. 7, 1901.
[12] The Baptismal register contains, in one case, a horoscope.
[13] **P** (Marriages only) 1569–1812. Gloucestershire Parish Registers, vol. 12, 1906.
[14] **P** 1561–1740. Yorkshire Parish Register Society, vol. 15, 1903.
[15] The register down to 1630 is much damaged by fire, the first four pages being mere fragments.
[16] **P** 1538–1636. Edited by J. W. Garrett-Pegge, 1904.
[17] **P** 1687–1812. Parish Register Society, vol. 52, 1904.

Parish.	County.	Date of Earliest Entry.	Parish.	County.	Date of Earliest Entry.
Chester,			Chigwell - -	Essex - -	1555
St. John the Baptist	- - -	1559	Chilbolton - -	Hants - -	1699
St. Martin - -	- - -	1680	Chilcomb - -	Hants - -	1556
St. Michael -	- - -	1581	Chilcombe - -	Dorset - -	1748
St. Olave - -	- - -	1612	Chilcompton - -	Somerset - -	1649
St. Peter - -	- - -	1559	Chilcote - -	Derby - -	1595
St. Mary - -	- - -	1628	Childerditch - -	Essex - -	1538
St. Oswald -	- - -	1580	Childrey - -	Berks - -	1558
Holy Trinity -	- - -	1654	Childwall - -	Lancaster -	1556
Chesterfield -	Derby - -	1558	Chilfrome - -	Dorset - -	[5] 1709
Chesterford, Great -	Essex -	1586	Chilham - -	Kent - -	1558
Chesterford, Little -	Essex - -	1559	Chillenden - -	Kent - -	1559
Chester-le-Street -	Durham - -	1582	Chillesford - -	Suffolk -	[6] 1740
Chesterton - - -	Cambridge -	1564	Chillingham - -	Northumberland	[7] 1696
Chesterton - -	Huntingdon -	1561	Chillington - -	Somerset - -	[8] 1750
Chesterton - - -	Oxford - -	1540	Chilmark - -	Wilts - -	1653
Chesterton - -	Warwick - -	[1] 1538	Chilthorne-Domer -	Somerset - -	1678
Cheswardine - -	Salop - -	1558	Chiltington, East -	Sussex - -	1651
Chetnole - -	Dorset - -	[2] —	Chiltington, West -	Sussex - -	1558
Chettisham - -	Cambridge -	1701	Chilton - -	Berks - -	1584
Chettle - - -	Dorset - -	1538	Chilton - -	Buckingham -	1730
Chetton - - -	Salop - -	1538	Chilton - -	Suffolk - -	1623
Chetwode - -	Buckingham -	1756	Chilton-Canteloe -	Somerset -	1714
Chetwynd - -	Salop - -	1585	Chilton-Foliatt - -	Wilts - -	1569
Cheveley - -	Cambridge -	1559	Chilton (Trinity) -	Somerset - -	[9] 1735
Chevening - - -	Kent - -	1561	Chilton-on-Polden -	Somerset -	1654
Cheverell, Great -	Wilts - -	1653	Chilvers-Coton - -	Warwick -	1654
Cheverell, Little -	Wilts - -	1653	Chilworth - -	Hants - -	1721
Chevington - -	Suffolk - -	1559	Chilworth (or St.	Surrey - -	1779
Chew, Magna - -	Somerset - -	1558	Martha on the		
Chew-Stoke - -	Somerset -	1663	Hill).		
Chewton-Mendip -	Somerset - -	1561	Chingford - -	Essex - -	1715
Chicheley - - -	Buckingham -	[3] 1539	Chinley - - -	Derby - -	1729
Chichester, All Saints -	Sussex - -	1557	Chinnock, East -	Somerset - -	1647
St. Andrew - -	- - -	1568	Chinnock, Middle -	Somerset -	1695
St. Martin -	- - -	1684	Chinnock, West -	Somerset - -	1678
St. Olave - -	- - -	1569	Chinnor - -	Oxford - -	1581
St. Pancras -	- - -	1559	Chippenham - -	Cambridge -	1559
St. Peter the Great -	- - -	1558	Chippenham - -	Wilts - -	1578
St. Peter the Less -	- - -	1679	Chipping - - -	Lancaster -	[10] 1559
St. Bartholomew -	- - -	1571	Chipstable - -	Somerset - -	1694
Chickerell, West -	Dorset - -	1723	Chipstead - -	Surrey - -	1656
Chicklade - -	Wilts - -	1721	Chirbury - - -	Salop - -	1629
Chickney - - -	Essex - -	1554	Chirk - - -	Denbigh - -	1611
Chiddingfold - -	Surrey - -	1563	Chirton - - -	Wilts - -	1585
Chiddingly - -	Sussex - -	1621	Chishall, Great -	Essex - -	1583
Chiddingstone - -	Kent - -	1558	Chishall, Little -	Essex - -	1577
Chideock - -	Dorset - -	[4] 1654	Chiselborough - -	Somerset - -	1558
Chidham - - -	Sussex - -	1652	Chisledon - -	Wilts - -	1641
Chieveley - -	Berks - -	1560	Chislehampton -	Oxford - -	1556
Chignal, St. James -	Essex - -	1723	Chislehurst - -	Kent - -	1558
Chignal-Smealy -	Essex - -	1600	Chislet - -	Kent - -	[11] 1538

[1] There are entries of baptisms commencing in 1529.
[2] Included in the registers of Yetminster (*q.v.*).
[3] **P** (Marriages only) 1559–1812. Buckinghamshire Registers, vol. 3, 1907.
[4] **P** (Marriages only) 1654–1812. Dorsetshire Parish Registers, vol. 2, 1907.
[5] **P** (Marriages only) 1709–1812. Dorsetshire Parish Registers, vol. 1, 1906.
[6] **P** 1740–1776. Edited by F. A. Crisp, 1886.
[7] **P** North Country Parish Registers by Robert Blair.
[8] Previous entries included in the Registers of Cudworth (*q.v.*).
[9] Previous entries included in the Registers of Bridgwater.
[10] **P** 1559–1694. Lancaster Parish Register Society, vol. 14.
[11] **P** 1538–1707. Edited by Robt. Hovenden, London, 1887.

Parish.	County.	Date of Earliest Entry.	Parish.	County.	Date of Earliest Entry.
Chiswick - - -	Middlesex -	[1] 1678	Clannaborough -	Devon - -	1696
Chithurst - -	Sussex - -	[2] 1739	Clapham - -	Bedford - -	1696
Chitterne - - -	Wilts - -	1653	Clapham - - -	Surrey - -	1552
Chittlehampton -	Devon - -	1575	Clapham - -	Sussex - -	1685
Chivelstone - -	Devon - -	1684	Clapham - - -	York - -	1596
Chivesfield - -	Herts - -	[3] —	Clapton - -	Cambridge -	[5] —
Chobham - - -	Surrey - -	1654	Clapton (Bourton-on-the-water).	Gloucester -	[6] —
Cholderton - -	Wilts - -	1616			
Cholesbury - -	Buckingham -	[4] 1583	Clapton - -	Northampton -	1558
Chollerton - -	Northumberland	1647	Clapton in Gordano -	Somerset - -	1558
Cholsey - - -	Berks - -	1540	Clarbeston - -	Pembroke -	1718
Chorley - - -	Lancaster -	1550	Clare - - -	Suffolk - -	1558
Chorlton - - -	Lancaster -	1737	Clareborough - -	Nottingham -	1563
Chorlton - - -	Stafford - -	1564	Clatford, Goodworth -	Hants - -	1538
Chrishall - -	Essex - -	1662	Clatford, Upper -	Hants - - -	1570
Christchurch - -	Monmouth -	1698	Clatworthy - -	Somerset - -	1558
Christchurch - -	Hants - -	1576	Claughton - -	Lancaster -	1701
Christ-Church - -	Surrey - -	1671	Claverdon - -	Warwick - -	1593
Christian-Malford -	Wilts - -	1653	Clavering - - -	Essex - -	1555
Christleton - -	Chester - -	1678	Claverley - -	Salop - -	[7] 1568
Christon - -	Somerset - -	1668	Claverton - - -	Somerset - -	1582
Christow - -	Devon - -	1557	Clawson, Long -	Leicester -	1558
Chudleigh - -	Devon - -	1558	Clawton - -	Devon - -	1694
Chulmleigh - -	Devon - -	1653	Claxby (Alford) -	Lincoln - -	1699
Churcham - -	Gloucester -	1541	Claxby (Market Rasen).	Lincoln - -	1556
Churchdown - -	Gloucester -	1653			
Churchill - - -	Oxford - -	1630	Claxby-Pluckacre -	- - -	[8] —
Churchill - - -	Somerset - -	1653	Claxton. See Clawson, Long.		
Churchill - - -	Worcester -	1540			
Churchill-in-Halfshire	Worcester -	1564	Claxton - -	Norfolk - -	1747
Church-Kirk - -	Lancaster -	1633	Claybrooke - -	Leicester -	[9] 1705
Church-Langton. See Langton Church.			Clay-Coton - -	Northampton -	1541
			Claydon - - -	Suffolk - -	1559
Churchover - -	Warwick - -	1658	Claydon, East -	Buckingham -	1584
Churchstanton -	Devon - -	1662	Claydon - - -	Oxford - -	1569
Churchstoke - -	Montgomery -	1558	Claydon, Middle -	Buckingham -	1630
Churchstow - -	Devon - -	1538	Claydon, Steeple-	Buckingham -	1575
Church Town. See Garstang.			Clayhanger - -	Devon - -	1538
			Clayhidon - -	Devon - -	1637
Churston-Ferrers -	Devon - -	1590	Claypole - -	Lincoln - -	1538
Chute - - -	Wilts - -	1580	Clayton - - -	Sussex - -	1601
Ciliau-Aeron - -	Cardigan -	1715	Clayton - -	York - -	1577
Cilycwm - -	Carmarthen -	1701	Clayton, West -	York - -	1720
Cirencester - -	Gloucester -	1560	Clayworth - -	Nottingham -	1545
Clacton, Great -	Essex - -	1542	Clears, St. - -	Carmarthen -	1681
Clacton, Little -	Essex - -	1538	Cleasby - -	York - -	1712
Claines - -	Worcester -	1538	Cleator - - -	Cumberland -	1572
Clandon, East -	Surrey - -	1558	Cleckheaton - -	York - -	1761
Clandon, West -	Surrey - -	1536	Clee - - -	Lincoln - -	1562
Clanfield - -	Oxford - -	1615	Clee, St. Margaret -	Salop - -	1634
Clanfield - -	Hants - -	1547	Cleer, St. - -	Cornwall -	[10] 1678

[1] **P** (Marriages only) 1678–1800. *See* Historical Collections relating to Chiswick. Edited by W. P. W. Phillimore, 1897.

[2] Previous to 1739 included in the Registers of Iping (*q.v.*).

[3] Included in the Registers of Gravely (*q.v.*).

[4] **P** (Marriages only) 1576–1812. Buckinghamshire Parish Registers, vol. 1, 1902.

[5] Included in the registers of Croydon (*q.v.*).

[6] Included in the registers of Bourton-on-the-Water (*q.v.*).

[7] **P** 1568–1685. Shropshire Parish Society, vol. 10.   [8] Included in the Registers of Moorby (*q.v.*).

[9] The original Register commencing 1563 is at Stanford Hall, Rugby. *See* Historical MSS. Commission, 10th Report.

[10] **P** (Marriages only) 1678–1812. Cornwall Parish Registers, vol. 8, 1905.

Parish.	County.	Date of Earliest Entry.	Parish.	County.	Date of Earliest Entry.
Cleeve, Bishop's. *See* Bishop's Cleeve.			Clodock - - -	Hereford - -	1714
			Cloford - - -	Somerset -	1561
Cleeve, Old - -	Somerset - -	1661	Clophill - -	Bedford -	1568
Cleeve, Prior - -	Worcester -	1598	Clopton - -	Suffolk -	1735
Clehonger - -	Hereford - -	1671	Closworth - -	Somerset -	1685
Clement's, St. - -	Cornwall	1543	Clothall - -	Hertford - -	1717
Clenchwharton -	Norfolk - -	1720	Clovelly - -	Devon - -	1686
Clent - - -	Stafford -	1562	Cloughton - -	York - -	[9] 1754
Cleobury-Mortimer -	Salop - -	1603	Clowne - -	Derby - -	1570
Cleobury, North -	Salop - -	1680	Clun - - -	Salop - -	1653
Clerkenwell, St. James	Middlesex	[1] 1560	Clunbury - -	Salop - -	[10] 1574
St. John	- - -	1723	Clungunford - -	Salop -	1559
Clether, St. - -	Cornwall	[2] 1640	Clutton - -	Somerset -	1693
Clevedon - - -	Somerset -	1727	Clydey - -	Pembroke -	1754
Clewer - - -	Berks - -	1653	Clymping - -	Sussex -	1678
Cley-next-the-Sea -	Norfolk -	1538	Clynnog - -	Carnarvon -	1646
Cliburn - - -	Westmorland -	1565	Clyro - - -	Radnor -	1667
Cliddesden - -	Hants - -	[3] 1636	Clyst, Broad-. *See* Broad-Clyst.		
Cliffe-by-Lewes -	Sussex - -	1606			
Cliffe-at-Hoo - -	Kent - -	1558	Clyst, St. George -	Devon - -	[11] 1565
Cliffe, King's. *See* King's-Cliffe.			St. Lawrence -	Devon - -	1539
			St. Mary -	Devon - -	1662
Cliffe-Pypard - -	Wilts - -	1576	Clyst-Honiton -	Devon -	1683
Cliffe, West - -	Kent - -	1576	Clyst-Hydon - -	Devon - -	1548
Clifford - - -	Hereford -	1690	Coaley - - -	Gloucester -	[12] 1582
Clifford-Chambers -	Gloucester -	[4] 1538	Coates - - -	Gloucester -	1566
Clifton - - -	Bedford - -	1538	Coates (Stow) -	Lincoln - -	1661
Clifton - - -	Gloucester -	1538	Coates - - -	Sussex - -	[13] —
Clifton - - -	Nottingham -	[5] 1573	Coates, Great -	Lincoln - -	1653
Clifton - - -	Westmorland -	1676	Coates, Little -	Lincoln - -	1726
Clifton-Campville -	Stafford -	1662	Coates, North -	Lincoln - -	1659
Clifton-Hampden -	Oxford - -	1578	Coberley - -	Gloucester -	1546
Clifton-Maybank -	Dorset - -	[6] —	Cobham - -	Kent - -	1653
Clifton-North - -	Nottingham -	1539	Cobham - -	Surrey - -	1562
Clifton-on-Dunsmore	Warwick - -	1594	Cockayne-Hatley. *See* Hatley-Cockayne.		
Clifton-on-Teme -	Worcester -	1598			
Clifton-Reynes -	Buckingham -	1653	Cockerham - -	Lancaster -	[14] 1594
Climping. *See* Clymping.			Cockerington, North -	Lincoln - -	1646
			Cockerington, South -	Lincoln - -	1670
Clippesby - -	Norfolk - -	1732	Cockermouth - -	Cumberland -	1632
Clipsham - -	Rutland - -	1726	Cockey. *See* Ainsworth.		
Clipston - -	Northampton -	1667	Cockfield - -	Durham -	1578
Clitheroe - -	Lancaster -	1570	Cockfield - -	Suffolk -	1561
Clive - - -	Salop - -	[7] 1667	Cocking - -	Sussex - -	1558
Cliviger. *See* Holme-in-Cliviger.			Cockington - -	Devon - -	1628
			Cockley-Cley - -	Norfolk -	1731
Clixby - - -	Lincoln -	[8] —	Cockshutt - -	Salop - -	1772
Clocaenog - -	Denbigh -	1672	Cockthorpe - -	Norfolk -	1560

[1] **P** 1551–1754. Harleian Society Registers, vols. 9, 10, 13, 17, 19, 20, 1884–94.

[2] **P** (Marriages only) 1640–1811. Cornwall Parish Registers, vol. 1, 1900.

[3] **P** (Marriages only) 1636–1812. Hampshire Parish Registers, vol. 1, 1899.

[4] **P** (Marriages only) 1538–1812. Gloucestershire Parish Registers, vol. 5, 1899.

[5] **P** (Marriages only) 1573–1812. Nottinghamshire Parish Registers, vol. 7, 1905.

[6] Included in the Registers of Bradford-Abbas (q.v.).

[7] **P** 1671–1812. Shropshire Parish Register Society, vol. 7.

[8] Included in the Registers of Caistor (q.v.).

[9] Other entries included in the Registers of Scalby (q.v.).

[10] **P** 1574–1812. Parish Register Society, vol. 38, 1901. Also Shropshire Parish Register Society, vol. 2.

[11] **P** 1565–1812. Parish Register Society, vol. 25. London, 1899.

[12] **P** (Marriages only) 1625–1812. Gloucestershire Parish Registers, vol. 5, 1899.

[13] Included in the Registers of Burton (q.v.).

[14] **P** 1595–1657. Lancashire Parish Register Society, 1904.

Parish.	County.	Date of Earliest Entry.	Parish.	County.	Date of Earliest Entry.
Coddenham - - -	Suffolk -	1539	Colerne - - -	Wilts - -	⁷1661
Coddington - -	Chester - -	¹1681	Colesborne - -	Gloucester -	1632
Coddington - -	Hereford - -	1675	Coleshill - -	Berks - -	1559
Coddington - -	Nottingham -	²1676	Coleshill - -	Warwick -	1538
Codford, St. Mary -	Wilts - -	1653	Coley - - -	York - -	⁸
St. Peter	Wilts - -	1680	Colkirk - -	Norfolk -	1538
Codicote - -	Hertford - -	1559	Collingbourn-Ducis -	Wilts - -	1653
Codsall - - -	Stafford - -	1587	Collingbourn-Kingston	Wilts - -	1653
Coed-Anna - -	Anglesea - -	1783	Collingham - -	York - -	1579
Coedkerne - -	Monmouth -	1733	Collingham, North -	Nottingham -	1558
Coffinswell - -	Devon - -	1560	Collingham, South -	Nottingham -	1558
Cofton-Hackett -	Worcester -	1550	Collington - -	Hereford -	1566
Cogan - - -	Glamorgan -	1785	Collingtree - -	Northampton -	1677
Cogenhoe - -	Northampton -	1558	Collyweston - -	Northampton -	1541
Coggeshall, Great -	Essex - -	1584	Colmer - -	Hants - -	⁹1563
Coggs - - -	Oxford - -	1653	Colmworth - -	Bedford -	1735
Coity. See Coyty.			Coln, St. Aldwins -	Gloucester -	1650
Coker, East - -	Somerset -	1560	Coln, St. Denis -	Gloucester -	1561
Coker, West - -	Somerset -	1697	Colne-Rogers - -	Gloucester -	¹⁰1754
Colan, St. - -	Cornwall -	1665	Colnbrook - -	Buckingham -	1760
Colaton-Raleigh -	Devon - -	1673	Colne - -	Huntingdon -	1668
Colby - - -	Norfolk -	1552	Colne - -	Lancaster -	¹¹1599
Colchester, All Saints -	Essex - -	1610	Colne, Earl's -	Essex - -	1559
Holy Trinity	- -	1696	Colne-Engain -	Essex - -	1629
St. Botolph -	- -	1560	Colne, Wakes -	Essex - -	1690
St. Giles -	- -	1692	Colne, White -	Essex - -	1558
St. James -	- -	1560	Colney - -	Norfolk -	1750
St. Leonard -	- -	³1542	Colsterworth -	Lincoln -	1572
St. Martin -	- -	1622	Colston-Basset -	Nottingham -	¹²1591
St. Mary Magdalen	- -	1721	Coltishall -	Norfolk -	1558
St. Mary the Virgin.	- -	1561	Colton - -	Lancaster -	¹³1623
St. Nicholas	- -	1541	Colton - -	Norfolk -	1542
St. Peter -	- -	1611	Colton - -	Stafford -	1647
St. Runwald -	- -	1576	Columb, St. Major -	Cornwall -	¹⁴1539
Coldred - -	Kent - -	1560	Columb, St. Minor -	Cornwall -	1560
Coldweston. See Weston, Cold.			Colva - -	Radnor -	1663
			Colwall - -	Hereford -	1651
Colebrooke - -	Devon - -	1558	Colwich - -	Stafford -	1590
Coleby - -	Lincoln -	⁴1561	Colwick - -	Nottingham -	¹⁵1569
Coleford - -	Gloucester -	⁵—	Colwinstone -	Glamorgan -	1766
Coleford - -	Somerset -	⁶—	Colyton - -	Devon - -	1538
Colemore. See Colmer.			Combe, St. Nicholas -	Somerset -	1678
Cole-Orton - -	Leicester -	1612	Combe - -	Hants - -	¹⁶1560
Coleridge - -	Devon -	1556	Combe-Florey -	Hants - -	1566
			Combe-Hay -	Hants - -	1538

¹ The Registers were destroyed by fire 5th May 1820, when the rectory was burnt down; one however, escaped, dating from 1681 to 1718. The Bishop's Transcripts commence 1597.
² **P** (Marriages only) 1676–1812. Nottinghamshire Parish Registers, vol. 3, 1900.
³ **P** 1670–1 (only). Edited by F. A. Crisp.
⁴ **P** 1561–1812. Parish Register Society, vol. 48, 1903.
⁵ Included in the Registers of Newland (q.v.).
⁶ Included in the Registers of Kilmersdon (q.v.).
⁷ **P** (Marriages only) 1661–1812. Wiltshire Parish Registers, vol. 4, 1907.
⁸ Included in the Registers of Halifax (q.v.).
⁹ **P** See note to Priors Dean, p. 128.
¹⁰ **P** (Marriages only) 1755–1812. Gloucestershire Parish Registers, vol. 12, 1906.
¹¹ **P** 1599–1653. Lancashire Parish Register Society, 1904.
¹² **P** (Marriages only) 1591–1811. Nottinghamshire Parish Registers, vol. 2, 1899.
¹³ **P** 1623–1812. Edited by A. A. Williams, Kendal, 1891.
¹⁴ **P** 1539–1780. Edited by A. J. Jewers, London, 1881.
¹⁵ **P** (Marriages only) 1569–1754. Nottinghamshire Parish Registers, vol. 10, 1907.
¹⁶ **P** (Marriages only), 1560–1812. Hampshire Parish Registers, vol. 2, 1900.

Parish.	County.	Date of Earliest Entry.	Parish.	County.	Date of Earliest Entry.
Combe-Long - -	Oxford - -	1646	Conwil-Cayo - -	Carmarthen -	1698
Combe-Martin -	Devon - -	1736	Cookbury - -	Devon - -	1749
Combe-Monkton -	Devon - -	1561	Cookham - - -	Berks - -	1656
Combe-Pyne - -	Somerset -	1681	Cookley - -	Suffolk -	1538
Combe-Raleigh -	Devon - -	1653	Cooling - - -	Kent - -	1707
Combe-in-Teignhead -	Devon - -	1653	Coombe-Bissett -	Wilts - -	1636
Comberton - -	Cambridge -	1560	Coombe-Keynes -	Dorset - -	1538
Comberton, Great -	Worcester -	1540	Coombes - -	Sussex - -	1538
Comberton, Little -	Worcester -	1540	Copdock - - -	Suffolk -	1701
Combroke - -	Warwick -	¹ 1701	Copford - -	Essex - -	1558
Combs - - -	Suffolk - -	1568	Copgrove - -	York - -	1586
Compton - -	Berks - -	1553	Cople - - -	Bedford - -	1563
Compton - -	Hants - -	1678	Copmanford - -	Huntingdon -	⁸ —
Compton - -	Surrey - -	1639	Copmanthorpe -	York - -	1759
Compton - - -	Sussex - -	1558	Copp - - -	Lancaster -	⁹ —
Compton, West -	Dorset - -	1538	Coppenhall - -	Chester -	1653
Compton-Abbas -	Dorset - -	1650	Coppenhall - -	Stafford - -	1678
Compton-Abdale -	Gloucester -	1720	Coppull - - -	Lancaster -	1765
Compton-Basset -	Wilts - -	1558	Corbridge - -	Northumberland	1657
Compton-Beauchamp	Berks - -	1552	Corby - - -	Lincoln - -	1561
Compton-Bishop -	Somerset -	1641	Corby - - -	Northampton -	1684
Compton - Chamberlayne.	Wilts - -	1538	Coreley - - -	Salop - -	1543
			Corfe - - -	Somerset - -	¹⁰ 1673
Compton-Dando -	Somerset -	1652	Corfe-Castle - -	Dorset - -	1653
Compton-Dundon -	Somerset -	1682	Corfe-Mullen - -	Dorset - -	1652
Compton-Fenny -	Warwick -	² 1626	Corhampton - -	Hants - -	1677
Compton-Greenfield -	Gloucester -	1583	Corley - - -	Warwick -	1540
Compton, Little -	Gloucester -	³ 1588	Cornard, Great -	Suffolk - -	1540
Compton, Long -	Warwick -	⁴ 1670	Cornard, Little -	Suffolk - -	1565
Compton-Martin -	Somerset -	1559	Cornelly - -	Cornwall -	1559
Compton-Nether -	Dorset - -	1538	Corney - - -	Cumberland -	1754
Compton-Over - -	Dorset - -	1726	Cornhill - -	Northumberland	1695
Compton - Pauncefoot.	Somerset -	1559	Cornhill - - -	Durham - -	1695
			Cornwell - -	Oxford - -	1662
Compton-Valence -	Dorset - -	1655	Cornwood - - -	Devon - -	1685
Compton-Wynyates -	Warwick -	1683	Cornworthy - -	Devon - -	1565
Condicote - -	Gloucester -	1663	Corpusty - -	Norfolk - -	1726
Condover - - -	Salop - -	⁵ 1570	Corringham - -	Essex - -	1558
Congerstone - -	Leicester -	1593	Corringham - -	Lincoln - -	1647
Congham - - -	Norfolk - -	1581	Corscombe - -	Dorset - -	1595
Congresbury - -	Somerset - -	1543	Corse - - -	Gloucester -	1661
Coningsby - -	Lincoln - -	1561	Corsenside - -	Northumberland	1726
Conington - -	Cambridge -	1538	Corsham - - -	Wilts - -	1553
Conington - -	Huntingdon -	1583	Corsley - - -	Wilts - -	1686
Conisborough -	York - -	1555	Corston - - -	Somerset -	1568
Coniscliffe - -	Durham - -	1590	Corston - - -	Wilts - -	¹¹ —
Conisholme - -	Lincoln - -	1559	Corton - - -	Suffolk - -	1579
Coniston - -	Lancaster -	1673	Corton-Denham -	Somerset -	1538
Conistone - - -	York - -	⁶ 1567	Corwen - - -	Merioneth -	1719
Constantine - -	Cornwall -	1581	Coryton - - -	Devon - -	1654
Convil-in-Elmet -	Carmarthen -	1743	Cosby - - -	Leicester -	1557
Conway - - -	Carnarvon -	⁷ 1541	Cosgrove - -	Northampton -	1691

¹ Bishops' Transcripts commence 1609. *See also* Kineton.
² **P** (Marriages only) 1627–1812. Warwickshire Parish Registers, vol. 1, 1904.
³ Bishops' Transcripts commence 1608. **P** (Marriages only) 1608–1681 and 1685–1812. Warwickshire Parish Registers, vol. 1, 1904.
⁴ **P** (Marriages only) 1685–1812. Warwickshire Parish Registers, vol. 1, 1904.
⁵ **P** 1570–1812. Shropshire Parish Register Society, vol. 6.
⁶ **P** 1567–1812. Edited by Rev. W. J. Stavert, Skipton, 1894.
⁷ **P** 1541–1793. Edited by A. Hadley, London, 1900.
⁸ Included in the Registers of Upton (*q.v.*).
⁹ Included in the Registers of St. Michael-on-Wyre.
¹⁰ **P** (Marriages only) 1687–1812. Somersetshire Parish Registers, vol. 7, 1906.
¹¹ Included in the Registers of Malmesbury (*q.v.*).

Parish.	County.	Date of Earliest Entry.	Parish.	County.	Date of Earliest Entry.
Cosheston - -	Pembroke -	1723	Cowarne, Little - -	Hereford - -	1563
Cosmus, St., and Da-			Cowarne, Much -	Hereford - -	1559
mian-in-the - Blean.			Cowbit - - -	Lincoln - -	1700
See Blean.			Cowbridge - -	Glamorgan -	1718
Cossall - - -	Nottingham -	[1] 1654	Cowden - - -	Kent - -	1566
Cossey (or Costessey) -	Norfolk -	1538	Cowes (Isle of Wight)	Hants - -	[10] 1679
Cossington - -	Leicester -	1544	Cowesby - - -	York - -	1679
Cossington - -	Somerset - -	1675	Cowfold - - -	Sussex - -	1558
Costock - - -	Nottingham -	[2] 1558	Cowley - - -	Gloucester -	1676
Coston - - -	Leicester - -	1561	Cowley - - -	Middlesex -	1562
Coston - - -	Norfolk -	1704	Cowley - - -	Oxford - -	1678
Cotesbach. See Cot-			Cowlinge - -	Suffolk - -	1559
tesbach.			Cowthorpe - -	York - -	1568
Cotgrave - -	Nottingham -	[3] 1559	Cowton, East - -	York - -	1754
Cotham - - -	Nottingham -	[4] 1587	Cowton, South -	York - -	1568
Cothelstone - -	Somerset - -	[5] 1664	Coxwell, Great -	Berks - -	1557
Cotheridge - -	Worcester -	[6] 1653	Coxwell, Little -	Berks - -	[11] — -
Cotleigh - - -	Devon - -	1653	Coxwold - -	York - -	1583
Coton - - -	Cambridge -	1538	Coychurch - -	Glamorgan -	1736
Cottam - - -	Nottingham -	1695	Coyty - - -	Glamorgan -	1791
Cottenham - -	Cambridge -	1572	Cradley - - -	Hereford - -	1560
Cottered - - -	Hertford - -	1558	Cradley - - -	Worcester -	1798
Cotterstock - -	Northampton -	1632	Crambe - - -	York - -	1710
Cottesbach - -	Leicester - -	1558	Cramlington - -	Northumberland	1665
Cottesbrooke - -	Northampton -	1630	Cranborne - -	Dorset - -	1602
Cottesmore - -	Rutland - -	1655	Cranbrook - -	Kent - -	1553
Cottingham - -	Northampton -	1574	Cranfield - -	Bedford - -	1653
Cottingham - -	York - -	1563	Cranford - -	Middlesex -	1564
Cottisford - - -	Oxford - -	1651	Cranford St. Andrew -	Northampton -	1695
Cotton - - -	Stafford - -	[7] —	St. John -	- - -	1627
Cotton - - -	Suffolk - -	1538	Cranham - -	Essex - -	1559
Coughton - -	Warwick - -	[8] 1673	Cranham - -	Gloucester -	1666
Coulsdon - - -	Surrey - -	1653	Cranleigh - -	Surrey - -	1608
Coulston, East -	Wilts - -	1714	Cranmore, East -	Somerset - -	1716
Cound - - -	Salop - -	[9] 1608	Cranmore, West -	Somerset - -	1563
Countesthorpe -	Leicester -	1577	Cranoe - - -	Leicester - -	1653
Countisbury - -	Devon - -	1676	Cransford - -	Suffolk - -	1653
Courland - - -	Somerset - -	1634	Cransley - -	Northampton -	1561
Courteenhall - -	Northampton -	1538	Crantock - -	Cornwall -	1559
Cove, North - -	Suffolk - -	1696	Cranwell - -	Lincoln - -	1564
Cove, South - -	Suffolk - -	1555	Cranwich - -	Norfolk - -	1732
Covehithe - -	Suffolk - -	1575	Cranworth - -	Norfolk - -	1653
Coveney - - -	Cambridge -	1676	Craswall - -	Hereford - -	[12] —
Covenham, St. Bar-	Lincoln - -	1566	Cratfield - -	Suffolk - -	1538
tholomew.			Crathorne - -	York - -	1723
St. Mary - -	- - -	1597	Crawford, Little. See		
Coventry St. Michael-	Warwick - -	1698	Tarrant Crawford.		
Holy Trinity -	- - -	1561	Crawley - - -	Hants - -	1649
St. John -	- - -	1734	Crawley - - -	Sussex - -	1653
Coverham - -	York - -	1707	Crawley, North -	Buckingham -	1558
Covington - -	Huntingdon -	1539	Cray St. Mary -	Kent - -	1579

[1] **P** (Marriages only) 1663-1812. Nottinghamshire Parish Registers, vol. 8, 1905.
[2] **P** (Marriages only) 1558-1812. Nottinghamshire Parish Registers, vol. 5, 1903.
[3] **P** (Marriages only) 1569-1812. Nottinghamshire Parish Registers, vol. 2, 1899.
[4] **P** (Marriages only) 1587-1812. Nottinghamshire Parish Registers, vol. 3, 1900.
[5] **P** (Marriages only) 1664-1812. Somersetshire Parish Registers, vol. 8, 1907.
[6] Bishop's Transcripts commence 1611.
[7] Included in the Registers of Alton.
[8] Bishop's Transcripts commence 1616.
[9] **P** 1562-1812. Shropshire Parish Register Society, vol. 2, 1902.
[10] Previous to 1679 included in the Registers of Northwood (q.v.).
[11] Included in the Registers of Faringdon (q.v.).
[12] Included in the Registers of Clodock (q.v.).

Parish.	County.	Date of Earliest Entry.	Parish.	County.	Date of Earliest Entry.
Cray, Foot's - -	Kent - -	1559	Cromer - - -	Norfolk - -	1689
Cray, North - -	Kent - -	1538	Cromhall - -	Gloucester -	1653
Cray, St. Paul's -	Kent - -	1579	Cromwell - -	Nottingham -	1650
Crayford - -	Kent - -	1558	Crondall - -	Hants - -	[7] 1569
Crayke - -	York - -	1538	Cronwere - -	Pembroke -	1725
Creacombe - -	Devon - -	1695	Crook - -	Westmorland -	1742
Creake, North -	Norfolk - -	1538	Croome d'Abitot -	Worcester -	1560
Creake, South - -	Norfolk - -	1538	Croome, Earl's -	Worcester -	[8] 1647
Creaton, Great -	Northampton -	1688	Croome-Hill -	Worcester -	[9] 1721
Credenhill - -	Hereford -	1671	Cropredy - -	Oxford - -	1538
Crediton - -	Devon - -	1564	Cropthorne - -	Worcester -	[10] 1557
Creech St. Michael -	Somerset -	[1] 1668	Cropton - -	York - -	1754
Creed - - -	Cornwall -	1653	Cropwell, Bishop -	Nottingham -	[11] 1539
Creeting, All Saints -	Suffolk - -	1705	Crosby-Garrett -	Westmorland -	1559
St. Mary -	Suffolk - -	1681	Crosby, Great -	Lancaster -	1749
St. Peter	Suffolk - -	1558	Crosby, Ravensworth	Westmorland -	1570
Creeton - -	Lincoln - -	1692	Crosby-on-Eden- -	Cumberland -	1649
Cregrina - -	Radnor - -	1685	Croscombe - -	Somerset - -	[12] 1558
Crendon, Long -	Buckingham -	1559	Cross-Canonby. See		
Cressage - -	Salop - -	[2] 1605	Canonby-Cross.		
Cressing - -	Essex - -	1733	Croscrake - -	Westmorland -	1796
Cressingham, Great -	Norfolk - -	[3] 1557	Crosstone - - -	York - -	1640
Cressingham, Little -	Norfolk - -	1681	Crosthwaite -	Cumberland -	1566
Cretingham - -	Suffolk - -	1558	Crosthwaite -	Westmorland -	1570
Crewkerne - -	Somerset - -	[4] 1551	Croston - -	Lancaster -	[13] 1543
Criccieth - -	Carnarvon -	1692	Crostwick - -	Norfolk - -	1562
Crich - - -	Derby - -	1600	Crostwright - -	Norfolk - -	1698
Crichel - - -	Dorset - -	1663	Croughton - -	Northampton- -	1663
Crick - - -	Northampton -	1559	Crowan - -	Cornwall -	1692
Crickadarn - -	Brecon - -	1734	Crowcombe - -	Somerset - -	1641
Cricket, St. Thomas -	Somerset -	1564	Crowell - -	Oxford - -	1594
Cricket-Malherbie -	Somerset - -	1723	Crowfield - -	Suffolk - -	[14] —
Crickhowell - -	Brecon - -	1633	Crowhurst - -	Surrey - -	1567
Cricklade, St. Mary -	Wilts - -	1683	Crowhurst - -	Sussex - -	1558
St. Sampson	Wilts - -	1673	Crowland - -	Lincoln - -	1639
Cricksea - -	Essex - -	1749	Crowle - -	Lincoln - -	1561
Criggion - - -	Montgomery -	[5] —	Crowle - -	Worcester -	1539
Crimplesham - -	Norfolk - -	1561	Crowmarsh-Giffard -	Oxford - -	1575
Cringleford - -	Norfolk - -	1560	Crownthorpe - -	Norfolk - -	1700
Croft - - -	Hereford - -	1565	Croxall - -	Derby - -	[15] 1586
Croft - - -	Leicester -	1583	Croxdale - -	Durham - -	1696
Croft - - -	Lincoln - -	1559	Croxden - -	Stafford - -	1648
Croft - - -	York - -	1617	Croxton - -	Cambridge -	1538
Crofton - -	York - -	1615	Croxton - -	Lincoln - -	1562
Crofton - -	Hants - -	[6] —	Croxton - -	Norfolk - -	[16] —
Croglin - -	Cumberland -	1644	Croxton (Thetford) -	Norfolk - -	1558

[1] **P** (Marriages only) 1665-1814. Somersetshire Parish Registers, vol. 7, 1906.
[2] **P** 1605-1812. Parish Register Society, London, 1900. *Also* **P** Shropshire Parish Register Society, vol. 2, 1902.
[3] **P** (Marriages only) 1557-1812. Norfolk Parish Registers, vol. 3, 1907.
[4] **P** (Marriages only) 1559-1812. Somersetshire Parish Registers, vol. 5, 1904.
[5] Included in the Registers of Alberbury (*q.v.*).
[6] Included in the Registers of Tichfield (*q.v.*).
[7] **P** (Marriages only) 1576-1812. Hampshire Parish Registers, vol. 4, 1902.
[8] Bishop's Transcripts commence 1612. [9] Bishop's Transcripts commence 1611.
[10] **P** 1557-1717. Edited by F. A. Crisp, London, 1896.
[11] **P** (Marriages only) 1539-1812. Nottinghamshire Parish Registers, vol. 2, 1899.
[12] The Churchwardens' account books for this parish date back to 1472.
[13] **P** 1543-1685. Lancashire Parish Register Society, 1900.
[14] Included in the Registers of Coddenham.
[15] **P** Baptisms and burials 1586-1812, marriages 1586-1753. "Sketch of Parish of Croxall," by Richard Ussher, 1881.
[16] Included in the Registers of Fulmodeston (*q.v.*).

F

Parish.	County.	Date of Earliest Entry.	Parish.	County.	Date of Earliest Entry.
Croxton-Kerrial -	Leicester -	1559	Cwmcarvan - -	Monmouth -	1660
Croxton, South -	Leicester -	1662	Cwmdauddwr -	Radnor -	1737
Croydon - -	Cambridge -	1672	Cwmyoy - -	Monmouth -	1708
Croydon - -	Surrey -	1538	Cyfeiliog -	Denbigh -	1636
Crudwell - -	Wilts -	[1] 1659			
Crundale - -	Kent -	1554			
Cruwys-Morchard -	Devon -	1572			
Crux-Easton -	Hants -	1702			
Cubberley. See Cober-ley.			**D.**		
Cubbington -	Warwick -	1559	Dacre - -	Cumberland -	1559
Cubert - -	Cornwall -	1653	Dadlington -	Leicester -	1734
Cubley - -	Derby -	1566	Dagenham -	Essex -	1598
Cublington -	Buckingham -	1566	Daglingworth -	Gloucester -	1561
Cuby - -	Cornwall -	[2] —	Dalbury -	Derby -	1545
Cuckfield -	Sussex -	1598	Dalby - -	Lincoln -	1721
Cucklington -	Somerset -	1558	Dalby -	York -	1657
Cuckney - -	Nottingham -	1632	Dalby Magna -	Leicester -	1591
Cuddesdon -	Oxford -	1541	Dalby-on-the-Wolds -	Leicester -	1725
Cuddington -	Buckingham -	1653	Dalby Parva -	Leicester -	1559
Cudham -	Kent -	1653	Dalderby -	Lincoln -	1690
Cudworth -	Somerset -	1699	Dale - -	Pembroke -	1735
Culbone -	Somerset -	1625	Dale Abbey -	Derby -	[9] 1667
Culford - -	Suffolk -	[3] 1560	Dalham - -	Suffolk -	1558
Culgaith -	Cumberland -	1758	Dallinghoe -	Suffolk -	1559
Culham -	Oxford -	1650	Dallington -	Northampton -	1577
Cullompton -	Devon -	1601	Dallington -	Sussex -	1643
Culmington -	Salop -	1575	Dalston - -	Cumberland -	[10] 1570
Culmstock -	Devon -	1645	Dalton-Holme -	York -	1653
Culpho - -	Suffolk -	[4] 1700	Dalton-in-Furness -	Lancaster -	1565
Culverthorpe -	Lincoln -	1559	Dalton-le-Dale -	Durham -	1653
Culworth -	Northampton -	1563	Dalton, North -	York -	1653
Cumberworth -	Lincoln -	1562	Dalwood -	Devon -	1568
Cumberworth -	York -	1653	Damerham, South -	Wilts -	1678
Cumnor - -	Berks -	1559	Danbury -	Essex -	1673
Cumrew - -	Cumberland -	1731	Danby - -	York -	1585
Cumwhitton -	Cumberland -	1694	Danby-Wiske -	York -	1631
Cundall - -	York -	[5] 1582	Darenth -	Kent -	1631
Curdworth -	Warwick -	1653	Daresbury -	Chester -	1617
Curland. See Cour-land.			Darfield -	York -	1628
			Darlaston -	Stafford -	1539
Curry-Mallet -	Somerset -	1682	Darley - -	Derby -	1541
Curry, North -	Somerset -	[6] 1539	Darlington -	Durham -	1590
Curry-Rivell -	Somerset -	[7] 1642	Darlton -	Notts -	1568
Cury - -	Cornwall -	1690	Darmsden -	Suffolk -	[11] —
Cusop - -	Hereford -	1754	Darnall -	York -	1719
Cutcombe -	Somerset -	1624	Darowen -	Montgomery -	1633
Cutsdean -	Worcester -	[8] 1696	Darrington -	York -	1568
Cuxham -	Oxford -	1577	Darsham -	Suffolk -	1539
Cuxton -	Kent -	1560	Dartford -	Kent -	1561
Cuxwold -	Lincoln -	1683	Dartington -	Devon -	1538
Cwm (or Combe) -	Flint -	1727	Dartmouth, St. Petrox	Devon -	1652

[1] **P** (Marriages only) 1662–1812. Wiltshire Parish Registers, vol. 3, 1906.
[2] Included in the Registers of Tregony (*q.v.*).
[3] These Registers are being printed.
[4] **P** 1721–1886. Edited by F. A. Crisp, 1886.
[5] **P** 1582–1780. Edited by H. D. Eshelby, 1898.
[6] **P** (Marriages only) 1539–1812. Somersetshire Parish Registers, vol. 2, 1899.
[7] **P** (Marriages only) 1642–1812. Somersetshire Parish Registers, vol. 3, 1901.
[8] Bishop's Transcripts commence 1634.
[9] **P** (Marriages only) 1667–1813. Derbyshire Parish Registers, vol. 1, 1906.
[10] **P** 1570–1812. Edited by J. Wilson, 1893.
[11] Included in the Registers of Barking (*q.v.*).

Parish.	County.	Date of Earliest Entry.	Parish.	County.	Date of Earliest Entry.
Darton - - -	York - -	1558	Dendron - -	Lancaster -	1788
Dasset, Avon. *See* Avon Dasset.			Denford - - -	Northampton -	1597
			Dengie - - -	Essex - -	1559
Dassett Burton. *See* Burton Dassett.			Denham - - -	Buckingham -	1653
			Denham (near Bury) -	Suffolk -	[5] 1539
Datchet - - -	Buckingham -	1559	Denham (near Eye) -	Suffolk -	1708
Datchworth - -	Hertford - -	1570	Dennington - -	Suffolk -	1570
Dauntsey - - -	Wilts - -	1653	Dennis, St. - -	Cornwall -	1687
Davenham - -	Chester - -	1560	Denston - -	Suffolk -	1561
Daventry - -	Northampton -	1560	Dent - - -	York - -	1611
David's, St. - -	Brecon - -	[1] —	Denton - -	Durham -	[6] 1586
David's, St. - -	Pembroke -	1724	Denton - - -	Huntingdon -	1546
Davidstow - -	Cornwall -	[2] 1710	Denton - -	Kent - -	1560
Davington - -	Kent - -	1549	Denton - - -	Lancaster -	1694
Dawley, Magna -	Salop - -	1666	Denton - - -	Lincoln - -	1558
Dawlish - - -	Devon - -	1627	Denton - - -	Norfolk -	1559
Daylesford - -	Worcester -	[3] 1674	Denton - - -	Northampton -	1540
Deal - - -	Kent - -	1559	Denton - - -	Sussex - -	1600
Dean - - -	Cumberland -	1542	Denton - - -	York - -	1754
Dean, East - -	Hants - -	1682	Denton, Nether -	Cumberland -	1703
Dean, East (near Chichester).	Sussex - -	1653	Denton, Upper -	Cumberland -	[7] —
			Denver - - -	Norfolk -	1653
Dean, Little - -	Gloucester -	1684	Deopham - -	Norfolk -	1560
Dean, Mitchell -	Gloucester -	1680	Depden - - -	Suffolk -	1538
Dean, Nether - -	Bedford - -	1566	Deptford, St. Nicholas	Kent - -	1563
Dean-Prior - -	Devon - -	1561	St. Paul -	- - -	1730
Dean, West (near Eastbourne).	Sussex - -	1554	Derby, St. Alkmund -	Derby - -	1538
			All Saints	- - -	1558
Dean, West (near Chichester).	Sussex - -	1631	St. Michael -	- - -	1559
			St. Peter -	- - -	1558
Dean, West - -	Wilts - -	1538	St. Werburgh -	- - -	1562
Deane - - -	Lancaster -	1637	Dereham, East -	Norfolk -	1538
Deane - - -	Hants - -	[4] 1659	Dereham, West -	Norfolk -	1558
Dearham - - -	Cumberland -	1662	Deritend - -	Warwick -	1699
Debach - - -	Suffolk -	1539	Dersingham - -	Norfolk -	1710
Debden - - -	Essex - -	1557	Derwen - -	Denbigh -	1632
Debenham - -	Suffolk -	1559	Desborough - -	Northampton -	1571
Debtling - -	Kent - -	1558	Desford - -	Leicester -	1559
Decumans, St. -	Somerset -	1600	Deuxhill - -	Salop - -	1655
Deddington - -	Oxford - -	1631	Devereux, St. - -	Hereford -	1669
Dedham - - -	Essex - -	1560	Deverill Longbridge -	Wilts - -	1682
Deene - - -	Northampton -	1558	Deverill Monkton -	Wilts - -	[8] 1695
Deeping, St. James -	Lincoln - -	1674	Devizes, St. John the Baptist.	Wilts - -	1559
Deeping, Market -	Lincoln -	1709			
Deeping, West -	Lincoln - -	1657	The Blessed Virgin Mary.	- - -	1569
Deerhurst - -	Gloucester -	1559	Devonport. *See* Plymouth.		
Defford - - -	Worcester -	1540			
Deighton Kirk -	York - -	1600	Devynock - - -	Brecon - -	1696
Deighton - -	York - -	1686	Dewchurch, Little -	Hereford -	1730
Dembleby - -	Lincoln -	1573	Dewchurch, Much -	Hereford -	1559
Denbigh - -	Denbigh -	1683	Dewlish - - -	Dorset - -	1627
Denbury - -	Devon - -	1559	Dewsall - - -	Hereford -	1582
Denby - - -	Derby - -	1577	Dewsbury - - -	York - -	[9] 1538
Denchworth - -	Berks - -	1570			

[1] Included in the Registers of Brecon.
[2] **P** (Marriages only) 1676-1811. Cornwall Parish Registers, vol. 1, 1900.
[3] Bishop's Transcripts commence 1624.
[4] **P** (Marriages only) 1679-1812. Hampshire Parish Registers, vol. 1, 1899.
[5] **P** 1539-1850. Edited by Rev. S. H. A. Hervey, 1904.
[6] **P** 1586-1662. Edited by J. R. Walbran, Ripon, 1842.
[7] From 1736 to 1812 recorded in the Registers at Lanercost (*q.v.*), and previous to that date at Nether Denton (*q.v.*).   [8] **P** (Marriages only) 1749-1812. Wiltshire Parish Registers, vol. 1, 1905.
[9] **P** 1538-1653. Edited by S. J. Chadwick, 1898.

Parish.	County.	Date of Earliest Entry.	Parish	County.	Date of Earliest Entry.
Dibden - - -	Hants - -	[1] 1664	Dobcross - -	York - -	1787
Dickleburgh - -	Norfolk - -	1540	Docking - -	Norfolk - -	1558
Didbrook - -	Gloucester -	1558	Docklow - -	Hereford -	1584
Didcot - - -	Berks - -	1562	Dodbrooke - -	Devon - -	1725
Diddington - -	Huntingdon -	1688	Doddenham -	Worcester -	[6] 1538
Diddlebury - -	Salop - -	1583	Dodderhill - -	Worcester -	1651
Didling - - -	Sussex - -	[2] —	Doddinghurst -	Essex - -	1560
Didlington - -	Norfolk -	1717	Doddington - -	Cambridge -	1681
Didmarton - -	Gloucester -	1567	Doddington - -	Lincoln - -	[7] 1690
Didsbury - - -	Lancaster -	[3] 1561	Doddington - -	Northumberland	1688
Digby - - -	Lincoln - -	1679	Doddington, Dry	Lincoln - -	[8] —
Digswell - - -	Hertford -	1538	Doddington, Great	Northampton -	1560
Dihewyd - - -	Cardigan - -	1718	Doddiscombsleigh -	Devon - -	1678
Dilham - - -	Norfolk -	1563	Dodford - -	Northampton -	1581
Dilhorne - - -	Stafford -	1558	Dodington - -	Kent - -	1589
Dilwyn - - -	Hereford -	1558	Dodington - -	Gloucester -	1575
Dinas - - -	Pembroke -	1676	Dodington - -	Somerset - -	[9] 1538
Dinder - - -	Somerset - -	1696	Dodleston - -	Chester -	1570
Dinedor - - -	Hereford -	1750	Dogmaels, St. -	Pembroke -	1713
Dingestow - -	Monmouth -	1755	Dogmersfield -	Hants - -	[10] 1695
Dingley - - -	Northampton -	1583	Dogwells, St. -	Pembroke -	1718
Dinnington - -	York - -	1730	Dolbenmaen -	Carnarvon -	[11] —
Dinnington - -	Somerset - -	1592	Dolgelly - -	Merioneth -	1640
Dinsdale, Low -	Durham - -	1556	Dolton - -	Devon - -	1608
Dinton - - -	Buckingham -	1562	Dolwyddelan -	Carnarvon -	1700
Dinton - - -	Wilts - -	1558	Dominic, St. -	Cornwall -	1539
Diptford - - -	Devon - -	1653	Donatts, St. -	Glamorgan -	1570
Discoed - - -	Radnor -	1718	Donatts, St., Welsh	Glamorgan -	1726
Diseworth - -	Leicester -	1656	Doncaster - -	York - -	1557
Dishley - - -	Leicester -	1681	Donhead, St. Andrew -	Wilts - -	1645
Disley - - -	Chester -	1591	St. Mary	Wilts - -	1678
Diss - - -	Norfolk -	1551	Donington - -	Lincoln - -	1642
Disserth - - -	Radnor -	1734	Donington - -	Salop - -	[12] 1556
Distington - -	Cumberland -	1653	Donington Castle -	Leicester - -	1539
Ditcheat - -	Somerset - -	1562	Donington-on-Bain -	Lincoln - -	1653
Ditchford - -	Warwick - -	[4] —	Donnington -	Hereford -	1690
Ditchingham - -	Norfolk -	1559	Donnington -	Sussex - -	1559
Ditchling - - -	Sussex - -	1556	Donyatt - -	Somerset - -	1719
Ditteridge - -	Wilts -	1584	Donyland, East -	Essex - -	1731
Dittisham - -	Devon - -	1650	Dorchester, All Saints	Dorset - -	1654
Ditton - - -	Kent - -	1663	Holy Trinity	- - -	1653
Ditton - - -	Buckingham -	[5] —	St. Peter	- - -	1653
Ditton, Fen- -	Cambridge -	1538	Dorchester - -	Oxford - -	1638
Ditton, Long -	Surrey - -	1564	Dore - -	Derby - -	[13] —
Ditton, Priors -	Salop - -	1673	Dorking - -	Surrey - -	1538
Ditton, Thames -	Surrey - -	1661	Dormston - -	Worcester -	[14] 1716
Ditton, Wood -	Cambridge -	1567	Dorney - -	Buckingham -	1538
Dixton, Newton -	Monmouth -	1661	Dorrington -	Lincoln - -	1655

[1] The earliest date on the cover of register is 1625, but all the entries before 1664 are missing from the book, and then irregular until 1731.
[2] Included in the Registers of Treyford (q.v.).
[3] P 1561-1757. Lancashire Parish Register Society, vol. 8, 1900.
[4] Included in the Registers of Stretton-on-the-Foss (q.v.).
[5] Included in the Registers of Stoke Poges (q.v.). [6] P Included in the Registers of Knightwick (q.v.).
[7] P 1562-1812. Parish Register Society, vol. 14, 1898.
[8] Included in the Registers of Westborough (q.v.).
[9] P (Marriages only) 1538-1805. Somersetshire Parish Registers, vol. 6, 1905.
[10] P (Marriages only) 1695-1812. Hampshire Parish Registers, vol. 3, 1902.
[11] Included in the Registers of Penmorva (q.v.).
[12] P 1556-1812. Shropshire Parish Register Society, vol. 3, 1901.
[13] Included in the registers of Dronfield up to 1813 for baptisms, 1844 for marriages, and 1829 for burials ; except for some incomplete baptismal entries dating from 1734 in a separate book which is preserved at Dore. [14] Bishop's Transcripts commence 1612.

Parish.	County.	Date of Earliest Entry.		Parish.	County.	Date of Earliest Entry.
Dorsington - -	Gloucester -	[1] 1593		Driffield - - -	Gloucester -	1561
Dorstone - -	Hereford - -	1733		Driffield, Great -	York - -	1556
Dorton - -	Buckingham -	1694		Driffield, Little - -	York - -	1578
Doulting - -	Somerset - -	1563		Drinkstone - -	Suffolk - -	1666
Dovercourt - -	Essex - -	1706		Droitwich, St. Andrew	Worcester -	1571
Doverdale - -	Worcester -	[2] 1755		St. Peter -	- - -	1544
Doveridge - -	Derby - -	1574		Dronfield - - -	Derby - -	1560
Dover, St. James -	Kent - -	1594		Droxford - - -	Hants - -	1633
St. Mary -	- - -	1557		Drypool - - -	York - -	1587
Dowdeswell - -	Gloucester -	1575		Ducklington - -	Oxford - -	[6] 1550
Dowland - -	Devon - -	1742		Duckmanton - -	Derby - - -	[7] —
Dowles - -	Salop - -	1572		Duddington - -	Northampton -	1733
Dowlish-Wake - -	Somerset -	1636		Dudleston - -	Salop - -	1693
Down - -	Kent - -	1538		Dudley, St. Thomas -	Worcester -	1541
Down, St. Mary -	Devon - -	1688		St. Edmund -	- - -	1540
Down, East - -	Devon - -	1538		Duffield - - -	Derby - -	[8] 1598
Down, West - -	Devon - -	1583		Dufton - - -	Westmorland -	1570
Downham - -	Cambridge -	1558		Dulas - - -	Hereford -	1770
Downham - -	Essex - -	1558		Dullingham - -	Cambridge -	1558
Downham - -	Lancaster -	1653		Duloe - - -	Cornwall -	1668
Downham-Market -	Norfolk - -	1554		Dulverton - -	Somerset -	1558
Downham Santon -	Suffolk - -	1576		Dulwich College -	Surrey - -	1616
Downhead - -	Somerset -	1695		Dumbleton - -	Gloucester -	1738
Downholme - -	York - -	1736		Dummer - - -	Hants - -	[9] 1540
Downton - -	Hereford -	1728		Dunchideock - -	Devon - -	1538
Downton - -	Wilts - -	1602		Dunchurch - -	Warwick -	1538
Dowsby - -	Lincoln - -	1670		Duncton - -	Sussex - -	1545
Doynton - -	Gloucester -	1566		Dundry - - -	Somerset -	1654
Draughton - -	Northampton -	1559		Dunham - - -	Nottingham -	1654
Drax - -	York - -	1597		Dunham, Great -	Norfolk - -	[10] 1539
Draycot-Cerne - -	Wilts - -	1691		Dunham, Little -	Norfolk - -	1562
Draycott-le-Moors -	Stafford - -	1669		Dunholme - -	Lincoln - -	1564
Drayton - -	Berks - -	1754		Dunkerton - -	Somerset -	1748
Drayton - - -	Norfolk - -	1558		Dunkeswell - -	Devon - -	1749
Drayton (near Wallingford).	Oxford - -	1568		Dunmow, Great -	Essex - -	1538
				Dunmow, Little -	Essex - -	1555
Drayton (near Banbury).	Oxford - -	1577		Dunnington - -	York - -	1583
				Dunsby - - -	Lincoln - -	1538
Drayton - -	Somerset -	[3] 1558		Dunsfold - -	Surrey - -	1628
Drayton-Bassett -	Stafford - -	1560		Dunsford - -	Devon - -	1599
Drayton-Beauchamp -	Buckingham -	1538		Dunstable - -	Bedford - -	1558
Drayton, Dry - -	Cambridge -	1564		Dunster - - -	Somerset -	1559
Drayton, East -	Nottingham -	1737		Dunstew - - -	Oxford - -	1654
Drayton Fenny -	Leicester -	1712		Dunston - - -	Lincoln - -	1691
Drayton, Fen -	Cambridge -	[4] 1573		Dunston - - -	Norfolk - -	1555
Drayton-Parslow -	Buckingham -	[5] 1559		Dunterton - -	Devon - -	1583
Drayton, West -	Middlesex -	1568		Dunton - - -	Bedford - -	1553
Drayton, West -	Nottingham -	1632		Dunton - - -	Buckingham -	1576
Drewsteignton -	Devon - -	1557		Dunton - - -	Essex - -	1538
Driby - - -	Lincoln - -	1622		Dunton - - -	Norfolk - -	1784
Drigg - - -	Cumberland -	1631		Dunton-Bassett -	Leicester -	1653

[1] **P** (Marriages only) 1602–1812. Gloucestershire Parish Registers, vol. 3, 1898.
[2] Bishop's Transcripts commence 1612.
[3] **P** (Marriages only) 1577–1812. Somersetshire Parish Registers, vol. 3, 1901.
[4] **P** (Marriages only) 1580–1812. Cambridgeshire Parish Registers, vol. 1, 1907.
[5] **P** (Marriages only) 1559–1812. Buckinghamshire Parish Registers, vol. 3, 1907.
[6] An Index to Surnames in Register, 1550–1880. Published by North Oxfordshire Archæological Society in 1881.
[7] Included in the Registers of Sutton (*q.v.*).
[8] **P** (Marriages only) 1766–1812. Derbyshire Parish Registers, vol. 3, 1907.
[9] **P** (Marriages only 1541–1812. Hampshire Parish Registers, vol. 1, 1899.
[10] **P** (Marriages only) 1538–1812. Norfolk Parish Registers, vol. 2, 1900.

Parish.	County.	Date of Earliest Entry.	Parish.	County.	Date of Earliest Entry.
Duntsbourne, Abbots	Gloucester -	[1] 1607	Easington - -	Oxford -	1583
Duntsbourne-Rouse -	Gloucester -	1545	Easington - -	York -	1585
Dunwich - -	Suffolk -	1672	Easington - -	York - -	1606
Durham, St. Giles -	Durham -	1584	Easingwold - -	York - -	1599
St. Margaret -	- -	[2] 1558	Eastbourne - -	Sussex - -	1558
St. Mary - -	- -	1571	Eastbridge - -	Kent - -	[10] —
St. Mary the Less -	- -	1559	East-Church - -	Kent - -	1677
St. Nicholas -	- -	1540	Eastdean - -	Sussex - -	1559
St. Oswald -	- -	[3] 1538	Easter, Good -	Essex - -	1538
The Cathedral Church.	- -	[4] 1609	Easter, High -	Essex - -	1654
			Eastergate - -	Sussex - -	1563
Durleigh - -	Somerset -	[5] 1683	Eastham - -	Chester -	[11] 1598
Durley - -	Hants -	1562	Eastham - -	Worcester -	1571
Durnford - -	Wilts -	[6] 1574	Easthampstead -	Berks -	1558
Durrington - -	Wilts -	[7] 1591	Easthope - -	Salop -	1624
Dursley - -	Gloucester -	[8] 1639	Easthorpe - -	Essex -	1572
Durston - -	Somerset -	1712	Eastington - -	Gloucester -	[12] 1558
Durweston - -	Dorset -	1793	Eastleach-Martin (or Burthorpe).	Gloucester -	1538
Duston - -	Northampton -	1692			
Duxford - -	Cambridge -	1685	Eastleach-Turville -	Gloucester -	1654
Dwygyfylchi -	Carnarvon -	1757	Eastling - -	Kent -	1558
Dymchurch - -	Kent -	1624	Eastnor - -	Hereford -	1561
Dymock - -	Gloucester -	1538	Easton - -	Hants -	1692
Dyrham - -	Gloucester -	1568	Easton - -	Huntingdon -	1708
Dyserth - -	Flint -	1602	Easton - -	Norfolk -	1678
			Easton-on-the-Hill	Northampton -	1579
			Easton - -	Suffolk -	1561
			Easton-Royal -	Wilts -	1580
			Easton-Bavent -	Suffolk -	[13] —
			Easton, Great -	Essex -	1561
E.			Easton, Great -	Leicester -	1722
			Easton, Grey -	Wilts -	1654
Eagle - -	Lincoln -	1588	Easton-in-Gordano -	Somerset -	1559
Eaglescliffe - -	Durham -	1539	Easton, Little -	Essex -	1559
Eakring - -	Nottingham -	1563	Easton-Maudit -	Northampton -	1539
Ealing - -	Middlesex -	1582	Easton-Neston -	Northampton -	1559
Eardisland - -	Hereford -	1614	Eastrington - -	York -	1563
Eardisley - -	Hereford -	1630	Eastrop - -	Hants -	[14] 1750
Earlham - -	Norfolk -	1621	Eastry - -	Kent -	1559
Earls Barton -	Northampton -	1558	Eastwell - -	Kent -	1538
Earnley - -	Sussex -	1562	Eastwell - -	Leicester -	1719
Earnshill - -	Somerset -	[9] —	Eastwick - -	Hertford -	[15] 1555
Earsdon - -	Northumberland	1589	Eastwood - -	Essex -	1685
Earsham - -	Norfolk -	1559	Eastwood - -	Nottingham -	[16] 1711
Easby - -	York -	1670	Eaton - -	Norfolk -	1568
Easebourne - -	Sussex -	1538	Eaton - -	Leicester -	1751
Easington -	Durham -	1571	Eaton - -	Nottingham -	1660

[1] **P** (Marriages only) 1607-1637. Gloucestershire Parish Registers, vol. 12, 1906.
[2] **P** 1558-1812. Durham and Northumberland Parish Register Society, vol. 9, 1904.
[3] **P** 1538-1751. Edited by Rev. A. W. Headlam, Durham, 1891.
[4] **P** 1609-1896. Harleian Society Registers, vol. 23, 1897.
[5] **P** (Marriages only) 1683-1807. Somersetshire Parish Registers, vol. 6, 1905.
[6] **P** 1574-1650. Printed by Sir T. Phillipps, 1823.
[7] **P** (Marriages only) 1591-1812. Wiltshire Parish Registers, vol. 2, 1906.
[8] **P** (Marriages only) 1636-1812. Gloucestershire Parish Registers, vol. 5.
[9] Included in the Registers of Hambridge (q.v.).
[10] Included in the Registers of Dymchurch (q.v.).
[11] **P** 1598-1700. Edited by Francis Sanders, London, 1891.
[12] **P** (Marriages only) 1558-1812. Gloucestershire Parish Registers, vol. 13, 1908.
[13] Included in the Registers of Benacre (q.v.).
[14] **P** (Marriages only) 1759-1807. Hampshire Parish Registers, vol. 5, 1903.
[15] **P** (Marriages only) 1556-1834. Hertfordshire Parish Registers, vol. 1, 1907.
[16] **P** (Marriages only) 1711-1812. Nottinghamshire Parish Registers, vol. 11, 1907.

Parish.	County.	Date of Earliest Entry.	Parish.	County.	Date of Earliest Entry.
Eaton-under-Heywood	Salop - -	1688	Edlesborough -	Buckingham - -	[10] 1567
Eaton-Bishop - -	Hereford -	1588	Edlingham - -	Northumberland	[11] 1659
Eaton-Bray - -	Bedford - -	1559	Edlington - -	Lincoln - -	1562
Eaton, Church - -	Stafford - -	1538	Edlington - - -	York - -	1731
Eaton-Constantine -	Salop - -	1684	Edmondbyers -	Durham - -	1700
Eaton-Hastings -	Berks - -	1574	Edmondsham - -	Dorset - -	1573
Eaton, Little - -	Derby - -	1791	Edmondthorpe -	Leicester - -	1560
Eaton-Socon - -	Bedford - -	1577	Edmonton - -	Middlesex -	1558
Ebberston - - -	York - -	[1] 1678	Edrens, St. -	Pembroke -	1785
Ebbesbourne-Wake -	Wilts - -	1653	Edstaston - -	Salop - -	1712
Ebchester - - -	Durham - -	[2] 1610	Edston, Great -	York - -	1557
Ebony - - -	Kent - -	1708	Edwalton - -	Nottingham -	[12] 1538
Ebrington - - -	Gloucester -	[3] 1653	Edwardstone -	Suffolk - -	1645
Eccles - - -	Lancaster -	1564	Edwin-Loach - -	Worcester -	1570
Eccles - - -	Norfolk - -	1678	Edwin-Ralph -	Worcester -	1748
Ecclesall-Bierlow -	York - -	1784	Edwinstow - -	Nottingham -	[13] 1634
Ecclesfield - -	York - -	[4] 1558	Edworth - -	Bedford - -	1552
Eccleshall - -	Stafford - -	1573	Effingham - -	Surrey - -	1565
Eccleston - -	Chester - -	1593	Egdean - - -	Sussex - -	1646
Eccleston - -	Lancaster -	[5] 1603	Egerton - - -	Kent - -	1684
Eckington - -	Derby - -	1558	Eggesford - -	Devon - -	1586
Eckington - -	Worcester -	[6] 1678	Egginton - -	Bedford - -	1553
Ecton - - -	Northampton -	1559	Egginton - -	Derby - -	1561
Edale - - -	Derby - -	1642	Egglestone - -	Durham - -	1795
Edburton - - -	Sussex - -	[7] 1558	Egham - - -	Surrey - -	1560
Edenbridge - -	Kent - -	1538	Egleton - -	Rutland - -	1538
Eden, Castle - -	Durham - -	1720	Eglingham - -	Northumberland	[14] 1662
Edenfield - -	Lancaster -	1728	Egloshayle - -	Cornwall -	[15] 1600
Edengale - -	Stafford - -	1573	Egloskerry - -	Cornwall -	[16] 1574
Edenhall - -	Cumberland -	1558	Eglwys-Brewis -	Glamorgan -	1750
Edenham - -	Lincoln - -	1654	Eglwys-Cummin -	Carmarthen -	1731
Edensor - -	Derby - -	1539	Eglwys-Fach -	Denbigh - -	1601
Edern - - -	Carnarvon -	1700	Eglwys-fair-Acherrig -	Carmarthen -	1761
Edgbaston - -	Warwick - -	1635	Eglwysilan - -	Glamorgan -	1689
Edgcote - -	Northampton -	1690	Eglwys-Newydd -	Cardigan -	1773
Edgecott - -	Buckingham -	1539	Eglwys-Rhos -	Carnarvon -	1754
Edgefield - -	Norfolk - -	1653	Eglwys-Wen. See		
Edgmond - -	Salop - -	1680	Whitechurch.		
Edgton - -	Salop - -	[8] 1722	Eglwyswrw - -	Pembroke -	1731
Edgware - -	Middlesex -	1717	Egmanton - -	Nottingham -	1653
Edgworth - -	Gloucester -	[9] 1554	Egremont - -	Carmarthen -	1751
Edingley - -	Nottingham -	1538	Egremont - -	Cumberland -	1630
Edingthorpe - -	Norfolk - -	1560	Egton - - -	York - -	1622
Edington - -	Wilts - -	1695	Egton - - -	Lancaster -	1791
Edith-Weston -	Rutland - -	1585	Eisey - - -	Wilts - -	1571
Edlaston - - -	Derby - -	1573	Elberton - - -	Gloucester -	1653

[1] The Registers of Ebberston and Allerston were printed in the parish magazine commencing with January 1887.

[2] **P** 1689–1812. Durham and Northumberland Parish Register Society, 1900.

[3] **P** (Marriages only) 1653–1812. Gloucestershire Parish Registers, vol. 6, 1900.

[4] **P** 1558–1621. Edited by A. S. Gatty, London, 1878.

[5] **P** 1603–1694. Lancashire Parish Register Society, vol. 15, 1903.

[6] Bishop's Transcripts commence 1612.

[7] **P** 1558–1673. Edited by Rev. C. H. Wilkie, 1884. Index to same by F. A. Crisp, 1887.

[8] **P** 1722–1812. Shropshire Parish Register Society, vol. 3.

[9] **P** (Marriages only) 1554–1812. Gloucestershire Parish Registers, vol. 12, 1906.

[10] **P** (Marriages only) 1568–1812. Buckinghamshire Parish Registers, vol. 1, 1902.

[11] **P** 1658–1812. Durham and Northumberland Parish Register Society, vol. 8, 1903.

[12] **P** (Marriages only) 1538–1812. Nottinghamshire Parish Registers, vol. 7, 1905.

[13] **P** 1634–1758. Edited by G. W. Marshall, 1891.

[14] **P** 1662–1812. Durham and Northumberland Parish Register Society, vol. 2, 1899.

[15] **P** (Marriages only) 1600–1812. Cornwall Parish Registers, vol. 6, 1904.

[16] **P** (Marriages only) 1574–1812. Cornwall Parish Registers, vol. 2, 1902.

Parish.	County.	Date of Earliest Entry.	Parish.	County.	Date of Earliest Entry.
Elden - - -	Hants - -	1651	Elmstead - -	Essex - -	1557
Eldersfield - -	Worcester -	[1] 1718	Elmsted - - -	Kent - -	[9] 1538
Elford - - -	Stafford -	1552	Elmstone - -	Kent - -	1552
Elham - - -	Kent - -	1566	Elmstone-Hardwick -	Gloucester -	1564
Eling - - -	Hants - -	[2] 1537	Elmswell - -	Suffolk - -	1659
Elkesley - -	Nottingham -	1628	Elmton - - -	Derby - -	1599
Elkington, North -	Lincoln - -	1757	Elsdon - -	Northumberland	[10] 1672
Elkington, South -	Lincoln -	1701	Elsenham - -	Essex - -	1730
Elkstone - -	Gloucester -	[3] 1592	Elsfield - -	Oxford - -	1686
Elkstone -	Stafford -	1791	Elsham - - -	Lincoln - -	1566
Ella, Kirk - -	York - -	1558	Elsing - - -	Norfolk - -	1558
Elland - -	York - -	[4] 1559	Elstead - -	Surrey - -	1540
Ellastone - -	Stafford -	1540	Elstead - -	Sussex - -	1571
Ellenbrook - -	Lancaster -	1765	Elston - - -	Nottingham -	[11] 1572
Ellenhall - -	Stafford -	1539	Elston Chapel -	Nottingham -	[12] 1584
Ellerburne - -	York - -	1691	Elstow - -	Bedford - -	1641
Ellerton-Priory -	York - -	1680	Elstree - -	Hertford -	1656
Ellesborough - -	Buckingham -	1603	Elsworth - -	Cambridge -	1538
Ellesmere - -	Salop - -	1653	Eltham - -	Kent - -	1583
Ellingham - -	Hants - -	1596	Eltisley - -	Cambridge -	1653
Ellingham - -	Norfolk - -	1538	Elton - - -	Derby - -	1691
Ellingham - -	Northumberland	1695	Elton - - -	Durham - -	1573
Ellingham, Great -	Norfolk - -	1630	Elton - - -	Hereford -	1657
Ellingham, Little -	Norfolk - -	1649	Elton - - -	Huntingdon -	1560
Ellington - -	Huntingdon -	1608	Elton-on-the-Hill -	Nottingham -	[13] 1592
Ellisfield - -	Hants - -	1540	Elvaston - -	Derby - -	1652
Ellough - - -	Suffolk - -	[5] 1540	Elveden or Elden -	Suffolk - -	1651
Elloughton - -	York - -	1657	Elvetham - -	Hants - -	[14] 1638
Elm - - -	Cambridge -	1539	Elvington - -	York - -	1600
Elm - - -	Somerset -	1697	Elvis, St. - -	Pembroke -	1797
Elmbridge - -	Worcester -	[6] 1570	Elwick-Hall -	Durham - -	1592
Elmdon - -	Essex - -	1618	Elworthy - -	Somerset -	1685
Elmdon - - -	Warwick -	1538	Ely, St. Mary -	Cambridge -	1670
Elmham, North - -	Norfolk -	[7] 1538	Holy Trinity	- -	1559
Elmham, South, All Saints.	Suffolk -	1708	Cathedral Church	- -	1691
			Emberton - -	Buckingham -	1659
Elmham, South, St. Margaret.	Suffolk - -	1679	Embleton - -	Cumberland -	1625
			Embleton -	Northumberland	1682
Elmham, South, St. Peter.	Suffolk -	1695	Emborrow - -	Somerset -	1569
			Emley or Elmley -	York - -	1600
Elmham, South, St. Michael.	Suffolk -	1559	Emmington - -	Oxford - -	1539
			Emneth - -	Norfolk - -	1681
Elmham, South, St. James.	Suffolk -	1705	Empingham - -	Rutland -	1559
Elmley-Castle -	Worcester -	[8] 1665	Empshott - -	Hants - -	1718
Elmley-Lovett -	Worcester -	1539	Emsworth. See Warblington.		
Elmore - -	Gloucester -	1560	Enborne - -	Berks - -	1666
Elmsett - -	Suffolk - -	1684	Endellion, St. - -	Cornwall -	[15] 1684

[1] Bishop's Transcripts commence 1611.
[2] **P** (Marriages only) 1539–1812. Hampshire Parish Registers, vol. 7, 1905.
[3] **P** (Marriages only) 1592–1812. Gloucestershire Parish Registers, vol. 6, 1900.
[4] **P** 1559–1640. Edited by J. W. Clay, Leeds, 1897.
[5] **P** 1540–1812. Edited by F. A. Crisp, London, 1886.
[6] **P** (Marriages only) 1570–1812. Worcestershire Parish Registers, vol. 1, 1901.
[7] **P** 1536–1631. Edited by Rev. A. G. Legge, Norwich, 1888.
[8] Bishop's Transcripts commence 1612.
[9] **P** 1552–1812. Edited by Rev. C. H. Wilkie, 1891.
[10] **P** 1672–1701. Society of Antiquaries, Newcastle-on-Tyne, 1903.
[11] **P** (Marriages only) 1573–1812. Nottinghamshire Parish Registers, vol. 3, 1900.
[12] **P** (Marriages only) 1584–1814. Nottinghamshire Parish Registers, vol. 3, 1900.
[13] **P** (Marriages only) 1593–1812. Nottinghamshire Parish Registers, vol. 1, 1898.
[14] **P** (Marriages only) 1639–1812. Hampshire Parish Registers, vol. 3, 1902.
[15] **P** (Marriages only) 1684–1812. Cornwall Parish Registers, vol. 4, 1903.

Parish.	County.	Date of Earliest Entry.	Parish.	County.	Date of Earliest Entry.
Enderby - -	Leicester - -	1559	Etwall - -	Derby - -	1558
Enderby, Bag -	Lincoln -	1561	Euston - - -	Suffolk -	1708
Enderby-Mavis -	Lincoln -	1579	Euxton - -	Lancaster -	1774
Enderby Wood -	Lincoln -	1561	Eval, St. - -	Cornwall -	1695
Endon - -	Stafford -	1730	Evedon - -	Lincoln -	1560
Enfield - - -	Middlesex -	1550	Evenechtyd -	Denbigh - -	1693
Enford - -	Wilts - -	1631	Evenley - -	Northampton -	1694
Englefield - -	Berks - -	1559	Evenlode - - -	Worcester -	1561
Englishcombe -	Somerset-	1728	Evercreech -	Somerset - -	1541
Enham, Knight's -	Hants - -	¹ 1683	Everdon - - -	Northampton -	1558
Enmore - -	Somerset -	² 1653	Everingham - -	York - -	1653
Ennerdale - -	Cumberland -	1643	Everley - - -	Wilts - -	1598
Enoder, St. - -	Cornwall -	1571	Eversden, Great -	Cambridge -	1541
Ensham - -	Oxford -	1653	Eversden, Little -	Cambridge -	1703
Enstone - - -	Oxford -	³ 1558	Eversholt - -	Bedford - -	1628
Enville - - -	Stafford -	1627	Evershot - -	Dorset - -	1694
Epperstone - -	Nottingham -	1582	Eversley - -	Hants - -	⁸ 1559
Epping - - -	Essex - -	1539	Everton - - -	Huntingdon -	⁹ —
Epsom - - -	Surrey -	1695	Everton - -	Nottingham -	1567
Epwell - - -	Oxford -	1577	Evesbatch - - -	Hereford -	1700
Epworth - -	Lincoln -	⁴ 1540	Evesham, All Saints -	Worcester -	1538
Erbistock - -	Flint - -	1679	St. Lawrence - -	-	1556
Ercall, Child's -	Salop -	1570	Evington - - -	Leicester -	1601
Ercall, High - -	Salop -	1585	Ewe, St. - - -	Cornwall -	¹⁰ 1559
Eriswell - -	Suffolk -	1669	Ewell (or Temple-	Kent - -	1581
Erith - - -	Kent - -	⁵ —	Ewell).		
Erlestoke. See Stoke,			Ewell - - -	Surrey -	1603
Erle.			Ewelme - - -	Oxford -	1599
Erme, St. - -	Cornwall -	1671	Ewenny - - -	Glamorgan -	1717
Ermington - -	Devon -	1603	Ewerby - - -	Lincoln -	1694
Erpingham - -	Norfolk -	1559	Ewhurst - -	Hants - -	¹¹ 1682
Erth, St. - -	Cornwall -	1563	Ewhurst - -	Surrey -	1614
Ervan, St. - -	Cornwall -	1674	Ewhurst - -	Sussex -	1558
Erwarton - -	Suffolk -	1558	Ewyas-Harold - -	Hereford -	1734
Eryholme - -	York -	1568	Exbourne - -	Devon -	1540
Escomb - -	Durham -	1545	Exeter, Allhallows,	Devon -	1561
Escrick - -	York -	1617	Goldsmith Street.		
Esh - - -	Durham -	⁶ 1567	Allhallows - on-	··	1694
Esher - - -	Surrey -	1678	the-Walls.		
Eskdale - - -	Cumberland -	1626	St. Edmund - -	-	1571
Eskdaleside - -	York -	1676	St. George - -	-	1681
Essendine - -	Rutland -	1600	St. John - -	-	1682
Essendon - -	Hertford -	1653	St. Kerrian - -	-	1558
Eston - - -	York -	1590	St. Petrock - -	-	1538
Etchilhampton -	Wilts - -	1630	St. Lawrence - -	-	1604
Etchingham - -	Sussex -	1564	St. Martin - -	-	1572
Eton - - -	Buckingham -	1594	St. Pancras - -	-	1664
Ettington - -	Warwick -	⁷ 1661	St. Mary-Arches -	-	1538
Etton - - -	Northampton -	1587	St. Mary-Major's -	-	1561
Etton - - -	York -	1557	St. Mary Steps -	-	1654

¹ **P** (Marriages only) 1683-1812. Hampshire Parish Registers, vol. 1, 1899.
² **P** (Marriages only) 1653-1812. Somersetshire Parish Registers, vol. 6, 1905.
³ "History of Enstone," by Rev. John Jordan, 1857, contains a list of surnames in Parish Register.
⁴ **P** 1563, &c. Epworth Parish Magazine, 1897, et seq.
⁵ Destroyed by fire in 1877. Extracts from Registers of Erith, edited by R. Hovenden, London, 1879.
⁶ **P** 1567-1812. Society of Antiquaries, Newcastle-on-Tyne, 1896.
⁷ **P** (Marriages only) 1623-1812. Warwickshire Parish Registers, vol. 1, 1904. Bishop's Transcripts commence 1621.
⁸ **P** (Marriages only) 1559-1812. Hampshire Parish Registers, vol. 3, 1902.
⁹ Included in the Registers of Tetworth (q.v.).
¹⁰ **P** (Marriages only) 1560-1812. Cornwall Parish Registers, vol. 10, 1906.
¹¹ **P** (Marriages only) 1682-1823. Hampshire Parish Registers, vol. 8, 1906.

Parish.	County.	Date of Earliest Entry.	Parish.	County.	Date of Earliest Entry.
Exeter—*cont.*			Fangfoss - -	York - -	1715
St. Olave - -	- - - -	1601	Farcett - - -	Huntingdon -	1650
St. Paul - -	- - -	1562	Fareham - -	Hants - -	1559
St. Stephen - -	- - -	1668	Farewell - -	Stafford -	1693
Holy Trinity -	- - -	1605	Farforth - -	Lincoln - -	1784
St. David - -	- - -	1559	Faringdon - -	Hants - -	1558
St. Sidwell - -	- - -	1569	Faringdon - -	Berks - -	1582
St. Leonard -	- - -	1768	Farington Gurney -	Somerset -	1680
St. Thomas - -	- - -	1554	Farlam - -	Cumberland -	1700
The Cathedral -	- - -	[1]1594	Farleigh, East - -	Kent - -	1580
Exford - - -	Somerset -	1609	Farleigh-Hungerford -	Somerset -	1673
Exhall (near Coventry)	Warwick -	1540	Farleigh, West -	Kent - -	1558
Exhall (near Alcester)	Warwick -	1539	Farley - - -	Surrey - -	1678
Exminster - -	Devon - -	1562	Farley. *See* Monkton		
Exning - - -	Suffolk - -	1558	Farley.		
Exton - - -	Hants - -	1579	Farley-Chamberlayne	Hants -	1593
Exton - - -	Rutland - -	1597	Farlington - -	Hants - -	1538
Exton - - -	Somerset -	1559	Farlington - -	York - -	1614
Eyam - - -	Derby - -	1630	Farlow - -	Salop - -	[4]—
Eydon - - -	Northampton -	1538	Farlsthorpe - -	Lincoln - -	1655
Eye - - -	Hereford - -	1573	Farmborough -	Somerset -	1559
Eye - - -	Northampton -	1543	Farmington - -	Gloucester -	1613
Eye - - -	Suffolk - -	1538	Farnborough -	Berks - -	1739
Eyke - - -	Suffolk - -	1538	Farnborough - -	Hants - -	[1]1584
Eynesbury - -	Huntingdon -	1539	Farnborough -	Warwick -	1558
Eynesford - -	Kent - -	1538	Farnborough - -	Kent - -	1558
Eythorne - -	Kent - -	1558	Farndish - -	Bedford -	1587
Eyton - - -	Hereford - -	1682	Farndon - -	Chester - -	1603
Eyton-on-the-Moors -	Salop - -	1698	Farndon - -	Nottingham -	[6]1559
Eyworth - - -	Bedford - -	1538	Farndon East -	Northampton -	1562
			Farnham - -	Dorset - -	1647
			Farnham - -	Essex - -	1558
			Farnham - -	Suffolk - -	1707
F.			Farnham - -	Surrey - -	1539
			Farnham - -	York - -	[7]1569
			Farnham-Royal -	Buckingham -	1635
Faccombe - -	Hants - -	[2]1585	Farnhurst - -	Sussex - -	1547
Faceby - - -	York - -	1707	Farningham - -	Kent - -	1589
Fagan, St. - -	Glamorgan -	1689	Farnley - -	York - -	1772
Fairfield - -	Derby - -	1738	Farnsfield - -	Nottingham -	1572
Fairfield - -	Kent - -	1558	Farnworth - -	Lancaster -	1538
Fairford - -	Gloucester -	[3]1617	Farringdon - -	Devon - -	1678
Fairlight - -	Sussex - -	1651	Farthinghoe -	Northampton -	1560
Fairstead - -	Essex - -	1537	Farthingstone -	Northampton -	1538
Fakenham - -	Norfolk - -	1719	Farway - -	Devon - -	1567
Fakenham Magna -	Suffolk - -	1559	Faulkbourne -	Essex - -	1574
Faldingworth - -	Lincoln - -	1560	Faversham - -	Kent - -	1620
Falkenham - -	Suffolk - -	1538	Fawkham - -	Kent - -	1568
Falmer - - -	Sussex - -	1642	Fawley - -	Berks - -	1540
Falmouth - -	Cornwall -	1663	Fawley - - -	Buckingham -	1573
Falstone - -	Northumberland	1742	Fawley - -	Hants - -	1673
Fambridge, North -	Essex - -	1556	Fawsley - -	Northampton -	1585
Fambridge, South -	Essex - -	1754	Faxton - -	Northampton -	[8]1653

[1] **P** 1594–1813. Devon and Cornwall Record Society, 1905-7.
[2] **P** (Marriages only) 1586–1812. Hampshire Parish Registers, vol. 2, 1900.
[3] The first Register book contains a few back entries, dated 1607-8-9-11, apparently the baptisms of the vicar's children.
[4] Included in the Registers of Stottesdon (*q.v.*).
[5] **P** (Marriages only) 1584–1812. Hampshire Parish Registers, vol. 3, 1902.
[6] **P** (Marriages only) 1559–1812. Nottinghamshire Parish Registers, vol. 3, 1900. Also **P** 1695-1718. Edited by T. M. Blagg, 1899 (from a book kept at Balderton).
[7] **P** 1569–1812. Parish Register Society, vol. 56, 1905.
[8] Transcripts commencing in 1563 in the Archdeacon's Registry at Leicester.

Parish.	County.	Date of Earliest Entry.	Parish.	County.	Date of Earliest Entry.
Featherstone - -	York - -	1558	Fillongley - -	Warwick -	[6]1538
Feckenham -	Worcester -	1538	Filton - - -	Gloucester -	[7]1654
Feering - - -	Essex - -	1563	Finborough, Great -	Suffolk -	1558
Felbrigge - - -	Norfolk -	1700	Finborough, Little -	Suffolk -	1558
Felixkirk - -	York - -	1598	Fincham - -	Norfolk -	1541
Felixstowe - -	Suffolk -	1653	Finchampstead -	Berks -	1653
Felkirk - -	York - -	[1]1701	Finchingfield - -	Essex - -	1617
Felmersham - -	Bedford -	1660	Finchley - -	Middlesex -	1560
Felmingham - -	Norfolk -	1754	Findern - -	Derby -	1558
Felpham - -	Sussex -	1557	Findon - - -	Sussex -	1566
Felsham - -	Suffolk -	1656	Finedon - -	Northampton -	1539
Felstead - -	Essex - -	1558	Fingest - -	Buckingham -	1607
Feltham - -	Middlesex -	1634	Finghall - -	York -	1593
Felthorpe - -	Norfolk -	1712	Fingringhoe - -	Essex - -	1653
Felton - -	Hereford -	1637	Finmere - -	Oxford -	1566
Felton - - -	Northumberland	1653	Finningham - -	Suffolk -	1560
Felton, West -	Salop -	1628	Finningley - -	Nottingham -	1557
Feltwell - -	Norfolk -	1562	Finsthwaite - -	Lancaster -	1725
Fenby - - -	Lincoln -	[2]—	Firbank - -	Westmorland -	[8]1746
Fen Drayton. See Drayton Fen.			Firbeck - -	York -	1721
			Firle, West -	Sussex -	1668
Feniton - -	Devon -	1549	Firsby - -	Lincoln -	1717
Fenny Drayton. See Drayton Fenny.			Firsby, East -	Lincoln -	1717
			Fishbourne, New -	Sussex -	1589
Fen-Stanton - -	Huntingdon -	1612	Fisherton-Anger -	Wilts -	1653
Fenton - - -	Lincoln -	1539	Fisherton-Delamere -	Wilts -	1561
Fenton-Kirk -	York -	1630	Fishguard - -	Pembroke -	1785
Feock, St. - -	Cornwall -	1671	Fishlake - -	York -	1561
Ferriby, North -	York -	[3]1730	Fishtoft - -	Lincoln -	1696
Ferriby, South -	Lincoln -	1538	Fiskerton - -	Lincoln -	1539
Ferring - -	Sussex -	1558	Fittleton - -	Wilts -	1623
Ferryside - -	Carmarthen -	[4]—	Fittleworth - -	Sussex -	1559
Fersfield - -	Norfolk -	1565	Fitz - - -	Salop -	[9]1559
Festiniog - -	Merioneth -	1695	Fitzhead - -	Somerset -	1558
Fetcham - -	Surrey -	1559	Fivehead - -	Somerset -	[10]1654
Fewston - -	York -	[5]1593	Fladbury - -	Worcester -	1560
Fiddington - -	Somerset -	1706	Flamborough - -	York -	1564
Field-Dalling -	Norfolk -	1538	Flamstead - -	Hertford -	1548
Fifehead-Magdalene -	Dorset -	1564	Flaunden - -	Hertford -	1729
Fifehead-Neville -	Dorset -	1573	Flawborough - -	Notts -	[11]1680
Fifield - - -	Oxford -	1712	Flaxley - -	Gloucester -	1648
Fifield Bavant -	Wilts -	1695	Fleckney - -	Leicester -	1637
Figheldean - -	Wilts -	1653	Fledborough - -	Nottingham -	1562
Filby - - -	Norfolk -	1599	Fleet - - -	Dorset -	1663
Filey - - -	York -	1573	Fleet - -	Lincoln -	[12]1652
Filgrave. See Tyringham.			Flemingston - -	Glamorgan -	1576
			Flempton - -	Suffolk -	1561
Filleigh - -	Devon -	1726	Fletching - -	Sussex -	1554
Fillingham - -	Lincoln -	1661	Fletton - -	Huntingdon -	1616

[1] **P** 1701–1812. Edited by A. N. J. Royds, 1894.
[2] Included in the Registers of Ashby (q.v.).
[3] There is an old Church Book containing entries from 1658, but the Registers proper, prior to 1730, are missing.
[4] Included in the Registers of St. Ishmael (q.v.).
[5] **P** 1593–1812. Edited by T. Parkinson, Skipton, 1899.
[6] **P** 1538–1653. Walsall, 1893.
[7] **P** (Marriages only) 1655–1812. Gloucestershire Parish Registers, vol. 13, 1908.
[8] Earlier included in the Registers of Kirkby Lonsdale (q.v.).
[9] **P** 1559–1812. Shropshire Parish Register Society, vol. 4, 1903 (Lichfield Diocese).
[10] **P** (Marriages only) 1656–1812. Somersetshire Parish Registers, vol. 5, 1904.
[11] **P** (Marriages only) 1680–1812. Nottinghamshire Parish Registers, vol. 4, 1902.
[12] **P** (Marriages only) 1561–1640 from Transcripts ; 1656–1812 from Registers. Lincolnshire Parish Registers, vol. 2, 1907.

Parish.	County.	Date of Earliest Entry.	Parish.	County.	Date of Earliest Entry.
Flimby - - -	Cumberland -	1696	Forest-Hill - -	Oxford -	1564
Flimstone. *See* Flemingstone.			Formby - - -	Lancaster -	1711
			Forncett - -	Norfolk -	1561
Flint - - -	Flint - -	1598	Fornham, All Saints -	Suffolk -	1558
Flintham - -	Nottingham -	¹ 1576	Fornham, St. Martin -	Suffolk -	1539
Flitcham - -	Norfolk -	1754	Forrabury - -	Cornwall -	³ 1710
Flitton - - -	Bedford -	1581	Forscote - -	Somerset -	1691
Flitwick - - -	Bedford -	1661	Forthampton - -	Gloucester -	⁹ 1678
Flixborough - -	Lincoln -	1660	Forton - - -	Stafford -	1558
Flixton - -	Lancaster -	1570	Fosdyke - - -	Lincoln -	1558
Flixton - -	Suffolk -	1544	Foston - -	Leicester -	1653
Flockton - -	York -	1716	Foston - -	Lincoln -	1560
Flookburgh -	Lancaster -	² —	Foston - -	York -	1587
Flordon - -	Norfolk -	1558	Foston-on-the-Wolds	York -	1653
Flore - -	Northampton -	1652	Fotherby - -	Lincoln -	1568
Florence, St. -	Pembroke -	1755	Fotheringhay - -	Northampton -	1557
Flowton - -	Suffolk -	1572	Foulden - -	Norfolk -	1538
Flyford-Flavel -	Worcester -	³ 1679	Foulmire - -	Cambridge -	1561
Flyford-Grafton -	Worcester -	⁴ 1676	Foulness - -	Essex -	1695
Fobbing -	Essex -	1539	Foulsham - -	Norfolk -	¹⁰ 1746
Foleshill - -	Warwick -	1564	Fovant - -	Wilts -	1541
Folke - -	Dorset -	1538	Fowey - -	Cornwall -	¹¹ 1543
Folkestone -	Kent -	1635	Fownhope - -	Hereford -	¹² 1538
Folkesworth -	Huntingdon -	1563	Foxcote - -	Buckingham -	1664
Folkingham -	Lincoln -	1583	Foxearth - -	Essex -	1551
Folkington -	Sussex -	1560	Foxholes - -	York -	1654
Folkton - -	York -	1665	Foxley - -	Norfolk -	1700
Fonthill-Bishop -	Wilts -	1754	Foxley - -	Wilts -	1713
Fonthill-Gifford -	Wilts -	1664	Foxton - -	Cambridge -	1678
Fontmell-Magna -	Dorset -	1653	Foxton - -	Leicester -	1690
Forcett - -	York -	1596	Foy - - -	Hereford -	1570
Ford. *See* Fordsbridge.			Fradswell - -	Stafford -	1578
			Framfield - -	Sussex -	1538
Ford - - -	Pembroke -	⁵ —	Framingham-Earl	Norfolk -	1721
Ford - -	Northumberland	1683	Framingham Pigot -	Norfolk -	1555
Ford - -	Salop -	⁶ 1589	Framlingham -	Suffolk -	1560
Ford - -	Sussex -	1627	Framlington, Long -	Northumberland	1653
Forden - -	Montgomery -	1598	Frampton - -	Dorset -	1654
Fordham - -	Cambridge -	1567	Frampton - -	Lincoln -	1538
Fordham - -	Essex -	1561	Frampton-Cotterell -	Gloucester -	1561
Fordham - -	Norfolk -	1576	Frampton-on-Severn -	Gloucester -	¹³ 1625
Fordingbridge -	Hants -	1642	Framsden - -	Suffolk -	1575
Fordington -	Lincoln -	⁷ —	Frankley - -	Worcester -	1598
Fordington -	Dorset -	1705	Frankton - -	Warwick -	1559
Fordley. *See* Middleton.			Fransham, Great -	Norfolk -	1560
			Fransham, Little -	Norfolk -	1538
Fordsbridge - -	Hereford -	1742	Frant - - -	Sussex -	1544
Fordwich - -	Kent -	1683	Frating - -	Essex -	1560
Foremark - -	Derby -	1662	Freckenham - -	Suffolk -	1550

¹ **P** (Marriages only) 1629–1812. Nottinghamshire Parish Registers, vol. 1, 1898.
² Included in the Registers of Cartmel (*q.v.*).
³ Bishop's Transcripts commence 1613.
⁴ Bishop's Transcripts commence 1612.
⁵ Included in the Registers of Hayscastle (*q.v.*).
⁶ **P** 1589–1812. Shropshire Parish Register Society, vol. 1 (Hereford Diocese). 1569–1812. Parish Register Society, vol. 29, 1900.
⁷ Included in the Registers of Ulceby (*q.v.*).
⁸ **P** (Marriages only) 1676–1812. Cornwall Parish Registers, vol. 1, 1900.
⁹ **P** (Marriages only) 1678–1812. Gloucestershire Parish Registers, vol. 1, 1896.
¹⁰ The first Register book of this parish, commencing in 1713, has been missing for some time.
¹¹ **P** (Marriages only) 1568–1812. Cornwall Parish Registers, vol. 8, 1905.
¹² **P** 1538–1673. Edited by F. A. Crisp, 1899.
¹³ **P** (Marriages only) 1625–1812. Gloucestershire Parish Registers, vol. 7, 1901.

Parish.	County.	Date of Earliest Entry.	Parish	County.	Date of Earliest Entry.
Freeby - - -	Leicester -	1604	Froyle - - -	Hants - -	1697
Freethorpe - -	Norfolk -	1755	Fryerning - - -	Essex - -	1595
Fremington - -	Devon -	1602	Fryston, Ferry -	York - -	⁶1674
Frensham - -	Surrey -	1649	Fryston-Monk - -	York - -	⁷1538
Frenze - - -	Norfolk -	1651	Fugglestone - -	Wilts - -	1568
Freshford - -	Somerset -	1705	Fulbeck - - -	Lincoln - -	1563
Freshwater (Isle of Wight).	Hants -	1576	Fulbourn - -	Cambridge -	1538
			Fulbrook - - -	Oxford - -	1615
Fressingfield - -	Suffolk -	1554	Fulford - - -	Stafford -	1800
Freston - - -	Suffolk -	¹1538	Fulford - - -	York - -	1653
Fretherne - -	Gloucester -	1631	Fulham - - -	Middlesex -	1674
Frettenham - -	Norfolk -	1558	Fulletby - - -	Lincoln - -	1750
Freystrop - -	Pembroke -	1729	Full-Sutton - -	York - -	1713
Frickley - - -	York -	1577	Fulmer - - -	Buckingham -	1688
Fridaythorpe - -	York -	1687	Fulmodeston - -	Norfolk - -	1555
Friermere - -	Lancaster -	1769	Fulstow - - -	Lincoln - -	1589
Friesthorpe - -	Lincoln -	1620	Fundenhall - -	Norfolk - -	1559
Frieston - - -	Lincoln -	1657	Funtington - -	Sussex - -	1564
Frilsham - -	Berks -	1711	Furtho - - -	Northampton -	1696
Frimley - - -	Surrey -	1590	Fyfield - - -	Berks - -	⁸—
Frindsbury - -	Kent -	1669	Fyfield - - -	Wilts - -	1732
Fringe - - -	Norfolk -	1671	Fyfield - - -	Essex - -	⁹1538
Fringford - -	Oxford -	1586	Fyfield - - -	Hants - -	1628
Frinsted - - -	Kent -	1714	Fylingdales - -	York - -	1653
Frinton - - -	Essex -	1754	Fylton. See Filton.		
Frisby-on-the-Wreak	Leicester -	1659			
Friskney - - -	Lincoln -	1558			
Friston - - -	Suffolk -	1543			
Friston - - -	Sussex -	1546			
Frithelstock - -	Devon -	1556			
Frittenden - -	Kent -	1558	**G.**		
Fritton - - -	Norfolk -	1558	Gaddesby - -	Leicester -	1698
Fritton - - -	Suffolk -	1706	Gaddesden, Great -	Hertford -	1559
Fritwell - - -	Oxford -	1558	Gaddesden, Little -	Hertford -	1681
Frocester - -	Gloucester -	³1559	Gainford - - -	Durham -	¹⁰1560
Frodesley - -	Salop -	³1547	Gainsborough - -	Lincoln - -	1564
Frodingham - -	Lincoln -	1638	Galby. See Gaulby.		
Frodingham, North -	York -	1559	Gamlingay - -	Cambridge -	1698
Frodsham - -	Chester -	1558	Gamston - - -	Nottingham -	1544
Frome-Selwood -	Somerset -	1558	Ganarew - - -	Hereford -	1635
Frome, Bishop's -	Hereford -	1564	Ganton - - -	York - -	1553
Frome, St. Quintin -	Dorset -	1653	Garboldisham - -	Norfolk - -	1609
Frome-Vauchurch -	Dorset -	1642	Garforth - - -	York - -	1663
Frome Whitfield -	Dorset -	⁴—	Gargrave - - -	York - -	¹¹1558
Frome, Canon -	Hereford -	1681	Garrigill - - -	Cumberland -	¹²1699
Frome Castle -	Hereford -	1678	Garsdale - - -	York - -	1608
Frostenden - -	Suffolk -	⁵1538	Garsdon - - -	Wilts - -	1737
Frowlesworth - -	Leicester -	1538	Garsington - -	Oxford - -	1562
Froxfield - -	Hants -	1545	Garstang - - -	Lancaster -	1567
Froxfield - - -	Wilts -	1561	Garston - - -	Lancaster -	1777

¹ Freston Parish Magazine, &c., 1887, contains an Index to the Register, 1538-1884. Edited by Rev. C. R. Durrant, rector.
² P (Marriages only) 1559-1800. Gloucestershire Notes and Queries, vol. 5.
³ P 1547-1812. Shropshire Parish Register Society, vol. 4, 1903 (Lichfield Diocese).
⁴ P 1538-1791. Edited by F. A. Crisp, 1887.
⁵ Included in the Registers of Holy Trinity, Dorchester (q.v.).
⁶ The earlier Registers, which dated to 1560, have been lost.
⁷ P 1538-1678. Parish Register Society, vol. 5, 1896.
⁸ The Registers were destroyed by fire in 1893.
⁹ P 1538-1700. Edited by F. A. Crisp, 1896.
¹⁰ Index to Registers, 1560-1784. London, 1889.
¹¹ P 1558-1812. Yorkshire Parish Register Society, vol. 28, 1907.
¹² P 1699-1730. Edited by Rev. C. Caine, 1901.

Parish.	County.	Date of Earliest Entry.	Parish.	County.	Date of Earliest Entry.
Garston, East -	Berks - -	1554	Giles, St., - on - the - Heath.	Devon - -	1653
Garth-Beibio - -	Montgomery	1718	Gileston - -	Glamorgan -	1701
Garthbrengy, St. David	Brecon - -	1732	Gilling - - -	York - -	1570
Gartheli - -	Cardigan -	[1] —	Gilling, East - -	York - -	1639
Garthorpe - -	Leicester - -	1568	Gillingham - -	Dorset - -	1559
Garton-in-Holderness	York - -	1593	Gillingham - -	Kent - -	1558
Garton-on-the-Wolds	York - -	1653	Gillingham - -	Norfolk - -	1541
Garveston - -	Norfolk -	1538	Gilmorton - -	Leicester -	1618
Garway - - -	Hereford -	1664	Gilston - - -	Hertford - -	1558
Gasthorpe - -	Norfolk -	[2] —	Gimingham - -	Norfolk -	1558
Gatcombe (Isle of Wight).	Hants - -	1560	Gipping - - -	Suffolk - -	[6] —
Gateforth - -	York - -	[3] —	Girton - - -	Cambridge -	1629
Gateley - - -	Norfolk -	1682	Girton - - -	Nottingham -	1680
Gateshead - -	Durham - -	1559	Gisburn - - -	York - -	1558
Gatton - - -	Surrey - -	1599	Gisleham - -	Suffolk - -	1559
Gaulby - - -	Leicester - -	1583	Gislingham - -	Suffolk - -	1558
Gautby - - -	Lincoln - -	1571	Gissing - - -	Norfolk - -	[7] —
Gawcott - -	Buckingham -	1806	Gittisham - -	Devon - -	1559
Gawsworth - -	Chester - -	1557	Givendale, Great -	York - -	1658
Gaydon - -	Warwick - -	1701	Gladestry - -	Radnor - -	1683
Gayhurst - -	Buckingham -	1728	Glaisdale - -	York - -	1758
Gayton - -	Norfolk - -	1702	Glandford - -	Norfolk -	1654
Gayton - - -	Northampton -	1558	Glandford Bridge -	Lincoln - -	[8] —
Gayton - - -	Stafford - -	1594	Glapthorne - -	Northampton -	1614
Gayton-le-Marsh -	Lincoln - -	1687	Glasbury - -	Brecon - -	[9] 1660
Gayton-le-Wold -	Lincoln - -	1773	Glascombe - -	Radnor - -	1720
Gayton-Thorpe -	Norfolk - -	1575	Glaston - -	Rutland - -	1555
Gaywood - - -	Norfolk -	1562	Glastonbury, St. John	Somerset -	1603
Gazeley - - -	Suffolk - -	1539	St. Benedict -	- -	1740
Gedding - - -	Suffolk - -	1543	Glatton - - -	Huntingdon -	1578
Geddington - -	Northampton -	1680	Glazeley - -	Worcester -	[10] —
Gedling - - -	Nottingham -	[4] 1558	Glemham, Great -	Suffolk - -	1569
Gedney - - -	Lincoln - -	1558	Glemham, Little -	Suffolk - -	1551
Gedney Hill - -	Lincoln - -	1693	Glemsford - -	Suffolk - -	1550
Geldeston - -	Norfolk - -	1657	Glen-Magna - -	Leicester -	1687
Gellygaer - -	Glamorgan -	1705	Glenfield - -	Leicester -	1604
Gennys, St. - -	Cornwall -	1702	Glentham - -	Lincoln - -	1690
George, St. (super Ely).	Glamorgan -	1693	Glentworth - -	Lincoln - -	1586
Georgeham - -	Devon - -	1538	Glinton - - -	Northampton -	1567
Germans, St. - -	Cornwall -	1590	Glooston - -	Leicester - -	1685
Germansweek - -	Devon - -	1652	Glossop - - -	Derby - -	1620
Germoe, St. - -	Cornwall -	[5] 1668	Gloucester, St. Aldate	Gloucester -	1572
Gerrans, St. - -	Cornwall -	1538	St. Catherine -	- -	1687
Gestingthorpe -	Essex - -	1609	St. John - -	- -	1558
Gidding, Great - -	Huntingdon -	1564	St. Mary-de-Crypt -	- -	1653
Gidding, Little -	Huntingdon -	1657	St. Mary-de-Lode -	- -	1675
Gidding, Steeple -	Huntingdon -	1571	Holy Trinity -	- -	1557
Gidleigh - -	Devon - -	1599	St. Michael - -	- -	1553
Giggleswick - -	York - -	1558	St. Nicholas -	- -	1558
Gilcrux - -	Cumberland -	1589	Cathedral Church -	- -	1661
Giles, St., - in - the - Wood.	Devon - -	1556	Gluvias, St. -	Cornwall -	1645
			Glympton - -	Oxford - -	1667

[1] Included in the Registers of Llanddewibrefi (*q.v.*).
[2] Included in the Registers of Riddlesworth (*q.v.*).   [3] Included in the Registers of Brayton (*q.v.*).
[4] **P** (Marriages only) 1558–1812. Nottinghamshire Parish Registers, vol. 10, 1907.
[5] **P** (Marriages only) 1674–1812. Cornwall Parish Registers, vol. 5, 1903.
[6] Included in the Registers of Stowmarket.
[7] The Registers have been destroyed by fire, with the exception of some fragments dating from the 16th century.
[8] Included in the Registers of Wrawby (*q.v.*).
[9] **P** 1660–1836. Parish Register Society, vol. 51, 1904.
[10] Included in the Registers of Chetton and Deuxhill (*q.v.*).

Parish.	County.	Date of Earliest Entry.	Parish	County.	Date of Earliest Entry.
Glyntaw - - -	Brecon - -	1776	Gosforth - -	Northumberland	1699
Glyn-Collwyn -	Brecon - -	[1] —	Gosport - -	Hants - -	1696
Glyncorrwg - -	Glamorgan -	1702	Gotham - - -	Nottingham -	[5] 1560
Glynde - - -	Sussex - -	1558	Goudhurst - -	Kent - -	1558
Gnosall - - -	Stafford - -	1572	Goulceby - -	Lincoln - -	1686
Goadby - -	Leicester - -	1745	Goxhill - - -	Lincoln - -	1590
Goadby - -	Leicester -	1656	Goxhill - - -	York - -	1561
Goathland - -	York - -	1669	Goytrey - - -	Monmouth -	1695
Goathill - -	Somerset -	1699	Grade - - -	Cornwall - -	1707
Goathurst - -	Somerset -	1559	Graffham - - -	Sussex - -	1665
Godalming - -	Surrey - -	[2] 1582	Graffham - -	Huntingdon -	1581
Godington - -	Oxford - -	1672	Grafton - - -	York - -	[9]
Godmanchester -	Huntingdon -	1604	Grafton-Regis -	Northampton -	1584
Godmanstone -	Dorset - -	1654	Grafton-Temple -	Warwick - -	[10] 1695
Godmersham -	Kent - -	1600	Grafton-Underwood -	Northampton -	1678
Godney - - -	Somerset -	1741	Grain, Isle of -	Kent - -	1653
Godshill (Isle of Wight)	Hants - -	1678	Grainsby - -	Lincoln - -	1561
Godstone - -	Surrey - -	1662	Grainthorpe - -	Lincoln - -	1653
Godwick - -	Norfolk - -	[3] —	Granborough - -	Buckingham -	1538
Goldcliff - -	Monmouth -	1728	Granby - - -	Nottingham -	[11] 1567
Goldhanger - -	Essex - -	1558	Grandborough - -	Warwick -	1581
Goldington - -	Bedford - -	1559	Gransden, Great -	Huntingdon -	1538
Goldsborough -	York - -	1707	Gransden, Little -	Cambridge -	1730
Goltho - - -	Lincoln - -	1672	Granston - -	Pembroke -	1778
Gonalston - -	Nottingham -	1538	Grantchester - -	Cambridge -	1539
Gonerby, Great -	Lincoln - -	1560	Grantham - -	Lincoln - -	1563
Gooderstone - -	Norfolk - -	1702	Grappenhall - -	Chester - -	1574
Goodleigh - -	Devon - -	1538	Grasby - - -	Lincoln - -	1653
Goodmanham -	York - -	1678	Grasmere - - -	Westmorland -	1571
Goodnestone - -	Kent - -	1569	Grately - - -	Hants - -	1624
Goodnestone next	Kent - -	1569	Gratwich - -	Stafford - -	1698
Wingham.			Graveley - - -	Cambridge -	1642
Goodrich - -	Hereford - -	1558	Graveley - -	Hertford - -	1551
Goodshaw - -	Lancaster -	1732	Graveney - -	Kent - -	[12] 1653
Goole - - -	York - -	[4] —	Gravenhurst, Lower -	Bedford - -	1705
Goosey - - -	Berks - -	[5] —	Gravenhurst, Upper -	Bedford - -	1567
Goosnargh - -	Lancaster -	1635	Gravesend - -	Kent - -	1547
Goostrey - -	Chester - -	1561	Grayingham - -	Lincoln - -	1576
Goran, St. - -	Cornwall - -	[6] 1661	Grayrigg - - -	Westmorland -	1724
Goring - - -	Oxford - -	1670	Grays. See Thurrock		
Goring - - -	Sussex - -	1560	Grays.		
Gorleston - -	Suffolk - -	1674	Greasbrough - -	York - -	1747
Gornal, Lower -	Stafford - -	[7] —	Greasley - - -	Nottingham -	[13] 1600
Gorton - - -	Lancaster -	1570	Greatham - -	Durham - -	1566
Gosbeck - -	Suffolk - -	1561	Greatham - - -	Hants - -	1571
Gosberton - -	Lincoln - -	1659	Greatham - -	Sussex - -	[14] —
Gosfield - - -	Essex - -	1538	Greatworth - -	Northampton -	1757
Gosforth - -	Cumberland -	1571	Greenford, Great -	Middlesex -	1539

[1] Included in the Registers of Llanfeigan (q.v.).
[2] **P** 1582–1688. Surrey Parish Register Society, vol. 2, 1905.
[3] Included in the Registers of Tittleshall (q.v.).
[4] Included in the Registers of Snaith (q.v.).   [5] Included in the Registers of Stanford (q.v.).
[6] **P** (Marriages only) 1668–1812. Cornwall Parish Registers, vol. 11, 1907.
[7] Included in the Registers of Sedgley (q.v.).
[8] **P** (Marriages only) 1560–1812. Nottinghamshire Parish Registers, vol. 5, 1903.
[9] Included in the Registers of Marton (q.v.).
[10] **P** (Marriages only) 1612–1812. Warwickshire Parish Registers, vol. 1, 1904. Bishop's Transcripts commence 1612.
[11] **P** (Marriages only) 1567–1812. Nottinghamshire Parish Registers, vol. 1, 1898.
[12] The Vicar of Graveney in 1769 certified that " the *old* Register was lost, through the fault, it is said, of a woman."
[13] **P** (Marriages only) 1600–1812. Nottinghamshire Parish Registers, vol. 8, 1905.
[14] Included in the Registers of Wiggonholt (q.v.).

Parish.	County.	Date of Earliest Entry.	Parish.	County.	Date of Earliest Entry.
Greenham - -	Berks - -	1607	Groton - - -	Suffolk -	1562
Green's Norton -	Northampton -	1565	Grove - - -	Berks - -	[10] —
Greenstead -	Essex - -	1676	Grove - - -	Buckingham -	[11] 1689
Greensted - - -	Essex - -	[1] 1561	Grove - - -	Nottingham -	1726
Greenwich - -	Kent - -	1615	Grundisburgh -	Suffolk -	1540
Greet - - -	Salop - -	[2] 1728	Guestling - -	Sussex -	1686
Greetham - -	Lincoln -	1653	Guestwick - - -	Norfolk -	1558
Greetham - -	Rutland - -	1576	Guildford, Holy	Surrey - -	1558
Greetwell - -	Lincoln -	1723	Trinity.		
Greinton - -	Somerset -	1728	St. Mary - -	- - -	1540
Grendon - -	Northampton -	1559	St. Nicholas -	- - -	1561
Grendon - -	Warwick -	1570	Guilsborough -	Northampton -	1560
Grendon-Bishop -	Hereford - -	1662	Guilsfield - -	Montgomery -	1573
Grendon-Underwood -	Buckingham -	1653	Guisborough -	York - -	1661
Gresford - - -	Denbigh - -	1660	Guiseley - -	York - -	1586
Gresham - -	Norfolk -	1560	Guist - - -	Norfolk -	1557
Gresley, Church -	Derby - -	1584	Guiting, Lower -	Gloucester -	[12] 1560
Gressenhall - -	Norfolk -	[3] 1538	Guiting, Temple -	Gloucester -	[13] 1647
Gressingham - -	Lancaster -	1710	Guldeford, East -	Sussex -	1705
Gretford - -	Lincoln -	1754	Gulval - - -	Cornwall -	[14] 1598
Gretton - - -	Gloucester -	[4] —	Gumfreston -	Pembroke -	1653
Gretton - -	Northampton -	1556	Gumley - - -	Leicester -	1694
Greystoke - -	Cumberland -	1559	Gunby, St. Nicholas -	Lincoln -	1715
Greywell - - -	Hants - -	1604	Gunby, St. Peter -	Lincoln -	1724
Grimley - -	Worcester -	1573	Gunthorpe - -	Norfolk -	1558
Grimoldby - -	Lincoln -	1563	Gunton - - -	Norfolk -	1723
Grimsby, Great -	Lincoln -	[5] 1538	Gunton - - -	Suffolk -	1759
Grimsby, Little -	Lincoln - -	1593	Gunwalloe - -	Cornwall -	1716
Grimstead, East -	Wilts - -	[6] —	Gussage, All Saints -	Dorset -	1560
Grimstead, West -	Wilts - -	1717	Gussage, St. Michael -	Dorset -	1653
Grimston - -	Norfolk -	1552	Guston - - -	Kent - -	1664
Grimston, North -	York - -	1686	Gwaenysgor -	Flint - -	1538
Grimstone - -	Leicester -	1635	Gwenddwr -	Brecon -	1724
Grindall - -	York - -	1592	Gwennap - -	Cornwall -	1658
Grindleton - -	York - -	1744	Gwernesney -	Monmouth -	1757
Grindon - - -	Durham - -	1565	Gwinear - -	Cornwall -	[15] 1560
Grindon - - -	Stafford -	1697	Gwithian - -	Cornwall -	[16] 1717
Gringley-on-the-Hill -	Nottingham -	1678	Gwnnws - -	Cardigan -	1754
Grinsdale - -	Cumberland -	1739	Gwyddelwern -	Merioneth -	1693
Grinshill - - -	Salop - -	[7] 1592	Gwytherin -	Denbigh -	1718
Grinstead, East -	Sussex -	1558	Gyffin - - -	Carnarvon -	1707
Grinstead, West -	Sussex -	1558	Gyfylliog - -	Denbigh -	1636
Grinton - - -	York - -	[8] 1640			
Griston - - -	Norfolk -	1652			
Grittleton - -	Wilts - -	[9] 1577			
Grosmont - -	Monmouth -	1589			

[1] **P** 1558–1812. Edited by F. A. Crisp, 1892.
[2] **P** 1728–1812. Shropshire Parish Register Society, vol. 5 (Hereford Diocese).
[3] In 1900 the old Registers of this parish were recovered after having been lost for 200 years.
[4] Included in the Registers of Winchcomb (q.v.).
[5] **P** 1538–1812. Edited by G. S. Stephenson, 1889.
[6] Included in the Registers of West Dean (q.v.).
[7] **P** 1592–1812. Shropshire Parish Register Society, vol. 2 (Lichfield Diocese), 1902.
[8] **P** 1640–1807. Yorkshire Parish Register Society, vol. 23, 1905.
[9] **P** (Marriages only) 1573–1812. Wiltshire Parish Registers, vol. 1, 1905.
[10] Included in the Registers of Wantage (q.v.).
[11] **P** (Marriages only) 1711–1812. Buckinghamshire Parish Registers, vol. 3, 1907.
[12] **P** (Marriages only) 1560–1812. Gloucestershire Parish Registers, vol. 4, 1898.
[13] **P** (Marriages only) 1676–1812. Gloucestershire Parish Registers, vol. 4, 1898.
[14] **P** 1598–1812. Edited by G. B. Miller, Penzance, 1893. **P** (Marriages only) 1686–1741. Cornwall Parish Registers, vol. 12, 1907.
[15] **P** (Marriages only) 1560–1812. Cornwall Parish Registers, vol. 12, 1907.
[16] **P** (Marriages only) 1560–1812. Cornwall Parish Registers, vol. 3, 1903.

Parish.	County.	Date of Earliest Entry.	Parish.	County.	Date of Earliest Entry.
			Halesowen	Worcester	1559
H.			Halesworth	Suffolk	1653
			Halford	Warwick	[6]1545
Habberley	Salop	[1]1670	Halifax	York	[7]1538
Habrough	Lincoln	1540	Halkin	Flint	1594
Haceby	Lincoln	1703	Hallam-Kirk	Derby	1700
Hacheston	Lincoln	1560	Hallam, West	Derby	[8]1545
Hackford (near Reepham).	Suffolk	1538	Hallaton	Leicester	1563
	Norfolk	1559	Hallen	Gloucester	[9] —
Hackford (near Wymondham).	Norfolk	1689	Halling	Kent	1705
Hackington			Hallingbury, Great	Essex	1538
Hackness	Kent	1567	Hallingbury, Little	Essex	1690
Hackney	York	[2]1567	Hallington	Lincoln	[10] —
Hackthorn	Middlesex	[3]1555	Halliwell	Lancaster	[11] —
Haconby	Lincoln	1653	Halloughton	Nottingham	1625
Haddenham	Buckingham	1653	Hallow	Worcester	1538
Haddenham	Cambridge	1574	Hallystone	Northumberland	[12] —
Haddiscoe	Norfolk	1558	Halsall	Lancaster	1606
Haddon	Huntingdon	1540	Halse	Somerset	[13]1558
Haddon, East	Northampton	1552	Halsham	York	1563
Haddon, West	Northampton	1653	Halstead	Essex	1564
Hadham, Much	Hertford	1559	Halstead	Kent	1561
Hadham, Little		1559	Halstock	Dorset	1698
Hadleigh	Essex	1568	Halston	Salop	[14]1686
Hadleigh	Suffolk	1557	Halstow, High	Kent	1662
Hadley Monken	Middlesex	1619	Halstow, Lower	Kent	1691
Hadlow	Kent	1558	Haltham-on-Bain	Lincoln	1561
Hadstock	Essex	1559	Halton	Northumberland	1654
Hadzor	Worcester	1554	Halton	Buckingham	1606
Hagbourne	Berks	1662	Halton	Chester	1732
Hagley	Worcester	1538	Halton	Lancaster	1592
Hagnaby	Lincoln	1684	Halton, East	Lincoln	1574
Hagworthingham	Lincoln	1562	Halton-Holgate	Lincoln	1567
Haile	Cumberland	1545	Halton, West	Lincoln	1538
Hailes	Gloucester	[4] —	Haltwhistle	Northumberland	1656
Hailey	Oxford	[5] —	Halvergate	Norfolk	1550
Hailsham	Sussex	1558	Halwell (Beaworthy)	Devon	1695
Hail-Weston	Huntingdon	1563	Halwell (Totnes)	Devon	1559
Hainton	Lincoln	1632	Ham	Kent	1552
Halam	Nottingham	1560	Ham	Wilts	1720
Halberton	Devon	1606	Ham, East	Essex	[15] —
Halden, High	Kent	1558	Ham, High	Somerset	[16]1569
Hale	Lancaster	1572	Ham, West	Essex	1653
Hale	Hants	1618	Hamble-le-Rice	Hants	1673
Hale-Magna	Lincoln	1538	Hambleden	Buckingham	1566
Hales	Norfolk	1674	Hambledon	Hants	1601
Hales, North. See Covehithe.			Hambledon	Surrey	1617
			Hambledon	Rutland	1558
			Hamerton	Huntingdon	1752

[1] P 1670-1822. Shropshire Parish Register Society, vol. 5 (Hereford Diocese).
[2] P 1557-1783. Yorkshire Parish Register Society, vol. 25, 1906.
[3] P (Baptisms only) 1555-1568. "Memorials of St. John Hackney," by R. Simpson, 1882.
[4] Included in the Registers of Didbroke (q.v.). [5] Included in the Registers of Witney (q.v.).
[6] P (Marriages only) 1552-1812. Warwickshire Parish Registers, vol. 3, 1906.
[7] P 1538-1541. Edited by W. J. Walker, 1885.
[8] See "The Oldest Register of West Hallam," by Rev. C. Kerry, Journal of the Derby Archæological Society, 1887.
[9] Included in the Registers of Henbury (q.v.). [11] Included in the Registers of Bolton (q.v.).
[10] Included in the Registers of Raithby (q.v.). [12] Included in the Registers of Alwinton.
[13] P (Marriages only) 1559-1812. Somersetshire Parish Registers, vol. 10, 1907.
[14] P 1686-1812. Shropshire Parish Register Society, vol. 2 (St. Asaph Diocese).
[15] Original Register lost, but an imperfect transcript has been preserved.
[16] P (Marriages only) 1569-1812. Somersetshire Parish Registers, vol. 1, 1898.

Parish	County	Date of Earliest Entry		Parish	County	Date of Earliest Entry
Hameringham	Lincoln	1744		Hanningfield, West	Essex	1558
Hammersmith	Middlesex	1751		Hannington	Hants	1771
Hammerton, Kirk	York	1714		Hannington	Northampton	1538
Hammerwich	Stafford	1720		Hannington	Wilts	1571
Hammoon	Dorset	1656		Hanslope	Buckingham	1570
Hampden, Great	Buckingham	¹1557		Hanwell	Middlesex	1571
Hampden, Little	Buckingham	1672		Hanwell	Oxford	1586
Hampnett	Gloucester	²1590		Hanwood	Salop	⁷—
Hampreston	Dorset	1617		Hanworth	Middlesex	1731
Hampstead	Middlesex	1560		Hanworth	Norfolk	1721
Hampstead-Marshall	Berks	1675		Hanworth, Cold	Lincoln	1725
Hampstead-Norreys	Berks	1538		Hanworth, Potter. See Potter Hanworth.		
Hampsthwaite	York	³1603		Happisburgh	Norfolk	1558
Hampton	Middlesex	1554		Hapton	Norfolk	1653
Hampton Bishop	Hereford	1669		Harberton	Devon	1621
Hampton-Gay	Oxford	1621		Harbledown	Kent	⁸1557
Hampton, Great and Little.	Worcester	1539		Harborne	Stafford	1538
Hampton, High-	Devon	1653		Harborough-Magna	Warwick	1540
Hampton-in-Arden	Warwick	1599		Harborough-Market	Leicester	1588
Hampton-Lovett	Worcester	⁴1666		Harbridge	Hants	1563
Hampton-Lucy	Warwick	1556		Harbury	Warwick	1564
Hampton-Meysey	Gloucester	1570		Harby	Leicester	1700
Hampton-Poyle	Oxford	1540		Harby	Nottingham	⁹—
Hamsey	Sussex	1583		Hardenhuish	Wilts	1730
Hamstall-Ridware	Stafford	⁵1598		Hardham	Sussex	1642
Hamsterley	Durham	1588		Hardingham	Norfolk	1557
Hanborough	Oxford	1560		Hardingstone	Northampton	1562
Hanbury	Stafford	1574		Hardington	Somerset	¹⁰—
Hanbury	Worcester	1577		Hardington - Mandeville.	Somerset	1687
Handley	Chester	1570		Hardley	Norfolk	1715
Handley	Dorset	1754		Hardmead	Buckingham	¹¹1556
Handsworth	Stafford	1558		Hardres, Lower	Kent	1558
Handsworth	York	1558		Hardres, Upper	Kent	1565
Hanford	Dorset	1669		Hardrow	York	1755
Hangleton	Sussex	1727		Hardwick	Norfolk	1561
Hanham-Abbots	Gloucester	1586		Hardwick, Prior's-	Warwick	¹²1660
Hankerton	Wilts	1699		Hardwick	Gloucester	¹³1566
Hanley	Stafford	1754		Hardwicke	Buckingham	1558
Hanley-Castle	Worcester	1538		Hardwicke	Cambridge	1564
Hanley-Child	Worcester	⁶—		Hardwicke	Oxford	1758
Hanley-William	Worcester	1586		Hardwycke	Northampton	1559
Hanmer	Flint	1563		Hareby	Lincoln	1587
Hannah	Lincoln	1559		Harefield	Middlesex	1538
Hanney, West	Berks	1565		Harescombe	Gloucester	¹⁴1741
Hanningfield, East	Essex	1612		Haresfield	Gloucester	1558
Hanningfield, South	Essex	1558				

¹ **P** 1557–1812. Edited by E. A. Ebblewhite, London, 1888.
² **P** Hampnett and Stowell. (Marriages only) 1737–1754. Gloucestershire Notes and Queries, vols. 1 and 2.
³ **P** 1603–1807. Yorkshire Parish Register Society, vol. 13, 1902.
⁴ Bishop's Transcripts commence 1615.
⁵ **P** 1598–1812. Staffordshire Parish Register Society, 1904.
⁶ Included in the Registers of Eastham (q.v.).
⁷ **P** 1559–1763. Shropshire Parish Register Society, vol. 1 (Hereford Diocese). The original Register was destroyed by fire in 1873.
⁸ **P** 1557–1800. Edited by J. Meadows Cowper, 1907.
⁹ Included in the Registers of North Clifton (q.v.).
¹⁰ Included in the Registers of Hemington (q.v.).
¹¹ **P** (Marriages only) 1575–1813. Buckinghamshire Parish Registers, vol. 2, 1904.
¹² **P** (Marriages only) 1662–1812. Warwickshire Parish Registers, vol. 1, 1904.
¹³ **P** (Marriages only) 1566–1812. Gloucestershire Parish Registers, vol. 12, 1906.
¹⁴ **P** (Marriages only) 1744–1812. Gloucestershire Parish Registers, vol. 10, 1905.

Parish.	County.	Date of Earliest Entry.	Parish.	County.	Date of Earliest Entry.
Harewood - -	Hereford - -	[1] 1671	Hart - - -	Durham - -	1577
Harewood - -	York - -	1614	Hartburn - -	Northumberland	1678
Harford - - -	Devon - -	1724	Hartest - - -	Suffolk -	1556
Hargham - -	Norfolk - -	1561	Hartfield - -	Sussex - -	1648
Hargrave - - -	Chester -	1631	Hartford - -	Huntingdon -	1538
Hargrave - -	Northampton -	1572	Hartgrove - -	Dorset - -	[5] —
Hargrave - - -	Suffolk - -	1710	Harthill - - -	Chester - -	1730
Harkstead - -	Suffolk - -	1654	Harthill - -	York - -	1586
Harlaston - - -	Stafford - -	[2] 1693	Harting - - -	Sussex - -	1567
Harlaxton - -	Lincoln - -	1558	Hartington - -	Derby - -	1610
Harle, Kirk - -	Northumberland	1692	Hartland - -	Devon - -	1578
Harlech - - -	Merioneth -	1695	Hartlebury - -	Worcester -	1540
Harleston - - -	Norfolk - -	1558	Hartlepool - -	Durham - -	1566
Harlestone - -	Northampton -	1570	Hartley - - -	Kent - -	1712
Harlestone - -	Suffolk - -	1561	Hartley-Mauditt - -	Hants - -	1672
Harleton - - -	Cambridge -	1636	Hartley-Wespall -	Hants - -	[6] 1558
Harley - - -	Salop - -	[3] 1745	Hartley-Wintney -	Hants - -	[7] 1658
Harling, East - -	Norfolk - -	1544	Hartlip - - -	Kent - -	1538
Harling, West - -	Norfolk - -	1583	Hartpury - - -	Gloucester -	1571
Harlington - -	Bedford - -	1647	Hartshead - -	York - -	[8] 1612
Harlington - -	Middlesex -	1540	Hartshorne - -	Derby - -	1594
Harsley, East - -	York - -	1693	Hartwell - - -	Buckingham -	[9] 1550
Harmondsworth -	Middlesex -	1670	Hartwell - -	Northampton -	1684
Harmon, St. - -	Radnor - -	1751	Hartwith - - -	York - -	1751
Harmston - - -	Lincoln - -	1563	Harty, Isle of - -	Kent - -	1679
Harnham - - -	Wilts - -	1568	Harvington - -	Worcester -	1573
Harnhill - - -	Gloucester -	1730	Harwell - - -	Berks - -	1558
Harpenden - -	Hertford - -	1562	Harwich - - -	Essex - -	1539
Harpford - - -	Devon - -	1569	Harwood, Great -	Lancaster -	1560
Harpham - - -	York - -	1720	Harworth - -	Nottingham -	1538
Harpley - - -	Norfolk - -	1722	Hascombe - -	Surrey - -	1646
Harpole - - -	Northampton -	1538	Haselbech - -	Northampton -	1653
Harpsden - - -	Oxford - -	1558	Haselbury-Bryan -	Dorset - -	1562
Harpswell - -	Lincoln - -	1559	Haseley - - -	Warwick - -	1588
Harptree, East - -	Somerset - -	1663	Haseley, Great -	Oxford - -	1538
Harptree, West -	Somerset -	1655	Haselor - - -	Warwick - -	1594
Harrietsham - -	Kent - -	1538	Haselton - - -	Gloucester -	1597
Harrington - -	Cumberland -	1653	Hasfield - - -	Gloucester -	1559
Harrington - -	Lincoln - -	1697	Hasguard - - -	Pembroke -	1756
Harrington - -	Northampton -	1673	Hasketon - - -	Suffolk - -	1545
Harringworth - -	Northampton -	1695	Haslebury-Plucknett -	Somerset -	1672
Harrogate - -	York - -	1758	Haslemere - -	Surrey - -	[10] 1594
Harrold - - -	Bedford - -	1598	Haslingden - -	Lancaster -	1620
Harroldston - -	Pembroke -	1765	Haslingfield - -	Cambridge -	1709
Harroldston, West	Pembroke -	1748	Haslington - -	Chester - -	1648
Harrow-on-the-Hill -	Middlesex -	[4] 1558	Hassingham - -	Norfolk - -	1563
Harrowden, Great	Northampton -	1672	Hastingleigh - -	Kent - -	1730
Harrowden, Little	Northampton -	1653	Hastings, All Saints -	Sussex - -	1559
Harston - - -	Cambridge -	1686	St. Clement	- - -	1558
Harston - - -	Leicester -	1707	Hatch-Beauchamp -	Somerset -	1760
Harswell - -	York - -	1653	Hatch, West - -	Somerset -	[11] 1606

[1] **P** 1671–1812. Edited by J. H. Parry, Devizes, 1900. [mentary Return of 1831.
[2] "Account of an earlier Register will be found in the Court of the Bishop of Lichfield." Parlia-
[3] **P** 1590–1812. Shropshire Parish Register Society, vol. 2, 1902 (Lichfield). 1745–1812. Parish
Register Society, vol. 23, 1899.
[4] **P** 1558–1653. Edited by W. O. Hewlett, Beverley, 1900.
[5] Included in the Registers of Fontmell Magna (q.v.).
[6] **P** (Marriages only) 1558–1812. Hampshire Parish Registers, vol. 9, 1907.
[7] **P** (Marriages only) 1658–1812. Hampshire Parish Registers, vol. 3, 1902.
[8] **P** 1612–1812. Yorkshire Parish Register Society, vol. 17, 1903.
[9] **P** (Marriages only) 1553–1812. Buckinghamshire Parish Registers, vol. 3, 1907.
[10] **P** 1594–1812. Parish Register Society, vol. 57, 1906.
[11] **P** (Marriages only) 1604–1812. Somersetshire Parish Registers, vol. 3, 1901.

Parish.	County.	Date of Earliest Entry.	Parish.	County.	Date of Earliest Entry.
Hatcliffe - -	Lincoln - -	1696	Hawkley - -	Hants - -	[7] 1797
Hatfield - -	Hereford -	1615	Hawkridge - -	Somerset - -	1655
Hatfield - - -	York - -	1566	Hawkshead - -	Lancaster - -	[8] 1568
Hatfield, Bishop's -	Hertford - -	1653	Hawksworth - -	Nottingham -	[9] 1569
Hatfield-Broad-Oak -	Essex - -	1558	Hawkwell - -	Essex - -	1692
Hatfield-Peverel -	Essex - -	1626	Hawling - -	Gloucester -	1677
Hatford - -	Berks - -	1538	Hawnby - -	York - -	[10] 1653
Hatherleigh - -	Devon - -	1558	Hawnes - -	Bedford - -	[11] 1596
Hatherley-Down -	Gloucester -	1563	Haworth - -	York - -	1645
Hathern - -	Leicester -	1563	Hawridge - -	Buckingham -	[12] 1725
Hatherop - -	Gloucester -	1670	Hawstead - -	Suffolk - -	1558
Hathersage - -	Derby - -	1627	Hawton - -	Nottingham -	[13] 1564
Hatley - -	Cambridge -	1589	Haxby - - -	York - -	1667
Hatley, Cockayne-	Bedford - -	1701	Haxey - -	Lincoln - -	1559
Hatley, East - -	Cambridge -	1585	Hay - - -	Brecon - -	1688
Hatton - - -	Lincoln - -	1552	Haydon - -	Dorset - -	1711
Hatton - - -	Warwick - -	[1] 1538	Haydon Bridge -	Northumberland	1654
Haugh - - -	Lincoln - -	1762	Haydor - -	Lincoln - -	[14] 1559
Haugham - -	Lincoln - -	1756	Hayes - -	Kent - -	1539
Haughley - -	Suffolk - -	1558	Hayes - -	Middlesex -	1638
Haughton - -	Stafford - -	[2] 1570	Hayfield - -	Derby - -	1622
Haughton-le-Skerne -	Durham - -	[3] 1569	Hayling - -	Hants - -	1571
Hault Hucknall. See			Haynes. See Hawnes.		
Ault Hucknall.			Haynford - -	Norfolk - -	1556
Hautbois, Great -	Norfolk - -	1563	Hayscastle - -	Pembroke -	1787
Hautbois, Little -	- - -	[4] —	Hayton - -	Cumberland -	1620
Hauxton - -	Cambridge -	1560	Hayton - - -	Nottingham -	1655
Hauxwell - -	York - -	1592	Hayton - -	York - -	1610
Havant - - -	Hants - -	1653	Hazeleigh - -	Essex - -	1575
Haverfordwest, St. Mary	Pembroke -	1678	Heacham - -	Norfolk - -	[15] 1558
St. Martin - -	- - -	1721	Headbourne Worthy -	Hants - -	1616
St. Thomas - -	- - -	1777	Headcorn - -	Kent - -	1560
Haverhill - -	Suffolk - -	1670	Headingley - -	York - -	1723
Havering-atte-Bower -	Essex - -	1671	Headington - -	Oxford - -	1683
Haveringland or Haver-	Norfolk - -	1694	Headley - -	Hants - -	1539
land.			Headley - -	Surrey - -	1663
Haversham - -	Buckingham -	1665	Headon - -	Nottingham -	[16] 1566
Hawarden - -	Flint - -	1585	Healaugh - -	York - -	1687
Hawerby - -	Lincoln - -	1598	Healing - -	Lincoln - -	1571
Hawes - - -	York - -	1695	Heanor - -	Derby - -	1559
Hawkchurch - -	Dorset - -	[5] 1663	Heanton-Punchardon -	Devon - -	1657
Hawkedon - -	Suffolk - -	1709	Heapham - -	Lincoln - -	1558
Hawkesbury - -	Gloucester -	[6] 1603	Heath - - -	Bedford - -	[17] —
Hawkhurst - -	Kent - -	1550	Heath - - -	Derby - -	[18] 1682
Hawkinge - -	Kent - -	1691	Heather - -	Leicester -	1619

[1] P (Marriages only) 1558–1812. Warwickshire Parish Registers, vol. 3, 1906.
[2] P 1570–1812. Staffordshire Parish Register Society, 1902.
[3] P "North Country Parish Registers," by Robert Blair.
[4] Included in the Registers of Lammas (q.v.).
[5] P (Marriages only) 1664–1812. Dorsetshire Parish Registers, vol. 2, 1907.
[6] P (Marriages only) 1603–1812. Gloucestershire Parish Registers, vol. 5, 1899.
[7] Earlier entries relating to this parish are in the Registers of Newton Valence.
[8] P 1568–1704. Edited by H. S. Cowper, London, 1897.
[9] P (Marriages only) 1569–1812. Nottinghamshire Parish Registers, vol. 1, 1898.
[10] P 1653–1722. Edited by E. E. Thoyts, Olney, 1890.
[11] P 1596–1812. Edited by William Brigg, Leeds, 1891.
[12] P (Marriages only) 1600–1812. Buckinghamshire Parish Registers, vol. 1, 1902.
[13] P (Marriages only) 1564–1812. Nottinghamshire Parish Registers, vol. 42, 1902.
[14] P 1559–1649. Parish Register Society, vol. 9, 1897.
[15] P (Marriages only) 1558–1812. Norfolk Parish Registers, vol. 2, 1900.
[16] P 1566–1812. Parish Register Society, vol. 43, 1902.
[17] Included in the Registers of Leighton Buzzard (q.v.).
[18] P (Marriages only) 1682–1812. Derbyshire Parish Registers, vol. 1, 1906.

Parish.	County.	Date of Earliest Entry.	Parish.	County.	Date of Earliest Entry.
Heathfield - -	Somerset -	[1] 1703	Hempstead - -	Norfolk - -	1558
Heathfield - -	Sussex - -	1582	Hempstead - -	Norfolk -	1707
Heaton, Kirk-. *See*			Hempstead, Hemel -	Hertford - -	1558
Kirk-Heaton.			Hempston, Broad -	Devon - -	1678
Heaton-Norris -	Lancaster -	1767	Hempston, Little -	Devon -	1539
Heavitree - -	Devon - -	1653	Hemsby - -	Norfolk -	1566
Hebburn - - -	Northumberland	1680	Hemswell - - -	Lincoln - -	1676
Heckfield - -	Hants - -	[2] 1538	Hemsworth - -	York - -	1685
Heckingham - -	Norfolk - -	1560	Hemyock - -	Devon - -	1635
Heckington - -	Lincoln -	1559	Henbury - -	Gloucester -	1538
Heddington - -	Wilts - -	1538	Henderskelf -	York - -	[5] —
Heddon-on-the-Wall -	Northumberland	1656	Hendon - -	Middlesex -	1653
Hedenham - -	Norfolk -	1559	Hendred, East -	Berks - -	1538
Hedgerley - - -	Buckingham -	1539	Hendred, West -	Berks - -	1559
Hedingham, Castle -	Essex - -	1558	Heneglwys - -	Anglesea -	1698
Hedingham, Sible -	Essex - -	1680	Henfield - -	Sussex - -	1596
Hedon - - -	York - -	1549	Henfynyw - -	Cardigan -	1718
Hedsor - - -	Buckingham -	1678	Hengrave - - -	Suffolk - -	[6] —
Heigham - -	Norfolk -	1563	Henham - -	Essex - -	1539
Heigham, Potter-	Norfolk - -	1538	Henley - -	Suffolk - -	1559
Heighington - -	Durham -	1559	Henley-in-Arden -	Warwick -	[7] 1672
Heighton, South -	Sussex - -	1700	Henley-on-Thames -	Oxford - -	1558
Helens, St. (Isle of Wight).	Hants - -	1653	Henllan - -	Denbigh -	1684
			Henllys - -	Monmouth -	1754
Helens, St. - -	Lancaster -	1713	Henlow - - -	Bedford -	1558
Helhoughton - -	Norfolk - -	1540	Hennock - - -	Devon - -	1544
Helidon - -	Northampton -	1571	Henny, Great - -	Essex - -	1695
Helland - - -	Cornwall, -	[3] 1722	Henry's Moat - -	Pembroke -	1755
Hellesdon - -	Norfolk -	1562	Hensingham - -	Cumberland -	1811
Hellingly - - -	Sussex - -	1618	Henstead - -	Suffolk - -	1539
Hellington - -	Norfolk - -	1562	Henstridge - -	Somerset -	1653
Helmdon - - -	Northampton -	1572	Hentland - -	Hereford - -	1558
Helmingham - -	Suffolk - -	1559	Heptonstall - -	York - -	1593
Helmsley - -	York - -	1575	Hepworth - - -	Suffolk - -	1688
Helmsley-gate -	York - -	1689	Herbranston - -	Pembroke -	1716
Helmsley, Upper -	York - -	1642	Hereford, All Saints -	Hereford - -	1669
Helperthorpe - -	York - -	1733	St. Martin -	- - -	1559
Helpringham - -	Lincoln -	1560	St. John-the-	- - -	1687
Helpstone - -	Northampton -	1685	Baptist.		
Helsington - -	Westmorland -	1728	St. Nicholas -	- - -	1556
Helston - - -	Cornwall -	1598	St. Owen -	- - -	1626
Hemblington - -	Norfolk - -	[4] 1562	St. Peter -	- - -	1556
Hemingborough -	York - -	1605	Hereford, Little - -	Hereford -	1725
Hemingby - -	Lincoln - -	1597	Hermitage - -	Dorset - -	1712
Hemingford, Abbots -	Huntingdon -	1693	Herne - - -	Kent - -	1558
Hemingford Grey -	Huntingdon -	1673	Hernhill - -	Kent - -	1557
Hemingstone - -	Suffolk - -	1553	Herriard - -	Hants - -	[8] 1666
Hemington - -	Northampton -	1563	Herringby - -	Norfolk -	[9] —
Hemington - -	Somerset - -	1539	Herringfleet - -	Suffolk - -	1706
Hemley - - -	Suffolk - -	1698	Herringswell - -	Suffolk - -	1748
Hempnall - -	Norfolk -	1560	Hertford, All Saints -	Hertford -	1559
Hempstead - -	Essex - -	1664	St. Andrew -	- - -	1560
Hempsted - -	Gloucester -	1558	Hertingfordbury -	Hertford - -	1679

[1] **P** (Marriages only) 1700–1812. Somersetshire Parish Registers, vol. 8, 1907.
[2] **P** (Marriages only) 1538–1812. Hampshire Parish Registers, vol. 4, 1903.
[3] **P** (Marriages only) 1677–1812. Cornwall Parish Registers, vol. 4, 1903.
[4] **P** (Marriages only) 1564–1812. Norfolk Parish Registers, vol. 1, 1899.
[5] One book of baptisms commencing in 1772.
[6] Included in the Registers of Flempton (*q.v.*).
[7] Bishop's Transcripts commence 1662.
[8] **P** (Marriages only) 1701–1812. Hampshire Parish Registers, vol. 8, 1906.
[9] Included in the Registers of Stokesby (*q.v.*).

Parish.	County.	Date of Earliest Entry.	Parish.	County.	Date of Earliest Entry.
Hesket-in-the-Forest -	Cumberland -	1662	Hilary, St. - -	Glamorgan -	1690
Hesketh - -	Lancaster -	1745	Hilary, St. - -	Cornwall -	ᵇ 1692
Hesleden, Monk- -	Durham -	1578	Hilborough - -	Norfolk - -	1561
Heslerton, West -	York -	1561	Hildersham -	Cambridge -	1560
Heslington -	York -	1653	Hilfield - -	Dorset - -	1565
Hessett - -	Suffolk -	1538	Hilgay - -	Norfolk -	1583
Hessle - -	York -	1561	Hill - -	Gloucester -	ᵉ 1653
Heston - - -	Middlesex -	1560	Hill-Deverill -	Wilts - -	1648
Heswall - -	Chester -	¹ 1559	Hill-Farrance -	Somerset -	⁷ 1702
Hethe - - -	Oxford -	1679	Hillesden - -	Buckingham -	1595
Hethel - -	Norfolk -	1710	Hillingdon -	Middlesex -	1549
Hethersett - -	Norfolk -	1616	Hillington -	Norfolk - -	1694
Heveningham -	Suffolk -	1539	Hillmorton -	Warwick -	1564
Hever - - -	Kent -	1632	Hilmarton -	Wilts - -	1645
Heversham - -	Westmorland -	1601	Hilperton -	Wilts - -	1694
Hevingham - -	Norfolk -	1654	Hilston - -	York - -	1654
Hewelsfield - -	Gloucester -	1664	Hilton - -	Dorset -	1603
Hewish. *See* Huish.			Hilton - -	Huntingdon -	1558
Heworth - -	Durham -	² 1808	Hilton-in-Cleveland -	York - -	1698
Hexham - -	Northumberland	1655	Himbleton -	Worcester -	⁸ 1713
Hexton - -	Hertford -	1538	Himley - -	Stafford -	1660
Hey (or Lees) -	Lancaster -	1743	Hinckley - -	Leicester -	1554
Heybridge - -	Essex -	1558	Hinderclay -	Suffolk -	1567
Heydon - -	Essex -	1538	Hinderwell -	York - -	1601
Heydon - -	Norfolk -	1538	Hindley - -	Lancaster -	1698
Heyford - -	Northampton -	1558	Hindlip - -	Worcester -	1612
Heyford, Lower -	Oxford -	1539	Hindolveston -	Norfolk -	1693
Heyford, Upper -	Oxford -	1558	Hindon - -	Wilts - -	1599
Heyope - -	Radnor -	1660	Hindringham -	Norfolk -	1660
Heysham - -	Lancaster -	1650	Hingham - -	Norfolk -	1601
Heyshott - -	Sussex -	1690	Hinksey, North -	Berks - -	1703
Heytesbury - -	Wilts -	1653	Hinksey, South -	Berks - -	1670
Heythrop - -	Oxford -	1607	Hinstock - -	Salop - -	1695
Heywood - -	Lancaster -	1733	Hintlesham -	Suffolk -	1652
Hibaldstow -	Lincoln -	1632	Hinton - -	Dorset -	1581
Hickleton -	York -	1694	Hinton, St. George -	Somerset -	1632
Hickling - -	Norfolk -	1654	Hinton-Admiral -	Hants - -	⁹ —
Hickling - -	Nottingham -	³ 1646	Hinton-Ampner -	Hants - -	1561
Higham - -	Kent -	1653	Hinton-Blewett -	Somerset -	1563
Higham - -	Suffolk -	1538	Hinton, Broad-	Wilts - -	1682
Higham, Cold-	Northampton -	1556	Hinton-Charterhouse	Somerset -	1546
Higham-Ferrers	Northampton -	1573	Hinton, Cherry-	Cambridge -	1538
Higham-Gobion	Bedford -	1558	Hinton-in-the-Hedges	Northampton -	1558
Higham-on-the-Hill -	Leicester -	1707	Hinton, Little -	Wilts - -	1649
High Bray -	Devon -	1735	Hinton, Little -	Dorset -	1621
Highclere - -	Hants -	⁴ 1656	Hinton-Martell -	Dorset -	1661
Highead. *See* Ivegill.			Hinton-on-the-Green	Gloucester -	¹⁰ 1735
Highgate - - -	Middlesex -	1633	Hinton, Tarrant-. *See*		
Highley - -	Salop -	1551	Tarrant-Hinton.		
Highway - -	Wilts -	1742	Hinton-Waldrist -	Berks - -	1551
Highweek - -	Devon -	1653	Hints - - -	Stafford -	1558
Highworth - -	Wilts -	1538	Hinxhill - -	Kent - -	1577

¹ **P** 1559–1729. Edited by T. H. Way, 1897.
² Earlier included in the Registers of Jarrow.
³ **P** (Marriages only) 1646–1812. Nottinghamshire Parish Registers, vol. 2, 1899.
⁴ **P** (Marriages only) 1656–1813. Hampshire Parish Registers, vol. 8, 1906.
⁵ **P** (Marriages only) 1676–1812. Cornwall Parish Registers, vol. 9, 1906.
⁶ **P** (Marriages only) 1653–1812. Gloucestershire Parish Registers, vol. 10, 1905.
⁷ **P** (Marriages only) 1701–1812. Somersetshire Parish Registers, vol. 8, 1907.
⁸ Bishop's Transcripts commence 1611.
⁹ Included in the Registers of Christchurch (*q.v.*).
¹⁰ **P** (Marriages only) 1735–1812. Gloucestershire Parish Registers, vol. 4, 1898.

Parish.	County.	Date of Earliest Entry.	Parish.	County.	Date of Earliest Entry.
Hinxton - -	Cambridge -	1538	Holme-Cultram -	Cumberland -	1581
Hinxworth - -	Hertford -	1739	Holme-Hale - -	Norfolk -	1538
Hipswell - -	York - -	1665	Holme-Lacy - -	Hereford - -	1562
Hirnant - - -	Montgomery -	1606	Holme-next-Runcton -	Norfolk - -	1562
Histon - - -	Cambridge -	1655	Holme - next - the -	Norfolk -	1704
Hitcham - - -	Buckingham -	1559	Sea.		
Hitcham - -	Suffolk - -	1575	Holme - on - Spalding-	York - -	1559
Hitchin - -	Hertford - -	1562	Moor.		
Hittisleigh - -	Devon - -	1676	Holme-on-the-Wolds -	York - -	1654
Hoath - -	Kent - -	1554	Holme-Pierrepoint -	Nottingham -	⁵1564
Hoathly, East - -	Sussex - -	1560	Holmer - -	Hereford - -	1712
Hoathly, West - -	Sussex - -	1645	Holmesfield - -	Derby - -	1730
Hoby - - -	Leicester - -	1562	Holmfirth - -	York - -	1797
Hockering - -	Norfolk - -	1561	Holmpton - -	York - -	1739
Hockerton - -	Nottingham -	1582	Holne - - -	Devon - -	1603
Hockham - -	Norfolk - -	1563	Holnest - -	Dorset - -	⁶1589
Hockley - -	Essex - -	1732	Holsworthy - -	Devon - -	1563
Hockliffe - -	Bedford - -	1620	Holt - - -	Denbigh - -	1662
Hockwold - -	Norfolk - -	1664	Holt - - -	Norfolk - -	1557
Hockworthy - -	Devon - -	1577	Holt - - -	Worcester - -	1538
Hoddesdon - -	Hertford - -	¹ —	Holt - - -	Wilts - -	1580
Hodgeston - -	Pembroke -	1755	Holtby - - -	York - -	1679
Hodnet - - -	Salop - -	1657	Holton - -	Oxford - -	1633
Hoggeston - -	Buckingham -	1547	Holton - -	Somerset - -	1558
Hognaston - -	Derby - -	1661	Holton, St. Mary -	Suffolk - -	1568
Hogsthorpe - -	Lincoln - -	1574	Holton, St. Peter -	Suffolk - -	1538
Holbeach - -	Lincoln - -	²1560	Holton-Beckering -	Lincoln - -	1560
Holbeck - -	York - -	1717	Holton-le-Clay - -	Lincoln - -	1750
Holbeton - -	Devon - -	1620	Holvestone - -	Norfolk - -	⁷ —
Holbrook - -	Suffolk - -	1559	Holwell - - -	Bedford - -	1560
Holcombe - -	Lancaster - -	1726	Holwell - - -	Dorset - -	1653
Holcombe - -	Somerset - -	1698	Holwell - - -	Oxford - -	⁸ —
Holcombe-Burnell -	Devon - -	1657	Holybourne - -	Hants - -	1690
Holcombe-Rogus -	Devon - -	1540	Holyhead - -	Anglesea -	1737
Holcott - -	Northampton -	1559	Holy-Island - -	Northumberland -	1578
Holcutt - -	Bedford - -	1658	Holywell - -	Lincoln - -	1558
Holdenby - -	Northampton -	1754	Holywell - -	Oxford - -	1653
Holdenhurst - -	Hants - -	1679	Holywell - -	Flint - -	1677
Holdgate - -	Salop - -	1662	Holywell - -	Huntingdon -	1667
Holford - -	Somerset - -	1558	Homersfield - -	Suffolk - -	1558
Holkham - -	Norfolk - -	³1542	Homington - -	Wilts - -	1675
Hollacombe - -	Devon - -	1638	Honeybourne, Church	Worcester -	1673
Holland, Great -	Essex - -	1539	Honey Church - -	Devon - -	1728
Holland, Little - -	Essex - -	⁴1561	Honiley - -	Warwick - -	1745
Hollesley - -	Suffolk - -	1623	Honing - -	Norfolk - -	1630
Hollinfare - -	Lancaster - -	1654	Honingham - -	Norfolk - -	1561
Hollingbourne - -	Kent - -	1556	Honington - -	Lincoln - -	1561
Hollington - -	Sussex - -	1636	Honington - -	Suffolk - -	1559
Hollinwood - -	Lancaster - -	1769	Honington - -	Warwick- -	⁹1571
Hollym - -	York - -	1564	Honiton - -	Devon - -	1598
Holme - -	Huntingdon -	1683	Honley - -	York - -	¹⁰ —
Holme - -	Nottingham -	1711	Hoo - - -	Norfolk - -	1733
Holme-in-Cliviger -	Lancaster -	1742	Hoo - - -	Suffolk - -	1653

¹ Included in the Registers of Broxbourn (q.v.).
² **P** 1606–1641. Edited by G. W. Macdonald, Lincoln, 1892.
³ **P** (Marriages only) 1542–1812. Norfolk Parish Registers, vol. 2, 1900.
⁴ Included in the Registers of Great Clacton.
⁵ **P** (Marriages only) 1564–1812. Nottinghamshire Parish Registers, vol. 2, 1899.
⁶ **P** 1589–1812. Edited by Rev. C. H. Mayo, 1894.
⁷ Included in the Registers of Burgh-Apton (q.v.).
⁸ Included in the Registers of Bradwell (q.v.).
⁹ **P** (Marriages only) 1571–1812. Warwickshire Parish Registers, vol. 1, 1904.
¹⁰ Included in the Registers of Aldmonbury (q.v.).

Parish.	County.	Date of Earliest Entry.	Parish.	County.	Date of Earliest Entry.
Hoo-Allhallows	Kent	1629	Horningtoft	Norfolk	1541
Hoo, St. Mary	Kent	1695	Hornsea	York	1654
Hoo, St. Werburgh	Kent	1587	Hornsey	Middlesex	1653
Hooe	Sussex	1609	Hornton	Oxford	1703
Hook	York	1683	Horringer. See Horn-		
Hoole	Lancaster	1673	ingsheath.		
Hooton-Pagnall	York	1538	Horseheath	Cambridge	1558
Hooton-Roberts	York	1702	Horsehouse	York	[9] —
Hope	Derby	1599	Horsell	Surrey	1653
Hope, or Estyn	Flint	1668	Horsendon	Buckingham	1637
Hope	Kent	[1] —	Horsepath	Oxford	1561
Hope-Bagot	Salop	1754	Horsey-next-the-Sea	Norfolk	1559
Hope-Bowdler	Salop	1564	Horsford	Norfolk	1597
Hope-Mansel	Hereford	1556	Horsforth	York	1693
Hope-under-Dinmore	Hereford	1701	Horsham	Norfolk	1695
Hopesay	Salop	1678	Horsham	Sussex	1540
Hopton-by-Thetford	Suffolk	1691	Horsington	Lincoln	1558
Hopton-by-Lowestoft	Suffolk	1673	Horsington	Somerset	1559
Hopton-Castle	Salop	[2] 1538	Horsley	Derby	1558
Hopton-Wafers	Salop	1729	Horsley	Gloucester	[10] 1587
Horbling	Lincoln	[3] 1653	Horsley, East	Surrey	1666
Horbury	York	[4] 1598	Horsley, Long	Northumberland	1668
Hordle	Hants	1754	Horsley, West	Surrey	1600
Hordley	Salop	1686	Horsmonden	Kent	1561
Horfield	Gloucester	1543	Horstead	Norfolk	[11] 1558
Horham	Suffolk	1594	Horsted-Keynes	Sussex	1638
Horksley, Great	Essex	1558	Horsted, Little	Sussex	1540
Horksley, Little	Essex	1568	Horton	Buckingham	1571
Horkstow	Lincoln	1562	Horton	Dorset	1653
Horley	Oxford	1538	Horton	Gloucester	[12] 1567
Horley	Surrey	1578	Horton	Northampton	1605
Hormead, Great	Hertford	1538	Horton	Northumberland	1648
Hormead, Little	Hertford	1588	Horton	Stafford	1653
Horn	Rutland	[5] —	Horton	Somerset	[13]
Hornblotton	Somerset	1763	Horton	York	1808
Hornby	Lancaster	1742	Horton - in - Ribbles-	York	1556
Hornby	York	1582	dale.		
Horncastle	Lincoln	[6] 1559	Horton-Kirby	Kent	1678
Hornchurch	Essex	1576	Horton, Monks	Kent	1558
Horndon, East	Essex	1558	Horwich	Lancaster	1695
Horndon-on-the-Hill	Essex	1672	Horwood	Devon	1653
Horndon, West	Essex	[7] —	Horwood, Great	Buckingham	1600
Horne	Surrey	1614	Horwood, Little	Buckingham	1568
Horning	Norfolk	1558	Hose	Leicester	1625
Horninghold	Leicester	1661	Hotham	York	1706
Horningsey	Cambridge	1628	Hothfield	Kent	1570
Horningsham	Wilts	1561	Hough-on-the-Hill	Lincoln	1646
Horningsheath	Suffolk	[6] 1558	Hougham	Kent	1659

[1] Included in the Registers of New Romney (q.v.).
P 1538–1812. Shropshire Parish Register Society, vol. 2 (Hereford Diocese). Also **P** Parish Register Society, vol. 40, 1901.
[3] **P** 1653–1837. Edited by H. Peet, Liverpool, 1895.
[4] **P** 1598–1812. Yorkshire Parish Register Society, vol. 3, 1900.
[5] Included in the Registers of Exton (q.v.).
[6] **P** 1559–1639. Edited by J. C. Hudson, 1892.
[7] Included in the Registers of Ingrave (q.v.).
[8] **P** 1558–1850. Edited by Rev. S. H. A. Hervey, Woodbridge, 1900.
[9] Included in the Registers of Coverham (q.v.).
[10] **P** (Marriages only) 1591–1812. Gloucestershire Parish Registers, vol. 12, 1906.
[11] **P** (Marriages only) 1558–1812. Norfolk Parish Registers, vol. 3, 1907.
[12] **P** (Marriages only) 1567–1811. Gloucestershire Parish Registers, vol. 13, 1908.
[13] Included in the Registers of Ilminster.

Parish.	County.	Date of Earliest Entry.	Parish.	County.	Date of Earliest Entry.
Hougham - -	Lincoln -	1562	Hullavington -	Wilts - -	1694
Houghton - -	Huntingdon -	1633	Hulme, Church-	Chester - -	1613
Houghton - -	Hants - -	1669	Hulton, Little -	Lancaster -	1768
Houghton - -	Sussex - -	1560	Humber - -	Hereford -	1588
Houghton-Conquest -	Bedford - -	1595	Humberstone -	Lincoln - -	1748
Houghton, Great -	Northampton -	1558	Humberstone -	Leicester -	1683
Houghton-in-the-Hole	Norfolk - -	1558	Humbleton -	York - -	1577
Houghton-le-Spring -	Durham -	1563	Hundleby -	Lincoln -	1707
Houghton, Little -	Northampton -	1540	Hundon - -	Suffolk - -	1538
Houghton, Long -	Northumberland	1646	Hungarton -	Leicester -	⁷ 1614
Houghton, New -	Norfolk - -	1654	Hungerford -	Berks and Wilts	1559
Houghton-on-the-Hill	Leicester -	1653	Hungerton -	Lincoln - -	1558
Houghton-on-the-Hill	Norfolk - -	1695	Hunmanby -	York - -	1584
Houghton-Regis -	Bedford - -	1538	Hunningham -	Warwick -	1718
Hound - - -	Hants - -	1660	Hunsdon - -	Hertford - -	1546
Hounslow - - -	Middlesex -	1708	Hunsingore -	York - -	1656
Hove - - -	Sussex - -	1538	Hunslet or Hunfleet -	York - -	1686
Hoveringham -	Nottingham -	1655	Hunstanton -	Norfolk -	1538
Hoveton St. John -	Norfolk - -	1673	Hunstanworth -	Durham - -	1724
Hoveton St. Peter -	Norfolk -	1624	Hunston - -	Suffolk -	1559
Hovingham - -	York - -	1642	Hunston - -	Sussex - -	1678
How-Caple - -	Hereford -	1677	Huntingdon, St. John	Huntingdon -	1585
Howden - - -	York - -	¹ 1543	All Saints -	- - -	1558
Howe - - -	Norfolk -	1734	St. Mary - -	- - -	1593
Howell - - -	Lincoln - -	1710	St. Benedict -	- - -	1574
Howick - - -	Northumberland	1678	Huntingfield -	Suffolk - -	1539
Hoxne - - -	Suffolk - -	1572	Huntington -	Hereford - -	1754
Hoyland, High -	York - -	1720	Huntington -	York - -	1592
Hoyland, Nether -	York - -	1740	Huntington -	Hereford -	1718
Hubberholme -	York - -	1663	Huntley - -	Gloucester -	1660
Hubberston - -	Pembroke -	1752	Hunton - -	Kent - -	1585
Hucking - - -	Kent - -	1556	Hunton - -	York - -	⁸ ----
Hucknall-Torkard -	Nottingham -	² 1559	Hunton - -	Hants - -	⁹ 1564
Huddersfield - -	York - -	1606	Huntsham -	Devon - -	1558
Huddington -	Worcester -	³ 1695	Huntshaw -	Devon - -	1746
Hudswell - -	York - -	1602	Huntspill - -	Somerset -	1654
Huggate - -	York - -	⁴ 1539	Hunworth -	Norfolk -	1653
Hugglescote - -	Leicester - -	1583	Hurley - -	Berks - -	1563
Hughenden - -	Buckingham -	1559	Hursley - -	Hants - -	1600
Hughley - -	Salop - -	⁵ 1576	Hurst - - -	Berks - -	1583
Hugill - - -	Westmorland -	1732	Hurstbourne-Priors -	Hants - -	¹⁰ 1604
Huish - - -	Wilts - -	1603	Hurstbourne-Tarrant -	Hants - -	¹¹ 1546
Huish - - -	Devon - -	1595	Hurstmonceaux -	Sussex -	1538
Huish-Champflower -	Somerset - -	1677	Hurst, Old - -	Huntingdon -	1653
Huish-Episcopi -	Somerset -	⁶ 1678	Hurstpierpoint -	Sussex - -	1558
Huish, North -	Devon - -	1655	Hurworth -	Durham - -	1559
Huish, South -	Devon - -	1576	Husborne-Crawley -	Bedford - -	1558
Hulcote - -	Buckingham -	1539	Husthwaite -	York - -	1674
Hull - -	York - -	1558	Huttoft - - -	Lincoln - -	1562
Hull, Bishop's - -	Somerset -	1562	Hutton - -	Essex - -	1654

¹ **P** 1543-1702. Yorkshire Parish Register Society, vol. 21, 1904; and vol. 24, 1905.
² **P** (Marriages only) 1560-1812. Nottinghamshire Parish Registers, vol. 9, 1906.
³ Bishop's Transcripts commence 1612.
⁴ **P** 1539-1812. Parish Register Society, vol. 36, 1901.
⁵ **P** 1576-1812. Shropshire Parish Register Society, vol. 1 (Hereford Diocese). Also **P** Parish Register Society, vol. 41, 1901.
⁶ **P** (Marriages only) 1698-1812. Somersetshire Parish Registers, vol. 1, 1898.
⁷ Included in the Registers of Harlaxton (q.v.).
⁸ Included in the Registers of Brompton Patrick (q.v.).
⁹ **P** (Marriages only) 1575-1812. Hampshire Parish Registers, vol. 9, 1907.
¹⁰ **P** (Marriages only) 1604-1812. Hampshire Parish Registers, vol. 1, 1899.
¹¹ **P** (Marriages only) 1546-1812. Hampshire Parish Registers. vol. 1, 1899.

Parish.	County.	Date of Earliest Entry.	Parish.	County.	Date of Earliest Entry.
Hutton - - -	Somerset - -	1715	Ightfield - -	Salop - -	1557
Hutton-Bonville -	York - -	1727	Ightham - -	Kent - -	1559
Hutton-Buscel - -	York - -	1572	Iken - - -	Suffolk - -	1669
Hutton-Cranswick -	York - -	1653	Ilam - - -	Stafford -	1656
Hutton-in-the-Forest -	Cumberland -	1729	Ilchester - -	Somerset -	1690
Hutton-Magna -	York - -	1670	Ilderton - -	Northumberland	1724
Hutton, New - -	Westmorland -	1741	Ilford, Little - -	Essex - -	1539
Hutton, Old - -	Westmorland -	1754	Ilfracombe - -	Devon - -	1567
Hutton-Roof - -	Westmorland -	¹ —	Ilkeston - -	Derby - -	1586
Hutton, Sand. *See*			Ilketshall St. Andrew -	Suffolk - -	1542
Sand Hutton.			St. John -	- - -	1538
Hutton, Sheriff *See*			St. Lawrence	- - -	1559
Sheriff Hutton.			St. Margaret	- - -	1538
Hutton's Ambo - -	York - -	1714	Ilkley - -	York - -	1597
Huxham - -	Devon - -	1667	Illington - -	Norfolk - -	1672
Huyton - - -	Lancaster -	1578	Illingworth - -	York - -	1695
Hykeham - -	Lincoln - -	1695	Illogan - - -	Cornwall -	1539
Hyssington - -	Montgomery -	1701	Ilmer - - -	Buckingham -	1660
Hythe - - -	Kent - -	1556	Ilmington - -	Warwick -	1588
Hythe, West - -	Kent - -	1730	Ilminster - -	Somerset -	1652
			Ilsington - -	Devon - -	1558
			Ilsley, East - -	Berks - -	1653
			Ilsley, West - -	Berks - -	1558
I.			Ilston - -	Glamorgan -	1729
			Ilston-on-the-Hill -	Leicester -	1654
Ibsley - -	Hants - -	1654	Ilton - - -	Somerset -	⁷ 1642
Ibstock - - -	Leicester -	1568	Imber - - -	Wilts - -	1709
Ibstone - - -	Oxford - -	1665	Immingham - -	Lincoln - -	1562
Ickenham - -	Middlesex -	1538	Impington - -	Cambridge -	1562
Ickford - -	Buckingham -	1561	Ince - - -	Chester -	1687
Ickham - - -	Kent - -	1557	Ingatestone - -	Essex - -	1558
Ickleford - -	Hertford -	1749	Ingestre - -	Stafford -	1691
Icklesham - -	Sussex - -	1669	Ingham - - -	Lincoln - -	1567
Ickleton - -	Cambridge -	1558	Ingham - - -	Norfolk - -	1801
Icklingham - -	Suffolk - -	1560	Ingham - - -	Suffolk - -	1538
Ickworth - -	Suffolk - -	² 1566	Ingleby-Arncliffe. *See*		
Icomb - - -	Gloucester -	³ 1545	Arncliffe Ingleby.		
Idbury - - -	Oxford - -	1754	Ingleby-Greenhow -	York - -	⁸ 1539
Iddesleigh - -	Devon - -	1540	Inglesham - -	Wilts - -	1589
Ide - - -	Devon - -	1653	Ingleton - - -	York - -	1607
Ideford - - -	Devon - -	1598	Ingoldisthorpe - -	Norfolk - -	1754
Iden - - -	Sussex - -	1559	Ingoldmells - -	Lincoln - -	1723
Idle - - -	York - -	⁴ —	Ingoldsby - - -	Lincoln - -	1566
Idlicote - -	Warwick -	⁵ 1556	Ingram - - -	Northumberland	⁹ 1682
Idmiston - -	Wilts - -	1577	Ingrave - - -	Essex - -	1560
Idsworth - -	Hants - -	⁶ —	Ingworth' - -	Norfolk - -	¹⁰ 1558
Iffley - - -	Oxford - -	1572	Inkberrow - -	Worcester -	¹¹ 1675
Ifield - - -	Kent - -	1751	Inkpen - - -	Berks - -	1633
Ifield - - -	Sussex - -	1568	Instow - - -	Devon - -	1717
Iford - - -	Sussex - -	1654	Intwood - -	Norfolk - -	1557
Igborough - -	Norfolk - -	1755	Inwardleigh - -	Devon - -	1699
			Inworth - -	Essex - -	1731

¹ Included in the Registers of Kirkby Lonsdale (*q.v.*).
² **P** 1566–1890. Rev. S. H. A. Hervey, Wells, 1894.
³ **P** (Marriages only) 1563–1812. Gloucestershire Parish Registers, vol. 13, 1908.
⁴ Included in the Registers of Calverley (*q.v.*).
⁵ **P** (Marriages only) 1557–1812. Warwickshire Parish Registers, vol. 1, 1904.
⁶ Included in the Registers of Charlton.
⁷ **P** (Marriages only) 1642–1811. Somersetshire Parish Registers, vol. 4, 1902.
⁸ **P** 1539–1800. Edited by J. Howell, 1889.
⁹ **P** 1682–1812. Durham and Northumberland Parish Register Society, vol. 7, 1903.
¹⁰ **P** (Marriages only) 1559–1812. Norfolk Parish Registers, vol. 1, 1899.
¹¹ Bishop's Transcripts commence 1613.

Parish.	County.	Date of Earliest Entry.	Parish.	County.	Date of Earliest Entry.
Iping - - -	Sussex - -	1664	Itchingfield - -	Sussex - -	1700
Ipplepen - -	Devon - -	1558	Itchington, Bishops -	Warwick - -	1559
Ippolyts, St. - -	Hertford - -	1710	Itchington, Long -	Warwick -	1653
Ipsden - - -	Oxford - -	1569	Itterringham - -	Norfolk - -	1560
Ipsley - - -	Warwick -	¹1615	Itton - - - -	Monmouth -	1773
Ipstone - - -	Bucks - -	1665	Ive, St. - - -	Cornwall- -	1651
Ipstones - - -	Stafford - -	1561	Ivegill - - -	Cumberland •	1709
Ipswich, St. Clement -	Suffolk - -	1563	Iver - - -	Buckingham -	1605
St. Helen - -	- - -	1677	Ives, St. - -	Cornwall -	1686
St. Lawrence -	- - -	1539	Ives, St. - -	Huntingdon -	1566
St. Margaret -	- - -	1538	Ivinghoe - - -	Buckingham -	⁷1559
St. Mary-at-Elms	- - -	1557	Ivychurch - -	Kent - -	⁸1564
St. Mary-at-the-Quay.	- - -	1559	Iwade - - -	Kent - -	1560
St. Mary-Stoke -	- - -	1565	Iwerne-Courtney -	Dorset - -	1562
St. Mary-le-Tower	- - -	1538	Iwerne-Minster - -	Dorset - -	⁹1742
St. Matthew -	- - -	1559	Ixworth - - -	Suffolk - -	1559
St. Nicholas -	- - -	²1539			
St. Peter - -	- - -	³1657			
St. Stephen -	- - -	1585			
Irby-in-the-Marsh -	Lincoln - -	1566	**J.**		
Irby-upon-Humber	Lincoln - -	⁴1558			
Irchester - - -	Northampton -	1622	Jackfield - - -	Salop - -	1759
Ireby - - -	Cumberland -	1705	Jacobstow - -	Cornwall -	1653
Ireleth - - -	Lancaster -	⁵—	Jacobstowe - -	Devon - -	1586
Irnham - - -	Lincoln - -	1559	Jarrow - - -	Durham - -	1572
Iron-Acton - -	Gloucester -	1570	Jeffreston - - -	Pembroke -	1723
Irstead - - -	Norfolk - -	1538	Jevington - -	Sussex - -	1661
Irthington - -	Cumberland -	1704	John's, St. - - -	Cornwall -	1616
Irthlingborough -	Northampton -	1562	John's, St., in the Vale	Cumberland -	1776
Irton - - -	Cumberland -	1697	Johnston - -	Pembroke -	1721
Isel - - - -	Cumberland -	1669	Juliot, St. - - -	Cornwall -	¹⁰1656
Isfield - - -	Sussex - -	1570	Just, St., in-Penwith -	Cornwall -	¹¹1599
Isham - - -	Northampton -	1701	Just, St., in-Roseland -	Cornwall -	1538
Ishmaels, St. - -	Carmarthen -	1571			
Ishmaels, St. - -	Pembroke -	1761			
Isle-Abbotts - -	Somerset - -	1558			
Isle-Brewers - -	Somerset -	⁶1705	**K.**		
Isleham - - -	Cambridge -	1566			
Isleworth - - -	Middlesex -	1566			
Isley Walton - -	Leicester - -	1710	Kea, St. - - -	Cornwall -	1701
Islington - - -	Middlesex -	1557	Keal, East - -	Lincoln -	¹²1708
Islington - - -	Norfolk - -	1588	Keal, West - -	Lincoln - -	1623
Islip - - - -	Northampton -	1695	Keddington - -	Lincoln -	1563
Islip - - - -	Oxford - -	1590	Kedington - -	Suffolk - -	1651
Issells, St. - -	Pembroke -	1753	Kedleston - -	Derby - -	1600
Issey, St. - - -	Cornwall -	1596	Keelby - - -	Lincoln -	1565
Itchen-Abbas - -	Hants - -	1586	Keele - - -	Stafford -	1540
Itchen-Stoke - -	Hants - -	1719	Keevil - - -	Wilts - -	1559
Itchenor, West - -	Sussex - -	1561	Kegidog (or St. George)	Denbigh -	¹³1694

¹ Bishop's Transcripts commence 1612.
² **P** 1539-1710. Parish Register Society, vol. 7, 1897.
³ **P** 1662-1700. Edited by F. A. Crisp, 1897.   ⁴ **P** 1558-1785. Edited by F. A. Crisp.
⁵ Included in the Registers of Dalton-in-Furness (q.v.).
⁶ **P** (Marriages only) 1705-1812. Somersetshire Parish Registers, vol. 4, 1902.
⁷ **P** (Marriages only) 1559-1812. Buckinghamshire Parish Registers, vol. 2, 1904.
⁸ The Registers of this parish before 1715 are preserved in the Diocesan Registry, Canterbury.
⁹ The earlier Registers were kept at Blandford and were burnt when that town was destroyed by fire in 1731.
¹⁰ **P** (Marriages only) 1656-1812. Cornwall Parish Registers, vol. 1, 1900.
¹¹ **P** (Marriages only) 1599-1812. Cornwall Parish Registers, vol. 3, 1903.
¹² Bishop's Transcripts commence 1562.
¹³ **P** 1694-1749. Edited by F. A. Crisp, 1890.

Parish.	County.	Date of Earliest Entry.	Parish.	County.	Date of Earliest Entry.
Kegworth - -	Leicester - -	1556	Kensington - -	Middlesex -	[7] 1539
Keighley - -	York - -	1562	Kensworth - -	Hertford - -	[8] 1615
Keinton-Mandeville -	Somerset - -	1731	Kentchurch - -	Hereford -	1686
Kelby - -	Lincoln -	[1] —	Kentford - -	Suffolk -	1709
Kelham - -	Nottingham -	1663	Kentisbeare - -	Devon - -	1695
Kellan - -	Cardigan -	1780	Kentisbury - -	Devon - -	1675
Kellaways - -	Wilts - -	1800	Kentmere - -	Westmorland -	1701
Kellet Over - -	Lancaster -	1653	Kenton - -	Devon - -	1694
Kelling - -	Norfolk -	1558	Kenton - -	Suffolk -	1538
Kellington - -	York -	1637	Kenwyn - - -	Cornwall -	1559
Kelloe - -	Durham - -	1693	Kerdiston - -	Norfolk -	[9] —
Kelly - - -	Devon - -	1653	Kerry - - -	Montgomery -	1619
Kelmarsh - -	Northampton -	1599	Kersey - -	Suffolk -	1542
Kelmscott - -	Oxford -	1601	Kerswell, King's -	Devon - -	1702
Kelsale - - -	Suffolk - -	[2] 1538	Kesgrave - -	Suffolk -	1658
Kelsey, North - -	Lincoln -	1621	Kessingland - -	Suffolk -	1561
Kelsey, South - -	Lincoln - -	1559	Keston - - -	Kent -	1541
Kelshall - -	Hertford -	1538	Keswick - -	Norfolk -	1538
Kelstern - -	Lincoln -	1651	Kettering - -	Northampton -	1637
Kelston - -	Somerset -	1538	Ketteringham -	Norfolk -	1558
Kelvedon - -	Essex - -	1558	Kettlebaston - -	Suffolk -	1578
Kelvedon-Hatch -	Essex - -	1561	Kettleburgh - -	Suffolk -	1561
Kemberton - -	Salop - -	1659	Kettlestone - -	Norfolk -	1540
Kemble - -	Gloucester -	1679	Kettlethorpe - -	Lincoln -	1653
Kemerton - -	Gloucester -	[3] 1572	Kettlewell - -	York - -	1698
Kemeys-Inferior -	Monmouth -	1701	Ketton - - -	Rutland -	1561
Kempley - -	Gloucester -	1677	Kevenllys (or Cefnllys)	Radnor -	1679
Kempsey - -	Worcester -	[4] 1688	Keverne, Saint - -	Cornwall -	1580
Kempsford - -	Gloucester -	[5] 1653	Kew - - -	Surrey -	1714
Kempston - -	Bedford - -	1570	Kew, Saint - -	Cornwall -	[10] 1564
Kempston - -	Norfolk -	1721	Kewstoke - -	Somerset -	1667
Kemsing - -	Kent - -	1561	Keyham - -	Leicester -	1563
Kenarth - -	Carmarthen -	1701	Keyingham - -	York - -	1618
Kenchester - -	Hereford - -	1757	Keymer - -	Sussex -	1601
Kencott - -	Oxford -	1584	Keyne, Saint - -	Cornwall -	1539
Kendal - -	Westmorland -	1558	Keynsham - -	Somerset -	1629
Kenderchurch -	Hereford -	1757	Keysoe - -	Bedford - -	1735
Kenelm, Saint -	Salop - -	1736	Keyston - -	Huntingdon -	1637
Kenilworth - -	Warwick -	1630	Keyworth - -	Nottingham -	[11] 1653
Kenley - - -	Salop - -	[6] 1682	Kibworth-Beauchamp	Leicester -	1574
Kenn - - -	Devon - -	1538	Kidderminster - -	Worcester -	[12] 1539
Kenn - - -	Somerset -	1540	Kiddington - -	Oxford -	1570
Kennardington -	Kent - -	1544	Kidlington - -	Oxford - -	[13] 1574
Kennerleigh - -	Devon - -	1645	Kidwelly - -	Carmarthen -	1586
Kennett - -	Cambridge -	1735	Kiffig (or Cyffic) -	Carmarthen -	1725
Kennett, East -	Wilts - -	1655	Kilburn - -	York - -	1600
Kenninghall - -	Norfolk -	1558	Kilby - - -	Leicester -	1653
Kennington - -	Kent - -	1671	Kildale - - -	York - -	[14] 1719

[1] Included in the Registers of Heydour or Haydor (q.v.).   [2] **P** 1538–1812. Edited by F. A. Crisp, 1887.
[3] **P** (Marriages only) 1575–1812. Gloucestershire Parish Registers, vol. 4, 1898.
[4] **P** (Marriages only) 1690–1812. Worcestershire Parish Registers, vol. 1, 1901. Bishop's Transcripts commence 1608.
[5] **P** 1653–1700. Edited by F. A. Crisp, 1887.
[6] **P** 1682–1812. Shropshire Parish Register Society, vol. 2, 1902. Lichfield Diocese.
[7] **P** 1539–1675. Harleian Society Registers, vol. 16, 1890.
[8] **P** (Marriages only) 1615–1812. Hertfordshire Parish Registers, vol. 1, 1907.
[9] Included in the Registers of Reepham (q.v.).
[10] **P** (Marriages only) 1564–1812. Cornwall Parish Registers, vol. 6, 1904.
[11] **P** (Marriages only) 1657–1812. Nottinghamshire Parish Registers, vol. 7, 1905.
[12] History of Kidderminster, by Rev. J. R. Burton, includes key to surnames 1539–1565; and extracts 1539–1660.
[13] **P** (Marriages only) 1574–1754. Oxfordshire Historical Society, vol. 24, 1893.
[14] Prior to this date included in the Registers of Ingleby-Greenhow (q.v.).

Parish.	County.	Date of Earliest Entry.	Parish.	County.	Date of Earliest Entry.
Kildwick - -	York -	1572	Kingsdon - -	Somerset -	[5] 1559
Kilgerran -	Pembroke -	1708	Kingsdown (Seven-	Kent -	1725
Kilham -	York -	1653	oaks).		
Kilken - -	Flint -	1576	Kingsdown (Sitting-	Kent -	1560
Kilkennin -	Cardigan -	1734	bourne).		
Kilkhampton -	Cornwall -	1539	Kingsey -	Bucks -	1538
Killamarsh -	Derby -	1638	Kingsland -	Hereford -	1538
Killingholme -	Lincoln -	1564	Kingsley -	Hants -	1568
Killington -	Westmorland -	1619	Kingsley -	Stafford -	1561
Kilmersdon -	Somerset -	1653	Kings-Lynn -	Norfolk -	1558
Kilmeston -	Hants -	1661	Kingsnorth -	Kent -	1538
Kilmington -	Devon -	[1] 1723	Kings Stanley. See		
Kilmington -	Somerset	1582	Stanley Kings.		
Kilnsea - -	York -	1711	Kingsthorpe -	Northampton -	1540
Kilnwick -	York -	1575	Kingston -	Cambridge -	1654
Kilnwick-Percy -	York -	1688	Kingston - -	Devon -	1630
Kilpeck -	Hereford -	1673	Kingston (Isle of	Hants -	1647
Kilrhedyn -	Carmarthen -	1733	Wight).		
Kilsby -	Northampton -	1754	Kingston - -	Kent -	[6] 1558
Kilton - -	Somerset -	1683	Kingston -	Sussex -	[7] 1570
Kilve - -	Somerset	1538	Kingston (near Taun-	Somerset -	1677
Kilverstone -	Norfolk -	1558	ton).		
Kilvington -	Nottingham -	[2] 1538	Kingston (near Ilmin-	Somerset -	1714
Kilvington, South	York -	1572	ster).		
Kilworth, North -	Leicester -	1553	Kingston-Bagpuize -	Berks -	1539
Kilworth, South -	Leicester -	1559	Kingston-by-Sea -	Sussex -	1591
Kilybebil -	Glamorgan -	1736	Kingston-Deverill -	Wilts -	[8] 1706
Kilymaenllwyd -	Carmarthen -	1740	Kingston-by-Lewes -	Sussex -	1654
Kimberley -	Norfolk -	1753	Kingston-Seymour -	Somerset -	1727
Kimble, Great -	Buckingham -	1701	Kingston-on-Hull -	York -	1564
Kimble, Little -	Buckingham -	1657	Holy Trinity -	- -	1558
Kimbolton -	Hereford -	1565	Kingston-on-Soar -	Nottingham -	[9] 1657
Kimbolton -	Huntingdon -	1647	Kingston-on-Thames -	Surrey -	1542
Kimcote -	Leicester -	1653	Kingstone - -	Stafford -	1571
Kimmeridge -	Dorset -	1700	Kingstone -	Hereford -	1659
Kimpton -	Hants -	1589	Kingswear -	Devon -	1601
Kimpton -	Hertford -	1559	Kingswinford -	Stafford -	1603
Kineton -	Warwick -	1538	Kingswood -	Gloucester -	[10] 1598
Kingerby -	Lincoln -	1765	Kington -	Wiltshire -	1563
Kingham -	Oxford -	1646	Kington -	Hereford -	1667
Kingsbridge -	Devon -	1612	Kington -	Worcester -	[11] 1587
King's-Bromley. See			Kington-Magna -	Dorset -	1670
Bromley, King's.			Kington, West -	Wilts -	1758
Kingsbury -	Middlesex -	1732	Kingweston -	Somerset -	1653
Kingsbury -	Warwick -	1537	Kinlet -	Salop -	1657
Kingsbury-Episcopi -	Somerset -	[3] 1557	Kinnerley -	Salop -	[12] 1677
King's-Caple -	Hereford -	1683	Kinnersley -	Hereford -	1626
Kingsclere -	Hants -	1538	Kinnersley -	Salop -	1691
King's-Cliffe -	Northampton -	1590	Kinoulton -	Nottingham -	[13] 1569
Kingscote -	Gloucester -	[4] 1651	Kinsham -	Hereford -	1594

[1] There is also an imperfect volume containing entries for 1577–1600.
[2] **P** (Marriages only) 1541–1812. Nottinghamshire Parish Registers, vol. 4, 1902.
[3] **P** (Marriages only) 1557–1812. Somersetshire Parish Registers, vol. 5, 1904.
[4] **P** (Marriages only) 1652–1812. Gloucestershire Parish Registers, vol. 8, 1902.
[5] **P** (Marriages only) 1540–1812. Somersetshire Parish Registers, vol. 1, 1898.
[6] **P** 1558–1837. Edited by Rev. C. H. Wilkie, 1893.
[7] Entered in the Registers of Ferring.
[8] **P** (Marriages only) 1706–1812. Wiltshire Parish Registers, vol. 1, 1905.
[9] **P** (Marriages only) 1755–1811. Nottinghamshire Parish Registers, vol. 5, 1903.
[10] **P** (Marriages only) 1598–1812. Gloucestershire Parish Registers, vol. 9, 1903.
[11] **P** (Marriages only) 1588–1836. Worcestershire Parish Registers, vol. 1, 1901.
[12] **P** 1677–1812. Shropshire Parish Register Society, vol. 3 (St. Asaph Diocese).
[13] **P** (Marriages only) 1569–1812. Nottinghamshire Parish Registers, vol. 2, 1899.

Parish.	County.	Date of Earliest Entry.	Parish.	County.	Date of Earliest Entry.
Kinson - - -	Dorset - -	[1] 1728	Kirkby Stephen - -	Westmorland -	1647
Kintbury - -	Berks - -	1558	Kirkby Thore - -	Westmorland -	1593
Kinver - -	Stafford -	1560	Kirkby Underwood -	Lincoln -	1569
Kinwarton - -	Warwick -	1556	Kirkby Wharfe - -	York - -	1583
Kippax - -	York - -	[2] 1539	Kirkdale - -	York - -	1579
Kirby-Bedon - -	Norfolk -	1558	Kirk-Ella - -	York - -	[6] 1558
Kirby-Bellars - -	Leicester -	1713	Kirkham - -	Lancaster -	1539
Kirby-Cane -	Norfolk - -	1538	Kirkharle. See Harle,		
Kirby-Grindalyth -	York - -	1722	Kirk.		
Kirby-Knowle	York - -	1556	Kirkhaugh - -	Northumberland	1686
Kirby-le-Soken -	Essex - -	1681	Kirkheaton - -	York - -	1653
Kirby-Misperton -	York - -	1789	Kirkheaton - -	Northumberland	[7] —
Kirby, Monks -	Warwick -	1678	Kirk-Ireton - -	Derby - -	[8] 1572
Kirby-Muxloe -	Leicester -	1639	Kirkland - -	Cumberland -	1620
Kirby-on-the-Moor	York - -	1607	Kirk-Leatham - -	York - -	1559
Kirby-Sigston -	York - -	1574	Kirk-Levington -	York - -	1734
Kirby-under-Dale -	York - -	1557	Kirkley - - -	Suffolk -	[9] 1751
Kirby, West -	Chester -	1692	Kirklington - -	Nottingham -	1578
Kirby-Wisk -	York - -	1615	Kirklington - -	York - -	1568
Kirdford - -	Sussex - -	1558	Kirklinton - -	Cumberland -	1650
Kirkandrews - on -	Cumberland -	1702	Kirk-Newton. See		
Eden.			Newton Kirk.		
Kirk - Andrews - on -	Cumberland -	1655	Kirkoswald - -	Cumberland -	[10] 1575
Esk.			Kirk-Sandall. See		
Kirkbampton - -	Cumberland -	1695	Sandall Kirk.		
Kirk-Bramwith -	York - -	1700	Kirk Smeaton. See		
Kirkbride - -	Cumberland -	1662	Smeaton Kirk.		
Kirkburn - -	York - -	1686	Kirkstead - -	Lincoln -	1739
Kirkburton - -	York - -	[3] 1540	Kirmington - -	Lincoln -	1698
Kirkby - - -	Lancaster -	1678	Kirmond-le-Mire -	Lincoln -	1751
Kirkby - - -	Lincoln -	1555	Kirstead - -	Norfolk -	1677
Kirkby, East -	Lincoln -	1583	Kirtling - -	Cambridge -	1585
Kirkby-Fleetham -	York - -	1591	Kirtlington - -	Oxford -	1558
Kirkby-Green -	Lincoln -	1722	Kirton - - -	Lincoln -	1562
Kirkby-in-Ashfield -	Nottingham -	[4] 1620	Kirton - - -	Suffolk -	1689
Kirkby-in-Cleveland -	York - -	1627	Kirton - - -	Nottingham -	1538
Kirkby-Ireleth -	Lancaster -	1607	Kirton-in-Lindsey -	Lincoln -	1585
Kirkby-la-Thorpe -	Lincoln -	1660	Kislingbury - -	Northampton -	1538
Kirkby-Lonsdale -	Westmorland -	1538	Kittisford - -	Somerset -	1694
Kirkby-Malham -	York - -	1597	Knaith - - -	Lincoln -	1576
Kirkby-Mallory -	Leicester -	1598	Knaptoft - - -	Leicester -	[11] —
Kirkby-Malzeard -	York - -	[5] 1653	Knapton - - -	Norfolk -	1687
Kirkby-Moorside -	York - -	1622	Knapton - - -	York - -	[12] 1760
Kirkby-on-Bain -	Lincoln -	1562	Knapwell - -	Cambridge -	[13] 1678
Kirkby Overblow -	York - -	1647	Knaresborough - -	York - -	1561
Kirkby Ravensworth -	York - -	1599	Knaresdale - -	Northumberland	[14] 1695
Kirkby, South -	York - -	1620	Knebworth - -	Hertford -	1606

[1] Earlier entries for this parish in the Registers of Canford (q.v.).
[2] P 1539-1812. Yorkshire Parish Register Society, vol. 10, 1901.
[3] P 1541-1711. Edited by F. A. Collins, 1887.
[4] P (Marriages only) 1620-1812. Nottinghamshire Parish Registers, vol. 11, 1907.
[5] This fine old eleventh century church was burnt down 9th February 1908, but the Registers were fortunately saved.
[6] P 1558-1841. Parish Register Society, vol. 11, 1897.
[7] Included in the Registers of Thockrington (q.v.).
[8] P (Marriages only) 1572-1812. Derbyshire Parish Registers, vol. 3, 1907.
[9] Earlier entries in the Registers of Pakefield.
[10] P 1577-1812. Edited by Rev. Canon Thornleigh, 1901.
[11] Included in the Registers of Mowsley (q.v.).
[12] Entries prior to this date are in the Registers of Wintringham (q.v.).
[13] P (Marriages only) 1695-1812. Cambridgeshire Parish Registers, vol. 1, 1907. (Supplemented by Bishop's Transcripts.)
[14] P "North Country Parish Registers," by Robert Blair.

Parish.	County.	Date of Earliest Entry.	Parish.	County.	Date of Earliest Entry.
Kneesall -	Nottingham -	1682	Lamberhurst - -	Kent - -	1563
Kneeton - - -	Nottingham -	[1] 1592	Lambeth - -	Surrey - -	1539
Knettishall - -	Suffolk - -	1772	Lambley - -	Northumberland	1742
Knighton - - -	Radnor - -	1600	Lambley - -	Nottingham' -	1560
Knighton - - -	Leicester -	1695	Lambourn - -	Berks - -	1560
Knighton-on-Teme -	Worcester -	1559	Lambourne - -	Essex - -	[5] 1582
Knighton, West -	Dorset - -	1693	Lambrook, East -	Somerset - -	[6] 1771
Knight's-Enham. See			Lambston - -	Pembroke -	1737
Enham Knight's.			Lamerton - -	Devon - -	1538
Knightwick - -	Worcester -	[2] 1539	Lamesley - -	Durham - -	1603
Knill - - -	Hereford - -	1585	Lammas - -	Norfolk - -	1538
Knipton - -	Leicester -	1562	Lamorran - -	Cornwall -	1573
Kniveton - - -	Derby - -	1591	Lampeter - Pont - -	Cardigan -	1695
Knockholt - -	Kent - -	1548	Stephen.		
Knockin - - -	Salop - -	1672	Lampeter-Velfrey -	Pembroke -	1755
Knoddishall - -	Suffolk - -	1566	Lamphey - -	Pembroke -	1755
Knook - - -	Wilts - -	1687	Lamplugh - -	Cumberland -	1581
Knossington - -	Leicester - -	1558	Lamport - -	Northampton -	1628
Knotting - - -	Bedford - -	1592	Lamyat - -	Somerset - -	1615
Knottingley - -	York - -	1724	Lancaster, St. Mary -	Lancaster -	1599
Knowle - - -	Somerset - -	[3] —	St. John -	- - -	1755
Knowle - - -	Warwick - -	1682	St. Ann -	- - -	1796
Knowle, Church-	Dorset - -	1547	Lanchester - -	Durham - -	1560
Knowlton - -	Kent - -	1550	Lancing - -	Sussex - -	1559
Knowstone - -	Devon - -	1538	Landbeach - -	Cambridge -	1538
Knoyle, East - -	Wilts - -	[4] 1538	Landcross - -	Devon - -	1608
Knutsford - - -	Chester - -	1581	Landewednack -	Cornwall -	1578
Kyloe - - -	Northumberland	1674	Landford - -	Wilts - -	1671
Kyme, South - -	Lincoln - -	1647	Landkey - -	Devon - -	1602
Kyre-Wyard (or Great	Worcester -	1694	Landrake - -	Cornwall -	1555
Kyre).			Landulph - -	Cornwall -	1540
			Landwade - -	Cambridge -	1700
			Laneast - - -	Cornwall -	[7] 1680
			Lane End - -	Stafford -	1764
L.			Laneham - -	Notts - -	1538
			Lanercost - -	Cumberland -	1684
			Langar - - -	Notts - -	[8] 1595
Laceby - - -	Lincoln - -	1538	Langdon, East -	Kent - -	1560
Lackford - -	Suffolk - -	1587	Langdon Hills -	Essex - -	1686
Lackington, White -	Somerset - -	1678	Langdon, West -	Kent - -	1590
Lacock - - -	Wilts - -	1559	Langenhoe - -	Essex - -	1660
Ladbroke - -	Warwick - -	1559	Langford - -	Bedford - -	1717
Ladock - - -	Cornwall -	1683	Langford - -	Oxford - -	1538
Laindon - - -	Essex - -	1653	Langford - -	Essex - -	1558
Laindon Hills. See			Langford - -	Norfolk - -	1770
Langdon Hills.			Langford - -	Notts - -	1692
Lakenham - -	Norfolk - -	1568	Langford Budville -	Somerset -	[9] 1538
Lakenheath - -	Suffolk - -	1712	Langford, Little -	Wilts - -	1699
Laleham - - -	Middlesex -	1538	Langford, Steeple-	Wilts - -	1674
Laleston - - -	Glamorgan -	1754	Langham - -	Essex - -	1638
Lamarsh - - -	Essex - -	1555	Langham - -	Rutland -	1559
			Langham - -	Suffolk -	1561
			Langham-Bishops -	Norfolk -	[10] 1695

[1] **P** (Marriages only) 1592-1812. Nottinghamshire Parish Registers, vol. 1, 1898.
[2] **P** 1538-1812. Edited by Rev. J. B. Wilson, London, 1891.
[3] Included in the Registers of Long Sutton (q.v.).
[4] **P** (Marriages only) 1538-1812. Wiltshire Parish Registers, vol. 3, 1906.
[5] **P** 1582-1709. Edited by F. A. Crisp, 1890.
[6] Baptisms only. Marriages and burials at the mother-church Kingsbury-Episcopi.
[7] **P** (Marriages only) 1680-1812. Cornwall Parish Registers, vol. 2, 1902.
[8] **P** (Marriages only) 1596-1812. Nottinghamshire Parish Registers, vol. 9, 1906.
[9] **P** (Marriages only) 1607-1812. Somersetshire Parish Registers, vol. 8, 1907.
[10] **P** (Marriages only) 1695-1812. Norfolk Parish Registers, vol. 3, 1907.

Parish.	County.	Date of Earliest Entry.	Parish.	County.	Date of Earliest Entry.
Langho (or Billington)	Lancaster	¹ 1733	Laughton - by - Gains-	Lincoln	1566
Langley	Essex	1678	borough.		
Langley	Kent	1664	Laughton	Sussex	1561
Langley	Norfolk	² 1695	Laughton-en-le-Morthen	York	1562
Langley-Abbots. See			Launcells	Cornwall	1642
Abbots-Langley.			Launceston	Cornwall	1559
Langley-Burrell	Wilts	1607	Launton	Oxford	1648
Langley, King's	Hertford	1558	Lavant, East	Sussex	1653
Langley, Kirk	Derby	1654	Lavant-Mid	Sussex	1567
Langley-Marish	Buckingham	1644	Lavendon	Buckingham	1574
Langpot	Somerset	³ 1728	Lavenham	Suffolk	1558
Langridge	Somerset	1756	Laver, High	Essex	1553
Langstone	Monmouth	1757	Laver, Little	Essex	1538
Langtoft	Lincoln	1668	Laver-Magdalen	Essex	1557
Langtoft	York	1587	Lavernock	Glamorgan	1733
Langton-by-Horncastle	Lincoln	1753	Laverstock	Wilts	1726
Langton-juxta-Partney	Lincoln	1558	Laverstoke	Hants	¹⁰ 1657
Langton-by-Wragby	Lincoln	1653	Laverton	Somerset	1678
Langton	York	1653	Lavington	Lincoln	1576
Langton, Church	Leicester	1559	Lavington, East	Wilts	1673
Langton-on-Swale	York	1695	Lavington, West	Wilts	1598
Langton-Herring	Dorset	1681	Lawford	Essex	1558
Langton-Long	Dorset	1591	Lawford, Church	Warwick	¹¹ 1575
Langton-Matravers	Dorset	1670	Lawhitton	Cornwall	1640
Langtree	Devon	1659	Lawrenny	Pembroke	1718
Languard Fort	Suffolk	⁴ 1761	Lawrence, St. Newland	Essex	1704
Langwathby	Cumberland	1695	Lawrence, St. (Isle of	Hants	1678
Langwith-Bassett	Derby	1685	Wight).		
Lanhydrock	Cornwall	⁵ 1559	Lawrence, St.	Pembroke	1760
Lanivet	Cornwall	⁶ 1608	Lawshall	Suffolk	1558
Lanlivery	Cornwall	⁷ 1600	Lawton, Church	Chester	1559
Lanreath	Cornwall	1555	Laxfield	Suffolk	1579
Lansalloes	Cornwall	1600	Laxton	Northampton	1689
Lanteglos-by-Fowey	Cornwall	1661	Laxton	Nottingham	1565
Lanteglos - by - Camel-	Cornwall	⁸ 1558	Laxton	York	1779
ford.			Layer-Breton	Essex	1755
Lapford	Devon	1567	Layer-de-la-Hay	Essex	1767
Lapley	Stafford	1538	Layer-Marney	Essex	1742
Lapworth	Warwick	⁹ 1561	Layham	Suffolk	1538
Larling	Norfolk	1678	Laysters	Hereford	1703
Lasham	Hants	1560	Layston	Hertford	1563
Lassington	Gloucester	1661	Lazonby	Cumberland	1538
Lastingham	York	1559	Lea	Gloucester	1706
Latchford	Lancaster	1777	Lea	Lincoln	1603
Latchingdon	Essex	1725	Lea	Wilts	1751
Lathbury	Buckingham	1690	Lea-Marston	Warwick	1570
Latimer	Buckingham	1756	Leadenham	Lincoln	1558
Latton	Essex	1567	Leafield	Oxford	1784
Latton	Wilts	1576	Leake	York	1570
Laugharne	Carmarthen	1639	Leake	Lincoln	1559
Laughton	Leicester	1754	Leake, East	Nottingham	¹² 1600

¹ For marriages see Blackburn.
² **P** (Marriages only) 1695-1812. Norfolk Parish Registers, vol. 1, 1899.
³ **P** (Marriages only) (1728-1812. Somersetshire Parish Registers, vol. 1, 1898.
⁴ Baptisms and burials only. For marriages see Felixstowe or Walton (Suffolk).
⁵ **P** (Marriages only) 1559-1812. Cornwall Parish Registers, vol. 4, 1903.
⁶ **P** (Marriages only) 1608-1812. Cornwall Parish Registers, vol. 2, 1902.
⁷ **P** (Marriages only) 1600-1812. Cornwall Parish Registers, vol. 10, 1906.
⁸ **P** (Marriages only) 1558-1812. Cornwall Parish Registers, vol. 1, 1900. [R. Hudson, 1904.
⁹ **P** Index to surnames in Registers 1561-1860, in "Memorials of a Warwickshire Parish," by
¹⁰ **P** (Marriages only) 1657-1812. Hampshire Parish Registers, vol. 9, 1907.
¹¹ Including Newnham-Regis.
¹² **P** (Marriages only) 1600-1812. Nottinghamshire Parish Registers, vol. 5, 1903.

Parish.	County.	Date of Earliest Entry.	Parish.	County.	Date of Earliest Entry.
Leake, West - -	Nottingham -	[1] 1580	Leigh - - -	Gloucester -	1569
Leamington, Hastings	Warwick -	1565	Leigh - - -	Kent -	1639
Leamington-Priors -	Warwick -	[2] 1702	Leigh - - -	Lancaster -	[11] 1560
Leasingham - -	Lincoln -	1695	Leigh - - -	Stafford -	1541
Leatherhead - -	Surrey -	1656	Leigh - - -	Surrey -	1579
Leathley - -	York -	1674	Leigh - - -	Worcester -	1538
Leaveland - -	Kent -	1553	Leigh, Abbots. See		
Leavington-Kirk. See			Abbots-Leigh.		
Kirk-Leavington.			Leigh-Delamere -	Wilts -	[12] 1626
Lechlade - -	Gloucester -	1686	Leigh, Little - -	Chester -	1782
Leck - - -	Lancaster -	[3] 1801	Leigh, North -	Devon -	1697
Leckford - -	Hants -	1757	Leigh, North -	Oxford -	1573
Leckhampstead	Buckingham -	1558	Leigh, South -	Oxford -	1612
Leckhampton -	Gloucester -	1682	Leigh, South -	Devon -	1718
Leckwith - -	Glamorgan -	1781	Leigh-on-Mendip -	Somerset -	1566
Leconfield - -	York -	1551	Leigh, West -	Devon -	1561
Ledbury - -	Hereford -	[4] 1538	Leighland -	Somerset -	[13] 1754
Ledsham - -	York -	[5] 1539	Leighs, Great -	Essex -	1556
Lee - - -	Buckingham -	1679	Leighs, Little -	Essex -	1679
Lee - - -	Kent -	[6] 1579	Leighton -	Salop -	1662
Lee - - -	Northumberland	1664	Leighton-Bromswold -	Hunts -	1653
Leebotwood -	Salop -	[7] 1547	Leighton-Buzzard -	Bedford -	1562
Lee Brockhurst	Salop -	1556	Leinthall, Earles -	Hereford -	1591
Leeds - -	Kent -	1557	Leinthall, Starkes -	Hereford -	1740
Leeds, St. Peter -	York -	[8] 1572	Leintwardine -	Hereford -	1547
St. John	- -	1725	Leire - -	Leicester -	1559
St. Paul	- -	1796	Leiston - -	Suffolk -	1538
Trinity Church	- -	1730	Lelant - -	Cornwall -	[14] 1679
Leek - -	Stafford -	1634	Lemington, Lower	Gloucester -	[15] 1685
Leek-Wootton. See			Lench, Church-	Worcester -	[16] 1696
Wootton, Leek.			Lench, Rous -	Worcester -	[17] 1538
Leeming - -	York -	[9] —	Lenham - -	Kent -	1558
Lees. See Hey.			Lenton - -	Nottingham -	[18] 1540
Legbourne - -	Lincoln -	1711	Leominster -	Hereford -	1559
Legsby - -	Lincoln -	1562	Leominster. See Ly-		
Leicester, All Saints -	Leicester -	1571	minster.		
St. Margaret	- -	1615	Leonard-Stanley. See		
St. Martin -	- -	1558	Stanley-Leonard.		
St. Nicholas	- -	1560	Leonard's, St. -	Sussex -	1636
St. Mary	- -	1600	Lesbury -	Northumberland	1689
Leigh - -	Dorset -	[10] —	Lesnewth -	Cornwall -	[19] 1563
Leigh - - -	Essex -	1684	Lessingham -	Norfolk -	1557

[1] **P** (Marriages only) 1617–1811. Nottinghamshire Parish Registers, vol. 5, 1903. " There is reason to believe that an earlier volume has been lost in recent years." See " Churches of Nottinghamshire," by J. T. Godfrey.

[2] **P** (Marriages only) 1704–1812. Warwickshire Parish Registers, vol. 1, 1904.

[3] Previously included in the Registers of Tunstall (*q.v.*).

[4] **P** 1556–1576. Parish Register Society, vol. 18, 1899.

[5] **P** 1539–1812. Yorkshire Parish Register Society, vol. 26, 1906.

[6] **P** 1579–1754. Edited by L. L. Duncan, 1888.

[7] **P** 1547–1812. Shropshire Parish Register Society, vol. 5 (Lichfield Diocese).

[8] **P** 1572–1722. 6 vols., Thoresby Society, 1889.

[9] Included in the Registers of Burneston (*q.v.*).   [10] Included in the Registers of Yetminster (*q.v.*).

[11] **P** 1559–1624. Edited by J. H. Hanning, 1882.

[12] **P** (Marriages only) 1735–1812. Wiltshire Parish Registers, vol. 1, 1905.

[13] Earlier entries are in the Registers of Old Cleeve.

[14] **P** (Marriages only) 1679–1812. Cornwall Parish Registers, vol. 9, 1906.

[15] **P** (Marriages only) 1701–1812. Gloucestershire Parish Registers, vol. 4, 1898.

[16] **P** (Marriages only) 1702–1812. Worcestershire Parish Registers, vol. 1, 1901.

[17] **P** (Marriages only) 1539–1811. Worcestershire Parish Registers, vol. 1, 1901.

[18] **P** (Marriages only) 1540–1812. Nottinghamshire Parish Registers, vol. 6, 1904. Also J. T. Godfrey, " History of Lenton."

[19] **P** (Marriages only) 1569–1812. Cornwall Parish Registers, vol. 1, 1900.

Parish.	County.	Date of Earliest Entry.	Parish.	County.	Date of Earliest Entry.
Letchworth - -	Hertford - -	[1] 1695	Lilbourne - -	Northampton -	1573
Letcombe-Bassett -	Berks - -	1564	Lilford - - -	Northampton -	1560
Letcombe-Regis -	Berks - -	1697	Lilleshall - -	Salop - -	1653
Letheringham -	Suffolk - -	[2] 1585	Lilley - - -	Hertford - -	1711
Letheringsett -	Norfolk - -	1653	Lillingstone-Dayrell -	Buckingham -	1584
Letterston - -	Pembroke -	[3] 1801	Lillingstone-Lovell -	Buckingham -	1558
Letton - - -	Hereford - -	1673	Lillington - - -	Dorset - -	1712
Letton - - -	Norfolk -	[4] —	Lillington - -	Warwick - -	1538
Levan, St. - -	Cornwall -	[5] 1694	Lilstock - - -	Somerset -	1654
Leven - - -	York - -	1628	Limber-Magna -	Lincoln - -	1561
Lever - - -	Lancaster -	1791	Limehouse - -	Middlesex -	1730
Leverington - -	Cambridge -	1558	Limington - -	Somerset -	[11] 1681
Leverton, North and South.	Lincoln -	1538	Limpenhoe - -	Norfolk -	1662
			Limpley-Stoke - -	Wilts - -	1707
Leverton, North -	Nottingham -	1669	Limpsfield - -	Surrey - -	1539
Leverton, South -	Nottingham -	1658	Linby - - -	Nottingham -	1692
Levington - -	Suffolk - -	1562	Linch - - -	Sussex - -	1701
Levisham - -	York - -	1700	Linchmere - -	Sussex - -	1566
Lew, North - -	Devon - -	1689	Lincoln, St. Benedict -	Lincoln - -	1645
Lewannick - -	Cornwall -	1660	St. Botolph - -	- - -	1561
Lewes, St. Michael -	Sussex - -	1589	St. John - -	- - -	1708
St. Peter and St. Mary -	- - -	1679	St. Margaret -	- - -	1538
			St. Mark - -	- - -	1681
St. John - -	- - -	1602	St. Martin - -	- - -	1548
All Saints -	- - -	1561	St. Mary, Wigford	- - -	1563
St. Thomas -	- - -	1606	St. Mary Magdalene.	- - -	1665
Lewisham - -	Kent - -	[6] —	St. Michael - -	- - -	1562
Lewknor - -	Oxford - -	1666	St. Nicholas -	- - -	1736
Lew Trenchard -	Devon - -	1706	St. Paul - -	- - -	1694
Lexden - - -	Essex - -	1560	St. Peter, at Arches.	- - -	1561
Lexham, East -	Norfolk - -	[7] 1538	St. Peter in Eastgate.	- - -	1662
Lexham, West -	Norfolk - -	1689	St. Peter, at Gowts	- - -	1538
Leybourne - -	Kent - -	1560	St. Swithin - -	- - -	1685
Leyland - -	Lancaster -	[8] 1653	Lindfield - - -	Sussex - -	1558
Leysdown - -	Kent - -	1701	Lindridge - - -	Worcester -	1648
Leyton - - -	Essex - -	1575	Lindsell - - -	Essex - -	1568
Lezant - - -	Cornwall -	[9] 1539	Lindsey - - -	Suffolk - -	1559
Leziat - - -	Norfolk - -	[10] —	Linford, Great -	Buckingham -	1654
Lichfield, St. Mary -	Stafford -	1566	Linford, Little -	Buckingham -	1757
St. Chad -	- - -	1635	Lingen - - -	Hereford -	1751
St. Michael -	- - -	1574	Lingfield - -	Surrey - -	1559
Cathedral Church	- - -	1660	Lingwood - -	Norfolk - -	1560
Liddington - -	Rutland -	1561	Linkenholt - -	Hants - -	[12] 1579
Liddington - -	Wilts - -	1692	Linkenhorne - -	Cornwall -	1616
Lidlington - -	Bedford - -	1705	Linley - - -	Salop - -	[13] —
Lifton - - -	Devon - -	1653			
Lightcliffe - -	York - -	1704			
Lighthorne - -	Warwick - -	1538			

[1] **P** (Marriages only) 1696–1805. Hertfordshire Parish Registers, vol. 1, 1907.
[2] **P** 1588–1812. Edited by P. C. Rushen, London, 1901.
[3] The old Registers were destroyed at the time of the French invasion.
[4] Included in the Registers of Cranworth (q.v.).
[5] **P** (Marriages only) 1694–1812. Cornwall Parish Registers, vol. 3, 1903.
[6] The greater part of the Registers were destroyed by fire in 1830. **P** 1558–1750. Edited by L. L. Duncan, 1891. (Compiled from various sources, including some fragments of the original Register.)
[7] **P** (Marriages only) 1541–1812. Norfolk Parish Registers, vol. 1, 1899.
[8] **P** 1653–1710. Record Society, Manchester, 1890, vol. 21.
[9] **P** (Marriages only) 1539–1812. Cornwall Parish Registers, vol. 11, 1907.
[10] Included in the Registers of Ashwicken (q.v.).
[11] **P** (Marriages only) 1695–1812. Somersetshire Parish Registers, vol. 2, 1899.
[12] **P** (Marriages only) 1579–1812. Hampshire Parish Registers, vol. 9, 1907.
[13] Included in the Registers of Broseley (q.v.).

Parish.	County.	Date of Earliest Entry.	Parish.	County.	Date of Earliest Entry.
Linslade, or Linchlade	Buckingham -	[1] 1690	Llanaelhaiarn	Carnarvon -	1749
Linstead-Magna	Suffolk - -	1655	Llanafan-fawr - -	Brecon -	1720
Linstead-Parva - -	Suffolk - -	1539	Llanafan-y-Trawsgoed	Cardigan -	1767
Linsted - -	Kent - -	1654	Llanallgo - - -	Anglesey -	1726
Linton - - -	Cambridge -	1559	Llananno - - -	Radnor - -	1754
Linton. *See* Lynton.			Llanarmon - -	Carnarvon -	1705
Linton - - -	Hereford -	1570	Llanarmon-yn-Jal -	Denbigh -	1683
Linton - - -	Kent - -	1560	Llanarmon - Dyfryn -	Denbigh - -	1625
Linton - - -	York - -	[2] 1562	Ceriog.		
Linwood - - -	Lincoln - -	1620	Llanarmon - Mynydd -	Denbigh -	1720
Lisfane - - -	Glamorgan -	1755	Mawr.		
Liskeard - - -	Cornwall -	1539	Llanarth - -	Cardigan -	1735
Liss - - - -	Hants - -	1590	Llanarth - -	Monmouth -	1598
Lisset - - -	York - - -	[3] 1661	Llanarthney - -	Carmarthen -	1720
Lissington - - -	Lincoln -	1562	Llanasa - - -	Flint - -	1629
Liston - - -	Essex - -	1599	Llanbabo - - -	Anglesey -	1740
Litcham - -	Norfolk - -	[4] 1550	Llanbadarn-Fawr -	Cardigan -	1678
Litchborough - -	Northampton -	1727	Llanbadarn-Fawr -	Radnor -	1696
Litchfield - -	Hants - -	[5] 1627	Llanbabarn-Odwyn -	Cardigan -	1777
Litlington - -	Cambridge -	1642	Llanbadarn - Tref -	Cardigan -	1724
Littleborough - -	Lancaster -	1758	Eglwys.		
Littleborough - -	Nottingham -	1539	Llanbadarn-y-Garreg -	Radnor -	1769
Littlebourne - -	Kent - -	[6] 1559	Llanbadock - -	Monmouth -	1710
Littlebury - - -	Essex - -	1544	Llanbadrig - -	Anglesey -	1732
Littleham, near Bide-	Devon - -	1538	Llanbeblig - -	Carmarthen -	1699
ford.			Llanbedr - - -	Brecon -	1675
Littleham, near Ex-	Devon -	1603	Llanbedr - -	Merioneth -	1627
mouth.			Llanbedr - Dyffryn -	Denbigh - -	1650
Littlehampton - -	Sussex - -	1573	Clwyd.		
Littleover - -	Derby - -	1683	Llanbedr-Goch -	Anglesey -	1801
Littleport - - -	Cambridge -	1753	Llanbedr-Painscastle -	Radnor - -	1726
Littleton - -	Middlesex -	1562	Llanbedr-y-Cenin -	Carnarvon -	1671
Littleton - - -	Hants - -	1736	Llanbedrog - -	Carnarvon -	1691
Littleton-Drew -	Wilts - -	1706	Llanberis - -	Carnarvon -	1726
Littleton, High -	Somerset - -	1658	Llanbeulan - -	Anglesey -	1754
Littleton, North and	Worcester -	[7] 1661	Llanbister - -	Radnor -	1682
Middle.			Llanblethian - -	Glamorgan -	1661
Littleton, South -	Worcester -	1538	Llanboidy - -	Carmarthen -	1752
Littleton-on-Severn -	Gloucester -	1701	Llanbrynmair -	Montgomery -	1663
Litlington - -	Sussex -	1695	Llancadwalladr -	Denbigh - -	1736
Litton - -	Somerset -	1584	Llancarfan - -	Glamorgan -	1619
Litton-Cheney - -	Dorset - -	1614	Llancillo - -	Hereford -	1728
Livermere - -	Suffolk - -	1538	Llancynfelin - -	Cardigan -	1754
Liverpool - - -	Lancaster -	[8] 1659	Llandaff - - -	Glamorgan -	1724
St. George - -	- - -	1734	Llandanwg - -	Merioneth -	1695
St. Thomas - -	- - -	1750	Llandawke - -	Carmarthen -	1771
St. Anne - -	- - -	1773	Llanddaniel-Fab -	Anglesey - -	1746
St. John - -	- - -	1767	Llanddarog - -	Carmarthen -	1732
Trinity - - -	- - -	1792	Llanddeiniol - -	Cardigan -	1754
St. Stephen - -	- - -	1792	Llanddeiniolen -	Carnarvon -	1575
St. Matthew - -	- - -	1798	Llandderfel - -	Merioneth -	1598
Christ Church -	- - -	1797	Llanddeusaint -	Carmarthen -	1784
All Saints - -	- - -	1796	Llanddew - -	Brecon - -	1709
Liverton - -	York -	1665	Llanddewi-in-Gower -	Glamorgan -	1718
Llanaber - - -	Merioneth -	1750	Llanddewi-Aberarth -	Cardigan -	1737

[1] **P** (Marriages only) 1575–1812. Buckinghamshire Parish Registers, vol. 3, 1907.
[2] **P** 1562–1812. Yorkshire Parish Register Society, vol. 5, 1900, and vol. 18, 1903.
[3] Earlier entries in Registers of Beeford (*q.v.*).
[4] **P** (Marriages only) 1555–1812. Norfolk Parish Registers, vol. 2, 1900.
[5] **P** (Marriages only) 1627–1812. Hampshire Parish Registers, vol. 8, 1906.
[6] Original Register Burials, 1678–1688. British Museum, Additional MS. 23748.
[7] Bishop's Transcripts commence 1611. *See also* Lansdowne MS. 1233.
[8] **P** 1660–1673. Edited by Henry Peet, 1873.

Parish.	County.	Date of Earliest Entry.	Parish.	County.	Date of Earliest Entry.
Llanddewi-Abergwes- sin.	Brecon - -	1738	Llandysilio-Gogo -	Cardigan -	1765
			Llandyssil - -	Cardigan -	1722
Llanddewi-Brefi -	Cardigan	1765	Llandyssil - -	Montgomery -	1699
Llanddewi-'r-Cwm -	Brecon - -	1755	Llanedarn - -	Glamorgan -	1700
Llanddewy-fach -	Radnor -	1754	Llanedwen -	Anglesey -	1747
Llanddewy-Velfrey -	Pembroke -	1727	Llanedy - -	Carmarthen -	1703
Llanddoget - -	Denbigh - -	1640	Llanefydd - -	Denbigh - -	1721
Llanddona - -	Anglesey -	1754	Llanegryn - -	Merioneth -	1754
Llanddulas - -	Denbigh - -	1754	Llanegwad - -	Carmarthen -	1701
Llanddwywe - -	Merioneth -	1674	Llaneilian - -	Anglesey -	1780
Llanddyfnan - -	Anglesey -	1768	Llanelian - -	Denbigh - -	1620
Llandebie - -	Carmarthen -	1695	Llanelidan - -	Denbigh -	1686
Llandecwyn - -	Merioneth -	1669	Llanelieu - -	Brecon - -	1746
Llandefaelog-fach -	Brecon -	1715	Llanellen - - -	Monmouth -	1756
Llandefalley - -	Brecon - -	1706	Llanelltyd - -	Merioneth -	1730
Llandefeilog - -	Carmarthen -	1695	Llanelly - -	Brecon - -	1701
Llandefeisant - -	Carmarthen -	1755	Llanelly - -	Carmarthen -	[1] 1684
Llandegai - - -	Carnarvon -	1674	Llanelwedd - -	Radnor - -	1773
Llandegfan - -	Anglesey -	1733	Llanenddwyn - -	Merioneth -	1694
Llandegla - - -	Denbigh - -	1710	Llanengan - -	Carnarvon -	1679
Llandeglay - -	Radnor - -	1727	Llanerch-Ayron -	Cardigan -	1730
Llandegveth - -	Monmouth -	1746	Llanerchymedd - -	Anglesey -	1740
Llandegwining - -	Carnarvon -	1779	Llanerfyl S. - -	Montgomery -	1623
Llandeloy - -	Pembroke -	1754	Llaneugrad - -	Anglesey -	1752
Llandenny - -	Monmouth -	1714	Llanfabon - -	Glamorgan -	1694
Llandewy-Ystradenny	Radnor - -	1732	Llanfachraeth - -	Anglesey -	1790
Llandilo-Abercowyn -	Carmarthen -	1695	Llanfachreth - -	Merioneth -	1636
Llandilo-Fawr - -	Carmarthen -	1721	Llanfaelog - -	Anglesey -	1689
Llandilo-Graban -	Radnor - -	1696	Llanfaelrhys - -	Carnarvon -	[4] —
Llandilo-Talybont -	Glamorgan -	1662	Llanfaes - - -	Anglesey -	1727
Llandilo-'r-Faen -	Brecon - -	1770	Llanfaethlu - -	Anglesey -	1743
Llandinabo - -	Hereford - -	[1] 1596	Llanfaglan S. Baglan	Carnarvon -	1695
Llandinam - -	Montgomery -	1594	Llanfair-ar-y-Bryn -	Carmarthen -	1735
Llandingat - -	Carmarthen -	1733	Llanfair-Caereinion -	Montgomery -	1602
Llandissilio - -	Carmarthen -	1720	Llanfair-Clydogan -	Cardigan -	1748
Llandogo - - -	Monmouth -	1694	Llanfair - Dyffryn -	Denbigh - -	1691
Llandough (near Cow- bridge).	Glamorgan -	1585	Clwyd.		
			Llanfair-Fechan -	Carnarvon -	1745
Llandough (near Car- diff).	Glamorgan -	1755	Llanfair-is-Gaer -	Carnarvon -	1675
			Llanfair-juxta-Harlech	Merioneth -	1695
Llandow - -	Glamorgan -	1688	Llanfair - Mathafarn -	Anglesey -	1801
Llandowror - -	Carmarthen -	1727	Eithaf.		
Llandrillo - -	Merioneth -	1686	Llanfair-Nantgwyn -	Pembroke -	1776
Llandrillo-yn-Rhos -	Denbigh - -	1693	Llanfair-Nant-y-Gôf -	Pembroke -	1801
Llandrindod - -	Radnor - -	1734	Llanfair-Orllwyn -	Cardigan -	1768
Llandrinio - -	Montgomery -	1662	Llanfair-yn-Eubwll -	Anglesey -	1768
Llandrygarn - -	Anglesey -	1739	Llanfair - Pwll -	Anglesey -	1757
Llandudno - -	Carnarvon -	1754	Gwyngyll.		
Llandulas - in - Tyr - Abbot.	Brecon - -	1729	Llanfair-Talhaiarn -	Denbigh - -	1668
			Llanfair-Ynghornwy -	Anglesey -	1732
Llanwrog - -	Carnarvon -	1590	Llanfair - yny - Cwm- mwd.	Anglesey -	[5] 1768
Llandyfodwg - -	Glamorgan -	1748			
Llandyfriog - -	Cardigan -	1725	Llanfallteg - -	Carmarthen -	1711
Llandyfrydog - -	Anglesey -	1600	Llanfawr - -	Merioneth -	1722
Llandygwydd - -	Cardigan -	1677	Llanfechan - -	Montgomery -	1603
Llandyrnog - -	Denbigh - -	1664	Llanfechell - -	Anglesey -	1691
Llandysilio - -	Anglesey -	[2] 1803	Llanferres - - -	Denbigh - -	1586
Llandysilio - -	Montgomery -	1662	Llanffinan - -	Anglesey -	1678

[1] **P** 1596-1812. Edited by J. H. Parry, 1900.
[2] Earlier entries at Llanfairpwllgwyngyll (q.v.).
[3] **P** (Marriages only) 1687-1837. See " A History of Llanelly Church," by A. Mee, 1888.
[4] Included in the Registers of Aberdaron (q.v.).
[5] Included with Registers of Llanidan (q.v.).

Parish.	County.	Date of Earliest Entry.	Parish.	County.	Date of Earliest Entry.
Llanfihangel - Aber - bythych.	Carmarthen -	1675	Llangar - -	Merioneth -	1614
Llanfihangel - Aber - cowin.	Carmarthen -	1754	Llangarren - -	Hereford - -	1569
			Llangasty-tal-y-llyn -	Brecon - -	1718
Llanfihangel - Aber - gwessin.	Brecon - -	1730	Llangathen - -	Carmarthen -	1747
			Llangattoc - nigh - Usk.	Monmouth -	1695
Llanfihangel-ar-Arth -	Carmarthen -	1756	Llangattock - -	Brecon - -	1703
Llanfihangel - Bâchel- laeth.	Carnarvon -	1692	Llangattock - -	Monmouth -	1597
			Llangattock-Lingoed	Monmouth -	1696
Llanfihangel - Bryn - Pabuan.	Brecon - -	1722	Llangattock - Vibon - Avel.	Monmouth -	1683
Llanfihangel-Cilfargen	Carmarthen -	1746	Llangedwyn - -	Denbigh - -	1672
Llanfihangel-Cwmdu	Brecon - -	1734	Llangefni - -	Anglesey -	1712
Llanfihangel-Geneu-'r-Glyn.	Cardigan -	1735	Llangeinor - -	Glamorgan -	1740
			Llangeinwen - -	Anglesey -	1688
Llanfihangel - Glyn-y-Myfyr.	Merioneth -	1662	Llangeitho - -	Cardigan -	1770
			Llangeler - -	Carmarthen -	1704
Llanfihangel-Helygen	Radnor - -	1732	Llangelynin - -	Carnarvon -	1733
Llanfihangel-Lledrod -	Cardigan -	1765	Llangelynin - -	Merioneth -	1618
Llanfihangel - Nant - Brân.	Brecon - -	1758	Llangendeirne - -	Carmarthen -	1735
			Llangennech - -	Carmarthen -	1741
Llanfihangel-Penbedw	Pembroke -	1680	Llangennith - -	Glamorgan -	1726
Llanfihangel - Rhôsy-corn.	Carmarthen -	1754	Llangenny - -	Brecon - -	1740
			Llangernieu - -	Denbigh -	1570
Llanfihangel - Rhydi-thon.	Radnor - -	1732	Llangeview - -	Monmouth -	1709
			Llangian - -	Carnarvon -	1693
Llanfihangel - Tal - y - Llyn.	Brecon - -	1700	Llangibby - -	Monmouth -	1678
			Llanginning - -	Carmarthen -	1736
Llanfihangel - Tyn - Sylwy.	Anglesey -	1754	Llanglydwen - -	Carmarthen -	1700
			Llangoed - -	Anglesey -	1763
Llanfihangel - Tre - 'r - Beirdd.	Anglesey -	1694	Llangoedmore -	Cardigan -	1725
			Llangollen - -	Denbigh -	1597
Llanfihangel-y-Creud-dyn.	Cardigan -	1781	Llangolman - -	Pembroke -	1755
			Llangorse - -	Brecon -	1688
Llanfihangel - yn - Gwynfa.	Montgomery -	1663	Llangoven - -	Monmouth -	1749
			Llangower - -	Merioneth -	1606
Llanfihangel - yn - Howyn.	Anglesey -	1788	Llangranog - -	Cardigan -	1730
			Llangristiolus -	Anglesey -	1721
Llanfihangel - y - Pen-nant.	Carnarvon -	1698	Llangua - -	Monmouth -	1714
			Llanguicke - -	Glamorgan -	1704
Llanfihangel - y - Pen-nant.	Merioneth -	1776	Llangunider - -	Brecon -	1736
			Llangunllo - -	Cardigan -	1754
Llanfihangel-Ysifeiog	Anglesey -	1703	Llangunllo - -	Radnor -	1744
Llanfihangel-Ystrad -	Cardigan -	1712	Llangunnock or Llan-gynog.	Carmarthen -	1775
Llanfihangel - y - Trae-than.	Merioneth -	1692			
			Llangunnor - -	Carmarthen -	1678
Llanfoist - - -	Monmouth -	1736	Llangurig - -	Montgomery -	1701
Llanfrechfa - -	Monmouth -	1727	Llangwm - -	Denbigh -	1738
Llanfrothen - -	Merioneth -	1693	Llangwm - -	Monmouth -	1663
Llanfwrog - -	Anglesey -	1743	Llangwm - -	Pembroke -	1716
Llanfwrog - -	Denbigh -	1638	Llangwyfan - -	Anglesey -	1754
Llanfyllin - -	Montgomery -	1664	Llangwyfan - -	Denbigh -	1723
Llanfynydd - -	Carmarthen -	1692	Llangwyllog - -	Anglesey -	1758
Llanfyrnach - -	Pembroke -	1754	Llangwnadl - -	Carnarvon -	1802
Llangadfan - -	Montgomery -	1630	Llangwstenin - -	Carnarvon -	1608
Llangadock-Fawr -	Carmarthen -	1750	Llangwyryfon - -	Cardigan -	1729
Llangadwaladr -	Anglesey -	1610	Llangybi - -	Cardigan -	1748
Llangaffo - -	Anglesey -	1659	Llangybi - -	Carnarvon -	1695
Llangain - - -	Carmarthen -	1772	Llangyfelach - -	Glamorgan -	1694
Llangammarch -	Brecon -	1763	Llangynfelyn - -	Cardigan -	1754
Llangan - -	Glamorgan -	1688	Llangynhafal - -	Denbigh -	1704
Llanganten - -	Brecon - -	1738	Llangyniew - -	Montgomery -	1583

Parish.	County.	Date of Earliest Entry.	Parish.	County.	Date of Earliest Entry.
Llangynog - -	Brecon - -	1755	Llansantffraid -	Cardigan -	1754
Llangynog -	Montgomery -	1720	Llansantffraid - Glan -	Denbigh - -	1660
Llangynwyd - -	Glamorgan -	1662	Conway.		
Llanhamllech - -	Brecon - -	1717	Llansantffraid - Glyn -	Denbigh	1754
Llanharan -	Glamorgan -	1615	Ceiriog.		
Llanharry -	Glamorgan -	1750	Llansantffraid - Glyn -	Monmouth -	1770
Llanhennock - -	Monmouth -	1695	Dyfrdwy.		
Llanhilleth -	Monmouth -	1733	Llansantffraid - yn -	Montgomery -	1582
Llanhowell - -	Pembroke -	1754	Mechan.		
Llanidan - -	Anglesey - -	1666	Llansantffread - in -	Radnor - -	1767
Llanidloes -	Montgomery -	1618	Elvel.		
Llaniestyn -	Anglesey - -	1755	Llansantffread -	Brecon - -	1718
Llaniestyn -	Carnarvon -	1754	Llansawell - -	Carmarthen -	1751
Llanigon -	Brecon - -	1712	Llansilin -	Denbigh - -	1706
Llanilar -	Cardigan -	1744	Llansoy - -	Monmouth -	1592
Llanilid - -	Glamorgan -	1714	Llanspythid -	Brecon - -	1699
Llanilterne -	Glamorgan -	1726	Llanstadwell -	Pembroke -	1714
Llaniltid -	Brecon - -	1776	Llanstephan -	Carmarthen -	1699
Llanina - -	Cardigan -	1780	Llanstephan -	Radnor - -	1666
Llanishen - -	Glamorgan -	1752	Llanstinan -	Pembroke -	1789
Llanishen -	Monmouth -	1591	Llanthetty -	Brecon - -	1693
Llanllawdog -	Carmarthen -	1719	Llanthewy-Rytherch -	Monmouth -	1733
Llanllechid -	Carnarvon -	1690	Llanthewy-Skirrid -	Monmouth -	1754
Llanlleonvel -	Brecon - -	1755	Llanthewy-Vach -	Monmouth -	1741
Llanllowell -	Monmouth -	1664	Llanthony-Abbey -	Monmouth -	1767
Llanllugan -	Montgomery -	1688	Llantillio-Crossenny -	Monmouth -	1719
Llanllwchaiarn -	Cardigan -	1720	Llantillio-Pertholey -	Monmouth -	1591
Llanllwchaiarn -	Montgomery -	1658	Llantrisaint -	Anglesey - -	1745
Llanllwni -	Carmarthen -	1739	Llantrisant -	Glamorgan -	1728
Llanllyfni -	Carnarvon -	1688	Llantrissent -	Monmouth -	1743
Llanmadock - -	Glamorgan -	1723	Llantrithyd -	Glamorgan -	1571
Llanmaes -	Glamorgan -	1583	Llantwit - juxta -	Glamorgan -	1695
Llanmartin -	Monmouth -	1755	Neath.		
Llanmerewig -	Montgomery -	1670	Llantwit Major -	Glamorgan -	1721
Llanmihangel -	Glamorgan -	1755	Llantwit-Vairdre -	Glamorgan -	1626
Llannon - -	Carmarthen -	1679	Llantysilio -	Denbigh - -	1677
Llannor -	Carnarvon -	1754	Llanuwchyllyn -	Monmouth -	1697
Llanover -	Monmouth -	1661	Llanvaches -	Monmouth -	1754
Llanpumpsaint -	Carmarthen -	1754	Llanvaes -	Brecon -	1730
Llanreithan -	Pembroke -	1786	Llanvair-Discoed -	Monmouth -	1680
Llanrhaiadr - in - Kin-	Denbigh -	1683	Llanvair-Kilgedin -	Monmouth -	1733
merch.			Llanvair-Waterdine -	Salop -	1606
Llanrhiadr - yn -Moch-	Denbigh	1679	Llanvapley -	Monmouth -	1699
nant.			Llanvareth -	Radnor -	1698
Llanrhian -	Pembroke -	1686	Llanveigan -	Brecon -	1747
Llanrhidian -	Glamorgan -	1730	Llanvetherine -	Monmouth -	1693
Llanrhydd -	Denbigh - -	1608	Llanveyno -	Hereford -	1714
Llanrhwydrys -	Anglesey -	1737	Llanvihangel - near -	Monmouth -	1753
Llanrhyddlad -	Anglesey -	1737	Roggiett.		
Llanrothal -	Hereford -	1740	Llanvihangel - Crucor-	Monmouth -	1629
Llanrûg -	Carnarvon -	1694	ney.		
Llanrwst -	Cardigan -	1613	Llanvihangel-Gobion	Monmouth -	1751
Llansadurnen -	Carmarthen -	1663	Llanvihangel-Llantar-	Monmouth -	1727
Llansadwrn -	Anglesey -	1584	nam.		
Llansadwrn -	Carmarthen -	1741	Llanvihangel - Nant -	Radnor -	1700
Llansaint -	Carmarthen -	1 —	Melan.		
Llansamlet -	Glamorgan -	1704	Llanvihangel-Pont-y-	Monmouth -	1742
Llansannan -	Denbigh - -	1666	Moile.		
Llansannor -	Glamorgan -	1750	Llanvihangel-Tor-y-	Monmouth -	1592
Llansantffraid -	Monmouth -	1753	Mynydd.		

1 Included in the Registers of St. Ishmaels (q.v.).
2 P 1666-1812. Edited by Rev. R. Ellis, 1904.
3 P 1571-1810. Edited by H. S. Hughes, London, 1888.

Parish.	County.	Date of Earliest Entry.	Parish.	County.	Date of Earliest Entry.
Llanvihangel - ystern - Llewern.	Monmouth -	1685	Lockerley - - -	Hants - -	1583
Llanvillo - - -	Brecon - -	1680	Locking - -	Somerset -	1750
Llanvrynach - -	Brecon - -	1695	Lockinge, East - -	Berks - -	1546
Llanwarne - -	Hereford -	1675	Lockington - -	Leicester -	1557
Llanwddyn - -	Montgomery -	1624	Lockington - -	York - -	1565
Llanwenarth-Citra -	Monmouth -	1725	Lockton - - -	York - -	1713
Llanwenllwyfo - -	Anglesey - -	1762	Loddington - -	Leicester -	1554
Llanwenog - -	Cardigan -	1722	Loddington - -	Northampton -	1622
Llanwern - - -	Monmouth -	1750	Loddiswell - -	Devon - -	1559
Llanwinio - -	Carmarthen -	1729	Loddon - - -	Norfolk -	1556
Llanwnda - - -	Carnarvon -	1600	Loders - - -	Dorset -	1636
Llanwnda - - -	Pembroke -	¹ 1697	Lodsworth - -	Sussex - -	1563
Llanwnen - -	Cardigan -	1763	Lofthouse - - -	York - -	1697
Llanwnog - - -	Montgomery -	1668	Lolworth - - -	Cambridge *	1565
Llanwnws. See Gwn-nws.			Londesborough -	York - -	1653
Llanwonno - -	Glamorgan -	1717	London :—		
Llanwrda - -	Carmarthen -	1684	Alban, St., Wood Street.	- - -	1566
Llanwrin - - -	Montgomery -	1676	Allhallows, Bark-ing.	- - -	1558
Llanwrthwl - -	Brecon - -	1713	Allhallows, Bread Street.	- - -	1539
Llanwrtyd - -	Brecon - -	1748	Allhallows the Great and Less.	- - -	1654
Llanwyddelan -	Montgomery -	1661	Allhallows, Honey Lane.	- - -	1538
Llanyblodwell - -	Salop - -	1695	Allhallows, Lom-bard Street.	- - -	1550
Llanybyther - -	Carmarthen -	1754	Allhallows, Lon-don Wall.	- - -	³ 1559
Llanychaer - -	Pembroke -	1785	Allhallows, Stain-ing.	- - -	1642
Llanychaeron See Llanerch-Ayron.			Alphage, St., Lon-don Wall.	- - -	1613
Llanychaiarn - -	Cardigan -	1754	Andrew, St., Hol-born.	- - -	1558
Llanychan - -	Denbigh - -	1696	Andrew, St., Hub-bard.	- - -	1791
Llanychlwydog - -	Pembroke -	1770	Andrew, St., Un-dershaft.	- - -	1558
Llanycil - -	Merioneth -	1616	Andrew, St., by the Wardrobe.	- - -	1558
Llanycrwys - -	Carmarthen -	1720	Anne, St., Black-friars.	- - -	1560
Llanymawddwy -	Merioneth -	1685	Anne and Agnes, SS.	- - -	1640
Llanymynoch - -	Salop - -	1668	Anne, St., Soho -	- - -	1686
Llanynghendl. See Llanfachraeth.			Antholin, St. -	- - -	⁴ 1538
Llanynys - - -	Brecon - -	1731	Augustine, St. -	- - -	1559
Llanynys - -	Denbigh - -	1626	Bartholomew, St., by Exchange.	- - -	1558
Llanyre - - -	Radnor - -	1735	Bartholomew, St., the Great.	- - -	1616
Llanystumdwy -	Carnarvon -	1708			
Llanywern - -	Brecon - -	1653	Bartholomew, St., the Less.	- - -	1547
Llawhaden - -	Pembroke -	1654			
Llechcynfarwy -	Anglesey - -	1745			
Llechrhyd - -	Cardigan -	1787			
Llechylched - -	Anglesey - -	1798			
Lledrod. See Llanfi-hangel-Lledrod.					
Llowes - - -	Radnor - -	1661			
Llysfaen - - -	Carnarvon -	1661			
Llyswen - -	Brecon - -	1787			
Llyswarney - -	Glamorgan -	1754			
Llys-y-fran - -	Pembroke -	1728			
Llywel - - -	Brecon - -	1695			
Load, Long - -	Somerset -	² 1711			

¹ The early Registers were destroyed at the time of the French invasion, 1797.
² These Registers contain baptisms and burials only. Marriages and previous entries for this Chapel were recorded in Martock Registers (q.v.). **P** (Marriages only) 1749–1808. Somersetshire Parish Registers, vol 3, 1901.
³ **P** 1559–1675. Edited by R. Hovenden and E. B. Jupp, London, 1878.
⁴ St. Antholin and St. John Baptist, Walbrook. **P** 1538–1754. Harleian Society Registers, vol. 8, 1883.

Parish.	County.	Date of Earliest Entry.	Parish.	County.	Date of Earliest Entry.
London—*continued.*			London—*continued.*		
Benet, St., Finck -	- - -	1538	Edmund, St., the King.	- - -	[8] 1670
Benet, St., Grace-church Street.	- - -	1558	Ethelburga -	- - -	1671
Benet, St., Paul's Wharf.	- - -	1619	Faith, St. -	- - -	1559
Benet, St., Shere-hog.	- - -	[1] —	Gabriel, St., Fen-church Street.	- - -	1571
Bethnal Green. *See* St. Matthew.			George, St., Bloomsbury.	- - -	1730
Botolph, St., Al-dersgate.	- - -	1638	George, St., the Martyr, Bloomsbury.	- - -	1707
Botolph, St., Aldgate.	- - -	1558	George, St., Botolph Lane.	- - -	[9] 1547
Botolph, St., Billingsgate.	- - -	1685	George, St., Hanover Square.	- - -	[10] 1725
Botolph, St., Bishopsgate.	- - -	[2] 1558	George, St., in the East.	- - -	1729
Bride, St. -	- - -	1653	Giles, St., Cripplegate.	- - -	1561
Bridewell Hospital and Precinct.	- - -	1666	Giles, St., in the Fields.	- - -	1561
Catherine, St. Coleman.	- - -	1559	Gray's Inn Chapel	- - -	[11] 1695
Charterhouse Chapel.	- - -	[3] 1671	Gregory, St., by St. Paul.	- - -	1559
Christchurch, Newgate Street.	- - -	[4] 1538	Helen, St., Bishopsgate.	- - -	[12] 1575
Christ Church, Spitalfields.	- - -	1729	James, St., Duke's Place.	- - -	[13] 1668
Christopher, St., -le-Stocks.	- - -	[5] 1558	James, St. Garlickhithe.	- - -	1538
Clement Danes, St.	- - -	1558	James, St., Piccadilly.	- - -	1685
Clement, St., Eastcheap.	- - -	1539	John, St., the Baptist.	- - -	[14] —
Dionis, St., Backchurch.	- - -	[6] 1538	John, St., the Evangelist.	- - -	[15] —
Duke Street Chapel, Westminster.	- - -	[7] 1745	John, St., the Evangelist, Westminster.	- - -	1728
Dunstan, St., in the East.	- - -	1558	John, St., Zachary.	- - -	1693
Dunstan, St., in the West.	- - -	1558	Katherine, St., by the Tower.	- - -	[16] 1584
			Katherine, St., Cree Church.	- - -	1663

[1] Included in the Registers of St. Stephen Walbrook (*q.v.*).
[2] **P** 1558–1753. Edited by Rev. A. W. C. Hallen, London, 1886–95.
[3] **P** 1671–1839. Harleian Society Registers, vol. 18, 1892.
[4] **P** 1538–1754. Harleian Society Registers, vol. 21, 1895.
[5] **P** 1558–1781. Edited by E. Freshfield, London, 1882.
[6] **P** 1538–1754. Harleian Society Registers, vol. 3, 1878.
[7] (Marriages only) 1745–1753.
[8] **P** 1670–1812. Edited by W. Brigg, Leeds, 1892.
[9] Marriages 1754–1812, included in the Registers of St. Botolph, Billingsgate.
[10] **P** (Marriages only) 1725–1837. Harleian Society Registers, vols. 11, 14, 22, 24, 1886, &c.
[11] **P** (Marriages only) 1695–1754. Edited by Joseph Foster, London, 1889.
[12] **P** 1575–1837. Harleian Society Registers, vol. 31, 1904.
[13] **P** (Marriages only) 1668–1837. Edited by W. P. W. Phillimore and G. E. Cokayne.
[14] Included in the Registers of St. Antholin (*q.v.*).
[15] Included in the Registers of Allhallows, Bread Street (*q.v.*).
[16] The College of St. Katherine, having been displaced by the Dock of that name, is now on the east side of Regent's Park.

Parish.	County.	Date of Earliest Entry.	Parish.	County.	Date of Earliest Entry.
London—*continued.*			London—*continued.*		
Lawrence, St., Jewry.	- - -	1538	Marylebone, St. -	- - -	1668
Lawrence, St., Pountney.	- - -	1538	Mary, St., -le-Bow	- - -	1538
Leonard, St., East-cheap.	- - -	[1] 1538	Mary, St., - le - Strand.	- - -	1558
Leonard, St., Foster Lane.	- - -	[2] —	Mary Magdalen, St., Milk Street.	- - -	1559
Leonard, St., Shoreditch.	- - -	1558	Mary Magdalen, St., Old Fish Street.	- - -	1712
Lincoln's Inn Chapel.	- - -	[3] 1695	Mary, St., Mount-haw.	- - -	1711
Luke, St., Old Street.	- - -	1733	Mary, St., Somer-set.	- - -	1711
Magnus, St., Martyr.	- - -	1557	Mary, St., Staining	- - -	[10] —
Margaret, St., Lothbury.	- - -	1558	Mary, St., White-chapel.	- - -	1558
Margaret, St., Moses.	- - -	1559	Mary, St., Wool-church.	- - -	1558
Margaret, St. New Fish Street.	- - -	[4] 1712	Mary, St., Wool-noth.	- - -	[11] 1538
Margaret, St., Pattens.	- - -	1559	Matthew, St., Bethnal Green.	- - -	1746
Margaret, St., Westminster.	- - -	1538	Matthew, St., Friday Street.	- - -	1538
Martin, St., in the Fields.	- - -	[5] 1550	Mayfair Chapel -	- - -	[12] 1728
Martin, St., Iron-monger Lane.	- - -	1539	Michael, St., Bassi-shaw.	- - -	1538
Martin, St., Lud-gate.	- - -	1539	Michael, St., Corn-hill.	- - -	[13] 1546
Martin, St., Orgar	- - -	1624	Michael, St., Crooked Lane.	- - -	1538
Martin, St., Out-wich.	- - -	[6] 1670	Michael, St., -le-Querne.	- - -	[14] 1669
Mary, St., Ab-church.	- - -	[7] 1558	Michael, St., Pater-noster Royal.	- - -	1558
Mary, St., Alder-manbury.	- - -	1538	Michael, St., Queenhithe.	- - -	1653
Mary, St., Alder-mary.	- - -	[8] 1558	Michael, St., Wood Street.	- - -	1559
Mary, St., at Hill-church.	- - -	1558	Mildred, St., Bread Street.	- - -	1658
Mary, St., Bothaw	- - -	[9] 1538	Mildred, St., Poultry.	- - -	1538
Mary, St., Cole -	- - -	1558	Nicholas, St.,Acons	- - -	[15] 1539

[1] Included in the Registers of St. Benet Finck (*q.v.*).
[2] Included in the Registers of Christchurch, Newgate Street (*q.v.*).
[3] **P** 1695–1852. Records of the Honourable Society of Lincoln's Inn, vol. 2, 1896.
[4] Included in the Registers of St. Magnus (*q.v.*).
[5] **P** 1550–1619. Harleian Society Registers, vol. 25, 1899.
[6] **P** 1670–1873. Harleian Society Registers, vol. 32, 1905.
[7] Included in the Registers of St. Lawrence Pountney (*q.v.*).
[8] **P** 1558–1754. Harleian Society Registers, vol. 5, 1880.
[9] Included in the Registers of St. Swithin (*q.v.*).
[10] Included in the Registers of St. Michael, Wood Street (*q.v.*).
[11] **P** 1538–1760, Edited by Rev. J. M. S. Brooke and Rev. A. W. C. Hallen, London, 1886.
[12] 1728–1754 in 9 vols., preserved at General Register Office, Somerset House. **P** 1735 1754. Harleian Society Registers Section, vol. 15, 1889.
[13] **P** 1546–1754. Harleian Society Registers, vol. 7, 1882.
[14] *See also* Registers of St. Vedast.
[15] **P** 1539–1812. Edited by W. Brigg, Leeds, 1890.

Parish.	County.	Date of Earliest Entry.	Parish.	County.	Date of Earliest Entry.
London—*continued.*			London—*continued.*		
Nicholas, St., Cole Abbey.	- - -	1538	Trinity, Holy, Minories.	- - -	1563
Nicholas, St. Olave	- - -	[1] 1704	Trinity, Holy, the Less.	- - -	1647
Olave, St., Hart Street.	- - -	1563	Vedast, St., Foster Lane.	- - -	[9] 1558
Olave, St., Jewry	- - -	1558	Westminster Abbey.	- - -	[10] 1606
Olave, St., Silver Street.	- - -	[2] —	Whitechapel. *See* St. Mary.		
Pancras, St.	- - -	1660	Whitehall, Chapel Royal.	- - -	[11] 1704
Pancras, St., Soper Lane.	- - -	1538	Londonthorpe	Lincoln - -	1539
Paul, St., Covent Garden.	- - -	[3] 1653	Longborough	Gloucester -	1676
Paul, St., Shadwell	- - -	1670	Longbridge - Deverill. *See* Deverill, Long-bridge.		
Paul's Cathedral, St.	- - -	[4] 1697	Longburton. *See* Bur-ton, Long.		
Peter, St., Cheap	- - -	[5] —	Longcot	Berks - -	[12] 1667
Peter, St., Cornhill	- - -	[6] 1538	Longdon	Salop - -	[13] —
Peter, St., -le-Poor	- - -	1651	Longdon - - -	Stafford - -	1681
Peter, St., Paul's Wharf.	- - -	1607	Longdon	Worcester -	1538
Peter, St., Tower of London.	- - -	1550	Longdon-on-Tern	Salop - -	[14] 1692
Savoy Chapel, The Strand.	- - -	1680	Longfield	Kent - -	1558
Sepulchre, St.	- - -	1662	Longfleet - - -	Dorset - -	[15] —
Shadwell. *See* St. Paul, Shadwell.			Longford	Derby - -	1538
Shoreditch. *See* St. Leonard, Shoreditch.			Longford - - -	Salop - -	1558
			Longham	Norfolk - -	1560
Spitalfields. *See* Christchurch, Spitalfields.			Longhope - - -	Gloucester -	1742
			Longhoughton. *See* Houghton, Long.		
Stephen, St. Cole-man Street.	- - -	1538	Longney - - -	Gloucester -	1660
			Longnor - - -	Salop - -	[16] 1586
Stephen, St. Wal-brook.	- - -	1557	Longnor - - -	Stafford - -	1694
			Longparish -	Hants - -	1654
Swithin, St.	- - -	1615	Longridge - -	Lancaster -	1760
Temple Church	- - -	[7] 1628	Long-Sleddale	Westmorland -	1670
Thomas, St., the Apostle.	- - -	[8] 1558	Longstock - - -	Hants - -	1718
			Longstone - -	Derby - -	1639
Trinity Chapel, Knightsbridge.	- - -	1658	Longstow. *See* Stow, Long.		
			Longton - - -	Lancaster -	[17] —
			Longtown - -	Hereford - -	[18] —

[1] Included in the Registers of St. Nicholas, Cole Abbey (*q.v.*).
[2] Included in the Registers of St. Alban's, Wood Street (*q.v.*).
[3] **P** 1653–1837. Harleian Society Registers, vols. 33 and 34, 1906.
[4] **P** 1697–1896. Harleian Society Registers, vol. 26, 1899.
[5] Included in the Registers of St. Matthew, Friday Street (*q.v.*).
[6] **P** 1538–1774. Harleian Society Registers, vols. 1 and 4, 1877 and 1879.
[7] **P** 1628–1853. Register of Burials at the Temple Church, London, 1905.
[8] **P** 1558–1754. Harleian Society Registers, vol. 6, 1881.
[9] **P** 1558–1837. Harleian Society Registers, vols. 29 and 30, 1902–3.
[10] **P** 1606–1875. Harleian Society Registers, vol. 10.
[11] One volume only, containing baptisms and marriages, 1704–1807.
[12] Including Farnham. Now with Shrivenham.   [13] Included in the Registers of Pontesbury (*q.v.*).
[14] **P** 1692–1812. Shropshire Parish Register Society, vol. 2, 1902 (Lichfield Diocese).
[15] Included in the Registers of Great Canford (*q.v.*).
[16] **P** 1586–1812. Shropshire Parish Register Society, vol. 5 (Lichfield Diocese).
[17] Prior to 1813 the Registers are very incomplete.
[18] Included in the Registers of Clodock (*q.v.*).

Parish.	County.	Date of Earliest Entry.	Parish.	County.	Date of Earliest Entry.
Longwood - - -	York - -	1797	Ludlow - - -	Salop - -	1558
Longworth - -	Berks - -	1559	Luffenham, North -	Rutland - -	1572
Looe, East - -	Cornwall -	¹ 1710	Luffenham, South -	Rutland -	1678
Loose - - -	Kent - -	1559	Luffincott - -	Devon -	1653
Lopen - - -	Somerset - -	1694	Lufton - -	Somerset -	1748
Lopham, North -	Norfolk -	1560	Lugwardine -	Hereford - -	1538
Lopham, South - -	Norfolk - -	1558	Lullingstone -	Kent - -	1578
Loppington - -	Salop - -	1654	Lullington - -	Derby - -	1560
Lorton - -	Cumberland -	1538	Lullington -	Somerset -	1712
Lostwithiel - -	Cornwall -	² 1609	Lullington - - -	Sussex - -	1721
Loughborough -	Leicester · -	1538	Lulsley - -	Worcester -	⁷ 1754
Loughor - -	Glamorgan -	1717	Lulworth, East - -	Dorset - -	1561
Loughton - -	Buckingham -	1707	Lulworth, West -	Dorset - -	1745
Loughton - -	Essex - -	1706	Lund - - -	York - -	1597
Lound - - -	Suffolk - -	1695	Lunds - - -	York - -	1755
Louth - - -	Lincoln -	1538	Luppitt - -	Devon -	1710
Loveston - -	Pembroke -	1777	Lurgashall - -	Sussex - -	1559
Lovington - -	Somerset -	1674	Lusby - - -	Lincoln -	1691
Lowdham - -	Nottingham -	³ 1559	Lustleigh - -	Devon - -	1631
Lowesby - -	Leicester -	1653	Luton - - -	Bedford -	1603
Lowestoft - -	Suffolk - -	⁴ 1561	Lutterworth - -	Leicester - -	1653
Loweswater - -	Cumberland -	1626	Lutton - - -	Northampton -	1653
Lowick - -	Lancaster -	1718	Lutton. See Sutton,		
Lowick - -	Northampton -	1542	Long, St. Nicholas.		
Lowick - - -	Northumberland	1718	Luxborough - -	Somerset - -	1557
Lowther - -	Westmorland -	1539	Luxulyan - -	Cornwall -	⁵ 1593
Lowthorpe - -	York - -	1546	Lydbury, North -	Salop - -	1558
Lowton - -	Lancaster -	1733	Lydd - - -	Kent - -	1542
Loxbeare - -	Devon - -	1560	Lydden - - -	Kent - -	1540
Loxhore - -	Devon -	1652	Lydeard, Bishop's -	Somerset -	1674
Loxley - - -	Warwick -	1540	Lydeard, St. Lawrence	Somerset - -	1573
Loxton - - -	Somerset -	1558	Lydford - -	Devon - -	1716
Lubenham - -	Leicester -	1559	Lydford, East - -	Somerset -	1730
Luccombe - -	Somerset - -	1690	Lydford, West -	Somerset -	1733
Lucker - -	Northumberland	1769	Lydgate - -	Suffolk - -	1547
Luckington - -	Wilts - -	1573	Lydgate - -	York - -	1788
Lucton - - -	Hereford -	1711	Lydham - - -	Salop - -	⁹ 1596
Ludborough - -	Lincoln -	1601	Lydiard-Millicent -	Wilts - -	1697
Ludchurch - -	Pembroke -	1732	Lydiard-Tregoz -	Wilts - -	1666
Luddenden - -	York - -	1653	Lydlinch - -	Dorset - -	¹⁰ 1559
Luddenham - -	Kent - -	1547	Lydney - - -	Gloucester -	1648
Luddesdown - -	Kent - -	1681	Lyford - - -	Berks - -	¹¹ —
Luddington - -	Lincoln -	1700	Lyme-Regis -	Dorset - -	1543
Luddington - in - the -	Northampton -	1635	Lyminge - -	Kent - -	¹² 1679
Brook.			Lymington -	Hants - -	1662
Ludford - - -	Salop - -	1643	Lyminster - -	Sussex - -	1566
Ludford - -	Lincoln - -	1696	Lymm - - -	Chester -	1568
Ludgershall - -	Buckingham -	1538	Lympne - -	Kent - -	1617
Ludgershall -	Wilts - -	1609	Lympsham - -	Somerset - -	1737
Ludgvan - - -	Cornwall -	⁵ 1563	Lympstone - -	Devon - -	1654
Ludham - - -	Norfolk - -	1583	Lyncombe - -	Somerset - -	1574

¹ Earlier entries are in the Registers of St. Martin-by-Looe.
² **P** (Marriages only) 1609–1812. Cornwall Parish Registers, vol. 8, 1905.
³ **P** (Marriages only) 1559–1812. Nottinghamshire Parish Registers, vol. 10, 1907.
⁴ **P** 1650–1750. Edited by F. A. Crisp, 1901.
⁵ **P** (Marriages only) 1563–1812. Cornwall Parish Registers, vol. 5, 1903.
⁶ **P** 1572–1812. Parish Register Society, vol. 4, 1896.
⁷ Bishop's Transcripts commence 1622.
⁸ **P** (Marriages only) 1594–1812. Cornwall Parish Registers, vol. 8, 1905.
⁹ **P** 1596–1812. Shropshire Parish Register Society, vol. 3 (Hereford Diocese).
¹⁰ **P** 1559–1812. Parish Register Society, vol. 17, 1899.
¹¹ Included in the Registers of Hanney (q.v.).
¹² Original Register, British Museum, 1538–1679. Additional MS. 33732.

Parish.	County.	Date of Earliest Entry.	Parish.	County.	Date of Earliest Entry.
Lyndhurst - -	Hants - -	1737	Maisemore - -	Gloucester -	1538
Lyndon - - -	Rutland - -	1580	Maker - - -	Cornwall -	1630
Lyneham - -	Wilts - -	1653	Malborough - -	Devon - -	1558
Lyng - - -	Norfolk - -	1538	Malden - - -	Surrey - -	1676
Lyng - - -	Somerset - -	1691	Maldon, All Saints	Esssex - -	1556
Lynn-Regis. See King's			St. Mary - -	- - -	1558
Lynn.			Mallerstang - -	Westmorland -	1714
Lynn, West - -	Norfolk - -	1695	Malling, East - -	Kent - -	1570
Lynton - - -	Devon - -	1568	Malling, South -	Sussex - -	1629
Lyonshall - -	Hereford -	1682	Malling, West -	Kent - -	1698
Lyss. See Liss.			Mallwyd - -	Merioneth -	1586
Lytchett-Matravers -	Dorset - -	1656	Malmesbury - -	Wilts - -	1590
Lytchett-Minster -	Dorset - -	1554	Malpas - - -	Chester - -	1561
Lytham - - -	Lancaster -	1679	Malpas - - -	Monmouth -	1733
Lythan's, St. - -	Glamorgan -	1748	Maltby - - -	York - -	1597
Lythe - - -	York - -	1637	Maltby-le-Marsh -	Lincoln - -	1644
			Malton, New - -	York - -	1570
			Malton, Old - -	York - -	1606
			Malvern, Great -	Worcester -	1556
M.			Mamble - - -	Worcester -	1590
			Mamhead - -	Devon - -	1556
Mabe - - -	Cornwall -	1653	Mamhilad - -	Monmouth -	1682
Mablethorpe - -	Lincoln - -	1650	Manaccan - -	Cornwall -	[7] 1615
Mabyn, St. - -	Cornwall -	[1] 1562	Manafon - -	Montgomery -	1596
Macclesfield - -	Chester - -	[2] 1572	Manaton - -	Devon - -	1653
Macclesfield-Forest -	Chester -	1669	Manby - - -	Lincoln - -	1679
Machen - - -	Monmouth -	1670	Mancetter - -	Warwick -	1576
Machynlleth - -	Montgomery -	1684	Manchester - -	Lancaster -	1573
Mackworth - -	Derby - -	[3] 1603	St. Ann - -	- - -	1736
Maddington - -	Wilts - -	1652	St. James - -	- - -	1788
Madehurst - -	Sussex - -	1639	St. John - -	- - -	1769
Madeley - - -	Salop - -	1645	St. Mary - -	- - -	1756
Madeley - - -	Stafford - -	1678	St. Michael - -	- - -	1789
Madingley - - -	Cambridge -	1691	Manea - - -	Cambridge -	1708
Madley - - -	Hereford - -	1558	Manfield - -	York - -	[8] 1594
Madresfield - -	Worcester -	[4] 1742	Mangotsfield - -	Gloucester -	1570
Madron - - -	Cornwall -	[5] 1577	Manningford-Abbas -	Wilts - -	1538
Maenclochog - -	Pembroke -	1770	Manningford-Bruce -	Wilts - -	1657
Maentwrog - -	Merioneth -	1695	Mannington - -	Norfolk - -	[9] —
Maer - - -	Stafford - -	1558	Manningtree - -	Essex - -	1695
Maesmynis - -	Brecon - -	1721	Manorbier - -	Pembroke -	1758
Maghull - - -	Lancaster -	1729	Manordivy - -	Pembroke -	1725
Magor - - -	Monmouth -	1799	Manorowen - -	Pembroke -	1783
Maiden-Bradley. See			Mansell-Gamage -	Hereford - -	1664
Bradley-Maiden.			Mansell-Lacy - -	Hereford - -	1714
Maiden-Newton -	Dorset - -	1553	Mansergh - -	Westmorland -	[10] —
Maidford - - -	Northampton -	1711	Mansfield - -	Nottingham -	1559
Maid's-Moreton. See			Mansfield-Woodhouse	Nottingham -	1653
Moreton Maid's.			Manston - - -	Dorset - -	1620
Maidstone - - -	Kent - -	[6] 1542	Manton - - -	Lincoln - -	1678
Maidwell - - -	Northampton -	1708	Manton - - -	Rutland - -	1573
Mainstone - - -	Salop - -	1604	Manuden - -	Essex - -	1561

[1] **P** (Marriages only) 1562-1812. Cornwall Parish Registers, vol. 2, 1902.
[2] **P** in Macclesfield Parish Magazine commencing 1886.
[3] **P** (Marriages only) 1603-1812. Derbyshire Parish Registers, vol. 1, 1906.
[4] Bishop's Transcripts commence 1611.
[5] **P** 1577-1726. Edited by G. B. Millett, 1877. **P** (Marriages only) 1674-1812. Cornwall Parish Registers, vol. 12, 1907.
[6] **P** 1542- . Edited by J. Cave Browne, 1890. (Marriages only, and only two parts issued.)
[7] **P** (Marriages only) 1633-1812. Cornwall Parish Registers, vol. 7, 1904.
[8] **P** 1594-1812. Edited by Rev. W. F. Stavert, 1898.
[9] Included in the Registers of Itteringham (q.v.).
[10] Included in the Registers of Kirkby-Lonsdale (q.v.).

MAP] 113 [MAR

Parish.	County.	Date of Earliest Entry.	Parish.	County.	Date of Earliest Entry.
Maperton - -	Somerset -	1559	Marland, Peter's -	Devon - -	1696
Maplebeck - -	Nottingham -	1562	Marlborough, St. Mary.	Wilts - -	⁸1602
Maplederwell - -	Hants - -	¹1618	St. Peter and St. Paul.	Wilts - -	⁴1611
Mapledurham - -	Oxford - -	1627			
Maplestead, Great -	Essex - -	1678	Marldon - -	Devon -	1598
Maplestead, Little -	Essex - -	1688	Marlesford - -	Suffolk - -	1661
Mapleton - -	Derby - -	1704	Marlingford - -	Norfolk - -	1558
Mapleton - -	York - -	1678	Marloes - - -	Pembroke -	1749
Mapperton - -	Dorset - -	²1669	Marlow, Great -	Buckingham -	⁵1592
Mappowder - -	Dorset - -	1653	Marlow, Little -	Buckingham -	1559
Marbury - -	Chester - -	1538	Marnham - -	Nottingham -	1601
March - - -	Cambridge -	1558	Marnhull - -	Dorset - -	1560
Marcham - - -	Berks - -	1658	Marple - - -	Chester - -	1655
Marchington - -	Stafford - -	1612	Marr - - -	York - -	1729
Marchwiel - -	Denbigh - -	1652	Marrick - - -	York - -	1687
Marcle, Little - -	Hereford - -	1748	Marros - - -	Carmarthen -	1738
Marcle, Much - -	Hereford -	1556	Marsden - -	York - -	1776
Mardale - - -	Westmorland -	1684	Marsham - -	Norfolk - -	⁶1538
Marden - - -	Hereford - -	1616	Marshfield - -	Gloucester -	⁷1562
Marden - - -	Kent - -	1559	Marshfield - -	Monmouth -	1656
Marden - - -	Wilts - -	1685	Marsh Chapel -	Lincoln -	1590
Marden, East - -	Sussex - -	1691	Marsh Gibbon -	Buckingham -	1577
Marden-Up - -	Sussex - -	1714	Marshwood - -	Dorset - -	⁸1614
Mareham-le-Fen - -	Lincoln - -	1562	Marske - - -	York - -	1594
Mareham - on - the - Hill.	Lincoln - -	1715	Marske-by-the-Sea -	York - -	⁹1569
Maresfield - -	Sussex - -	1538	Marston - - -	Lincoln - -	1707
Marfleet - - -	York - -	1713	Marston - - -	Oxford - -	1654
Margam - -	Glamorgan -	1672	Marston - - -	Stafford - -	1556
Margaret, St. - -	Hereford - -	1702	Marston-Bigott -	Somerset -	1654
Margaret, St., at Cliffe	Kent - -	1558	Marston, Butler's -	Warwick -	¹⁰1538
Margaret-Marsh - -	Dorset - -	1682	Marston Chapel -	Worcester -	¹¹1767
Margaret-Roding. See Roding, Margaret.			Marston, Fleet -	Buckingham -	1630
			Marston, Long -	York - -	1648
Margaretting - -	Essex - -	1628	Marston-Magna -	Somerset -	1566
Margate - - -	Kent - -	1559	Marston-Meysey -	Wilts - -	1742
Marham - -	Norfolk - -	1562	Marston-Montgomery -	Derby -	166c
Marhamchurch - -	Cornwall - -	1558	Marston-Morteyne -	Bedford -	1703
Marholm - - -	Northampton -	1566	Marston, North -	Buckingham -	1724
Mariansleigh - -	Devon - -	1727	Marston-on-Dove -	Derby - -	1654
Mark - - -	Somerset - -	1647	Marston, Potters -	Leicester -	¹²
Markby - - -	Lincoln - -	1558	Marston, Priors-	Warwick -	1689
Markfield - -	Leicester - -	1571	Marston St. Lawrence -	Northampton -	1653
Markham, East - -	Nottingham -	1561	Marston-Sicca -	Gloucester -	¹³1680
Markham, Clinton -	Nottingham -	1651	Marston, South -	Wilts - -	1539
Marksbury - -	Somerset - -	1563	Marston-Trussel -	Northampton -	1561
Markshall - -	Essex - -	1585	Marstow - -	Hereford -	1707
Mark's Tey. See Tey, Marks.			Marsworth (or Masworth).	Buckingham -	¹⁴1720

¹ **P** (Marriages only) 1629–1812. Hampshire Parish Registers, vol. 9, 1907.
² **P** (Marriages only) 1669–1812. Dorset Parish Registers, vol. 1, 1906.
³ **P** (Marriages only) 1602–1812. Wiltshire Parish Registers, vol. 2, 1906.
⁴ **P** (Marriages only) 1611–1812. Wiltshire Parish Registers, vol. 2, 1906.
⁵ **P** 1592–1611. Buckinghamshire Parish Register Society, vol. 3, 1904.
⁶ **P** 1538–1836. Edited by A. T. Michell, 1889.
⁷ **P** 1558–1693. Edited by F. A. Crisp, 1893.
⁸ Included in the Registers of Whitechurch-Canonicorum (*q.v.*).
⁹ **P** 1569–1812. Yorkshire Parish Register Society, vol. 16, 1903.
¹⁰ **P** (Marriages only) 1538–1812. Warwickshire Parish Registers, vol. 1, 1904.
¹¹ Earlier entries in the Registers of Yardley (*q.v.*).
¹² Included in the Registers of Barwell (*q.v.*).
¹³ **P** (Marriages only) 1680–1812. Gloucestershire Parish Registers, vol. 10, 1905.
¹⁴ **P** (Marriages only) 1574–1812. Buckinghamshire Parish Registers, vol. 1, 1902.

Parish.	County.	Date of Earliest Entry.	Parish.	County.	Date of Earliest Entry.
Martha, St., -on-the-Hill. *See* Chilworth.			Mawnan - -	Cornwall -	⁶1553
Martham - -	Norfolk -	1558	Maxey - -	Northampton -	⁷1538
Martin - -	Lincoln -	1562	Maxstoke - -	Warwick -	1653
Martin - -	Wilts -	1590	Mayfield - -	Stafford -	1576
Martin, St., -by-Looe -	Cornwall -	1653	Mayfield - -	Sussex -	1570
Martin, St. -	Salop -	1601	Mayland - -	Essex -	1748
Martin, St., in Meneage	Cornwall -	1571	Meare - -	Somerset -	1560
Martindale - -	Westmorland -	1633	Measham - -	Derby -	1681
Martinhoe - -	Devon -	1632	Meavy - -	Devon -	1659
Martin-Hussingtree -	Worcester -	1538	Medbourne -	Leicester -	1588
Martlesham - -	Suffolk -	1653	Medmenham -	Buckingham -	1654
Martletwy - -	Pembroke -	1718	Medomsley -	Durham -	1608
Martley - -	Worcester -	1625	Medstead - -	Hants -	1560
Martock - -	Somerset -	¹1558	Meerbrook -	Stafford -	1738
Marton - -	Chester -	1563	Meesden - -	Hertford -	1737
Marton - -	Lincoln -	1651	Meeth - -	Devon -	1752
Marton - -	Warwick -	1660	Meifod - -	Montgomery -	1649
Marton-in-Cleveland -	York -	1572	Melbourn - -	Cambridge -	1558
Marton-in-Craven -	York -	1548	Melbourne -	Derby -	1653
Marton-in-the-Forest -	York -	1539	Melbury-Abbas -	Dorset -	1716
Marton, Long -	Westmorland -	1586	Melbury-Bubb -	Dorset -	1678
Marton with Grafton -	York -	1648	Melbury-Osmond -	Dorset -	1580
Martyr-Worthy. *See* Worthy, Martyr.			Melbury-Sampford -	Dorset -	1606
			Melchbourne -	Bedford -	1706
Marwood - -	Devon -	1602	Melcombe-Horsey -	Dorset -	1690
Mary Church, St. -	Devon -	1641	Melcombe-Regis -	Dorset -	1606
Marychurch, St. -	Glamorgan -	1577	Meldon - -	Northumberland	1706
Mary Hill, St. -	Glamorgan -	1751	Meldreth - -	Cambridge -	1681
Mary, St., in the Marsh	Kent -	1675	Melford, Long -	Suffolk -	1559
Maryport - -	Cumberland -	1760	Meliden - -	Flint -	1602
Marystow - -	Devon -	1654	Meline - -	Pembroke -	1702
Masham - -	York -	1599	Melksham - -	Wilts -	1568
Mashbury - -	Essex -	1539	Melling, near Lancaster	Lancaster -	1626
Massingham, Great -	Norfolk -	1564	Melling, near Liverpool	Lancaster -	1680
Massingham, Little -	Norfolk -	1558	Mellion, St -	Cornwall -	1558
Matching - -	Essex -	1558	Mellis - -	Suffolk -	1559
Matherne - -	Monmouth -	1565	Mellon, St. -	Monmouth -	1722
Mathon - -	Worcester -	²1631	Mellor - -	Derby -	⁸1624
Mathry - -	Pembroke -	1729	Mells - -	Somerset -	1567
Matlask - -	Norfolk -	1558	Melmerby -	Cumberland -	1701
Matlock - -	Derby -	1637	Melsonby -	York -	1573
Matson - -	Gloucester -	³1553	Meltham -	York -	1669
Matterdale - -	Cumberland -	1645	Melton -	Suffolk -	1691
Mattersey - -	Nottingham -	1542	Melton -	York -	⁹
Mattingley - -	Hants -	⁴—	Melton-Constable -	Norfolk -	1561
Mattishall - -	Norfolk -	1656	Melton, Great -	Norfolk -	1558
Maughan, St. -	Monmouth -	⁵1733	Melton, High -	York -	1538
Maulden - -	Bedford -	1558	Melton, Little -	Norfolk -	1734
Mautby - -	Norfolk -	1663	Melton-Mowbray -	Leicester -	1547
Mawgan-in-Meneage -	Cornwall -	1559	Melton-Ross -	Lincoln -	1568
Mawgan-in-Pyder -	Cornwall -	1686	Melverley -	Salop -	¹⁰1723
			Membury -	Devon -	1637

¹ **P** (Marriages only) 1559–1812. Somersetshire Parish Registers, vol. 3, 1901.
² Bishop's Transcripts commence 1613.
³ **P** (Marriages only). Gloucestershire Parish Registers, vol. 3, 1898.
⁴ Included in the Registers of Heckfield (*q.v.*).
⁵ *See also* Llangattock-Vibon-Avel.
⁶ **P** (Marriages only) 1553–1812. Cornwall Parish Registers, vol. 7, 1904.
⁷ **P** 1538–1713. Edited by Rev. W. D. Sweeting, 1892.
⁸ **P** (Marriages only) 1678–1755. Derbyshire Parish Registers, vol. 3, 1907.
⁹ Included in the Registers of Welton (*q.v.*).
¹⁰ **P** 1723–1812. Shropshire Parish Register Society, vol. 1. **P** 1723–1812. Parish Register Society, vol. 24, 1899.

Parish.	County.	Date of Earliest Entry.	Parish.	County.	Date of Earliest Entry.
Mendham - -	Norfolk and Suffolk.	1678	Methwold - - -	Norfolk -	1685
			Mettingham - -	Suffolk -	1664
Mendlesham - -	Suffolk - -	1558	Metton - - -	Norfolk -	1738
Menheniot - -	Cornwall -	[1] 1554	Mevagissey - -	Cornwall -	1598
Mentmore - -	Buckingham -	[2] 1685	Mewan, St. - -	Cornwall -	1693
Meole-Brace. *See* Brace Meole.			Mexborough - -	York -	1562
			Meylltyrne - -	Carnarvon -	1740
Meols, North - -	Lancaster -	1594	Michael, St., -on-Wyre	Lancaster -	1659
Meon, East - -	Hants -	1560	Michael, St., Caerhays	Cornwall -	1580
Meon-Stoke - -	Hants - -	1599	Michael, St., Penkevil	Cornwall -	1516
Meon, West - -	Hants -	[3] 1538	Michaelchurch - -	Hereford -	[10] —
Meopham - -	Kent -	1573	Michaelchurch - on - Arrow.	Radnor -	1741
Mepal - - -	Cambridge -	1659			
Meppershall - -	Bedford -	1653	Michaelchurch, St. -	Somerset -	1695
Mere - - -	Wilts -	1561	Michaelchurch-Eskley	Hereford -	1719
Merevale - -	Leicester and Warwick.	1727	Michaelston-le-Pit -	Glamorgan -	1783
			Michaelston - super - Avon.	Glamorgan -	1785
Mereworth - -	Kent -	1560			
Meriden - - -	Warwick -	1646	Michaelston - super - Ely.	Glamorgan -	1754
Merrington, Kirk -	Durham -	[4] 1578			
Merriott - - -	Somerset -	1646	Michaelstone-y-Vedw -	Glamorgan and Monmouth.	1661
Merrow - - -	Surrey -	1538			
Merryn, St. - -	Cornwall -	[5] 1688	Michaelstow - -	Cornwall -	[11] 1544
Mersea, East - -	Essex -	1720	Micheldean - -	Gloucester -	[12] 1680
Mersea, West - -	Essex - -	1625	Micheldever - -	Hants -	1538
Mersham - -	Kent -	1558	Michelmersh - -	Hants -	1558
Merstham - - -	Surrey -	[6] 1538	Mickfield - -	Suffolk -	1558
Merston - -	Sussex -	1751	Mickleham - -	Surrey -	1549
Merther - - -	Cornwall -	1658	Mickleover - -	Derby -	1607
Merthyr - -	Carmarthen -	1678	Mickleton - -	Gloucester -	[13] 1590
Merthyr-Cynog - -	Brecon -	[7] 1756	Middle. *See* Myddle.		
Merthyr-Dovan -	Glamorgan -	1754	Middleham - -	York -	1604
Merthyr-Mawr - -	Glamorgan -	1749	Middlesbrough - -	York -	[14] —
Merthyr-Tydfil -	Glamorgan -	1704	Middlesmoor - -	York -	1700
Merton - - -	Devon -	1687	Middleton, St. George	Durham -	[15] —
Merton - -	Norfolk -	1566	Middleton - -	Essex -	1700
Merton - -	Oxford -	1635	Middleton - -	Lancaster -	[16] 1541
Merton - - -	Surrey -	1559	Middleton - -	Norfolk -	1560
Meshaw - - -	Devon -	1581	Middleton - -	Suffolk -	1653
Messing - - -	Essex -	1538	Middleton - -	Sussex -	1551
Messingham - -	Lincoln -	[8] 1562	Middleton - -	Warwick -	1671
Metfield - - -	Suffolk -	1559	Middleton - -	Westmorland -	[17] —
Metheringham - -	Lincoln -	1538	Middleton - -	Westmorland -	1678
Methley - - -	York -	[9] 1560	Middleton-Cheney -	Northampton -	1551

[1] **P** (Marriages only) 1554–1812. Cornwall Parish Registers, vol. 10, 1906.
[2] **P** (Marriages only) 1575–1812. Buckinghamshire Parish Registers, vol. 1, 1902.
[3] **P** (Marriages only) 1538–1800. Hampshire Parish Registers, vol. 3, 1905.
[4] "North Country Parish Registers," by Robert Blair.
[5] **P** (Marriages only) 1689–1812. Cornwall Parish Registers, vol. 4, 1903.
[6] **P** 1538–1812. Parish Register Society, vol. 42, 1902.
[7] Very imperfect until 1800.
[8] The early Register book, which was rebound in 1812, has been found to be not in chronological order, and it is possible that it contains an entry of an earlier date than 1562.
[9] **P** 1560–1812. Thoresby Society, vol. 12, 1903.
[10] Included in the Registers of Tretyre (*q.v.*).
[11] **P** (Marriages only) 1548–1812. Cornwall Parish Registers, vol. 1, 1900.
[12] **P** (Marriages only) 1680–1812. Gloucestershire Parish Registers, vol. 9, 1903.
[13] **P** (Marriages only) 1594–1812. Gloucestershire Parish Registers, vol. 3, 1898.
[14] The early Registers of this parish are entered in the Register Book of Acklam (*q.v.*), but kept quite distinct.
[15] **P** 1616–1812. Durham and Northumberland Parish Register Society, 1906.
[16] **P** 1541–1663. Lancashire Parish Register Society, vol. 10, 1902.
[17] **P** Included in the Registers of Kirkby-Lonsdale (*q.v.*).

Parish.	County.	Date of Earliest Entry.	Parish.	County.	Date of Earliest Entry.
Middleton-in-Teesdale	Durham - -	1578	Milverton - -	Somerset -	1538
Middleton-on-Leven -	York - -	1614	Milverton - -	Warwick - -	1742
Middleton-on-the-Hill	Hereford - -	1650	Milwich - -	Stafford -	⁵ 1573
Middleton - on - the - Wolds.	York - -	1678	Mimms, North - -	Hertford - -	1565
			Mimms, South	Middlesex -	1558
Middleton-Scriven -	Salop - -	1728	Minchinhampton -	Gloucester -	⁶ 1558
Middleton-Stoney -	Oxford - -	1598	Minehead - -	Somerset -	1548
Middleton-Stony -	Derby - -	1715	Minety - -	Wilts - -	1663
Middleton-Tyas - -	York - -	1539	Miningsby - -	Lincoln -	1695
Middlewich - -	Chester - -	1613	Minshull, Church -	Chester - -	1651
Middlezoy - -	Somerset -	1754	Minstead - -	Hants - -	1682
Midgham - -	Berks - -	1622	Minster - -	Cornwall -	⁷ 1676
Midhope - - -	York - -	1772	Minster-in-Sheppey -	Kent - -	1703
Midhurst - -	Sussex - -	1565	Minster (Thanet) -	Kent - -	1557
Milborne, St. Andrew -	Dorset - -	1570	Minster-Lovell -	Oxford - -	1754
Milborne-Port - -	Somerset -	1539	Minster, South -	Essex - -	1702
Milbrook - -	Bedford - -	1558	Minsterley - -	Salop - -	⁸ —
Milburn - - -	Westmorland -	1678	Minsterworth - -	Gloucester -	1633
Milcombe - -	Oxford - -	¹ —	Minterne Magna -	Dorset -	1635
Milden - - -	Suffolk - -	1558	Minting - -	Lincoln -	1561
Mildenhall - -	Suffolk - -	1559	Minver, St. - -	Cornwall -	⁹ 1558
Mildenhall - -	Wilts - -	1653	Mirfield - -	York - -	1559
Mile-End (or Myland)	Essex - -	1674	Miserden - -	Gloucester -	1574
Mileham - - -	Norfolk - -	1538	Missenden, Great -	Buckingham -	1678
Milford-Haven -	Pembroke -	1808	Missenden, Little -	Buckingham -	1559
Milford - - -	Hants - •	1594	Misson - -	Nottingham -	1653
Millbrook - -	Hants - -	1633	Misterton - -	Leicester -	1558
Millington - -	York - -	1609	Misterton - -	Nottingham -	1540
Millom - - -	Cumberland -	1598	Misterton - -	Somerset -	1558
Milnrow - - -	Lancaster -	1722	Mistley - -	Essex - -	1559
Milson - - -	Salop - -	1678	Mitcham - -	Surrey -	1563
Milstead - - -	Kent - -	1543	Mitchel-Troy -	Monmouth -	1590
Milston - - -	Wilts - -	² 1539	Mitford - -	Northumberland	1667
Milton - - -	Berks - -	1654	Mitton. See Mytton.		
Milton - - -	Cambridge -	1707	Mitton, Lower -	Worcester -	¹⁰ 1693
Milton - - -	Hants - -	1654	Mixbury - -	Oxford - -	1645
Milton - - -	Kent - -	³ 1746	Mobberley - -	Chester -	1578
Milton-Abbey -	Dorset - -	⁴ 1650	Moccas - -	Hereford -	1673
Milton, Abbot -	Devon - -	1653	Mochdre. See Mough- trey.		
Milton-Bryan -	Bedford -	1559			
Milton-Clevedon -	Somerset -	1595	Modbury - -	Devon - -	1601
Milton-Damerel -	Devon - -	1754	Molash - -	Kent - -	1557
Milton-Ernest -	Bedford - -	1538	Mold - - -	Flint - -	1612
Milton, Great -	Oxford - -	1550	Molesey, East -	Surrey - -	1668
Milton-Keynes -	Buckingham -	1559	Molesey, West -	Surrey - -	1729
Milton-Lilborne -	Wilts - -	1686	Molesworth - -	Huntingdon -	1564
Milton-Malzor -	Northampton -	1558	Molland - -	Devon - -	1538
Milton, next Graves-end.	Kent - -	1558	Mollington - -	Oxford - -	1562
			Molton, North -	Devon - -	1542
Milton, next Sitting-bourne.	Kent - -	1538	Molton, South -	Devon - -	1601
			Monckton, Bishop's	York - -	¹¹ —
Milton, South - -	Devon - -	1686	Monckton-Tarrant -	Dorset - -	1697

¹ Included in the Registers of Bloxham (q.v.).
² **P** (Marriages only) 1540–1812. Wiltshire Parish Registers, vol. 3, 1906.
³ Before this date included in the Registers of Thanington (q.v.).
⁴ **P** (Marriages only) 1559–1812. Dorset Parish Registers, vol. 1., 1906.
⁵ **P** 1573–1711. Staffordshire Parish Register Society, vol. 3, 1904.
⁶ **P** (Marriages only) 1566–1812. Gloucestershire Parish Registers, vol. 11, 1905.
⁷ **P** (Marriages only). Cornwall Parish Registers, vol. 1, 1900.
⁸ Included in the Registers of Westbury (q.v.).
⁹ **P** (Marriages only) 1559–1812. Cornwall Parish Registers, vol. 4, 1903.
¹⁰ Bishop's Transcripts commence 1603.
¹¹ Included in the Registers of Ripon (q.v.).

Parish	County.	Date of Earliest Entry.	Parish.	County.	Date of Earliest Entry.
Monewden - -	Suffolk - -	1705	Moreton-in-the-Marsh	Gloucester -	[9] 1643
Mongeham, Great -	Kent - -	1685	Moreton, Maids' -	Buckingham -	1558
Mongewell - - -	Oxford - -	1682	Moreton-Morrell -	Warwick - -	1538
Monington - -	Pembroke -	1784	Moreton, North - -	Berks - -	1558
Monk-Hesleden. See			Moreton-on-Lugg -	Hereford - -	1759
Hesleden, Monk.			Moreton-Pinkney -	Northampton -	1641
Monk - Fryston. See			Moreton-Say - -	Salop - -	1691
Fryston, Monk-.			Moreton, South - -	Berks - -	1599
Monk-Hopton - -	Salop - -	[1] 1698	Moreton-Valence -	Gloucester -	1681
Monkland - -	Hereford - -	1582	Morland - -	Westmorland -	1539
Monkleigh - -	Devon - -	1548	Morley - - -	Derby - -	1543
Monks-Eleigh - -	Suffolk - -	1557	Morley, St. Botolph -	Norfolk - -	1539
Monksilver - -	Somerset - -	1653	Morley, St. Peter -	Norfolk -	1590
Monkswood - -	Monmouth -	1783	Morningthorpe - -	Norfolk - -	1557
Monkton - -	Devon - -	1737	Morpeth - - -	Northumberland	1584
Monkton - -	Kent - -	1700	Morston - - -	Norfolk - -	1548
Monkton Deverill. See			Mortehoe - -	Devon - -	1726
Deverill, Monkton.			Mortlake - - -	Surrey - -	1599
Monkton-Farleigh -	Wilts - -	1570	Morton - - -	Derby - -	1570
Monkton-Moor -	York - -	1681	Morton - - -	Lincoln - -	1597
Monkton-Nun - -	York - -	1708	Morton - - -	Nottingham -	1640
Monkton, West - -	Somerset - -	[2] 1710	Morton, Abbott's -	Worcester -	1728
Monmouth - -	Monmouth -	1598	Morton-Bagot - -	Warwick - -	[10] 1663
Monnington-on-Wye -	Hereford -	1684	Morton-Jefferies -	Hereford -	1711
Montacute - -	Somerset - -	1558	Morton-on-the-Hill -	Norfolk - -	1720
Montford - -	Salop - -	[3] 1661	Morvah - - -	Cornwall -	[11] 1617
Montgomery - -	Montgomery -	1694	Morval - - -	Cornwall -	1538
Monxton - -	Hants - -	[4] 1716	Morville - - -	Salop - -	1562
Monyash - - -	Derby - -	1707	Morwenstow - -	Cornwall -	1558
Moorby - - -	Lincoln - -	1561	Moseley - - -	Worcester -	1758
Moorlinch - - -	Somerset -	1578	Mosser - - -	Cumberland -	1783
Morborne - -	Huntingdon -	1724	Mossley - - -	Lancaster -	[12]
Morchard-Bishop -	Devon - -	1660	Mosterton - -	Dorset - -	1655
Morcott - - -	Rutland - -	1539	Motcomb - - -	Dorset - -	1676
Morden - - -	Dorset - -	1575	Mothvey - - -	Carmarthen -	1653
Morden - - -	Surrey - -	[5] 1634	Mottisfont - -	Hants - -	1701
Morden, Guilden- -	Cambridge -	1553	Mottiston (Isle of Wight).	Hants - -	1680
Morden, Steeple- -	Cambridge -	1675			
Mordiford - -	Hereford - -	1621	Mottram -in-Longden- dale.	Chester -	1559
More - - - -	Salop - -	[6] 1569			
Morebath - -	Devon - -	1558	Moughtrey - -	Montgomery -	1682
Moreleigh - - -	Devon - -	1659	Moulsford - -	Berks - -	1679
Moresby - - -	Cumberland -	1717	Moulsoe - - -	Buckingham -	1559
Morestead - - -	Hants - -	1549	Moulton - - -	Lincoln - -	1558
Moreton - - -	Dorset - -	1741	Moulton - - -	Northampton -	[13] 1565
Moreton - - -	Essex - -	[7] 1558	Moulton - - -	Suffolk - -	1560
Moreton-Corbet -	Salop - -	[8] 1580	Moulton, Great - -	Norfolk -	1557
Moreton-Hampstead -	Devon - -	1603	Moulton, Little -	Norfolk - -	1539

[1] **P** 1698-1812. Shropshire Parish Register Society, vol. 3.
[2] **P** (Marriages only) 1710-1812. Somersetshire Parish Registers, vol. 8, 1907.
[3] **P** 1559-1812. Shropshire Parish Register Society, vol. 7.
[4] **P** (Marriages only) 1716-1812. Hampshire Parish Registers, vol. 1, 1899.
[5] **P** 1634-1812. Parish Register Society, vol. 37, 1901.
[6] **P** 1570-1812. Shropshire Parish Register Society, vol. 2. **P** 1569-1812. Parish Register Society, vol. 34, 1900.
[7] **P** 1558-1759. Edited by F. A. Crisp, 1890.
[8] **P** 1580-1812. Shropshire Parish Register Society, vol. 1, 1900. **P** 1580-1812. Parish Register Society, vol. 39, 1901.
[9] **P** (Marriages only) 1672-1812. Gloucestershire Parish Registers, vol. 5, 1899.
[10] Bishop's Transcripts commence 1614.
[11] **P** (Marriages only) 1617-1812. Cornwall Parish Registers, vol. 12, 1907.
[12] Included in the Registers of Ashton-under-Lyne (q.v.).
[13] **P** (Baptisms only) 1565-1812. Parish Register Society, vol. 47, 1901.

I

Parish.	County.	Date of Earliest Entry.	Parish.	County.	Date of Earliest Entry.
Mount - - -	Cardigan -	1778			
Mountfield - -	Sussex - -	1558	**N.**		
Mountnessing -	Essex - -	1654			
Mounton - -	Monmouth -	1790	Naburn - - -	York - -	1653
Mountsorrel -	Leicester -	1677	Nackington - -	Kent - -	1563
Mowsley - -	Leicester -	1660	Nacton - - -	Suffolk - -	1562
Moylgrove - -	Pembroke -	1771	Nafferton - -	York - -	1653
Moze - - -	Essex - -	[1] 1551	Nafford - - -	Worcester -	[6] —
Muchelney - -	Somerset -	[2] 1703	Nailsea - - -	Somerset - -	1554
Mucking - -	Essex -	1558	Nailstone - - -	Leicester -	1694
Mucklestone - -	Salop and Stafford.	1556	Nailsworth - -	Gloucester -	[7] 1794
			Nannerch - - -	Flint and Denbigh.	1664
Muckton - -	Lincoln -	1695			
Mudford - - -	Somerset -	1563	Nantcwnlle - -	Cardigan -	1765
Mugginton - -	Derby -	1674	Nantddu - -	Brecon -	1779
Muggleswick - -	Durham -	1730	Nantglyn - -	Denbigh - -	1719
Muker - - -	York - -	1638	Nantmel - - -	Radnor -	1742
Mulbarton - -	Norfolk - -	1547	Nantwich - -	Chester - -	[8] 1539
Mullion - - -	Cornwall -	1598	Napton-on-the-Hill -	Warwick -	1604
Mumby - - -	Lincoln -	1573	Narberth - -	Pembroke -	1685
Muncaster - -	Cumberland -	1720	Narborough - -	Leicester - -	1599
Munden, Great -	Hertford - -	1578	Narburgh - -	Norfolk -	[9] 1558
Munden, Little - -	Hertford -	1680	Narford - - -	Norfolk - -	[10] 1559
Mundesley - -	Norfolk - -	[3] 1756	Naseby - - -	Northampton -	1563
Mundford - -	Norfolk -	1699	Nash - - -	Monmouth -	1733
Mundham - -	Norfolk -	1559	Nash - - -	Pembroke -	1742
Mundham, North	Sussex - -	1553	Nassington - -	Northampton -	1654
Mundon - -	Essex - -	1741	Nateley-Scures -	Hants - -	1666
Mungrisdale - -	Cumberland -	1745	Nateley-Up - -	Hants - -	[11] 1692
Munsley - - -	Hereford - -	[4] 1708	Natland - - -	Westmorland -	1735
Munslow - -	Salop - -	1559	Naughton - -	Suffolk - -	1561
Mursley - - -	Buckingham -	1578	Naunton - - -	Gloucester -	1540
Murston - - -	Kent - -	1561	Naunton-Beauchamp -	Worcester -	[12] 1696
Musbury - - -	Devon - -	1653	Navenby - - -	Lincoln -	1681
Musgrave, Great	Westmorland -	1562	Navestock - - -	Essex - -	1538
Muskham, North	Nottingham -	1704	Nayland - - -	Suffolk - -	1558
Muskham, South	Nottingham -	1589	Nazeing - - -	Essex - -	1559
Muston - - -	Leicester - -	1561	Neath - - -	Glamorgan -	1692
Muston - - -	York - -	1542	Neatishead - -	Norfolk - -	1676
Mutford - - -	Suffolk - -	1554	Necton - - -	Norfolk -	1558
Myddle - - -	Salop - -	1541	Nedging - - -	Suffolk - -	1559
Mydrim - - -	Carmarthen -	1653	Needham - - -	Norfolk - -	1643
Myland. *See* Mile End			Neen-Savage - -	Salop - -	1575
Mylor - - -	Cornwall -	[5] 1673	Neen-Sollars - -	Salop - -	1678
Mynachlogdu - -	Pembroke -	1802	Neenton - - -	Salop - -	[13] 1558
Mynwere - - -	Pembroke -	1783	Nempnett-Thrubwell -	Somerset -	1556
Mynyddyslwyn -	Monmouth -	1664	Neot, St. - - -	Cornwall -	1549
Myton-upon-Swale -	Monmouth -	1654	Neot's, St. - -	Huntingdon -	1691
Mytton - - -	Monmouth -	1611	Nerquis - - -	Flint -	1665

[1] **P** 1551–1678. Edited by F. A. Crisp, 1899.
[2] **P** (Marriages only) 1703–1812. Somersetshire Parish Registers, vol. 1, 1898.
[3] **P** (Marriages only) 1724–1812. Norfolk Parish Registers, vol. 3, 1907.
[4] **P** 1662–1812. Parish Register Society, vol. 46, 1903.
[5] **P** (Marriages only) 1673–1812. Cornwall Parish Registers, vol. 7, 1904.
[6] Church demolished and now included with Birlingham. Bishop's Transcripts commence 1610.
[7] Was formerly a chapelry in the parishes of Avening, Horsley, and Minchinhampton, so that the Registers of those places must be searched for entries before 1794.
[8] *See* James Hall's "History of Nantwich."
[9] **P** (Marriages only) 1558–1812. Norfolk Parish Registers, vol. 1, 1899.
[10] **P** (Marriages only) 1559–1812. Norfolk Parish Registers, vol. 2, 1900.
[11] **P** (Marriages only) 1696–1750. Hampshire Parish Registers, vol. 2, 1900.
[12] Bishop's Transcripts commence 1611.
[13] **P** 1558–1812. Shropshire Parish Register Society, vol. 3.

Parish.	County.	Date of Earliest Entry.	Parish.	County.	Date of Earliest Entry.
Ness, Great - -	Salop - -	1589	Newchurch-Kenyon -	Lancaster -	⁴1599
Ness, Little - -	Salop - -	¹1605	Newdigate - -	Surrey - -	1559
Neston - -	Chester -	1559	Newenden - -	Kent - -	⁵1559
Netheravon - -	Wilts - -	1582	Newent - -	Gloucester -	1673
Netherbury - -	Dorset - -	1592	Newhaven - -	Sussex - -	1553
Nether-Exe - -	Devon - -	1731	Newick - -	Sussex - -	1558
Netherwent - -	Monmouth -	1754	Newington next Sit-	Kent - -	1558
Netteswell - -	Essex - -	1558	tingbourne.		
Nettlebed - -	Oxford -	1653	Newington - -	Oxford - -	1572
Nettlecombe - -	Somerset -	1540	Newington, St. Mary -	Surrey - -	1707
Nettleden - -	Buckingham -	² —	Newington-Bagpath -	Gloucester -	⁶1686
Nettleham - -	Lincoln - -	1583	Newington, next	Kent - -	1559
Nettlestead - -	Kent - -	1640	Folkestone.		
Nettlestead - -	Suffolk - -	1618	Newington, South -	Oxford - -	1538
Nettleton - -	Lincoln -	1679	Newington, Stoke -	Middlesex -	1559
Nettleton - -	Wilts -	1556	Newland. See St.		
Nevendon - -	Essex - -	1669	Lawrence.		
Nevern - - -	Pembroke -	1663	Newland - -	Gloucester -	1560
Nevin, or Nefyn -	Carnarvon -	1694	Newland - - -	Worcester -	1562
Newark-on-Trent -	Nottingham -	³1599	Newland - -	Lancaster -	⁷ —
Newbald - -	York - -	1600	Newlands - -	Cumberland -	1749
Newbiggin -	Westmorland -	1572	Newlyn - -	Cornwall -	1559
Newbiggin -	Northumberland	1665	Newmarket - -	Suffolk -	1638
Newbold-on-Avon -	Warwick - -	1558	Newmarket - -	Cambridge -	1622
Newbold-Pacey -	Warwick -	1554	Newmarket - -	Flint -	1696
Newbold-Verdon -	Leicester - -	1542	New Moat - -	Pembroke -	1754
Newborough -	Stafford -	1601	Newnham - -	Gloucester -	1547
Newborough - -	Anglesey -	1721	Newnham - -	Hants - -	⁸1754
Newbottle - -	Northampton -	1538	Newnham - -	Hertford -	1676
Newbourne - -	Suffolk - -	1561	Newnham - -	Kent -	1722
Newbrough - -	Northumberland	1695	Newnham - - -	Northampton -	1678
Newburn - -	Northumberland	1659	Newnham-Murren -	Oxford - -	1678
Newbury - -	Berks - -	1538	Newnton, Long - -	Wilts - -	⁹1648
Newcastle - -	Glamorgan -	1745	Newton-Longville -	Buckingham -	1560
Newcastle - on - Tyme,	Northumberland	1558	Newport - -	Essex - -	1558
St. Nicholas.			Newport (Isle of	Hants - -	1541
All Saints - -	- - -	1600	Wight).		
St. Andrew -	- -	1597	Newport - -	Monmouth -	1702
St. John - -	- -	1587	Newport - -	Salop - -	1569
Newcastle, Little -	Pembroke -	1783	Newport - -	Pembroke -	1741
Newcastle-under-Lyme	Stafford -	1563	Newport-Pagnell -	Buckingham -	1558
Newchapel - -	Stafford -	1723	Newtimber - -	Sussex -	1558
Newchurch - -	Carmarthen -	1719	Newton (near Cam-	Cambridge -	1560
Newchurch (Isle of	Hants - -	1692	bridge).		
Wight).			Newton (near Wisbech)	Cambridge -	1653
Newchurch - -	Kent - -	1684	Newton - -	Lancaster -	1723
Newchurch - -	Monmouth -	1710	Newton - - -	Lincoln -	1612
Newchurch - -	Radnor -	1708	Newton - -	Pembroke -	1757
Newchurch-in-Pendle	Lancaster -	1574	Newton-Blossomville -	Buckingham -	1730
Newchurch-in-Rossen-	Lancaster -	1654	Newton-Bromswold -	Northampton -	1749
dale.			Newton-by-Castleacre	Norfolk -	1771
Newchurch - in - Tyr -	Brecon - -	1729	Newton-by-Toft -	Lincoln -	1592
Abbot.			Newton-Ferrers ⌋ -	Devon - -	1600

¹ See also Registers of Baschurch.
² Included in the Registers of Great Gaddesden (q.v.).
³ P (Marriages only) 1599-1754. Nottinghamshire Parish Registers, vol. 4, 1902.
⁴ P 1599-1812. Lancashire Parish Register Society, vol. 18, 1905.
⁵ P 1559-1813. Parish Register Society, vol. 10, 1897.
⁶ P (Marriages only) 1686-1812. Gloucestershire Parish Registers, vol. 7, 1901 ; and (Marriages only) 1599-1685. Gloucestershire Parish Registers, vol. 12, 1906.
⁷ Included in the Registers of Ulverston (q.v.).
⁸ P (Marriages only) 1754-1812. Hampshire Parish Registers, vol. 8, 1906.
⁹ P (Marriages only) 1653-1812. Wiltshire Parish Registers, vol. 3, 1906.

Parish.	County.	Date of Earliest Entry.	Parish.	County.	Date of Earliest Entry.
Newton-Flotman -	Norfolk - -	1558	Nocton - - -	Lincoln -	1582
Newton-Harcourt -	Leicester - -	[1] —	Noke - - -	Oxford - -	1574
Newton-in-Cleveland -	York - -	1725	Nolton - - -	Pembroke -	1695
Newton-in-Makerfield	Lancaster -	1735	Nolton -	Glamorgan -	* —
Newton-in-the-Willows	Northampton -	1687	Nonington -	Kent -	1525
Newton, Kirk -	Northumberland	[2] 1789	Norbury -	Chester -	* —
Newton, Kyme - -	York - -	1633	Norbury - -	Derby - -	1686
Newton, Long - -	Durham -	1564	Norbury - -	Salop - -	1560
Newton, near Sudbury	Suffolk - -	1558	Norbury - -	Stafford - -	1538
Newton, North - -	Somerset -	1778	Norham - - -	Durham - -	1653
Newton, North -	Wilts - -	1755	Normanby -	Lincoln -	1653
Newton-Nottage -	Glamorgan -	1715	Normanby -	York - -	1699
Newton, Old - -	Suffolk - -	1677	Normanby - on - the-	Lincoln -	1561
Newton-on-Ouze -	York - -	1651	Wold.		
Newton-on-Trent -	Lincoln - -	1658	Normanton -	Derby - -	[10] 1769
Newton-Poppleford -	Devon - -	[3] —	Normanton -	Lincoln -	1669
Newton-Purcell -	Oxford - -	1681	Normanton -	Rutland -	1755
Newton-Regis -	Warwick -	1657	Normanton - -	York - -	1538
Newton-Reigny -	Cumberland -	1572	Normanton-le-Heath -	Leicester - -	1695
Newton-Solney -	Derby - -	1667	Normanton-on-Soar -	Nottingham -	[11] 1559
Newton, South -	Wilts - -	1695	Normanton-on-Trent -	Nottingham -	1673
Newton, St. Cyres -	Devon - -	1554	Normanton, South -	Derby - -	1540
Newton, St. Loe -	Somerset -	1538	Northallerton - -	York - -	1593
Newton-St. Petrock -	Devon - -	1578	Northam - - -	Devon - -	1538
Newton-Tony - -	Wilts - -	[4] 1568	Northampton, All	Northampton -	1560
Newton-Tracey -	Devon - -	1562	Saints.		
Newton-Valence -	Hants - -	1569	St. Giles - -	- - -	1559
Newton-Water -	Huntingdon -	1687	St. Peter - -	- - -	1578
Newton, Welsh -	Hereford - -	1758	St. Sepulchre -	- - -	1566
Newton, West -	Norfolk -	1560	Northaw - -	Hertford - -	[12] —
Newton-Wold -	Lincoln - -	1578	Northborough - -	Northampton -	1538
Newton-Wold -	York - -	1709	Northbourne - -	Kent - -	1586
Newton-Wood -	Northampton -	1588	Northchapel - -	Sussex - -	1717
Newtown - -	Montgomery -	1660	Northenden - -	Chester -	1564
Newtown - -	Hants - -	[5] 1666	Northfield - -	Worcester -	1560
Newtown - -	Salop - -	1780	Northfleet - -	Kent - -	1539
Newtown-Linford -	Leicester - -	[6] 1654	North-Hales. See Cove-		
Nibley, North -	Gloucester -	1567	hithe.		
Nichol-Forest - -	Cumberland -	1761	North-Hill - -	Cornwall -	1555
Nicholas, St. - -	Devon - -	1622	North-Holme -	Lincoln -	[13]
Nicholas, St. -	Glamorgan -	1755	Northiam - -	Sussex - -	1558
Nicholas, St. -	Pembroke -	1783	Northill - -	Bedford - -	1562
Nicholas, St., at Wade	Kent - -	1653	Northington - -	Hants - -	1579
Nicholaston - -	Glamorgan -	1766	Northleach - -	Gloucester -	1556
Nidd - - -	York - -	[7] 1678	Northleigh. See Leigh,		
Ninebanks - -	Northumberland	1767	North.		
Ninfield - -	Sussex - -	1663	Northmoor - -	Oxford - -	1654
Niton (Isle of Wight)	Hants - -	1559	Northolt - -	Middlesex -	1560
Nockholt. See Knock-			Northop - - -	Flint - -	1590
holt.			Northorpe - -	Lincoln - -	1594

[1] Included in the Registers of Wistow (q.v.).
[2] The early Registers were destroyed by fire in 1789, with the exception of a few pages containing fragments of entries from 1657.
[3] Included in the Registers of Aylesbear (q.v.).
[4] **P** (Marriages only) 1591–1812. Wiltshire Parish Registers, vol. 3, 1906.
[5] **P** (Marriages only) 1679–1812. Hampshire Parish Registers, vol. 8, 1906.
[6] **P** 1677–1679. Edited by F. A. Crisp, 1884.
[7] The earlier Registers were destroyed by fire in 1678.
[8] Included in the Registers of Coyty (q.v.).
[9] Included in the Registers of Poynton (q.v.).   [10] Earlier entries at S. Peter's, Derby.
[11] **P** (Marriages only) 1599–1812. Nottinghamshire Parish Registers, vol. 5, 1903.
[12] Church burnt with Registers, February 1881.
[13] Included in the Registers of Wainfleet, All Saints (q.v.).

Parish.	County.	Date of Earliest Entry.	Parish.	County.	Date of Earliest Entry.
Northover - -	Somerset -	[1] 1722	Norwich—continued.		
Northwick - -	Gloucester -	[2] 1667	St. George, Tomb- -	- -	[6] 1538
Northwold - -	Norfolk - -	1656	land.		
Northwood (Isle of	Hants - -	1539	St. Giles - -	- - -	1538
Wight).			St. Gregory - -	- - -	1571
Norton - -	Derby - -	1560	St. Helens -	- - -	1678
Norton - -	Durham - -	1574	St. John, Madder-	- - -	1558
Norton - - -	Gloucester -	1686	market.		
Norton - -	Hertford - -	1571	St. John-de-Sepul-	- - -	1636
Norton - - -	Kent - -	1559	chre.		
Norton - -	Northampton -	1678	St. John, Timber-	- - -	1559
Norton - - -	Radnor - -	1704	hill.		
Norton (St. Philip) -	Somerset -	1680	St. James - -	- - -	1556
Norton - -	Suffolk - -	1539	St. Paul - -	- - -	1567
Norton - - -	Worcester -	1538	St. Lawrence -	- - -	1558
Norton - -	York - -	1560	St. Margaret-de-	- - -	1559
Norton-Bavant - -	Wilts - -	1616	Westwick.		
Norton, Bishop -	Lincoln - -	1587	St. Martin - at -	- - -	1538
Norton-Brize - -	Oxford - -	1585	Palace.		
Norton-Canes - -	Stafford - -	1566	St. Martin-at-Oak	- - -	1704
Norton, Canon -	Hereford - -	1716	St. Mary, Coslany	- - -	[7] 1557
Norton, Chipping- -	Oxford - -	1563	St. Mary-in-the-	- - -	1591
Norton, Cold - -	Essex - -	1539	Marsh.		
Norton-Coleparle -	Wilts - -	1663	St. Michael, Cos-	- - -	1558
Norton-Disney -	Lincoln - -	1578	lany.		
Norton, East - -	Leicester - -	1721	St. Michael at	- - -	[8] 1538
Norton-Fitzwarren -	Somerset -	[3] 1556	Plea.		
Norton, Hook- - -	Oxford - -	1566	St. Michael at	- - -	1562
Norton-in-Hales -	Salop - -	1573	Thorn.		
Norton-in-the-Moors -	Stafford - -	1576	St. Peter, Hungate	- - -	1596
Norton-juxta-Kempsey	Worcester -	1538	St. Peter, Mancroft	- - -	1538
Norton - juxta - Twy-	Leicester - -	1686	St. Peter, Mounter-	- - -	1538
cross.			gate.		
Norton, King's - -	Leicester -	1588	St. Peter, South-	- - -	1558
Norton, King's -	Worcester -	1546	gate.		
Norton-Lindsey - -	Warwick - -	[4] 1742	St. Saviour - -	- -	1555
Norton-Malreward -	Somerset -	1554	St. Simon and St.	- -	1539
Norton-Mandeville -	Essex - -	[5] 1783	Jude.		
Norton, Midsomer -	Somerset -	1677	St. Stephen - -	- - -	1538
Norton-Subcorse -	Norfolk - -	1560	St. Swithin -	- - -	1700
Norton-sub-Hambdon	Somerset -	1558	Norwood - -	Middlesex -	1654
Norwell - -	Nottingham -	1685	Notgrove - - -	Gloucester -	1660
Norwich - - -	Norfolk - -		Notley, Black - -	Essex - -	1570
St. Julian - -	- - -	1589	Notley, White - -	Essex - -	1541
All Saints - -	- - -	1573	Nottingham, St. Mary	Nottingham -	[9] 1566
St. Andrew - -	- - -	1557	St. Nicholas -	- - -	[10] 1562
St. Augustine - -	- - -	1558	St. Peter - -	- - -	[11] 1572
St. Benedict - -	- - -	1562	Nowton - - -	Suffolk - -	1559
St. Clement - -	- - -	1538	Nuffield - -	Oxford - -	1570
St. Edmund - -	- - -	1550	Nunburnholme - -	York - -	1586
St. Etheldred - -	- - -	1665	Nuneaton - -	Warwick - -	1577
St. George Cole-	- - -	1538	Nuneham-Courtney -	Oxford - -	1715
gate.			Nunkeeling - -	York - -	1559

[1] **P** (Marriages only) 1531–1812. Somersetshire Parish Registers, vol. 1, 1898.
[2] Included in the Registers of Henbury (q.v.).
[3] **P** (Marriages only) 1565–1812. Somersetshire Parish Registers, vol. 8, 1907.
[4] Bishop's Transcripts commence 1607.
[5] Earlier destroyed by damp.
[6] **P** 1538–1707. Edited by G. B. Jay, Norwich, 1891.
[7] **P** (Marriages only) 1557–1812. Norfolk Parish Registers, vol. 3, 1907.
[8] **P** 1538–1695. Edited by T. R. Tallack, Norwich, 1892.
[9] **P** (Marriages only) 1566–1813. Nottingham City Parish Registers, vols. 1 and 2, 1900.
[10] **P** (Marriages only) 1562–1812. Nottingham City Parish Registers, 1902.
[11] **P** (Marriages only) 1572–1812. Nottingham City Parish Registers, 1901.

Parish.	County.	Date of Earliest Entry.	Parish.	County.	Date of Earliest Entry.
Nunney - - -	Somerset	1547	Ockham - -	Surrey - -	1567
Nunnington - -	York -	1539	Ockley - - -	Surrey - -	1539
Nunthorpe - in - Cleveland.	York -	—	Ocle-Pychard - -	Hereford -	1773
			Odcombe - - -	Somerset - -	1669
Nunton - - -	Wilts -	1672	Oddingley - -	Worcester -	[7] 1661
Nursling - -	Hants -	1617	Oddington - -	Gloucester -	1549
Nursted - - -	Kent -	1561	Oddington - -	Oxford - -	1572
Nutfield - -	Surrey -	1674	Odell - - -	Bedford - -	1604
Nuthurst - -	Sussex -	1563	Odiham - -	Hants - -	[8] 1538
Nutley - -	Hants -	1688	Odstock - - -	Wilts - -	1541
Nuttall - -	Nottingham -	[1] 1657	Offchurch - -	Warwick -	1669
Nymet (St. George) -	Devon -	1599	Offenham - - -	Worcester -	[9] 1538
Nymett-Rowland -	Devon -	1719	Offham - -	Kent - -	1538
Nympsfield -	Gloucester -	[2] 1678	Offley - -	Hertford - -	[10] 1653
Nympton, Bishop's -	Devon -	1556	Offley, High -	Stafford -	1689
Nympton, King's -	Devon -	1538	Offord-Cluny -	Huntingdon -	1598
Nynehead -	Somerset -	[3] 1670	Offord-Darcy - -	Huntingdon -	1697
			Offton - - -	Suffolk - -	1558
			Offwell - - -	Devon - -	1551
O.			Ogbourne, St. Andrew	Wilts - -	1664
			Ogbourne, St. George	Wilts - -	1538
Oadby - -	Leicester - -	1653	Ogwell, East - -	Devon - -	1674
Oake - - -	Somerset -	1630	Ogwell, West -	Devon - -	1681
Oakford - -	Devon - -	1568	Okeford, Childe-	Dorset - -	1652
Oakham - - -	Rutland -	1564	Okeford-Fitzpaine -	Dorset - -	1592
Oakington - -	Cambridge -	1561	Okehampton - -	Devon - -	1634
Oakley - - -	Bedford -	1680	Okehampton-Monk -	Devon - -	1653
Oakley - -	Buckingham -	1704	Okeover - - -	Stafford -	1737
Oakley. *See* Ugley.			Okewood - -	Surrey - -	1700
Oakley - - -	Suffolk -	1538	Old - - -	Northampton -	1539
Oakley, Church-	Hants - -	[4] 1559	Oldberrow - -	Worcester -	[11] 1649
Oakley, Great -	Essex -	1559	Oldbury - -	Salop - -	1583
Oakley, Great -	Northampton -	1562	Oldbury - -	Worcester -	1714
Oakley, Little -	Essex -	1558	Oldbury-on-the-Hill -	Gloucester -	[12] 1567
Oakley, Little -	Northampton -	1679	Oldbury-on-Severn -	Gloucester -	[13]
Oaksey - - -	Wilts -	1670	Oldcastle - -	Monmouth -	1783
Oare - - -	Kent - -	1714	Oldham - - -	Lancaster -	[14] 1558
Oare - - -	Somerset -	1674	Oldswinford - -	Worcester -	1602
Oborne - - -	Dorset -	1567	Ollerton - -	Nottingham -	[15] 1592
Oby - - -	Norfolk - -	[5] —	Olney - - -	Buckingham -	[16] 1665
Occold - - -	Suffolk -	1681	Olveston - -	Gloucester -	1560
Ockbrook - -	Derby - -	[6] 1630	Ombersley - -	Worcester -	1574
Ockendon, North -	Essex -	1570	Onecote - -	Stafford -	1755
Ockendon, South -	Essex -	1538	Onehouse - -	Suffolk - -	1552
			Ongar, Chipping -	Essex - -	[17] 1558

[1] **P** (Marriages only) 1663–1812. Nottinghamshire Parish Registers, vol. 8, 1905.
[2] **P** (Marriages only) 1679–1812. Gloucestershire Parish Registers, vol. 1, 1896; and **P** (Marriages only) 1609–1678. Gloucestershire Parish Registers, vol. 12, 1906.
[3] **P** (Marriages only) 1670–1812. Somersetshire Parish Registers, vol. 8, 1907.
[4] **P** (Marriages only) 1565–1812. Hampshire Parish Registers, vol. 3, 1902.
[5] Included in the Registers of Ashby (*q.v.*).
[6] **P** (Marriages only) 1631–1812. Derbyshire Parish Registers, vol. 1, 1906.
[7] Bishop's Transcripts commence 1611.
[8] **P** (Marriages only) 1538–1812. Hampshire Parish Registers, vol. 6, 1904.
[9] **P** (Marriages only) 1543–1812. Worcestershire Parish Registers, vol. 1, 1901.
[10] **P** (Marriages only) 1654–1812. Hertfordshire Parish Registers, vol. 1, 1907.
[11] Bishop's Transcripts commence 1613.
[12] **P** (Marriages only) 1568–1812. Gloucestershire Parish Registers, vol. 9, 1905.
[13] Included in the Registers of Thornbury (*q.v.*).
[14] **P** 1558–1661. Edited by Giles Shaw, Oldham, 1889. *Also*, 1558–1658. Local Notes and Gleanings, vols. 1, 2, 3, Oldham, 1887.
[15] **P** 1592–1812. Edited by G. W. Marshall, Exeter, 1896.
[16] **P** 1665–1812. Buckinghamshire Parish Register Society, vol. 6.
[17] **P** 1558–1750. Edited by F. A. Crisp, 1886.

Parish.	County.	Date of Earliest Entry.	Parish.	County.	Date of Earliest Entry.
Ongar, High - -	Essex - -	1538	Oswestry - -	Salop - -	[9]1558
Onibury - - -	Salop - -	1577	Osyth, St. - -	Essex - -	1666
Orby - - -	Lincoln -	1725	Otford - - -	Kent - -	1630
Orchard, East - -	Dorset - -	[1]—	Otham - - -	Kent - -	1538
Orchard-Portman -	Somerset -	[2]1538	Othery - - -	Somerset -	1560
Orchard, West - -	Dorset - -	1754	Otley - - -	Suffolk - -	1734
Orchardleigh - -	Somerset -	1623	Otley - - -	York - -	1562
Orcheston, St. George	Wilts - -	1647	Otterbourne - -	Hants - -	1648
Orcheston, St. Mary -	Wilts - -	1688	Otterden - -	Kent - -	1660
Orcop - - -	Hereford -	1672	Otterford - -	Somerset -	[10]1558
Ordsall - - -	Nottingham -	1538	Otterham - -	Cornwall -	[11]1687
Ore - - -	Sussex - -	1558	Otterhampton -	Somerset -	[12]1636
Orford - - -	Suffolk -	1538	Otterington, North -	York - -	1591
Orlestone - -	Kent - -	1554	Otterington, South -	York - -	1718
Orleton - - -	Hereford -	1565	Otterton - -	Devon - -	1559
Orleton - - -	Worcester -	[3]—	Ottery, St. Mary -	Devon - -	1601
Orlingbury - -	Northampton -	1564	Ottery, Upper -	Devon - -	1560
Ormsby, Nun - -	Lincoln - -	1741	Ottery, Venn - -	Devon - -	1681
Ormsby, South - -	Lincoln -	1561	Ottringham - -	York - -	1566
Ormesby - -	York - -	1599	Oulton - - -	Norfolk - -	1706
Ormesby, St. Margaret	Norfolk -	1675	Oulton - - -	Suffolk - -	1659
Ormesby, St. Michael -	Norfolk -	1568	Oundle - - -	Northampton -	1625
Ormshed - -	Westmorland -	1562	Ousby - - -	Cumberland	1663
Ormskirk - -	Lancaster -	[4]1557	Ousden - - -	Suffolk - -	1675
Orpington - -	Kent - -	[5]1560	Ouseburn, Great -	York - -	1662
Orsett - - -	Essex - -	1669	Ouseburn, Little -	York - -	1564
Orston - - -	Nottingham -	[6]1589	Outwell - - -	Norfolk and Cambridge.	1559
Orton - - -	Northampton -	[7]—			
Orton - - -	Westmorland -	1595	Over - - -	Cambridge -	1577
Orton, Great - -	Cumberland -	1569	Over - - -	Chester -	1558
Orton-Longueville -	Huntingdon -	1559	Overbury - -	Worcester -	1557
Orton-on-the-Hill -	Leicester -	1657	Overchurch. See Upton		
Orton-Waterville -	Huntingdon -	1539	(Cheshire).		
Orwell - - -	Cambridge -	1560	Overstone - -	Northampton -	1680
Osbaldwick - -	York - -	1581	Overstrand - -	Norfolk - -	1558
Osbournby - -	Lincoln -	1682	Overton - - -	Flint - -	1602
Osgathorpe - -	Leicester -	1683	Overton - - -	Lancaster -	1724
Osmaston - by - Ash-	Derby - -	1606	Overton - - -	Hants - -	[13]1645
bourne.			Overton - - -	Wilts - -	1682
Osmaston-by-Derby -	Derby - -	1743	Overton - - -	York - -	1593
Osmington - -	Dorset - -	1678	Overton, Cold -	Leicester -	1556
Osmotherley - -	York - -	1696	Overton, Market -	Rutland -	1573
Ospringe - -	Kent - -	1561	Oving - - -	Buckingham -	1678
Ossett - - -	York - -	[8]1792	Oving - - -	Sussex - -	1561
Ossington - -	Nottingham -	1594	Ovingdean - -	Sussex - -	[14]1719
Oswaldkirk - -	York - -	1538	Ovingham - -	Northumberland	1679

[1] Included in the Registers of Iwerne-Minster (q.v.).
[2] **P** (Marriages only) 1538-1812. Somersetshire Parish Registers, vol. 7, 1906.
[3] Included in the Registers of Eastham (q.v.).
[4] **P** 1557-1626. Lancashire Parish Register Society, vol. 13, 1902.
[5] **P** 1560-1754. Edited by H. C. Kirby, London, 1895.
[6] **P** (Marriages only) 1592-1812. Nottinghamshire Parish Registers, vol. 1, 1898.
[7] Included in the Registers of Rowell (q.v.).
[8] Baptisms only, which before this date were entered in Dewsbury Registers (q.v.).
[9] **P** 1558-1630. Shropshire Parish Register Society, St. Asaph Diocese, vol. 4.
[10] These Registers are very incomplete, especially the entries of marriages. According to the Parliamentary Return of 1831, one of the Churchwardens at the beginning of the last century, who was a shopkeeper, used some of the Registers for waste paper to enfold his goods.
[11] **P** (Marriages only) 1687-1811. Cornwall Parish Registers, vol. 1, 1900.
[12] **P** (Marriages only) 1656-1749. Somersetshire Parish Registers, vol. 6, 1905.
[13] **P** (Marriages only) 1640-1812. Hampshire Parish Registers, vol. 2, 1900.
[14] Some Registers of baptisms beginning in 1794, which had taken place at Ovingdean have been found in the Registers of Falmer.

Parish.	County.	Date of Earliest Entry.	Parish.	County.	Date of Earliest Entry.
Ovington - - -	Essex - -	1559			
Ovington -	Hants - -	1591			
Ovington - - -	Norfolk -	1654	**P.**		
Owermoigne -	Dorset - -	1569			
Owersby - - -	Lincoln -	1559	Packington - -	Leicester - -	1677
Owlpen - -	Gloucester -	[1] 1677	Packington, Great -	Warwick -	1538
Owmby-by-Spital	Lincoln - -	1700	Packington, Little -	Warwick - -	1628
Owslebury - - -	Hants - -	1678	Packwood - -	Warwick -	1668
Owston - - -	Lincoln -	1605	Padbury - - -	Buckingham -	1538
Owston - -	York - -	1683	Paddington - -	Middlesex -	1701
Owston - -	Leicester - -	1701	Paddlesworth - -	Kent - -	1715
Owthorne - -	York - -	1574	Padiham - - -	Lancaster -	[4] 1573
Owthorpe - - -	Nottingham -	[2] 1731	Padstow - - -	Cornwall -	[5] 1599
Oxburgh - -	Norfolk -	1538	Padworth - -	Berks - -	[6] 1693
Oxendon, Great -	Northampton -	1564	Pagham - - -	Sussex - -	1707
Oxenhall - -	Gloucester -	1665	Paglesham - -	Essex - -	1719
Oxenton - - -	Gloucester -	1678	Paignton - - -	Devon -	1559
Oxford, St. Aldate -	Oxford - -	1678	Painswick - -	Gloucester -	[7] 1548
Christ Church Cathedral.	- - -	1639	Pakefield - - -	Suffolk -	1678
			Pakenham - -	Suffolk -	[8] 1670
All Saints - -	- - -	1559	Palgrave - - -	Suffolk -	1559
St. Clement -	- - -	1666	Palling-next-the-Sea -	Norfolk -	1616
St. Cross - -	- - -	1653	Pamber - - -	Hants - -	1661
St. Ebbe - -	- - -	1557	Pampisford - -	Cambridge -	1565
St. Giles - -	- - -	1576	Pancras, St. See London.		
St. John - -	- - -	1616			
St. Martin - -	- - -	1569	Pancras-Wyke - -	Devon - -	1694
St. Mary Magdalene.	- - -	1602	Panfield - -	Essex - -	1569
			Pangbourn - -	Berks - -	1556
St. Mary - the - Virgin.	- - -	1599	Pannall - - -	York - -	1586
			Panteg - - -	Monmouth -	1598
St. Michael - -	- - -	1558	Panton - - -	Lincoln -	1736
St. Peter - le - Bailey.	- - -	1585	Papplewick - -	Nottingham -	1661
			Papworth-St. Agnes -	Cambridge and Huntingdon.	1558
St. Peter-in-the-East.	- - -	1653			
			Papworth-Everard -	Cambridge - -	[9] 1695
St. Thomas - -	- - -	1655	Parham - - -	Suffolk -	1538
Oxhill - - -	Warwick - -	1568	Parham - - -	Sussex - -	1538
Oxhead - - -	Norfolk -	1573	Parkham - - -	Devon - -	[10] 1538
Oxted - - -	Surrey - -	1603	Parkstone - -	Dorset - -	[11] —
Oxton - - -	Nottingham -	1564	Parley, West - -	Dorset - -	[12] 1715
Oxwich - - -	Glamorgan -	1655	Parndon, Great -	Essex - -	1547
Oxwick - - -	Norfolk -	1538	Parndon, Little -	Essex - -	1660
Oystermouth - -	Glamorgan -	1719	Parracombe - -	Devon - -	1687
Ozleworth - -	Gloucester -	[3] 1698	Parson-Drove - -	Cambridge -	1657
			Partney - - -	Lincoln - -	1699
			Partrishow - -	Brecon - -	1728
			Parwich - - -	Derby - -	1730

[1] **P** (Marriages only) 1697-1837. Gloucestershire Parish Registers, vol. 1, 1896 ; and (Marriages only) 1837-1897. Gloucestershire Parish Registers, vol. 2, 1897.
[2] **P** (Marriages only) 1733-1812. Nottinghamshire Parish Registers, vol. 2, 1899.
[3] **P** (Marriages only) 1698-1812. Gloucestershire Parish Registers, vol. 12, 1906.
[4] **P** 1573-1653. Lancashire Parish Register Society, vol. 16, 1903.
[5] **P** (Marriages only) 1599-1812. Cornwall Parish Registers, vol. 6, 1904.
[6] Bishop's Transcripts commence 1607.
[7] **P** (Marriages only) 1548-1812. Gloucestershire Parish Registers, vol. 8, 1902.
[8] **P** 1564-1766. Edited by F. A. Crisp, 1888.
[9] Original Register 1565-1692 in British Museum, Additional M.S. 31854.
[10] **P** 1538-1812. Devon and Cornwall Register Society, 1906.
[11] Included in the Registers of Great Canford (q.v.).
[12] There is a tradition in the parish that the earlier Registers were used in a dairy-shop to wrap up pats of butter for customers.

Parish.	County.	Date of Earliest Entry.	Parish.	County.	Date of Earliest Entry.
Passenham - -	Northampton -	1695	Penboyr - - -	Carmarthen -	1752
Paston - -	Norfolk - -	1538	Penbryn - -	Cardigan -	1726
Paston - - -	Northampton -	1644	Pencarreg - - -	Carmarthen -	1754
Patcham - -	Sussex - -	1558	Pencombe - -	Hereford - -	1543
Patching - -	Sussex - -	1560	Pencoyd - -	Hereford -	[5] 1564
Pateley-Bridge -	York - -	1552	Penderyn - -	Brecon - -	1754
Patney - -	Wilts - -	1592	Pendleton - -	Lancaster -	1776
Patrington - -	York - -	[1] 1570	Pendock - -	Worcester -	1558
Patrixbourne - -	Kent - -	1556	Pendomer - -	Somerset -	1729
Patshull - -	Stafford - -	1559	Pendoylan - -	Glamorgan -	1727
Patterdale - -	Westmorland -	1611	Penegoes - - -	Montgomery -	1679
Pattingham - -	Salop and Stafford.	1559	Penhow - - -	Monmouth -	1725
			Penhurst - -	Sussex - -	1559
Pattishall - -	Northampton -	1556	Penistone - -	York - -	1644
Pattiswick - -	Essex - -	1677	Penkridge - -	Stafford - -	1572
Paul, St. - -	Cornwall -	[2] 1595	Penley - - -	Flint - -	1752
Paulers Pury -	Northampton -	1557	Penllech - -	Carnarvon -	1777
Paull - - -	York - -	1657	Penmachno - -	Carnarvon -	[6] —
Paulton - - -	Somerset -	1733	Penmaen - - -	Glamorgan -	1765
Pauntley - -	Gloucester -	1538	Penmaenmawr. See		
Pavenham - -	Bedford - -	1560	Dwygyfylchi.		
Pawlett - -	Somerset -	1667	Penmark - - -	Glamorgan -	1751
Paxton, Great -	Huntingdon -	1583	Penmon - - -	Anglesea -	1695
Paxton, Little -	Huntingdon -	1567	Penmorva - -	Carnarvon -	1672
Peak Forest - -	Derby - -	[3] 1678	Pennynnedd - -	Anglesea -	1741
Peakirk - -	Northampton -	1560	Penn - - -	Buckingham -	1563
Peasemore - - -	Berks - -	1538	Penn - - -	Stafford - -	1569
Peasenhall - -	Suffolk - -	1558	Pennal - - -	Merioneth -	1721
Peasmarsh - -	Sussex - -	1568	Pennant - - -	Montgomery -	1680
Peatling-Magna -	Leicester -	1565	Pennard, East -	Somerset -	1608
Peatling-Parva -	Leicester -	1711	Pennard, West -	Somerset -	1538
Pebmarsh - -	Essex - -	1648	Pennington - -	Lancaster -	1623
Pebworth - - -	Gloucester -	[4] 1595	Pennycross - -	Devon - -	1634
Peckham, East -	Kent - -	1558	Penrhos - -	Carnarvon -	[7] —
Peckham, West -	Kent - -	1561	Penrhos - -	Monmouth -	1718
Peckleton - -	Leicester -	1567	Penrhoslligwy -	Anglesey -	1766
Pedmore - - -	Worcester -	1539	Penrice - - -	Glamorgan -	1721
Peel - - -	Lancaster -	1760	Penrieth - - -	Pembroke -	1755
Peldon - - -	Essex - -	1725	Penrith - - -	Cumberland -	[8] 1556
Pelham, Brent- -	Hertford - -	1539	Pensax - - -	Worcester -	1563
Pelham, Furneaux- -	Hertford -	1560	Pen-Selwood -	Somerset -	1721
Pelham, Stocking- -	Hertford - -	1695	Penshaw - -	Durham - -	1754
Pelsall - -	Stafford -	1763	Penshurst - -	Kent - -	1558
Pelynt - - -	Cornwall -	1678	Penstrowed - -	Montgomery -	1628
Pembrey - -	Carmarthen -	1700	Penterry - - -	Monmouth -	1721
Pembridge - -	Hereford - -	1564	Pentir - - -	Carnarvon -	[9] —
Pembroke, St. Mary -	Pembroke -	1711	Pentlow - - -	Essex - -	1539
Pembroke, St. Michael	Pembroke -	1748	Pentney - - -	Norfolk - -	1730
Pembroke, St. Nicholas	Pembroke -	1748	Penton-Mewsey -	Hants - -	[10] 1642
Pembury - - -	Kent - -	1561	Pentraeth - -	Anglesey -	1740
Penalley - - -	Pembroke -	1738	Pentrevoelas -	Denbigh -	1772
Penalt - - -	Monmouth -	1765	Pentrich - - -	Derby - -	1653
Penarth - - -	Glamorgan -	1768	Pentridge - - -	Dorset - -	1714

[1] **P** 1570–1731. Yorkshire Parish Register Society, vol. 6, 1900.
[2] **P** (Marriages only) 1595–1812. Cornwall Parish Registers, vol. 9, 1906.
[3] **P** Edited by G. W. Marshall, Worksop, 1901.
[4] **P** (Marriages only) 1595–1700. Gloucestershire Notes and Queries, vol. 1.
[5] **P** 1564–1812. Edited by G. J. H. Parry, 1900.
[6] There are some old Registers, but now totally illegible.
[7] Included in the Registers of Abererch (q.v.).
[8] **P** 1556–1601. Edited by Geo. Watson, Penrith, 1893.
[9] Original Register 1616–1712. In British Museum, Additional MS. 32644.
[10] **P** (Marriages only) 1649–1812. Hampshire Parish Registers, vol. 1, 1899.

Parish.	County.	Date of Earliest Entry.	Parish.	County.	Date of Earliest Entry.
Pentyrch - -	Glamorgan -	1670	Pewsey - -	Wilts - -	1568
Penwortham - -	Lancaster -	[1] —	Peyhembury -	Devon - -	1559
Pen-y-Clawdd -	Monmouth -	1727	Phillack - -	Cornwall -	[3] 1560
Penzance - -	Cornwall -	1789	Philleigh - -	Cornwall -	1733
Peopleton - -	Worcester -	[2] 1632	Pickenham, North -	Norfolk -	1678
Peover, Lower -	Chester -	1570	Pickenham, South -	Norfolk -	1694
Peover, Over -	Chester -	1688	Pickering - -	York - -	1559
Peper-Harrow -	Surrey -	1697	Pickhill - -	York - -	[9] 1567
Perivale - -	Middlesex -	1707	Pickwell - -	Leicester -	1572
Perlethorpe - -	Nottingham -	[3] 1538	Pickworth - -	Lincoln -	1538
Perran-Arworthal -	Cornwall -	[4] 1754	Pickworth - -	Rutland -	1660
Perranuthnoe -	Cornwall -	1562	Piddinghoe - -	Sussex -	1540
Perranzabuloe -	Cornwall -	[5] 1566	Piddington - -	Northampton -	1573
Perrot, North -	Somerset -	1684	Piddington - -	Oxford -	1654
Perrot, South -	Dorset -	1538	Piddle, North -	Worcester -	1565
Pershore, St. Andrew -	Worcester -	[6] 1641	Piddle, Wyre -	Worcester -	[10] 1670
Pershore, Holy Cross -	Worcester -	1540	Piddle-Hinton -	Dorset -	1539
Pertenhall -	Bedford -	1582	Piddle Town -	Dorset -	1538
Peterchurch - -	Hereford -	1711	Piddle Trenthide -	Dorset -	1646
Peterborough Cathedral.	Northampton -	1615	Pidley - -	Huntingdon -	1558
			Pierre, St. -	Monmouth -	[11] 1686
Peterborough, St. John Baptist.	Northampton -	1558	Pilham - -	Lincoln -	1677
			Pillaton -	Cornwall -	1557
Petersfield - -	Hants -	1558	Pillerton-Hersey -	Warwick -	1539
Petersham - -	Surrey -	1574	Pillerton-Priors -	Warwick -	1604
Peter's, St. (Isle of Thanet).	Kent -	1582	Pilleth - -	Radnor -	1772
			Pilling - -	Lancaster -	1638
Peters Marland. See Marland Peters.			Pilsdon - -	Dorset -	1754
			Pilton - -	Devon -	1569
Peterstone-super-Montem.	Glamorgan -	1745	Pilton - -	Northampton -	1569
			Pilton - -	Rutland -	1548
Peterstone - Wentloog	Monmouth -	1707	Pilton - -	Somerset -	1558
Peterston-super-Ely -	Glamorgan -	[7] 1749	Pimperne - -	Dorset -	1559
Peterstow - -	Hereford -	1538	Pinchbeck - -	Lincoln -	[12] 1560
Petham - -	Kent -	1559	Pinhoe - -	Devon -	1561
Petherick, Little -	Cornwall -	1706	Pinner - -	Middlesex -	1654
Petherton, North -	Somerset -	1558	Pinnock - -	Gloucester -	[13] —
Petherton, South -	Somerset -	1574	Pinnock, St. -	Cornwall -	1566
Petherwyn, North -	Devon -	1653	Pinvin - -	Worcester -	1552
Petherwyn, South -	Cornwall -	1656	Pinxton - -	Derby -	1561
Petrockstowe -	Devon -	1695	Pipe - -	Hereford -	1558
Petrox, St. -	Pembroke -	1640	Pirbright - -	Surrey -	1574
Pett - -	Sussex -	1675	Pirton - -	Hertford -	1558
Pettaugh - -	Suffolk -	1653	Pirton - -	Oxford -	1598
Pettistree - -	Suffolk -	1539	Pirton - -	Worcester -	1538
Petton - -	Salop -	1677	Pishill - -	Oxford -	1765
Petworth - -	Sussex -	1559	Pistyll - -	Carnarvon -	[14] —
Pevensey - -	Sussex -	1565	Pitchcombe - -	Gloucester -	[15] 1709

[1] The early Registers were destroyed by fire in 1857.
[2] Bishop's Transcripts commence 1612.
[3] **P** 1538-1812. Edited by G. W. Marshall, Worksop. 1887.
[4] **P** (Marriages only) 1684-1812. Cornwall Parish Registers, vol. 7, 1904.
[5] The Registers very incomplete until 1640.
[6] Bishop's Transcripts commence 1608.
[7] **P** Edited by A. F. C. C. Langley, London, 1888.
[8] **P** (Marriages only) 1572-1812. Cornwall Parish Registers, vol. 2, 1902.
[9] **P** 1567-1812. Yorkshire Parish Register Society, vol. 20, 1904.
[10] Bishop's Transcripts commence 1615.
[11] See also Portskewett.
[12] **P** (Marriages only) 1560-1812. Lincolnshire Parish Registers, vol. 2, 1907.
[13] Included in the Registers of Didbrooke (q.v.).
[14] Included in the Registers of Edern (q.v.).
[15] **P** (Marriages only) 1709-1742. Gloucestershire Notes and Queries, vol. 3, 268.

Parish.	County.	Date of Earliest Entry.	Parish.	County.	Date of Earliest Entry.
Pitchcott - -	Buckingham -	1680	Ponsonby - -	Cumberland -	1723
Pitchford - -	Salop - -	[1]1558	Pontefract - -	York - -	1585
Pitchley. See Pytchley			Ponteland - -	Northumberland	1602
Pitcomb - -	Somerset - -	1538	Pontesbright (or	Essex - -	1538
Pitminster - -	Somerset -	[2]1542	Chappel).		
Pitney - -	Somerset - -	[3]1699	Pontesbury - -	Salop - -	1538
Pitsea - - -	Essex - -	1688	Ponton, Great -	Lincoln - -	1622
Pitsford - -	Northampton -	1560	Ponton, Little -	Lincoln - -	1729
Pitstone - -	Buckingham -	[4]1653	Pool, South -	Devon - -	1664
Pittington - -	Durham - -	1574	Poole - -	Dorset - -	1538
Pixley - - -	Hereford -	1745	Poole - - -	York - -	[10]
Plaistow - -	Sussex - -	[5]—	Poole-Keynes -	Wilts - -	1632
Plaitford - -	Wilts - -	1710	Poorstock - -	Dorset - -	[11]1568
Plaxtol - -	Kent - -	1648	Poorton, North -	Dorset - -	[12]1695
Playden - -	Sussex - -	1714	Popham - -	Hants - -	[13]1628
Playford - -	Suffolk - -	1660	Poplar - -	Middlesex -	1711
Pleasley - -	Derby - -	1553	Poppleton-Nether -	York - -	1640
Plemstall - -	Chester - -	1558	Poppleton-Upper -		
Pleshey - -	Essex - -	1656	Poringland, Great -	Norfolk -	1560
Pluckley - -	Kent - -	1560	Poringland, Little -	Norfolk - -	[14]—
Plumbland - -	Cumberland -	1677	Porlock - -	Somerset -	1625
Plumpton - -	Northampton -	1682	Portbury - -	Somerset - -	1719
Plumpton - -	Sussex - -	1558	Portchester - -	Hants - -	1607
Plumpton-Wall -	Cumberland -	[6]—	Portesham - -	Dorset - -	1573
Plumstead - -	Kent - -	1654	Port-Eynon - -	Glamorgan -	1740
Plumstead - -	Norfolk - -	1556	Porthkerry - -	Glamorgan -	1724
Plumstead, Little -	Norfolk - -	1559	Portishead - -	Somerset - -	1554
Plumstead, Great -	Norfolk - -	1558	Portland - -	Dorset - -	1591
Plumtree - -	Nottingham -	1558	Portlemouth - -	Devon - -	1563
Plungar - -	Leicester - -	1695	Portsea - -	Hants - -	1653
Plymouth St. Andrews	Devon - -	1581	Portskewet - -	Monmouth -	1593
King Charles the	Devon - -	1653	Portslade - -	Sussex - -	1666
Martyr.			Portsmouth - -	Hants - -	[15]1653
Plympton (St. Mary) -	Devon - -	[7]1603	Poslingford - -	Suffolk - -	1678
Plympton (St. Maurice)	Devon - -	[8]1616	Postling - -	Kent - -	1687
Plymstock - -	Devon - -	1591	Postwick - -	Norfolk - -	1570
Plymtree - -	Devon - -	1538	Potsgrove - -	Bedford - -	1663
Pocklington - -	Devon - -	1559	Potter-Hanworth -	Lincoln - -	1683
Podymore-Milton -	Somerset -	[9]1635	Potter-Heigham. See		
Pointington. See			Heigham, Potter.		
Poyntington.			Potterne - -	Wilts - -	1557
Polebrook - -	Northampton -	1653	Potterspury - -	Northampton -	1671
Polesworth - -	Warwick - -	1631	Potton - -	Bedford - -	1614
Poling - -	Sussex - -	1653	Pott-Shrigley - -	Chester - -	1630
Polstead - -	Suffolk - -	1538	Poughill - -	Cornwall -	1538
Poltimore - -	Devon - -	1718	Poughill - -	Devon - -	1567

[1] P 1558-1812. Shropshire Parish Register Society (Lichfield Diocese), vol. 1, 1900, and Parish Register Society, vol. 31, 1900.
[2] P (Marriages only) 1542-1812. Somersetshire Parish Registers, vol. 7, 1906.
[3] P (Marriages only) 1623-1812. Somersetshire Parish Registers, vol. 2, 1899.
[4] P (Marriages only) 1576-1812. Buckinghamshire Parish Registers, vol. 1, 1902.
[5] Included in the Registers of Kirdford (q.v.).
[6] Included in the Registers of Lazonby (q.v.).
[7] P 1603-1683. In Parish Magazine, commencing 1891.
[8] P 1616-1812. In Parish Magazine, commencing from January 1888 to December 1890.
[9] P (Marriages only) 1744-1811. Somersetshire Parish Registers, vol. 2, 1899.
[10] Included in the Registers of Otley (q.v.).
[11] P (Marriages only) 1568-1812. Dorset Parish Registers, vol. 1, 1906.
[12] P (Marriages only) 1761-1812. Dorset Parish Registers, vol. 1, 1906. P (Marriages only) 1698-1747. Dorset Parish Registers, vol. 2, 1907.
[13] P (Marriages only) 1628-1812. Hampshire Parish Registers, vol. 9, 1907.
[14] Included in the Registers of Howe (q.v.).
[15] P (Marriages only) 1653-1812. Hampshire Parish Registers, vol. 10, 1907.

Parish.	County.	Date of Earliest Entry.	Parish.	County.	Date of Earliest Entry.
Poulshot - -	Wilts - -	1627	Princetown - -	Devon - -	1807
Poulton-le-Fylde -	Lancaster -	[1] 1591	Prior's-Hardwick. See		
Poulton-le-Sands -	Lancaster -	1747	Hardwick, Prior's.		
Poulton - -	Wilts - -	1695	Prior's-Lee - -	Salop - -	[9] —
Poundstock - -	Cornwall -	1615	Prior's-Dean - -	Hants - -	[10] 1538
Powderham - -	Devon - ·	1558	Priston - -	Somerset - -	1764
Powerstock. See Poor-			Prittlewell - -	Essex - -	1645
stock.			Privett - - -	Hants - -	1538
Powick - -	Worcester -	[2] 1662	Probus - -	Cornwall -	1641
Poxwell - -	Dorset - -	1674	Publow - -	Somerset -	1569
Poynings - -	Sussex - -	1558	Puckington - -	Somerset -	[11] 1693
Poyntington -	Dorset - -	1618	Pucklechurch - -	Gloucester -	1590
Poynton - -	Chester -	1723	Puddington - -	Bedford - -	1662
Preen-Church - ·	Salop - -	1680	Puddington - -	Devon - -	1684
Prees - - -	Salop - -	1597	Pudlestone - -	Hereford - -	1566
Prendergast - -	Pembroke -	1696	Pudsey - -	York - -	[12] —
Prescot - -	Lancaster -	1580	Pulborough - -	Sussex - -	1595
Preshute - -	Wilts - -	[3] 1607	Pulford - -	Chester -	1559
Prestbury - -	Chester - -	[4] 1560	Pulham, St. Mary the	Norfolk - -	1539
Prestbury - -	Gloucester -	1633	Virgin.		
Presteign - -	Hereford -	1561	Pulham, St. Mary	Norfolk - -	1538
Preston - - -	Dorset - -	1693	Magdalen.		
Preston (near Ciren-	Gloucester -	1677	Pulham - - -	Dorset - -	1734
cester).			Pulloxhill - -	Bedford - -	1706
Preston (near Led-	Gloucester -	1665	Pulverbatch - -	Salop - -	1542
bury).			Puncheston - -	Pembroke -	1797
Preston-by-Faversham	Kent - -	1559	Puncknowle - -	Dorset - -	1630
Preston (near Elm-	Kent - -	1558	Puriton - -	Somerset -	1558
ston).			Purleigh - -	Essex - -	1592
Preston - - -	Lancaster -	[5] 1611	Purley - - -	Berks - -	1662
Preston - - -	Rutland - -	1560	Purton - -	Wilts - -	1558
Preston - - -	Somerset -	1741	Pusey - -	Berks - -	1661
Preston - - -	Suffolk - -	1628	Putford, East -	Devon - -	1671
Preston - - -	Sussex - -	1538	Putford, West -	Devon - -	1668
Preston-in-Holderness	York - -	1559	Putley - -	Hereford -	1561
Preston-Bagot -	Warwick - -	[6] 1677	Putney - -	Surrey - -	1620
Preston-Bissett -	Buckingham -	1662	Puttenham - -	Hertford - -	1678
Preston-Capes -	Northampton -	1613	Puttenham - -	Surrey - -	1562
Preston-Deanery -	Northampton -	1670	Puxton - -	Somerset -	1542
Preston, East -	Sussex - -	1573	Pwllcrochan -	Pembroke -	1695
Preston-Gobalds -	Salop - -	1602	Pyecombe - -	Sussex - -	1561
Preston, Long -	York - -	1563	Pyle - -	Glamorgan -	1695
Preston-Patrick -	Westmorland -	1703	Pylle - -	Somerset -	1591
Preston-on-Stour -	Gloucester -	[7] 1540	Pyon, Kings -	Hereford -	1538
Preston-on-the-Weald	Salop - -	1693	Pyrford - -	Surrey - -	1666
Moors.			Pytchley - -	Northampton -	1695
Preston-on-Wye -	Hereford - -	1574	Pyworthy - -	Devon - -	1653
Preston-Wynne -	Hereford -	[8] 1730			
Prestwich - -	Lancaster -	1603			
Prestwold - -	Leicester - -	1560			
Priddy - - -	Somerset -	1761			

[1] **P** 1591–1677. Lancashire Parish Register Society, vol. 16, 1904.
[2] Bishop's Transcripts commence 1611.
[3] **P** (Marriages only) 1606–1812. Wiltshire Parish Registers, vol. 4, 1907.
[4] **P** 1560–1636. Lancashire and Cheshire Record Society, vol. 5, 1881.
[5] **P** 1611–1631. In Records of Parish Church, Preston, by T. C. Smith, Preston, 1892.
[6] Bishop's Transcripts commence 1612.
[7] **P** (Marriages only) 1541–1812. Gloucestershire Parish Registers, vol. 4, 1898.
[8] The entries for this parish from 1573 to 1730 were made in the Registers of Withington.
[9] Included in the Registers of Shiffnal (q.v.).
[10] **P** 1538–1812 (including Colmer). Edited by Rev. T. Hervey, 1886.
[11] **P** (Marriages only) 1695–1812. Somersetshire Parish Registers, vol. 4, 1902.
[12] Included in the Registers of Calverley (q.v.).

Parish.	County.	Date of Earliest Entry.	Parish.	County.	Date of Earliest Entry.
Q.			Radway - -	Warwick -	1600
			Radwell - -	Hertford - -	1590
			Radwinter - -	Essex -	1638
Quadring - -	Lincoln -	1583	Radyr - -	Glamorgan -	1725
Quainton - -	Buckingham -	1599	Ragdale - -	Leicester - -	1668
Quantoxhead, East -	Somerset -	1654	Raglan - -	Monmouth -	1711
Quantoxhead, West -	Somerset -	1558	Ragnall - -	Nottingham -	1700
Quarley - - -	Hants - -	1559	Rainford -	Lancaster - -	1718
Quarndon - -	Derby - -	1754	Rainham - -	Kent - -	1592
Quarnford - - .	Stafford -	1744	Rainham - -	Essex - -	1570
Quarrington - -	Lincoln -	1558	Rainham, East -	Norfolk -	1627
Quatford - -	Salop - -	1577	Rainham, West -	Norfolk - -	1539
Quatt-Malvern -	Salop - -	1672	Rainham, South -	Norfolk -	1740
Quedgeley -	Gloucester -	[1] 1559	Rainow - - -	Chester -	1765
Queenborough - -	Kent - -	1719	Raithby (Spilsby) -	Lincoln -	1558
Queen-Camel. *See*			Raithby (South) -	Lincoln - -	1654
Camel, Queen-.			Rame - - -	Cornwall -	1653
Queen-Charlton. *See*			Rampisham - -	Dorset - -	1576
Charlton, Queen-.			Rampton - - -	Cambridge -	1674
Queenhill - -	Worcester -	[2] 1733	Rampton - -	Nottingham -	1565
Quendon - -	Essex - -	1687	Ramsbury - -	Wilts - -	1678
Queniborough - -	Leicester - -	1561	Ramsden-Bellhouse -	Essex -	[6] 1562
Quenington - -	Gloucester -	1653	Ramsden-Crays -	Essex - -	1558
Quethiock - -	Cornwall -	1574	Ramsey - -	Essex - -	1645
Quiddenham - -	Norfolk - -	1538	Ramsey - -	Huntingdon -	1559
Quinton - -	Gloucester -	[3] 1547	Ramsholt - -	Suffolk -	1706
Quinton - -	Northampton -	1648	Ranby - - -	Lincoln -	1569
Quorndon - -	Leicester -	1576	Rand - - -	Lincoln - -	1661
			Randwick - - -	Gloucester -	1662
			Rangeworthy - -	Gloucester -	1704
			Ranworth - -	Norfolk - -	[7] 1558
R.			Rasen-Market - -	Lincoln -	1561
			Rasen-Middle-Drax -	Lincoln - -	1754
Rackenford - -	Devon - -	1597	Rasen - Middle - Tup-holme.	Lincoln -	1708
Rackheath - -	Norfolk - -	1660			
Racton - -	Sussex - -	1680	Rasen, West - -	Lincoln - -	1683
Radbourne - -	Derby - -	1572	Raskelf - - -	York - -	[8] 1754
Radcliffe-on-Trent -	Nottingham -	[4] 1632	Rastrick - -	York - -	1614
Radcliffe - -	Lancaster -	1555	Ratby - - -	Leicester -	1754
Radclive - -	Buckingham -	1594	Ratcliffe-Culey -	Leicester - -	1585
Raddington - -	Somerset - -	1583	Ratcliffe-on-Soar -	Nottingham -	[9] 1597
Radford - -	Nottingham -	[5] 1563	Ratcliffe-on-the-Wreak	Leicester -	1698
Radford-Semele -	Warwick -	1565	Ratley - - -	Warwick -	1701
Radipole - -	Dorset - -	1560	Ratlinghope - -	Salop - -	1702
Radley - -	Berks - -	1599	Rattery - -	Devon - -	1654
Radnage - -	Buckingham -	1574	Rattlesden - -	Suffolk - -	[10] 1558
Radnor, New - -	Radnor - -	1644	Rauceby - -	Lincoln - -	1688
Radnor, Old - -	Radnor -	1682	Raughton-Head -	Cumberland -	1663
Radstock - -	Somerset - -	1719	Raunds - -	Northampton -	1581
Radstone - -	Northampton -	1565	Raveley, Great -	Huntingdon -	[11] —

[1] **P** (Marriages only) 1559-1836. Gloucestershire Parish Registers, vol. 1, 1896.
[2] Bishop's Transcripts commence 1608.
[3] **P** (Marriages only) 1547-1812. Gloucestershire Parish Registers, vol. 6, 1900.
[4] **P** (Marriages only) 1633-1812. Nottinghamshire Parish Registers, vol. 2, 1899.
[5] **P** (Marriages only) 1563-1812. Nottinghamshire Parish Registers, vol. 9, 1906.
[6] **P** With Stock-Harward (*q.v.*).
[7] **P** (Marriages only) 1559-1812. Norfolk Parish Registers, vol. 3, 1907.
[8] Registers of Marriages only prior to 1813. The more ancient Registers were destroyed by fire.
[9] **P** (Marriages only) 1624-1812. Nottinghamshire Parish Registers, vol. 7, 1905.
[10] **P** 1558-1758. Edited by Rev. J. R. Olorenshaw, Peterborough, 1900.
[11] Included in the Registers of Upwood (*q.v.*).

Parish.	County.	Date of Earliest Entry.	Parish.	County.	Date of Earliest Entry.
Raveley, Little -	Huntingdon -	1576	Reedham - -	Norfolk -	1754
Ravendale - -	Lincoln - -	1723	Reepham - -	Lincoln -	1633
Ravenfield - -	York - -	1563	Reepham - -	Norfolk -	1538
Raveningham -	Norfolk - -	1691	Reigate - -	Surrey - -	1556
Ravensden - -	Bedford -	1558	Reighton - -	York - -	1559
Ravensthorpe -	Northampton -	1539	Remenham - -	Berks - -	1697
Ravenstone - -	Buckingham -	1568	Rempstone - -	Nottingham -	[8] 1570
Ravenstone - -	Derby and Leicester.	1705	Rendcombe - -	Gloucester -	[9] 1566
			Rendham - -	Suffolk - -	1554
Ravenstonedale -	Westmorland -	[1] 1571	Rendlesham - -	Suffolk - -	1722
Rawcliffe - -	York - -	1689	Renhold - -	Bedford -	1654
Rawdon - - -	York - -	1783	Rennington - -	Northumberland	1768
Rawmarsh - -	York - -	1653	Renwick - -	Cumberland -	1649
Rawreth - - -	Essex - -	1539	Repps - - -	Norfolk -	1563
Raydon - - -	Suffolk - -	1562	Repps, North -	Norfolk -	1558
Rayleigh - -	Essex - -	1548	Repps, South -	Norfolk -	1558
Rayne - - -	Essex - -	1558	Repton - - -	Derby - -	1580
Raynham. See Rainham.			Reston, North -	Lincoln - -	1562
			Reston, South -	Lincoln -	1757
Reach. See Heath (Beds).			Retford, East -	Nottingham -	1573
			Retford, West -	Nottingham -	[10] 1772
Reading, St. Giles -	Berks - -	1599	Rettendon - -	Essex - -	1678
St. Lawrence	- - -	1605	Revelstoke - -	Devon - -	1653
St. Mary	- - -	[2] 1538	Revesby - -	Lincoln - -	1595
Rearsby - - -	Leicester -	1648	Rewe - - -	Devon - -	1686
Reculver - - -	Kent - -	1602	Reydon - - -	Suffolk - -	1712
Redberth - -	Pembroke -	1807	Reymerston - -	Norfolk -	1559
Redbourn - - -	Hertford - -	1626	Reynoldston - -	Glamorgan -	1713
Redbourne - -	Lincoln -	1558	Rhayader - -	Radnor - -	1759
Redcliffe, St. Mary. See Bristol.			Rhiw - - -	Carnarvon -	1793
			Rhoscolyn - -	Anglesey -	1732
Redditch - -	Worcester -	[3] 1770	Rhos-Crowther -	Pembroke -	1731
Rede - - -	Suffolk - -	1538	Rhossili - -	Glamorgan -	1642
Redenhall - -	Norfolk -	[4] —	Rhosmarket - -	Pembroke -	1772
Redgrave - -	Suffolk - -	1538	Rhuddlan - -	Flint - -	1681
Redisham, Great -	Suffolk - -	1713	Ribbesford - -	Worcester -	[11] 1574
Redisham, Little -	Suffolk - -	[5] —	Ribby - - -	Lancaster -	[12] —
Redlingfield - -	Suffolk - -	1739	Ribchester - -	Lancaster -	[13] 1598
Redmarley-d'Abitot -	Worcester -	1539	Riby - - -	Lincoln -	1559
Redmarshall - -	Durham -	1559	Riccal - - -	York - -	1613
Redmile - -	Leicester - -	1653	Richard's Castle -	Hereford - -	1559
Redmire - -	York - -	[6] —	Richmond - -	Surrey - -	[14] 1582
Redruth - - -	Cornwall -	[7] 1560	Richmond - -	York - -	1556
Redwick - -	Monmouth -	1787	Rickinghall-Inferior -	Suffolk - -	1652
Reed - - -	Hertford -	1539	Rickinghall-Superior -	Suffolk -	1557

[1] **P** 1571–1812. Edited by Rev. R. W. Metcalfe, 3 vols. Kendal, 1893–4. (Anglican, Presbyterian, and Quaker.)

[2] **P** 1538–1812. Edited by G. P. Crawlurd, Reading, 1892.

[3] **P** (Marriages only) 1808–1812. Worcestershire Parish Registers, vol. 1, 1901. Marriages previous to 1808 included in the Registers of Tardebigge (q.v.).

[4] Included in the Registers of Harleston (q.v.).

[5] Included in the Registers of Ringsfield (q.v.).

[6] Included in the Registers of Bolton Castle (q.v.).

[7] **P** 1560–1716. Edited by F. C. Peter, Redruth, 1894.

[8] **P** (Marriages only) 1571–1812. Nottinghamshire Parish Registers, vol. 5, 1903.

[9] **P** (Marriages only) 1566–1812. Gloucestershire Parish Registers, vol. 1, 1896.

[10] The ancient Registers of this parish, which commenced in 1538, have disappeared.

[11] See I. R. Burton's History of Ribbesford.

[12] Included in the Registers of Kirkham (q.v.).

[13] **P** 1598–1608. In History of Ribchester by T. C. Smith and Rev. J. Shortt.

[14] **P** 1583–1720. Surrey Parish Register Society, vols. 1 and 3, 1905.

Parish.	County.	Date of Earliest Entry.	Parish.	County.	Date of Earliest Entry.
Rickling	Essex	1660	River	Kent	1620.
Rickmansworth	Hertford	1653	Rivington	Lancaster	1703
Riddlesworth	Norfolk	1686	Road	Somerset	1587
Ridge	Hertford	1558	Roade	Northampton	1587
Ridgewell	Essex	1562	Roath	Glamorgan	1731
Ridgmont	Bedford	1539	Robeston, Wathen	Pembroke	1737
Ridley	Kent	1626	Robeston, West	Pembroke	1741
Ridlington	Norfolk	1559	Roborough	Devon	1619
Ridlington	Rutland	1559	Rocester	Stafford	[7] 1568
Ridware - Hamstall. See Hamstall - Ridware.			Roch	Pembroke	1694
			Roche	Cornwall	1572
			Rochdale	Lancaster	[8] 1582
Ridware-Mavesyn	Stafford	1538	Rochester Cathedral	Kent	[9] 1657
Ridware-Pipe	Stafford	[1] 1561	St. Margaret's	-	1640
Rigsby	Lincoln	1686	St. Nicholas	-	1624
Rillington	York	1638	Rochford	Essex	1678
Rilston	York	[2] 1559	Rochford	Worcester	1569
Rimpton	Somerset	1538	Rock	Northumberland	1768
Ringland	Norfolk	1688	Rock	Worcester	1548
Ringley	Lancaster	1719	Rockbeare	Devon	1645
Ringmer	Sussex	1605	Rockbourne	Hants	1561
Ringmore	Devon	1719	Rockfield	Monmouth	1696
Ringsfield	Suffolk	1751	Rockhampton	Gloucester	1565
Ringshall	Suffolk	1539	Rockingham	Northampton	1562
Ringstead	Northampton	1570	Rockland, All Saints	Norfolk	1696
Ringstead	Norfolk	1546	St. Mary	-	1656
Ringway	Chester	1751	St. Peter	-	1538
Ringwood	Hants	1561	Rocliffe	Cumberland	1679
Ringwould	Kent	1569	Rodborne-Cheney	Wilts	1663
Ripe	Sussex	1538	Rodborough	Gloucester	1692
Ripley	Surrey	[3] —	Rodden	Somerset	1659
Ripley	York	1560	Roding-Abbess	Essex	1560
Ripon	York	1587	Roding-Aythorpe	Essex	1559
Rippingale	Lincoln	1633	Roding - Beauchamp. See Beauchamp-Roding.		
Ripple	Kent	1560			
Ripple	Worcester	1568	Roding-Berners. See Berners-Roding.		
Ripponden	York	1684			
Ripton-Abbots	Huntingdon	1559	Roding, High	Essex	1538
Ripton, King's	Huntingdon	1633	Roding-Leaden	Essex	1572
Risborough, Monk's	Buckingham	1587	Roding-Margaret	Essex	1538
Risborough, Prince's	Buckingham	1561	Roding, White	Essex	1547
Risby	Lincoln	[4] —	Rodington	Salop	1678
Risby	Suffolk	1674	Rodmarton	Gloucester	1605
Risca	Monmouth	1736	Rodmell	Sussex	1704
Rise	York	1559	Rodmersham	Kent	1538
Riseley	Bedford	1628	Rodney - Stoke. See Stoke-Rodney.		
Rishangles	Suffolk	1593			
Risington, Great	Gloucester	1538	Rogate	Sussex	1558
Risington, Little	Gloucester	1543	Rogiett	Monmouth	1750
Risington, Wick	Gloucester	[5] 1739	Rokeby	York	1598
Risley	Derby	[6] 1667	Rollesby	Norfolk	1558
Riston, Long	York	1653	Rolleston	Leicester	1599
Rivenhall	Essex	1639			

[1] **P** 1561–1812. Staffordshire Parish Register Society, 1905.
[2] **P** 1559–1812. Edited by C. H. Lowe, Leeds, 2 vols., 1895-6.
[3] Included in the Registers of Send (q.v.).
[4] Included in the Registers of Roxby (q.v.).
[5] **P** (Marriages only) 1605–1838. Gloucestershire Parish Registers, vol. 13, 1908.
[6] **P** (Marriages only) 1720–1812. Derbyshire Parish Register Society, vol. 1, 1906.
[7] **P** 1566–1705. Staffordshire Parish Register Society, 1906.
[8] **P** 1582–1641. Edited by Henry Fishwick, Rochdale, 1888-9, 2 vols.
[9] **P** 1657–1837. Edited by Thos. Shindler, Canterbury, 1892.

Parish.	County.	Date of Earliest Entry.	Parish.	County.	Date of Earliest Entry.
Rolleston	Nottingham	1559	Rowlestone	Hereford	1723
Rolleston	Stafford	1589	Rowley	York	1653
Rollright, Great	Oxford	1560	Rowley-Regis	Stafford	1539
Rollright, Little	Oxford	1754	Rowner	Hants	[5] 1590
Rollstone	Wilts	1653	Rowston	Lincoln	1561
Rolvenden	Kent	1561	Roxby	Lincoln	1689
Romald-Kirk	York	1578	Roxby	York	1758
Romansleigh	Devon	1539	Roxham	Norfolk	[6] —
Romford	Essex	1561	Roxton	Bedford	1684
Romney, New	Kent	1662	Roxwell	Essex	1558
Romney, Old	Kent	1538	Roydon	Essex	1567
Romsey	Hants	1569	Roydon (Diss)	Norfolk	1559
Romsley	Worcester	1736	Roydon (Lynn)	Norfolk	1721
Ronton	Stafford	1655	Royston	Hertford	1662
Roos	York	[1] 1571	Roystone	York	1563
Ropley	Hants	1538	Royton	Lancaster	1755
Ropsley	Lincoln	1558	Ruabon	Denbigh	1559
Rose-Ash	Devon	1591	Ruan-Lanihorne	Cornwall	1685
Rosedale	York	1616	Ruan-Major	Cornwall	1682
Rosemarket. See Rhos-			Ruan-Minor	Cornwall	1653
market.			Ruardean	Gloucester	1540
Rosliston	Derby	1768	Ruckinge	Kent	1538
Ross	Hereford	1671	Ruckland	Lincoln	1757
Rossington	York	1538	Rudbaxton	Pembroke	1730
Rostherne	Chester	1595	Rudby-in-Cleveland	York	1584
Rothbury	Northumberland	1658	Ruddington	Nottingham	[7] 1636
Rotherby	Leicester	1561	Ruddry	Glamorgan	1640
Rotherfield	Sussex	1539	Rudford	Gloucester	1729
Rotherfield-Greys	Oxford	1591	Rudgwick	Sussex	1558
Rotherfield-Peppard	Oxford	1571	Rudham, East	Norfolk	1562
Rotherham	York	[2] 1556	Rudham, West	Norfolk	1565
Rotherhithe	Surrey	1556	Rudstone	York	1550
Rothersthorpe	Northampton	1563	Rufford	Lancaster	1669
Rotherwick	Hants	1561	Rufforth	York	1655
Rothley	Leicester	1562	Rugby	Warwick	1620
Rothwell	Lincoln	1560	Rugeley	Stafford	1569
Rothwell	Northampton	1708	Ruishton	Somerset	[8] 1754
Rothwell	York	[3] 1538	Ruislip	Middlesex	1689
Rottingdean	Sussex	1558	Rulen	Radnor	1773
Rougham	Norfolk	1783	Rumboldswyke	Sussex	1669
Rougham	Suffolk	1567	Rumburgh	Suffolk	1558
Roughton	Lincoln	1564	Rumney	Monmouth	1744
Roughton	Norfolk	1562	Runcorn	Chester	1558
Rounton, East	York	1595	Runcton, North	Norfolk	1563
Rounton, West	York	1725	Runhall	Norfolk	1566
Rousdon	Devon	1685	Runham	Norfolk	1539
Rousham	Oxford	1544	Runnington	Somerset	1586
Rous-Lench. See			Runton	Norfolk	1743
Lench, Rous-.			Runwell	Essex	1558
Routh	York	1633	Ruscombe	Berks	1559
Rowberrow	Somerset	1723	Rushall	Norfolk	[9] 1560
Rowde	Wilts	1606	Rushall	Stafford	1686
Rowington	Warwick	[4] 1638	Rushall	Wilts	1651

[1] **P** Edited by R. B. Machell, vol. 1, Hull, 1888.
[2] **P** 1542-1563. Edited by John Guest.
[3] **P** 1538-1689. Yorkshire Parish Register Society, vol. 27, 1906.
[4] **P** 1612-1812. Parish Register Society, vol. 21, 1899.
[5] **P** (Marriages only) 1590-1812. Hampshire Parish Registers, vol. 8, 1906.
[6] Included in the Registers of Royston (q.v.).
[7] **P** (Marriages only) 1655-1813. Nottinghamshire Parish Registers, vol. 7, 1905.
[8] **P** (Marriages only) 1679-1812. Somersetshire Parish Registers, vol. 8, 1907.
[9] **P** 1686-1812. "Records of Rushall," by F. W. Wilmore, Walsall, 1892.

Parish.	County.	Date of Earliest Entry.	Parish.	County.	Date of Earliest Entry.
Rushbrook - -	Suffolk - -	[1] 1568	Salford, St. Stephen -	Lancaster -	1794
Rushbury - -	Salop - -	1538	Salhouse - -	Norfolk -	1561
Rushden - -	Hertford - -	1607	Saling, Great - -	Essex - -	1715
Rushden - -	Northampton -	1559	Saling, Little. *See*		
Rushford - -	Norfolk - -	1762	Bardfield Saling.		
Rushmere (Ipswich) -	Suffolk - -	1582	Salisbury, St. Edmund	Wilts - -	1560
Rushmere (Beccles) -	Suffolk - -	1718	Cathedral Church	- - -	1564
Rushock - -	Worcester -	[2] 1661	St. Martin - -	- - -	1620
Rushton - -	Northampton -	1625	St. Thomas - -	- - -	1570
Rushton-Spencer -	Stafford - -	1700	Salkeld, Great -	Cumberland -	1583
Ruskington - -	Lincoln - -	1668	Sall - - -	Norfolk - -	1558
Rusland - - -	Lancaster -	[3] —	Salmonby - -	Lincoln -	1558
Rusper - - -	Sussex - -	1560	Salperton - -	Gloucester -	1629
Rustington - -	Sussex - -	1568	Saltash - -	Cornwall -	1697
Ruston East - -	Norfolk - -	1558	Saltby - -	Leicester -	1565
Ruston-Parva -	York - -	1720	Saltersford - -	Chester -	1770
Ruston, South -	Norfolk - -	1708	Saltfleetby, All Saints -	Lincoln - -	1558
Ruthin - -	Denbigh -	1592	Saltfleetby, St. Clement	Lincoln -	1718
Ruyton-in-the-Eleven	Salop - -	[4] 1719	Saltfleetby, St. Peter -	Lincoln -	1653
Towns.			Saltford - -	Somerset -	1712
Ryarsh - -	Kent - -	1539	Salthouse - -	Norfolk -	1544
Ryburgh, Great -	Norfolk -	1547	Salton - -	York - -	1573
Ryburgh, Little -	Norfolk -	1688	Saltwood - -	Kent - -	1560
Ryde (Isle of Wight) -	Hants - -	[5] —	Salwarpe - -	Worcester -	[6] 1666
Rye - - -	Sussex - -	1538	Samlesbury - -	Lancaster -	1722
Ryhall - -	Rutland -	1674	Sampford-Arundel -	Somerset -	1695
Ryme-Intrinseca -	Dorset - -	1631	Sampford-Brett -	Somerset -	1654
Ryston - -	Norfolk -	1687	Sampford-Courtenay -	Devon - -	1558
Ryther - -	York - -	1550	Sampford, Great -	Essex - -	1559
Ryton - -	Durham - -	[6] 1581	Sampford, Little -	Essex - -	1563
Ryton - -	Salop - -	1659	Sampford-Peverell -	Devon - -	1672
Ryton-on-Dunsmoor -	Warwick - -	1538	Sampford-Spiney -	Devon - -	1659
			Sampson, St. - -	Cornwall -	[10] 1568
S.			Sancreed - -	Cornwall -	[11] 1559
			Sancton - -	York - -	1538
Sacombe - -	Hertford -	1726	Sandal, Magna - -	York - -	1652
Sadberge - -	Durham -	1662	Sandal Parva (or Kirk	York - -	1679
Saddington - -	Leicester -	1538	Sandal).		
Saddleworth - -	York - -	[7] 1613	Sandbach - -	Chester -	1562
Saffron-Walden -	Essex - -	1558	Sanderstead - -	Surrey -	1564
Saham-Toney -	Norfolk -	1547	Sandford - -	Devon - -	1603
Saintbury - -	Gloucester -	[8] 1585	Sandford - -	Oxford -	1695
Salcombe-Regis -	Devon - -	1702	Sandford-on-Thames -	Oxford -	1572
Salcott Virley -	Essex - -	1628	Sandford-Orcas -	Dorset -	1538
Saleby - -	Lincoln -	1554	Sandhurst - -	Berks -	1603
Salehurst - -	Sussex - -	1575	Sandhurst - -	Gloucester -	1538
Salesbury - -	Lancaster -	1807	Sandhurst - -	Kent - -	1563
Salford - -	Lancaster -	1708	Sand Hutton - -	York - -	1706
Salford - -	Bedford -	1558	Sandiacre - -	Derby - -	[12] 1570
Salford - -	Oxford -	1754	Sandon - -	Essex -	1554
Salford-Priors -	Warwick -	1568	Sandon - -	Hertford -	1678
			Sandon - -	Stafford -	1635

[1] P 1567-1850. Edited by Rev. S. H. A. Hervey, Woodbridge, 1903.
[2] Bishop's Transcripts commence 1608. [3] Included in the Registers of Colton (*q.v.*).
[4] P 1719-1812. Shropshire Parish Register Society, vol. 5.
[5] Included in the Registers of Newchurch (*q.v.*).
[6] P 1581-1812. Durham and Northumberland Parish Register Society, vol. 6, 1902.
[7] P 1613-1800. Edited by J. Radcliffe, 1788-1891.
[8] P (Marriages only) 1585-1812. Gloucestershire Parish Registers, vol. 4, 1898.
[9] Bishop's Transcripts commence 1613.
[10] P (Marriages only) 1568-1812. Cornwall Parish Registers, vol. 6, 1904.
[11] P (Marriages only) 1559-1812. Cornwall Parish Registers, vol. 5, 1903.
[12] P (Marriages only) 1581-1812. Derbyshire Parish Registers, vol 1, 1906.

K

Parish.	County.	Date of Earliest Entry.	Parish.	County.	Date of Earliest Entry.
Sandridge - -	Hertford -	1559	Scarborough - -	York - -	1672
Sandringham - -	Norfolk - -	[1] 1558	Scarcliff - - -	Derby - -	1680
Sandwich, St. Clement	Kent - -	1563	Scarle, North - -	Lincoln - -	1571
St. Mary -	- - -	1538	Scarle, South - -	Nottingham -	1684
St. Peter -	- - -	1538	Scarning - -	Norfolk - -	1538
Sandy - - -	Bedford - -	1538	Scarrington - -	Nottingham -	[5] 1570
Sankey, Great - -	Lancaster -	1728	Scartho - -	Lincoln - -	1560
Santon - -	Norfolk - -	1770	Scawby - - -	Lincoln - -	1558
Sapcote - - -	Leicester -	1564	Scawton - -	York - -	1721
Sapey-Pritchard (or	Worcester -	1674	Scole - - -	Norfolk - -	1561
Lower Sapey).			Scopwick - -	Lincoln - -	1605
Sapey, Upper -	Hereford -	1679	Scorborough - -	York - -	[6] 1653
Sapiston - -	Suffolk - -	1680	Scothorne - -	Lincoln -	1630
Sapperton - -	Gloucester -	1662	Scotter - -	Lincoln - -	1563
Sarnesfield - -	Hereford -	[2] 1755	Scotton - -	Lincoln -	1560
Sarratt - - -	Hertford -	1560	Scottow - -	Norfolk -	1558
Sarsden - -	Oxford - -	1575	Scoulton - -	Norfolk - -	1550
Satley - - -	Durham - -	1797	Scraptoft - -	Leicester -	1538
Satterleigh - -	Devon - -	1570	Scratby - -	Norfolk -	[7] —
Satterthwaite - -	Lancaster -	1766	Scrayfield - -	Lincoln - -	[8] —
Saul - - -	Gloucester -	[3] 1760	Scrayingham - -	York - -	1648
Saundby - -	Nottingham -	1558	Scredington - -	Lincoln - -	1738
Saunderton - -	Buckingham -	1728	Scremby - -	Lincoln - -	1716
Sausthorpe - -	Lincoln - -	1745	Screveton - -	Nottingham -	[9] 1640
Sawbridgeworth -	Hertford - -	1558	Scrivelsby - -	Lincoln - -	1565
Sawley - -	Derby - -	1654	Scrooby - -	Nottingham -	1695
Sawley - - -	York - -	[4] —	Scropton - -	Derby - -	1680
Sawston - -	Cambridge -	1640	Scruton - -	York - -	1572
Sawtry, All Saints -	Huntingdon -	1591	Sculcoates - -	York - -	1576
Sawtry, St. Andrew -	Huntingdon -	1662	Sculthorpe - -	Norfolk - -	1561
Saxby - - -	Leicester -	1678	Seaborough - -	Somerset -	1562
Saxby, St. Helen -	Lincoln -	1666	Seaford - -	Sussex - -	1559
Saxby, All Saints -	Lincoln - -	1719	Seaforth - -	Lancaster -	[10] —
Saxelby - -	Leicester -	1538	Seagrave - -	Leicester -	1682
Saxham, Great - -	Suffolk - -	1555	Seagry - -	Wilts - -	1610
Saxham, Little - -	Suffolk - -	1559	Seaham - -	Durham - -	1646
Saxilby - -	Lincoln - -	1563	Seal - - -	Kent - -	1654
Saxlingham - -	Norfolk -	1558	Seale - - -	Surrey - -	1539
Saxlingham-Nethergate	Norfolk - -	1556	Seale, Nether and Over	Derby - -	1566
Saxmundham - -	Suffolk - -	1538	Seamer - -	York - -	1588
Saxsted - -	Suffolk - -	1546	Seamer-in-Cleveland -	York - -	1638
Saxthorpe - -	Norfolk - -	1720	Searby - -	Lincoln - -	1558
Saxton - - -	York - -	1538	Seasalter - -	Kent - -	1588
Scalby - - -	York - -	1656	Seasoncote - -	Gloucester -	[11] —
Scaldwell - -	Northampton -	1560	Seathwaite - -	Lancaster -	1684
Scaleby - -	Cumberland -	1724	Seaton - - -	Devon - -	1583
Scalford - -	Leicester -	1558	Seaton Rutland -	Rutland - -	1538
Scamblesby - -	Lincoln -	1570	Seaton Ross - -	York - -	1653
Scammonden - -	York - -	1746	Seavington, St. Mary -	Somerset -	1716
Scampston - -	York - -	1756	Seavington, St. Michael	Somerset -	1558
Scampton - -	Lincoln - -	1548	Sebergham - -	Cumberland -	1694

[1] **P** (Marriages only) 1561–1812. Norfolk Parish Registers, vol. 2, 1900.
[2] **P** 1660–1897. Parish Register Society, vol. 13, 1898.
[3] The older Registers were destroyed in a flood.
[4] Included in the Registers of Ripon (q.v.).
[5] **P** (Marriages only) 1572–1812. Nottinghamshire Parish Registers, vol. 1, 1898.
[6] **P** 1653–1800. Yorkshire Parish Register Society, vol. 8, 1901.
[7] Included in the Registers of Ormesby St. Margaret (q.v.).
[8] Included in the Registers of Hameringham (q.v.).
[9] **P** (Marriages only) 1640–1812. Nottinghamshire Parish Registers, vol. 1, 1898.
[10] Included in the Registers of Sephton (q.v.).
[11] Included in the Registers of Longborough (q.v.).

Parish.	County.	Date of Earliest Entry.	Parish.	County.	Date of Earliest Entry.
Seckington - -	Warwick -	1612	Shalbourn - -	Berks - -	1678
Sedbergh - -	York - -	1595	Shalden - - -	Hants - -	1686
Sedgeberrow - -	Worcester -	1566	Shalfleet (Isle of Wight)	Hants - -	1695
Sedgebrook - -	Lincoln - -	¹ 1559	Shalford - - -	Essex - -	1558
Sedgefield - -	Durham - -	1580	Shalford - - -	Surrey - -	1564
Sedgeford - -	Norfolk - -	1560	Shalstone - -	Buckingham -	1538
Sedgehill - - -	Wilts - -	1758	Shangton - -	Leicester -	1580
Sedgeley - -	Stafford - -	1558	Shanklin (Isle of Wight)	Hants - -	1724
Sedlescomb - -	Sussex - -	1558	Shap - - -	Westmorland -	1563
Seend - - -	Wilts - -	1612	Shapwick - -	Dorset - -	1654
Seething - - -	Norfolk - -	1561	Shapwick - -	Somerset -	1590
Sefton - - -	Lancaster -	1597	Shareshill - -	Stafford -	1565
Seighford - -	Stafford - -	1560	Sharnbrook - -	Bedford -	1596
Selattyn - -	Salop - -	² 1557	Sharnford - -	Leicester -	1671
Selborne - - -	Hants - -	1556	Sharrington - -	Norfolk -	1672
Selby - - -	York - -	1590	Shaugh-Prior - -	Devon - -	1565
Sele. See Beeding, Upper.			Shaw (or Crompton) -	Lancaster -	1704
Selham - - -	Sussex - -	1565	Shaw - - -	Berks - -	1646
Sellack - - -	Hereford - -	1566	Shawbury - -	Salop - -	1561
Selling - - -	Kent - -	1558	Shawell - - -	Leicester -	1558
Sellinge - - -	Kent - -	1559	Shearsby - -	Leicester -	1658
Selmeston - -	Sussex - -	1667	Shebbear - -	Devon - -	1576
Selsey - - -	Sussex -	⁰ 1662	Sheen - - -	Stafford -	1595
Selside - - -	Westmorland -	1753	Sheepshed - -	Leicester -	1538
Selston - - -	Nottingham -	³ 1557	Sheepstor - -	Devon - -	1691
Selworthy - -	Somerset - -	1672	Sheepwash - -	Devon - -	1673
Semer - - -	Suffolk - -	1538	Sheepy, Great - -	Leicester -	⁷ 1607
Semington - -	Wilts - -	1589	Sheering - - -	Essex - -	1558
Semperingham - -	Lincoln - -	1558	Sheerness-on-Sea -	Kent - -	⁸ 1695
Send - - - -	Surrey - -	1653	Sheffield - -	York - -	1560
Sennen - - -	Cornwall -	⁴ 1700	Shefford, East - -	Berks - -	1603
Sephton. See Sefton.			Shefford, Great -	Berks - -	1571
Sessay - - -	York - -	1612	Sheinton - -	Salop - -	⁹ 1658
Setchey - - -	Norfolk - -	⁵ —	Sheldon - - -	Derby - -	1745
Setmurthy - -	Cumberland -	1759	Sheldon - - -	Devon - -	1721
Settrington - -	York - -	1559	Sheldon - - -	Warwick -	1558
Sevenhampton - -	Gloucester -	1588	Sheldwich - -	Kent - -	1558
Sevenhampton -	Wilts - -	1538	Shelfanger - -	Norfolk -	1686
Sevenoaks - -	Kent - -	1559	Shelford - -	Nottingham -	¹⁰ 1563
Sevington - -	Kent - -	1554	Shelford, Great -	Cambridge -	1557
Shabbington - -	Buckingham -	1714	Shelford, Little -	Cambridge -	1686
Shackerstone - -	Leicester -	⁶ 1630	Shelland - -	Suffolk -	1721
Shadingfield - -	Suffolk - -	1538	Shelley - - -	Essex - -	1687
Shadoxhurst - -	Kent - -	1538	Shelley - - -	Suffolk -	1747
Shaftesbury, Holy Trinity.	Dorset - -	1695	Shellingford - -	Berks - -	1579
			Shellow-Bowels - -	Essex - -	1555
St. Peter - -	- - -	1623	Shelsley-Beauchamp -	Worcester -	1538
St. James - -	- - -	1559	Shelswell - -	Oxford - -	¹¹ —

¹ ℙ (Marriages only) 1559–1812. Lincolnshire Parish Registers, vol. 2, 1907.
² ℙ 1557–1812. Shropshire Parish Register Society, vol. 58 (St. Asaph Diocese), 1557–1812. Parish Register Society, vol. 55, 1906.
³ ℙ (Marriages only) 1559–1812. Nottinghamshire Parish Registers, vol. 11, 1907.
⁴ ℙ (Marriages only) 1669–1812. Cornwall Parish Registers, vol. 3, 1903.
⁵ Included in the Registers of North Runcton (q.v.).
⁶ Original Register, 1558–1630, in Bodleian Library, Oxford. ℙ Leicestershire Archæological Society Transactions, vol. 5.
⁷ Earlier entries in Ratcliffe Culey Registers (q.v.).
⁸ Marriages not solemnized at this chapel.
⁹ ℙ 1658–1812. Shropshire Parish Register Society, vol. 2, 1902 (Lichfield Diocese). ℙ 1658–1812. Parish Register Society, vol. 28, 1900.
¹⁰ ℙ (Marriages only) 1563–1812. Nottinghamshire Parish Registers, vol. 2, 1899.
¹¹ Included in the Registers of Newton Purcell (q.v.).

Parish.	County.	Date of Earliest Entry.	Parish.	County.	Date of Earliest Entry.
Shelton	Bedford	1565	Shilton-Rood	Oxford	1662
Shelton	Norfolk	1595	Shilton	Warwick	1695
Shelton	Nottingham	¹ 1595	Shimpling	Norfolk	1538
Shelve	Salop	1583	Shimplingthorne	Suffolk	1538
Shenfield	Essex	1539	Shinfield	Berks	1649
Shenington	Oxford	² 1721	Shingay	Cambridge	⁹ —
Shenley	Buckingham	1653	Shingham	Norfolk	1762
Shenley	Hertford	1657	Shipbourne	Kent	1656
Shenstone	Stafford	1579	Shipdham	Norfolk	1558
Shenton	Leicester	1625	Shipham	Somerset	1560
Shephall	Hertford	1560	Shiplake	Oxford	1672
Shepperton	Middlesex	1574	Shipley	Sussex	1609
Shepreth	Cambridge	1734	Shipmeadow	Suffolk	1561
Shepton-Beauchamp	Somerset	³ 1558	Shipston-on-Stour	Worcester	¹⁰ 1571
Shepton-Mallett	Somerset	1634	Shipton	Salop	¹¹ 1538
Shepton-Montague	Somerset	1560	Shipton	York	1675
Sherborne	Dorset	1538	Shipton-Bellinger	Hants	1540
Sherborne	Gloucester	1572	Shipton-George	Dorset	¹² —
Sherborne, St. John	Hants	⁴ 1652	Shipton Moyne	Gloucester	¹³ 1570
Sherborne, Monk	Hants	1601	Shipton-Oliffe	Gloucester	1653
Sherborne	Warwick	1587	Shipton-on-Cherwell	Oxford	1653
Sherburn	York	1653	Shipton-under-Wych-	Oxford	1538
Sherburn-in-Elmet	York	1639	wood.		
Shere	Surrey	1547	Shirburn	Oxford	1587
Shereford	Norfolk	1721	Shire-Newton	Monmouth	1730
Sherfield-English	Hants	1640	Shireshead	Lancaster	¹⁴ —
Sherfield-on-Loddon	Hants	⁵ 1574	Shirland	Derby	1678
Sherford	Devon	1713	Shirley	Derby	1663
Sheriff-Hales	Salop	1557	Shobdon	Hereford	1556
Sheriff-Hutton	York	1628	Shobrooke	Devon	1538
Sheringham	Norfolk	1670	Shocklach	Chester	1538
Sherington	Buckingham	⁶ 1698	Shoebury, North	Essex	1680
Shermanbury	Sussex	1653	Shoebury, South	Essex	1704
Shernbourne	Norfolk	1749	Shopland	Essex	1741
Sherrington	Wilts	1677	Shoreham	Kent	1558
Sherston Magna	Wilts	⁷ 1653	Shoreham, New	Sussex	1566
Sherwell	Devon	1538	Shoreham, Old	Sussex	1566
Sheviock	Cornwall	⁸ 1666	Shorncott	Wilts	1708
Shields, South	Durham	1653	Shorne	Kent	1640
Shifnall	Salop	1678	Shorthampton	Oxford	1650
Shilbottle	Northumberland	1690	Shorwell (Isle of Wight)	Hants	1676
Shillingford	Devon	1565	Shotesham, All Saints	Norfolk	1538
Shillingstone	Dorset	1654	St. Botolph and		1687
Shillington	Bedford	1544	St. Mary.		
Shilton, Earl	Leicester	1552	Shotley	Northumberland	1670

¹ **P** (Marriages only) 1606–1812. Nottinghamshire Parish Registers, vol. 4, 1902. **P** 1595–1812. Edited by T. M. Blagg, Worksop, 1900.

² The Registers before this date were destroyed in a fire which consumed the greater part of the village in 1720.

³ **P** (Marriages only) 1558–1812. Somersetshire Parish Registers, vol. 4, 1902.

⁴ **P** (Marriages only) 1653–1812. Hampshire Parish Registers, vol. 3, 1902.

⁵ **P** (Marriages only) 1574–1812. Hampshire Parish Registers, vol. 9, 1907.

⁶ **P** (Marriages only) 1688–1812. Buckinghamshire Parish Registers, vol. 3, 1907.

⁷ **P** (Marriages only) 1653–1812. Wiltshire Parish Registers, vol. 1, 1905.

⁸ **P** (Marriages only) 1570–1812. Cornwall Parish Registers, vol. 4, 1903.

⁹ Included in the Registers of Wendy (q.v.).

¹⁰ **P** (Marriages only) 1571–1812. Worcestershire Parish Registers, vol. 1, 1901.

¹¹ **P** 1538–1812. Shropshire Parish Register Society, vol. 1 (Hereford Diocese). **P** 1538–1812. Parish Register Society, vol. 22, 1899.

¹² Included in the Registers of Burton-Bradstock (q.v.).

¹³ **P** (Marriages only) 1587–1812. Gloucestershire Parish Registers, vol. 9, 1903.

¹⁴ Included in the Registers of Cockerham (q.v.).

Parish.	County.	Date of Earliest Entry.	Parish.	County.	Date of Earliest Entry.
Shotley - -	Suffolk - -	1571	Silchester - -	Hants - -	[1] 1653
Shottesbrook -	Berks - -	1556	Sileby - -	Leicester - -	1568
Shotteswell -	Warwick - -	1564	Silian - - -	Cardigan -	1788
Shottisham -	Suffolk - -	1618	Silkstone - -	York - -	1558
Shotwick -	Chester -	1551	Silsden - -	York - -	1768
Shoulden - -	Kent - -	1591	Silton - -	Dorset - -	1653
Shouldham -	Norfolk -	1653	Silton, Over -	York - -	1678
Shouldham-Thorpe -	Norfolk -	1737	Silverdale - -	Lancaster -	[8] —
Shrawardine -	Salop -	[1] 1645	Silverstone -	Northampton -	[9] —
Shrawley -	Worcester -	1537	Silverton - -	Devon - -	1626
Shrewsbury, St. Alk-	Salop -	1560	Silvington -	Salop - -	1716
mond.			Simonburn -	Northumberland -	[10] 1681
St. Chad -	- - -	1616	Simpson -	Buckingham -	1719
Holy Cross -	- - -	[2] 1541	Singleton - -	Sussex -	1664
St. Julian -	- - -	1559	Singleton, Great	Lancaster -	[11] —
St. Mary -	- - -	1584	Sinnington -	York - -	1517
Shrewton - -	Wilts - -	1651	Siston - -	Gloucester -	[12] 1576
Shrivenham -	Berks - -	1575	Sithney, St. -	Cornwall -	[13] 1664
Shropham -	Norfolk -	1720	Sittingbourne -	Kent - -	1561
Shuckburgh, Lower -	Warwick -	1678	Sixhills - -	Lincoln - -	1672
Shuckburgh, Upper -	Warwick -	1757	Sizeland - -	Norfolk -	1558
Shudy-Camps -	Cambridge -	1558	Skeckling -	York - -	1747
Shurdington -	Gloucester -	1561	Skeffington -	Leicester -	1514
Shustoke -	Warwick -	1538	Skeffling -	York - -	1585
Shute - - -	Devon - -	1561	Skegby - -	Nottingham -	[14] 1569
Shutford - -	Oxford - -	1698	Skegness -	Lincoln - -	1653
Shuttington -	Warwick -	1557	Skelbrooke -	York - -	1592
Sibbertoft -	Northampton -	1680	Skellingthorpe -	Lincoln - -	1563
Sibdon-Carwood -	Salop -	[3] 1580	Skelton -	Cumberland -	[15] 1580
Sibertswold -	Kent - -	1563	Skelton-by-York	York - -	1538
Sibford - -	Oxford - -	[4] —	Skelton - in - Cleve-	York - -	1698
Sibsey - -	Lincoln -	1566	land.		
Sibson (or Sibstone) -	Leicester -	1558	Skendleby - -	Lincoln -	1723
Sibthorpe -	Nottingham -	[5] 1720	Skenfrith - -	Monmouth -	1662
Sibton - -	Suffolk - -	1552	Skerne - -	York - -	1561
Sidbury - -	Devon - -	1559	Skeyton - -	Norfolk -	1706
Sidbury - -	Salop - -	[6] 1560	Skidbrooke -	Lincoln -	1558
Siddington -	Chester -	1720	Skidby - -	York - -	1655
Siddington -	Gloucester -	1606	Skilgate - -	Somerset -	1674
Side. See Syde.			Skillington -	Lincoln -	1542
Sidestrand - -	Norfolk -	1558	Skinnand - -	Lincoln -	1791
Sidlesham -	Sussex - -	1566	Skipsea - -	York - -	1720
Sidmouth - -	Devon - -	1589	Skipton - -	York - -	[16] 1592
Sigglesthorne -	York - -	1562	Skipwith - -	York - -	1718
Sigston, Kirby -	York - -	1574	Skirbeck - -	Lincoln -	1661

[1] **P** 1645-1812. Shropshire Archæological Society, vol. 7, 1895.
[2] See Shropshire Archæological Society, vol. 1.
[3] **P** 1582-1812. Shropshire Parish Register Society, vol. 2 (Hereford Diocese). **P** 1583-1812. Parish Register Society, vol. 20, 1899.
[4] **P** Included in the Registers of Swalcliffe (q.v.).
[5] **P** (Marriages only) 1721-1812. Nottinghamshire Parish Registers, vol. 4, 1902.
[6] **P** 1560-1812. Shropshire Parish Register Society, vol. 1 (Hereford Diocese).
[7] **P** (Marriages only) 1653-1812. Hampshire Parish Registers, vol. 7, 1905.
[8] Included in the Registers of Warton (q.v.).
[9] Included in the Registers of Whittlebury (q.v.).
[10] **P** "North Country Parish Registers," by Robert Blair.
[11] Included in the Registers of Kirkham (q.v.).
[12] **P** 1576-1641. Edited by H. B. McCall, 1901.
[13] **P** (Marriages only) 1654-1812. Cornwall Parish Registers, vol. 7, 1904.
[14] **P** (Marriages only) 1569-1812. Nottinghamshire Parish Registers, vol. 11, 1907.
[15] Included in the Registers of Ripon (q.v.).
[16] **P** 1592-1812. Edited by Rev. W. J. Stavert, 1894-1896.

Parish.	County.	Date of Earliest Entry.	Parish.	County.	Date of Earliest Entry.
Skirlaugh	York	1719	Snetterton	Norfolk	1669
Skirpenbeck	York	1660	Snettisham	Norfolk	[7] 1682
Slaidburn	York	1653	Snitterby	Lincoln	[8] —
Slaithwaite	York	1684	Snitterfield	Warwick	[9] 1561
Slaley	Northumberland	1714	Snodland	Kent	1559
Slapton	Buckingham	[1] 1653	Snoring, Great	Norfolk	1560
Slapton	Devon	1634	Snoring, Little	Norfolk	1559
Slapton	Northampton	1573	Snowshill	Gloucester	[10] 1593
Slaugham	Sussex	1654	Soberton	Hants	1539
Slaughter, Lower	Gloucester	[2] —	Sockburn	Durham	1588
Slaughter, Upper	Gloucester	1538	Sodbury, Chipping-	Gloucester	[11] 1661
Slaughterford	Wilts	1702	Sodbury, Little	Gloucester	1703
Slawston	Leicester	1559	Sodbury, Old	Gloucester	[12] 1684
Sleaford, New	Lincoln	1575	Soham	Cambridge	1559
Sleaford, Old	Lincoln	[3] —	Soham, Earl-	Suffolk	1558
Slebech	Pembroke	1758	Soham, Monk-	Suffolk	1712
Sledmere	York	1696	Solihull	Warwick	[13] 1538
Slimbridge	Gloucester	[4] 1635	Soller's Hope	Hereford	1695
Slindon	Sussex	1558	Somborne, King's	Hants	1672
Slinfold	Sussex	1558	Somerby	Leicester	1751
Slingsby	York	1687	Somerby (near Brigg)	Lincoln	1661
Slipton	Northampton	1671	Somerby (near Grantham).	Lincoln	[14] 1730
Sloley	Norfolk	1560			
Smallburgh	Norfolk	1561	Somercoates, North	Lincoln	1558
Smarden	Kent	1632	Somercoates, South	Lincoln	1558
Smeaton, Great	York	1650	Somerford, Great (or Broad Somerford).	Wilts	1707
Smeaton, Kirk-	York	1604			
Smeeth	Kent	1662	Somerford-Keynes	Wilts	1560
Smethcote	Salop	[5] 1609	Somerford, Little	Wilts	1708
Smethwick	Stafford	1732	Somerleyton	Suffolk	1558
Smisby	Derby	1720	Somersal-Herbert	Derby	1538
Snailwell	Cambridge	1629	Somersby	Lincoln	1730
Snaith	York	1568	Somersham	Huntingdon	1558
Snape	Suffolk	1560	Somersham	Suffolk	1675
Snareston	Leicester	1559	Somerton	Oxford	1627
Snarford	Lincoln	1718	Somerton	Somerset	[15] 1697
Snargate	Kent	1553	Somerton	Suffolk	1538
Snave	Kent	1619	Somerton, East	Norfolk	[16]
Snead	Montgomery	1665	Somerton, West	Norfolk	1736
Sneaton	York	1581	Sompting	Sussex	1546
Sneinton	Nottingham	[6] 1650	Sonning	Berks	1592
Snelland	Lincoln	1654	Sopley	Hants	[17] 1678
Snelston	Derby	1574	Sopworth	Wilts	[18] 1697

[1] P (Marriages only) 1653-1812. Buckinghamshire Parish Registers, vol. 1, 1902.
[2] Included in the Registers of Bourton-on-the-Water (q.v.).
[3] Included in the Registers of Quarrington (q.v.).
[4] P (Marriages only) 1635-1812. Gloucestershire Parish Registers, vol. 1, 1896 ; also P (Marriages only) 1571-1740, from Bishop's Transcripts. Gloucestershire Parish Registers, vol. 11, 1905.
[5] P 1609-1812. Shropshire Parish Register Society, vol. 1, 1900 (Lichfield Diocese). P 1609-1812. Parish Register Society, vol. 26, 1899.
[6] P (Marriages only) 1655-1812. Nottinghamshire Parish Registers, vol. 10, 1907.
[7] P (Marriages only) 1682-1812. Norfolk Parish Registers, vol. 2, 1900.
[8] Included in the Registers of Waddingham (q.v.).
[9] P (Marriages only) 1561-1812. Warwickshire Parish Registers, vol. 3, 1906.
[10] P (Marriages only) 1593-1812. Gloucestershire Parish Registers, vol. 4, 1898.
[11] P (Marriages only) 1661-1812. Gloucestershire Parish Registers, vol. 11, 1905.
[12] P (Marriages only) 1684-1812. Gloucestershire Parish Registers, vol. 9, 1903.
[13] P 1538-1668. Parish Register Society, vol. 51, 1904.   [Additional MS. 24,802.
[14] P 1601-1715. Leicestershire Archæological Society, vol. 5. Original Register in British Museum.
[15] P (Marriages only) 1697-1812. Somersetshire Parish Registers, vol. 2, 1899.
[16] Included in the Registers of Winterton (q.v.).
[17] P (Marriages only) 1682-1812. Hampshire Parish Registers, vol. 7, 1905.
[18] P (Marriages only) 1698-1812. Wiltshire Parish Registers, vol. 1, 1905.

Parish.	County.	Date of Earliest Entry.	Parish.	County.	Date of Earliest Entry.
Sotby - - -	Lincoln -	1658	Sowerby (near Thirsk)	York - -	1569
Sotherton - - -	Suffolk -	1675	Sowerby-Bridge -	York - -	1709
Sotterley - -	Suffolk -	1557	Sowerby, Castle- -	Cumberland -	1711
Sotwell - - -	Berks -	1684	Sowerby, Temple- -	Westmorland -	1669
Soulbury - -	Buckingham -	¹ 1624	Sowton - - -	Devon - -	1560
Soulderne - - -	Oxford - -	1668	Spalding - -	Lincoln -	⁸ 1538
Souldrop - -	Bedford -	1670	Spaldwick - -	Huntingdon -	1688
Sourton - -	Devon - -	1722	Spanby - - -	Lincoln - -	1681
Southacre - -	Norfolk -	¹ 1575	Sparham - -	Norfolk -	1573
Southam - -	Warwick -	³ 1539	Sparkford - -	Somerset - -	1729
Southampton, All Saints.	Hants -	1650	Sparsholt - -	Berks - -	1558
			Sparsholt - -	Hants - -	1602
Holy Rhood - -	- - -	1653	Spaxton - -	Somerset -	⁹ 1558
St. Lawrence -	- - -	1751	Speen - - -	Berks - -	1629
St. Mary -	- - -	1675	Speeton - -	York - -	¹⁰ —
St. Michael -	- - -	1552	Speldhurst - -	Kent - -	1559
Southbroom - -	Wilts - -	1572	Spelsbury - -	Oxford - -	1539
Southchurch - -	Essex - -	1695	Spennithorne - -	York - -	1573
Southease - - -	Sussex - -	1538	Spernall - -	Warwick -	¹¹ 1676
Southery - -	Norfolk - -	1706	Spetchley - -	Worcester -	1539
Southfleet - - -	Kent - -	1558	Spetisbury - -	Dorset -	1705
Southgate - -	Middlesex -	⁴ —	Spexhall - -	Suffolk - -	1538
South-hill - - -	Cornwall -	1538	Spilsby - - -	Lincoln -	1562
Southill - -	Bedford - -	1538	Spittal - - -	Pembroke -	1783
Southleigh. See Leigh, South.			Spixworth - -	Norfolk -	1551
			Spofforth - -	York - -	1599
Southminster - -	Essex - -	1702	Spondon - -	Derby - -	¹² 1653
Southoe - -	Huntingdon -	1670	Sporle - - -	Norfolk -	1562
Southolt - - -	Suffolk - -	1538	Spratton - -	Northampton -	1538
Southover - -	Sussex - -	1558	Spreyton - -	Devon - -	1563
Southport - - -	Lancaster -	1594	Spridlington - -	Lincoln - -	1556
Southrop - -	Gloucester -	⁵ 1656	Springfield - -	Essex - -	1653
Southtown - -	Suffolk - -	⁶ —	Springthorpe - -	Lincoln -	1588
Southwark, Christ-church.	Surrey - -	1671	Sproatley - -	York - -	1647
			Sprotborough -	York - -	1559
St. George the Martyr.	- - -	1602	Sproughton - -	Suffolk -	1541
			Sprowston - -	Norfolk -	1690
St. John, Horsley-down.	- ·· -	1732	Sproxton - -	Leicester -	1640
			Stackpole-Elidor -	Pembroke -	1724
St. Olave - - -	- - -	1685	Stadhampton - -	Oxford - -	1567
St. Saviour -	- - -	⁷ 1570	Stafford, St. Mary -	Stafford -	1559
St. Thomas -	- - -	1614	St. Chadd -	- - -	1636
Southwell - -	Nottingham -	1559	Stafford, West -	Dorset - -	1570
Southwick - -	Hants - -	1628	Stagsden - -	Bedford -	1670
Southwick - -	Northampton -	1732	Stainburn - -	York - -	1803
Southwick - -	Sussex - -	1653	Stainby - -	Lincoln - -	1653
Southwold - -	Suffolk -	1602	Staindrop - -	Durham -	1635
Southwood - -	Norfolk - -	1630	Staines - -	Middlesex -	¹³ 1644
Sowe - - -	Warwick -	1538	Stainfield - -	Lincoln -	1680
Sowerby (near Halifax)	York - -	1643	Stainland - -	York - -	1782

¹ **P** (Marriages only) 1575–1812. Buckinghamshire Parish Registers, vol. 1, 1902.
² **P** (Marriages only) 1576–1812. Norfolk Parish Registers, vol. 1, 1899.
³ **P** 1539–1657. In "History of Southam," by W. L. Smith, 1894.
⁴ Included in the Registers of Edmonton (*q.v.*).
⁵ **P** (Marriages only) 1656–1837. Gloucestershire Parish Registers, vol. 13, 1908.
⁶ Included in the Registers of Gorleston (*q.v.*).
⁷ St. Saviour. See "The Genealogist," vols. 6–9.
⁸ **P** (Marriages only) 1550–1812. Lincolnshire Parish Registers, vol. 1, 1905.
⁹ **P** (Marriages only) 1558–1812. Somersetshire Parish Registers, vol. 6, 1905.
¹⁰ Included in the Registers of Bridlington (*q.v.*).
¹¹ Bishop's Transcripts commence 1612.
¹² **P** (Marriages only) 1653–1812. Derbyshire Parish Registers, vol. 3, 1907.
¹³ **P** 1644–1694. Edited by F. A. Crisp, 1887.

Parish.	County.	Date of Earliest Entry.	Parish.	County.	Date of Earliest Entry.
Stainley, South - -	York - -	1658	Stanford-Rivers -	Essex - -	1538
Stainmore - -	Westmorland -	1708	Stangate - -	Essex - -	[7]
Stainton (near Conisborough).	York - -	1566	Stanground - -	Huntingdon -	1538
			Stanhoe - - -	Norfolk - -	1558
Stainton (near Thornaby-on-Tees).	York - -	1551	Stanhope - -	Durham - -	[1] 1595
			Stanion - - -	Northampton -	1703
Stainton - by - Langworth.	Lincoln -	1720	Stanley - - -	Derby - -	[9] 1675
			Stanley, King's- -	Gloucester -	[10] 1573
Stainton, Great -	Durham - -	1561	Stanley, Leonard- -	Gloucester -	[11] 1570
Stainton-le-Vale -	Lincoln -	1757	Stanmer - - -	Sussex - -	1558
Stainton, Market, St. Michael.	Lincoln -	1689	Stanmore, Great -	Middlesex -	1600
			Stanmore, Little -	Middlesex -	1558
Stalbridge - -	Dorset - -	1691	Stanningfield -	Suffolk - -	1561
Stalham - -	Norfolk - -	1561	Stannington - -	Northumberland	1658
Stalisfield - -	Kent - -	1699	Stansfield - -	Suffolk - -	1538
Stallingborough -	Lincoln -	1549	Stanstead - -	Kent - -	1564
Stalling-Busk -	York - -	1742	Stanstead - -	Suffolk - -	1570
Stalmine - -	Lancaster -	1593	Stanstead-Abbots -	Hertford - -	1678
Stalybridge - -	Chester - -	1776	Stansted-Montfichet -	Essex - -	1558
Stambourne - -	Essex - -	1559	Stanton - - -	Gloucester -	[12] 1572
Stambridge, Great -	Essex - -	1563	Stanton, All Saints -	Suffolk - -	1584
Stambridge, Little -	Essex - -	1659	Stanton, St. John the Baptist.	Suffolk - -	1579
Stamford, All Saints -	Lincoln -	[1] 1560			
St. George - -	- - -	1560	Stantonbury - -	Buckingham -	1653
St. John Baptist -	- - -	1561	Stanton-by-Bridge -	Derby - -	1664
St. Mary - -	- - -	1569	Stanton - by - Dale Abbey.	Derby - -	[13] 1604
St. Michael - -	- - -	1560			
Stamford-Baron -	Northampton -	[2] 1572	Stanton-Drew - -	Somerset - -	1653
Stamfordham - -	Northumberland	1662	Stanton-Fitzwarren -	Wilts - -	1542
Stanbridge - -	Bedford - -	1560	Stanton-Harcourt -	Oxford - -	1568
Standerwick - -	Somerset - -	[3] —	Stanton-Lacy - -	Salop - -	[14] 1561
Standish - -	Gloucester -	[4] 1559	Stanton, Long, All Saints'.	Cambridge -	1672
Standish - -	Lancaster -	1558			
Standlake - -	Oxford - -	1560	Stanton, Long, St. Michael.	Cambridge -	1559
Standon - -	Hertford - -	1671			
Standon - -	Stafford - -	[5] 1558	Stanton - on - Hine-Heath.	Salop - -	1655
Stanfield - -	Norfolk - -	1558			
Stanford - -	Kent - -	1556	Stanton-on-the-Wolds	Nottingham -	1735
Stanford - -	Norfolk - -	1754	Stanton-Prior - -	Somerset - -	1572
Stanford-Bishop -	Hereford -	1699	Stanton, St. Bernard -	Wilts - -	1568
Stanford-Dingley -	Berks - -	1538	Stanton, St. John's -	Oxford - -	1654
Stanford-in-the-Vale -	Berks - -	1558	Stanton, St. Quintin -	Wilts - -	1679
Stanford-le-Hope -	Essex - -	1680	Stanton, Stoney- -	Leicester -	1558
Stanford-on-Avon -	Leicester -	1607	Stanton-under-Bardon	Leicester -	[15] —
Stanford-on-Soar -	Nottingham -	[6] 1635	Stanway - - -	Essex - -	1704
Stanford-on-Teme -	Worcester -	1595	Stanway - -	Gloucester -	1 3

[1] See "The Reliquary." St. George, vol. 8; St. John, vols. 20, 21, 22, 24; St. Mary, vols. 9-11; St. Michael, vols. 14-20.
[2] See "The Reliquary," vols. 12 and 13.
[3] Included in the Registers of Beckington (q.v.).
[4] **P** (Marriages only) 1559-1812. Gloucestershire Parish Registers, vol. 6, 1900.
[5] **P** 1558-1812. Staffordshire Parish Register Society, 1902.
[6] **P** (Marriages only) 1633-1812. Nottinghamshire Parish Registers, vol. 5, 1903.
[7] Included in the Registers of Steeple (q.v.).
[8] **P** (Marriages only) 1613-1812. Durham and Northumberland Parish Register Society, vol 3, 1900.
[9] **P** (Marriages only) 1754-1812. Derbyshire Parish Registers, vol. 1, 1906.
[10] **P** (Marriages only) 1573-1812. Gloucestershire Parish Registers, vol. 1, 1896.
[11] **P** (Marriages only) 1570-1812. Gloucestershire Parish Registers, vol. 2, 1897.
[12] **P** (Marriages only) 1572-1812. Gloucestershire Parish Registers, vol. 4, 1898.
[13] **P** (Marriages only) 1605-1812. Derbyshire Parish Registers, vol. 1, 1906.
[14] **P** 1561-1812. Shropshire Parish Register Society, vol. 4 (Hereford Diocese).
[15] Included in the Registers of Thornton (q.v.).

Parish.	County.	Date of Earliest Entry.	Parish.	County.	Date of Earliest Entry.
Stanwell	Middlesex	1632	Stean	Northampton	[9] —
Stanwick	Northampton	1550	Stebbing	Essex	1712
Stanwick	York	1693	Stedham	Sussex	1538
Stanwix	Cumberland	1660	Steep	Hants	1610
Stapenhill	Derby	1680	Steeping, Great	Lincoln	1711
Staple	Kent	1544	Steeping, Little	Lincoln	1559
Staple-Fitzpaine	Somerset	1684	Steeple	Dorset	1548
Stapleford	Cambridge	1707	Steeple	Essex	1666
Stapleford	Hertford	1578	Steepleton-Iwerne	Dorset	1755
Stapleford	Leicester	1579	Stelling	Kent	1557
Stapleford	Lincoln	1695	Stenigot	Lincoln	1562
Stapleford	Nottingham	[1] 1655	Stephens, St., by Launceston.	Cornwall	1569
Stapleford	Wilts	1637			
Stapleford-Abbotts	Essex	1653	Stephens, St.	Hertford	1552
Stapleford-Tawney	Essex	[2] 1558	Stephens, St., by Saltash	Cornwall	1545
Staplegrove	Somerset	1558	Stephens, St., in-Brannel.	Cornwall	[10] 1694
Staplehurst	Kent	1538			
Stapleton	Cumberland	1725	Stepney	Middlesex	[11] 1568
Stapleton	Gloucester	1720	Steppingley	Bedford	1562
Stapleton	Leicester	[3] —	Sterndale, Earl-	Derby	1765
Stapleton	Salop	[4] 1630	Sternfield	Suffolk	1558
Starston	Norfolk	1558	Stert	Wilts	[12] 1579
Startforth	York	1668	Stetchworth	Cambridge	1666
Stathern	Leicester	1567	Stevenage	Hertford	1538
Staughton, Great	Huntingdon	1540	Steventon	Berks	1558
Staughton, Little	Bedford	1598	Steventon	Hants	[13] 1604
Staunton	Gloucester	1653	Stevington	Bedford	1653
Staunton	Nottingham	[5] 1654	Stewkley	Buckingham	[14] 1545
Staunton	Worcester	1559	Stewton	Lincoln	1711
Staunton Chapel	Nottingham	[6] 1663	Steyning	Sussex	1565
Staunton, Long	Salop	1568	Steynton	Pembroke	1637
Staunton-on-Arrow	Hereford	1558	Stibbard	Norfolk	1733
Staunton-on-Wye	Hereford	1677	Stibbington	Huntingdon	[15] —
Staunton, White-	Somerset	[7] 1606	Stickford	Lincoln	1663
Staveley	Derby	1702	Stickney	Lincoln	1643
Staveley	York	1558	Stiffkey	Norfolk	1548
Staveley	Westmorland	1651	Stifford	Essex	[16] 1568
Staveley-in-Cartmel	Lancaster	[8] —	Stillingfleet	York	1598
Staverton	Devon	1614	Stillington	York	1666
Staverton	Gloucester	1542	Stilton	Huntingdon	1660
Staverton	Northampton	1564	Stinchcombe	Gloucester	[17] 1582
Staverton	Wilts	1675	Stinsford	Dorset	1579
Stawell	Somerset	1685	Stirchley	Salop	[18] 1638
Stawley	Somerset	1653	Stisted	Essex	1538

[1] **P** (Marriages only) 1656-1812. Nottinghamshire Parish Registers, vol. 8, 1905.
[2] **P** 1558-1752. Edited by F. A. Crisp, 1892.
[3] Included in the Registers of Barwell (q.v.).
[4] **P** 1635-1812. Shropshire Parish Register Society, vol. 1, 1900 (Lichfield Diocese). **P** 1546-1812. Parish Register Society, vol. 35, 1901.
[5] **P** (Marriages only) 1655-1812. Nottinghamshire Parish Registers, vol. 4, 1902.
[6] **P** (Marriages only) 1663-1802. Nottinghamshire Parish Registers, vol. 4, 1902.
[7] **P** (Marriages only) 1606-1811. Somersetshire Parish Registers, vol. 4, 1902.
[8] Included in the Registers of Cartmel (q.v.).
[9] Included in the Registers of Hinton (q.v.).
[10] **P** (Marriages only) 1681-1812. Cornwall Parish Registers, vol. 10, 1906.
[11] **P** (Marriages only) 1568-1696. Edited by T. Colyer Ferguson, 1898.
[12] **P** (Marriages only) 1579-1812. Wiltshire Parish Registers, vol. 4, 1907.
[13] **P** (Marriages only) 1604-1812. Hampshire Parish Registers, vol. 1, 1899.
[14] **P** 1545-1653. Edited by Rev. R. B. Dickson, 1897.
[15] Included in the Registers of Sibson (q.v.).
[16] **P** 1568-1783. Edited by F. A. Crisp.
[17] **P** (Marriages only) 1583-1812. Gloucestershire Parish Registers, vol. 2, 1897, and vol. 6, 1900.
[18] **P** 1638-1812. Shropshire Parish Register Society, vol. 5, 1904.

Parish.	County.	Date of Earliest Entry.	Parish.	County.	Date of Earliest Entry.
Stithian, St. -	Cornwall -	[1] 1623	Stoke-Dry - -	Leicester and Rutland.	1559
Stivichall -	Warwick -	1653			
Stixwold - - -	Lincoln -	1541	Stoke, East - -	Dorset - -	1742
Stoak - -	Chester -	1543	Stoke, East - -	Nottingham -	[10] 1553
Stock - -	Worcester -	1562	Stoke-Edith - -	Hereford -	1538
Stock-Harward -	Essex -	[2] 1563	Stoke-Erle -	Wilts - -	1681
Stock-Gaylard -	Dorset -	1567	Stoke-Ferry - -	Norfolk -	1736
Stockbridge -	Hants -	1663	Stoke-Fleming -	Devon -	1538
Stockbury -	Kent -	1653	Stoke-Gabriel -	Devon -	1539
Stockerston -	Leicester -	1574	Stoke-Gifford -	Gloucester -	1556
Stockland -	Dorset -	1640	Stoke-Golding -	Leicester -	1656
Stockland-Bristol -	Somerset -	[3] 1538	Stoke-Goldington -	Buckingham -	1538
Stockleigh-English -	Devon -	1610	Stoke-Hammond -	Buckingham -	1538
Stockleigh-Pomeroy -	Devon -	1556	Stoke-Lacy - -	Hereford -	1567
Stocklinch - Magda-lene.	Somerset -	[4] 1712	Stoke-Lane - -	Somerset -	1644
			Stoke-Lyne - -	Oxford -	1665
Stocklinch-Ottersey -	Somerset -	[5] 1560	Stoke-Mandeville -	Buckingham -	1699
Stockport - -	Chester -	[6] 1584	Stoke-next-Guildford	Surrey -	1662
Stockton - -	Norfolk -	1561	Stoke, North - -	Oxford -	1740
Stockton -	Salop -	1558	Stoke, North - -	Somerset -	1649
Stockton -	Warwick -	1567	Stoke, North - -	Sussex -	1678
Stockton - -	Wilts -	[7] 1589	Stoke-Pero - -	Somerset -	1712
Stockton-on-Tees -	Durham -	1621	Stoke-Poges - -	Buckingham -	1563
Stockton-on-Teme -	Worcester -	1539	Stoke-Prior - -	Hereford -	1678
Stockton - on - the-Forest.	York -	1653	Stoke-Prior - -	Worcester -	1557
			Stoke-Rivers -	Devon -	1553
Stodmarsh -	Kent -	1558	Stoke-Rodney - -	Somerset -	1654
Stody - - -	Norfolk -	1661	Stoke-Severn -	Worcester -	1538
Stogumber - -	Somerset -	1559	Stoke, South - -	Lincoln -	1660
Stogursey -	Somerset -	1660	Stoke, South - -	Oxford -	1557
Stoke - -	Warwick -	1574	Stoke, South - -	Somerset -	1691
Stoke - -	Kent -	1666	Stoke, South - -	Sussex -	1553
Stoke -	Norfolk -	1538	Stoke-Talmage -	Oxford -	1754
Stoke, St. Gregory St. Mary	Somerset -	1561	Stoke-Trister -	Somerset -	1751
	- -	[8] 1676	Stoke-in-Teignhead -	Devon -	1538
Stoke -	Salop -	1654	Stoke-under-Hamdon	Somerset -	1558
Stoke-Abbot -	Dorset -	1559	Stoke-upon-Terne -	Salop -	1654
Stoke-Albany -	Northampton -	1575	Stoke-upon-Trent -	Stafford -	1689
Stoke-Ash -	Suffolk -	1538	Stoke-Wake - -	Dorset -	1546
Stoke-Bliss -	Hereford and Worcester.	1571	Stoke, West - -	Sussex -	1564
			Stokeham -	Nottingham -	1672
Stoke-Bruerne -	Northampton -	1560	Stokenchurch -	Oxford -	1707
Stoke-by-Clare -	Suffolk -	1538	Stokenham -	Devon -	1578
Stoke-by-Nayland -	Suffolk -	1558	Stokesay - -	Salop -	1558
Stoke-Canon -	Devon -	1654	Stokesby - -	Norfolk -	1560
Stoke-Charity -	Hants -	[9] 1544	Stokesley - -	York -	[11] 1571
Stoke-Climsland -	Cornwall -	1538	Stondon-Massey -	Essex -	1708
Stoke d'Abernon -	Surrey -	1619	Stondon, Upper -	Bedford -	1683
Stoke-Damerel -	Devon -	1689	Stone - -	Buckingham -	[12] 1538
Stoke-Doyle -	Northampton -	1560	Stone - -	Gloucester -	[13] 1594

[1] **P** (Marriages only) 1654–1812. Cornwall Parish Registers, vol. 7, 1904.
[2] **P** 1563–1700. Edited by Rev. E. P. Gibson, London, 1881.
[3] **P** (Marriages only) 1538–1807. Somersetshire Parish Registers, vol. 6, 1905.
[4] **P** (Marriages only) 1712–1776. Somersetshire Parish Registers, vol. 4, 1902.
[5] **P** (Marriages only) 1558–1812. Somersetshire Parish Registers, vol. 4, 1902.
[6] **P** 1584–1620. Edited by E. W. Bulkeley, 1889.
[7] **P** (Marriages only) 1590–1812. Wiltshire Parish Registers, vol. 3, 1906.
[8] **P** (Marriages only) 1679–1812. Somersetshire Parish Registers, vol. 7, 1906.
[9] **P** (Marriages only) 1542–1812. Hampshire Parish Registers, vol. 9, 1907.
[10] **P** (Marriages only) 1559–1812. Nottinghamshire Parish Registers, vol. 5, 1900.
[11] **P** 1571–1750. Yorkshire Parish Register Society, vol. 7, 1901.
[12] **P** (Marriages only) 1538–1812. Buckinghamshire Parish Registers, vol. 3, 1907.
[13] **P** (Marriages only) 1594–1812. Gloucestershire Parish Registers, vol. 3, 1898.

Parish.	County.	Date of Earliest Entry.	Parish.	County.	Date of Earliest Entry.
Stone (near Rye) -	Kent - -	1604	Stower-Provost - -	Dorset - -	1701
Stone - - -	Stafford -	1568	Stower, West -	Dorset - -	1654
Stone - -	Worcester -	1601	Stowey - -	Somerset -	1584
Stone-Easton - -	Somerset - -	1572	Stowey, Nether - -	Somerset - -	1640
Stone (near Dartford)	Kent - -	1718	Stowey, Over - -	Somerset -	⁶ 1558
Stonegrave - -	York - -	1584	Stowford - - -	Devon - -	1707
Stoneham, North -	Hants - -	1640	Stowting - -	Kent - -	1539
Stoneham, South -	Hants - -	1663	Stradbroke - -	Suffolk - -	1538
Stonehouse - -	Gloucester -	¹ 1558	Stradishall - -	Suffolk - -	1548
Stonehouse, East -	Devon - -	1754	Stradsett - - -	Norfolk - -	1559
Stoneleigh - -	Warwick -	1634	Stragglesthorpe -	Lincoln -	1765
Stonesby - -	Leicester - -	1625	Stranton - -	Durham - -	1580
Stonesfield - -	Oxford -	1571	Strata-Florida - -	Cardigan -	1750
Stonham-Aspal - -	Suffolk - -	1558	Stratfield-Mortimer -	B e r k s a n d	1681
Stonham-Earl -	Suffolk - -	1654		Hants.	
Stonham-Parva -	Suffolk - -	1542	Stratfieldsaye - -	Hants - -	⁷ 1539
Stonton-Wyville -	Leicester -	1538	Stratfield-Turgiss -	Hants - -	⁸ 1672
Stoodleigh - -	Devon - -	1597	Stratford, Fenny -	Buckingham -	1730
Stopham - -	Sussex - -	1544	Stratford, St. Andrew	Suffolk - -	1720
Storrington - -	Sussex - -	1547	St. Mary -	- - -	1562
Stortford, Bishops. *See*			Stratford-on-Avon -	Warwick -	⁹ 1558
Bishops-Stortford.			Stratford, Stony- -	Buckingham -	1738
Stotfold - -	Bedford - -	1703	Stratford-sub-Castle -	Wilts - -	1654
Stottesdon - -	Salop - -	1565	Stratford, Tony - -	Wilts - -	1562
Stoughton - -	Sussex - -	1675	Stratford Water- -	Buckingham -	1596
Stoughton - -	Leicester - -	1538	Stratton - - -	Cornwall -	1687
Stoulton - -	Worcester -	1542	Stratton - - -	Dorset - -	1560
Stourmouth - -	Kent - -	1538	Stratton - - -	Gloucester -	1600
Stourpaine - -	Dorset - -	² 1631	Stratton - - -	Norfolk - -	1558
Stourton - -	Wilts - -	³ 1570	Stratton - - -	Wilts - -	¹⁰ 1608
Stoven - - -	Suffolk - -	1653	Stratton-Audley - -	Oxford - -	1696
Stow - - -	Lincoln - -	1561	Stratton, East - -	Hants - -	1540
Stow - - -	Cambridge -	1650	Stratton, Long - -	Norfolk - -	1547
Stow-Bardolph -	Norfolk - -	1559	Stratton-on-the-Fosse	Somerset -	1710
Stow-Bedon - -	Norfolk - -	1722	Stratton-Strawless -	Norfolk - -	1562
Stowlangtoft - -	Suffolk - -	1559	Streatham - - -	Surrey - -	1538
Stow-Long - -	Cambridge -	1569	Streatley - - -	Bedford - -	1693
Stow, Longa - -	Huntingdon -	1591	Streatley - - -	Berks - -	1679
Stow-Maries - -	Essex - -	1559	Street - - -	Somerset - -	¹¹ 1639
Stowmarket - -	Suffolk - -	1559	Street - - -	Sussex - -	1560
Stow-on-the-Wold -	Gloucester -	1558	Strelley - - -	Nottingham -	¹² 1665
Stow-Upland - -	Suffolk - -	1693	Strensall - - -	York - -	1580
Stow, West - -	Suffolk - -	⁴ 1558	Strensham - - -	Worcester -	1569
Stowe - -	Salop - -	1576	Stretford - - -	Hereford - -	1720
Stowe - -	Buckingham -	1568	Stretford - - -	Lancaster -	1598
Stowe - - -	Lincoln - -	⁵ —	Strethall - - -	Essex - -	1739
Stowe - -	Stafford -	1577	Stretham - - -	Cambridge -	1558
Stowe-Nine-Churches-	Northampton -	1560	Stretton - - -	Rutland - -	1631
Stowell - - -	Gloucester -	1590	Stretton - - -	Stafford - -	1659
Stowell - - -	Somerset - -	1745	Stretton Church- -	Salop - -	1662
Stower, East - -	Dorset - -	1598	Stretton-en-le-Field -	Derby - -	1695

¹ **P** (Marriages only) 1558–1812. Gloucestershire Parish Registers, vol. 2, 1897.
² **P** 1631–1799. Edited by E. A. Fry, 1900.
³ **P** 1570–1800. Harleian Society Registers, vol. 12.
⁴ **P** 1558–1856. Edited by the Rev. S. H. Hervey, 1905.
⁵ Included in the Registers of Barholm (*q.v.*).
⁶ **P** (Marriages only) 1558–1812. Somersetshire Parish Registers, vol. 6, 1905.
⁷ **P** (Marriages only) 1539–1812. Hampshire Parish Registers, vol. 5, 1903.
⁸ **P** (Marriages only) 1672–1812. Hampshire Parish Registers, vol. 6, 1904.
⁹ **P** 1558–1812. Parish Register Society, vols. 6 and 16, 1897–8.
¹⁰ **P** Edited by Sir Thos. Phillipps.
¹¹ **P** 1559–1762. Edited by A. J. Jewers, 1898.
¹² **P** (Marriages only) 1665–1812. Nottinghamshire Parish Registers, vol. 8, 1905

Parish.	County.	Date of Earliest Entry.	Parish.	County.	Date of Earliest Entry.
Stretton-Grandison -	Hereford - -	1558	Sundon - - -	Bedford -	1582
Stretton, Little - -	Leicester -	1592	Sundridge - - -	Kent - -	1579
Stretton-Magna -	Leicester -	1603	Sunninghill - -	Berks - -	1560
Stretton-on-Dunsmore	Warwick -	1681	Sunningwell - -	Berks - -	1543
Stretton-on-the-Foss -	Warwick -	1538	Surfleet - - -	Lincoln -	1662
Stretton-Sugwas -	Hereford -	1733	Surlingham - -	Norfolk - -	1561
Stringston - - -	Somerset - -	1623	Sustead - - -	Norfolk -	1558
Strixton - - -	Northampton -	1730	Sutcombe - - -	Devon -	1684
Strood - - -	Kent - -	1565	Sutterby - - -	Lincoln -	1595
Stroud - - -	Gloucester -	1624	Sutterton - - -	Lincoln - -	1538
Stroxton - - -	Lincoln - -	1735	Sutton - - -	Bedford - -	1538
Strubby - - -	Lincoln -	1558	Sutton - - -	Cambridge -	1558
Strumpshaw - -	Norfolk - -	[1] 1562	Sutton - - -	Derby - -	1662
Stubton - - -	Lincoln -	[2] 1660	Sutton - - -	Essex - -	1741
Stuchbury - -	Northampton -	[3] —	Sutton - - -	Norfolk - -	1558
Studham - - -	Bedford and Hertford.	1570	Sutton - - -	Northampton -	[9] 1758
			Sutton - - -	Salop - -	[10] —
Studland - - -	Dorset - -	1581	Sutton - - -	Suffolk - -	1554
Studley - - -	Warwick -	[4] 1663	Sutton - - -	Surrey - -	1636
Studley-Hall - -	York - -	[5] —	Sutton - - -	Sussex -	1656
Stukeley, Great -	Huntingdon -	1569	Sutton-at-Hone - -	Kent - -	1607
Stukeley, Little -	Huntingdon -	1655	Sutton-Bassett - -	Northampton -	1576
Stuntney - -	Cambridge -	1545	Sutton-Benger -	Wilts - -	1653
Sturmer - - -	Essex - -	1733	Sutton-Bingham -	Somerset -	1742
Sturminster-Marshall -	Dorset - -	[6] 1562	Sutton, Bishop's. See		
Sturminster-Newton -	Dorset - -	1681	Bishop's Sutton.		
Sturry - - -	Kent - -	1538	Sutton-Bonnington, St.	Nottingham -	[11] 1560
Sturston - - -	Norfolk -	[7] —	Anne.		
Sturton - - -	Nottingham -	1638	St. Michael -	Nottingham -	[12] 1558
Sturton, Great -	Lincoln -	1679	Sutton-by-Dover -	Kent - -	1538
Stuston - - -	Suffolk -	1630	Sutton-Cheney -	Leicester -	1674
Stutton - - -	Suffolk -	1665	Sutton-Coldfield -	Warwick -	1603
Suckley - - -	Worcester -	[8] 1695	Sutton-Courtney -	Berks - -	1539
Sudborne - -	Suffolk -	1661	Sutton, East - -	Kent - -	1648
Sudborough - -	Northampton -	1660	Sutton, Full-. See Full-		
Sudbrooke - -	Lincoln -	1579	Sutton.		
Sudbury - - -	Derby - -	1673	Sutton-Guilden - -	Chester -	1595
Sudbury, All Saints' -	Suffolk -	1564	Sutton-in-Ashfield -	Nottingham -	[13] 1572
St. Gregory -	- -	1653	Sutton-in-Holderness -	York - -	1558
St. Peter -	- -	1593	Sutton-in-the-Marsh -	Lincoln -	1685
Sudeley-Manor -	Gloucester -	1705	Sutton, King's -	Northampton -	1582
Suffield - - -	Norfolk -	1558	Sutton, Long -	Hants - -	[14] 1561
Sulgrave - -	Northampton -	1668	Sutton, Long -	Lincoln - -	1672
Sulham - - -	Berks - -	1720	St. Edmund -	- -	1706
Sulhampstead-Abbots-	Berks - -	1602	St. James - -	- -	1570
Sulhampstead-Banister	Berks - -	1654	St. Nicholas (or	- -	1538
Sullington - - -	Sussex - -	1555	Sutton).		
Sully - - -	Glamorgan -	1754	Sutton, Long - -	Somerset -	[15] 1558
Sunbury - - -	Middlesex -	1565	Sutton-Maddock -	Salop - -	1559
Sunderland - -	Durham - -	1719	Sutton-Mallet -	Somerset -	1683

[1] **P** (Marriages only) 1562–1812. Norfolk Parish Registers, vol. 1, 1899.
[2] **P** 1577–1628. Edited by F. A. Crisp, 1883.
[3] Included in the Registers of Helmdon (q.v.).
[4] Bishop's Transcripts commence 1613.   [5] Included in the Registers of Aldfield (q.v.).
[6] **P** 1563–1812. Edited by Edith Hobday, Exeter, 1901.
[7] Included in the Registers of Tottington (q.v.).   [8] Bishop's Transcripts commence 1613.
[9] Earlier Registers at Caistor, the mother church (q.v.).
[10] Included in the Registers of Meole Brace (q.v.).
[11] **P** (Marriages only) 1560–1812. Nottinghamshire Parish Registers, vol. 5, 1903.
[12] **P** (Marriages only) 1559–1812. Nottinghamshire Parish Registers, vol. 5, 1903.
[13] **P** (Marriages only) 1572–1812. Nottinghamshire Parish Registers, vol. 11, 1907.
[14] **P** (Marriages only) 1561–1812. Hampshire Parish Registers, vol. 5, 1903.
[15] **P** (Marriages only) 1559–1812. Somersetshire Parish Registers, vol. 1, 1898.

Parish.	County.	Date of Earliest Entry.	Parish.	County.	Date of Earliest Entry.
Sutton-Mandeville -	Wilts - -	1748	Swindon - -	Gloucester -	⁴1606
Sutton-Montis -	Somerset -	1701	Swindon - - -	Wilts - -	1640
Sutton-on-Lound -	Nottingham -	1538	Swine - - -	York - -	1706
Sutton-on-the-Forest -	York - -	1557	Swineshead - -	Lincoln -	1639
Sutton-on-the-Hill -	Derby - -	1575	Swinfleet - -	York - -	⁵—
Sutton-on-Trent -	Nottingham -	1584	Swinford - -	Leicester -	1559
Sutton, St. Michael -	Hereford -	1678	Swinford, Old -	Worcester -	1602
Sutton, St. Nicholas -	Hereford -	1586	Swingfield - -	Kent - -	1698
Sutton-under-Brails -	Gloucester -	¹1578	Swinhope - -	Lincoln -	1697
Sutton - upon - Derwent.	York - -	1593	Swinnerton - -	Stafford -	1558
			Swinstead - -	Lincoln -	1648
Sutton-Valence -	Kent - -	1576	Swinton - -	Lancaster -	1791
Sutton-Veney -	Wilts - -	1653	Swithland - -	Leicester -	1676
Sutton-Waldron -	Dorset - -	1678	Swyncombe - -	Oxford -	1568
Swaby - -	Lincoln - -	1660	Swynshed - -	Bedford -	1550
Swaffham - -	Norfolk -	1559	Swyre - - -	Dorset -	1718
Swaffham-Bulbeck -	Cambridge -	1558	Syde - - -	Gloucester -	⁶1686
Swaffham-Prior -	Cambridge -	1559	Sydenham - -	Oxford -	1705
Swafield - -	Norfolk -	1660	Sydenham-Damerel -	Devon -	1539
Swainsthorpe -	Norfolk -	1558	Syderstone - -	Norfolk -	1585
Swainswick - -	Somerset -	1557	Sydling - -	Dorset -	1565
Swalcliffe - -	Oxford - -	1558	Syerston - -	Nottingham -	⁷1567
Swalecliffe - -	Kent - -	1558	Sykehouse - -	York - -	⁸1700
Swallow - -	Lincoln - -	1672	Syleham - -	Suffolk -	1539
Swallowcliffe -	Wilts - -	1760	Symondsbury -	Dorset -	⁹1558
Swallowfield -	Berks - -	1539	Syresham - -	Northampton -	1668
Swanage - -	Dorset - -	1563	Syston - - -	Leicester -	1644
Swanbourne -	Buckingham -	1566	Syston - - -	Lincoln -	1561
Swannington -	Norfolk -	1538	Sywell - - -	Northampton -	1571
Swanscombe -	Kent - -	1559			
Swansea - -	Glamorgan -	1631			
Swanton-Abbot -	Norfolk -	1538			
Swanton-Morley -	Norfolk -	1548			
Swanton-Novers -	Norfolk -	1667			
Swarby - -	Lincoln -	1678			
Swardeston -	Norfolk -	1538	**T.**		
Swarkeston -	Derby - -	1604			
Swarraton -	Hants - -	1754	Tachbrook, Bishop's.		
Swaton - - -	Lincoln -	1681	*See* Bishop's Tachbrook.		
Swavesey - -	Cambridge -	1576			
Swayfield - -	Lincoln - -	1724	Tackley - - -	Oxford - -	1559
Sweffling - -	Suffolk -	1679	Tacolneston -	Norfolk -	1653
Swell - -	Somerset -	²1559	Tadcaster - -	York - -	1570
Swell, Nether -	Gloucester -	³1678	Taddington -	Derby - -	1643
Swell, Upper -	Gloucester -	1543	Tadley - - -	Hants - -	¹⁰1683
Swepston - -	Leicester -	1561	Tadlow - - -	Cambridge -	1653
Swerford - -	Oxford -	1577	Tadmarton -	Oxford -	1548
Swettenham -	Chester -	1570	Taf-Fechan -	Brecon -	1772
Swilland - -	Suffolk -	1678	Takeley - - -	Essex -	1662
Swillington -	York -	1553	Talachddu -	Brecon -	1756
Swimbridge -	Devon -	1562	Talaton - - -	Devon -	1621
Swinbrook -	Oxford -	1684	Talbenny - -	Pembroke -	1764
Swinderby -	Lincoln -	1568	Talgarth - -	Brecon -	1695

¹ **P** (Marriages only) 1578–1812. Gloucestershire Parish Registers, vol. 4, 1898.
² **P** (Marriages only) 1559–1812. Somersetshire Parish Registers, vols. 4 and 5, 1902–4.
³ **P** (Marriages only) 1686–1812. Gloucestershire Parish Registers, vol. 3, 1898.
⁴ **P** (Marriages only) 1638–1837. Gloucestershire Parish Registers, vol. 1, 1896.
⁵ Included in the Registers of Whitgift (*q.v.*).
⁶ **P** (Marriages only) 1686–1812. Gloucestershire Parish Registers, vol. 12, 1906.
⁷ **P** (Marriages only) 1568–1812. Nottinghamshire Parish Registers, vol. 4, 1902.
⁸ Earlier entries in Registers at Fishlake (*q.v.*).
⁹ **P** (Marriages only) 1558–1812. Dorset Parish Registers, vol. 2, 1907.
¹⁰ **P** (Marriages only) 1691–1812. Hampshire Parish Registers, vol. 6, 1904.

Parish.	County.	Date of Earliest Entry.	Parish.	County.	Date of Earliest Entry.
Talk-o'-th'-Hill	Stafford	[1] —	Taverham	Norfolk	1713
Talliaris	Carmarthen	[2] —	Tavistock	Devon	1614
Talland	Cornwall	1651	Tavy, St. Mary	Devon	1560
Talley	Carmarthen	1686	Tavy, St. Peter	Devon	1614
Tallington	Lincoln	1690	Tawstock	Devon	1538
Talyllyn	Merioneth	1683	Tawton, Bishop's. *See*		
Tamerton-Foliot	Devon	1794	Bishop's-Tawton.		
Tamerton, North	Cornwall	1556	Tawton, North	Devon	1538
Tamworth	Stafford	1558	Tawton, South	Devon	1540
Tandridge	Surrey	1680	Taxall	Chester	1612
Tanfield	Durham	[3] 1719	Taynton	Gloucester	1538
Tanfield, West	York	1653	Taynton	Oxford	1538
Tangley	Hants	[4] 1675	Tealby	Lincoln	1714
Tangmere	Sussex	1539	Teath, St.	Cornwall	[11] 1558
Tankersley	York	1598	Tedburn	Devon	1558
Tannington	Suffolk	[5] 1539	Teddington	Middlesex	1558
Tansor	Northampton	1639	Teddington	Worcester	[12] 1560
Tanworth	Warwick	1558	Tedstone-de-la-Mere	Hereford	1690
Taplow	Buckingham	1710	Tedstone-Wafer	Hereford	1729
Tardebigge	Worcester and Warwick.	1566	Teffont-Ewyas	Wilts	[13] 1577
			Teffont-Magna	Wilts	—
Tarleton	Lancaster	1719	Teigh	Rutland	1572
Tarporley	Chester	1558	Teignmouth, East	Devon	1665
Tarrant-Crawford	Dorset	1597	Teignmouth, West	Devon	1706
Tarrant-Gunville	Dorset	1719	Teignton Bishop's. *See*		
Tarrant-Hinton	Dorset	[6] 1545	Bishop's Teignton.		
Tarrant-Keynston	Dorset	1737	Teignton, King's	Devon	1670
Tarrant-Monckton	Dorset	1760	Teigngrace	Devon	1683
Tarrant-Rawston	Dorset	1749	Tellisford	Somerset	1539
Tarrant-Rushton	Dorset	1696	Telscombe	Sussex	1684
Tarring-Neville	Sussex	1569	Temple, Ewell. *See*		
Tarring, West	Sussex	1559	Ewell.		
Tarrington	Hereford	1561	Templeton	Devon	1556
Tarvin	Chester	1563	Tempsford	Bedford	1604
Tasburgh	Norfolk	1558	Tenbury	Worcester	1653
Tasley	Salop	[7] 1563	Tenby	Pembroke	1711
Tatenhill	Stafford	[8] 1563	Tendring	Essex	1538
Tatham	Lancaster	1558	Tenterden	Kent	1544
Tatham-Fell	Lancaster	1745	Terling	Essex	1538
Tathwell	Lincoln	1625	Terrington	York	[14] 1599
Tatsfield	Surrey	[9] 1690	Terrington, St. Clement	Norfolk	1597
Tattenhall	Chester	1654	Terrington, St. John	Norfolk	1538
Tattenhoe	Buckingham	1733	Terwick	Sussex	1577
Tatterford	Norfolk	1560	Teston	Kent	1538
Tatterset	Norfolk	1558	Tetbury	Gloucester	[15] 1631
Tattershall	Lincoln	1569	Tetcott	Devon	1599
Tattingstone	Suffolk	1654	Tetford	Lincoln	1709
Taunton, St. James	Somerset	1626	Tetney	Lincoln	1730
St. Mary Magdalen		[10] 1558	Tetsworth	Oxford	1604

[1] Included in the Registers of Audley (*q.v.*).   [2] Included in the Registers of Llandilo-fawr (*q.v.*).
[3] The Registers before this date have been lost.
[4] **P** (Marriages only) 1703–1812. Hampshire Parish Registers, vol. 2, 1900.
[5] **P** 1539–1714. Edited by F. A. Crisp, 1884.
[6] **P** 1545–1812. Parish Register Society, vol. 44, 1902.
[7] **P** 1563–1812. Shropshire Parish Register Society, vol. 1 (Hereford Diocese).
[8] **P** 1563–1812. Staffordshire Parish Register Society, 1905.
[9] **P** 1690–1812. Surrey Parish Register Society, vol. 4, 1906.
[10] **P** (Marriages only) 1558–1812. Somersetshire Parish Registers, vols. 9 and 10, 1907.
[11] **P** (Marriages only) 1558–1812. Cornwall Parish Registers, vol. 1, 1900.
[12] From 1726 to 1730 the entries are recorded in the Overbury Register.
[13] Included in the Registers of Dinton (*q.v.*).
[14] **P** 1599–1812. Yorkshire Parish Register Society, vol. 29, 1907.
[15] **P** (Marriages only) 1631–1812. Gloucestershire Parish Registers, vol. 10, 1905.

Parish	County.	Date of Earliest Entry.		Parish.	County.	Date of Earliest Entry.
Tettenhall-Regis	Stafford	1602		Thoresby, South	Lincoln	1665
Tetworth	Huntingdon	[1] —		Thoresway	Lincoln	1727
Teversall	Nottingham	[2] 1571		Thorganby	Lincoln	1561
Teversham	Cambridge	1592		Thorganby	York	1653
Tew, Great	Oxford	1609		Thorington	Suffolk	[3] 1561
Tewin	Hertford	1559		Thorington	Essex	1553
Tewkesbury	Gloucester	1559		Thorley (Isle of Wight)	Hants	1666
Tey, Great	Essex	1559		Thorley	Hertford	1539
Tey, Little	Essex	1660		Thormanby	York	1658
Tey, Marks	Essex	1560		Thornage	Norfolk	1560
Teynham	Kent	1539		Thornborough	Buckingham	1602
Thakeham	Sussex	1628		Thornbury	Devon	1652
Thame	Oxford	1601		Thornbury	Gloucester	1538
Thanet, Isle of, St. Lawrence.	Kent	[3] 1560		Thornbury	Hereford	1538
				Thornby	Northampton	1649
St. Peter's	-	1582		Thorncombe	Dorset	[7] 1551
Thanington	Kent	1558		Thorndon	Suffolk	1538
Tharston	Norfolk	1560		Thorne	York	1565
Thatcham	Berks	1561		Thorne-Coffin	Somerset	1690
Thaxted	Essex	1558		Thorne-Falcon	Somerset	[8] 1725
Theberton	Suffolk	1548		Thorne, St. Margaret	Somerset	1715
Theddingworth	Leicester	1635		Thorner	York	1622
Theddlethorpe, All Saints.	Lincoln	1561		Thorney-Abbey	Cambridge	1653
				Thorney	Nottingham	1562
Theddlethorpe, St. Helen.	Lincoln	1716		Thorney, West	Sussex	1530
				Thornford	Dorset	1676
Thelbridge	Devon	1612		Thornham	Kent	1625
Thelnetham	Suffolk	1538		Thornham	Norfolk	1716
Thelveton	Norfolk	1538		Thornham-Magna	Suffolk	1555
Thelwall	Chester	1782		Thornham Little	Suffolk	1766
Themelthorpe	Norfolk	1715		Thornhaugh	Northampton	1562
Thenford	Northampton	1562		Thornhill	York	[9] 1580
Therfield	Hertford	1538		Thornthwaite	Cumberland	1775
Thetford	Cambridge	1654		Thornthwaite	York	[10] —
Thetford, St. Cuthbert	Norfolk	1672		Thornton	Buckingham	[11] 1562
St. Peter	-	1672		Thornton	Leicester	1559
St. Mary	-	1653		Thornton	Lincoln	1561
Theydon-Bois	Essex	1717		Thornton	York	1651
Theydon-Garnon	Essex	1558		Thornton	York	1678
Theydon-Mount	Essex	[4] 1564		Thornton-in-Craven	York	1566
Thimbleby	Lincoln	1695		Thornton-Curtis	Lincoln	1568
Thirkleby	York	1611		Thornton-Dale	York	1539
Thirne	Norfolk	[5] —		Thornton-in-Lonsdale	York	1576
Thirsk	York	1556		Thornton-in-the-Moors	Chester	1574
Thistleton	Rutland	1574		Thornton-le-Moor	York	1735
Thockrington	Northumberland	1715		Thornton-le-Street	York	1600
Thomas, St., the Apostle	Cornwall	1673		Thornton-Steward	York	1563
Thompson	Norfolk	1538		Thornton-Watlass	York	1574
Thompson Winterbourne.	Dorset	1802		Thoroton	Nottingham	[12] 1583
				Thorp-Acre	Leicester	[13] —
Thoresby, North	Lincoln	1546		Thorp-Arch	York	1595

[1] Included in the Registers of Everton (q.v.).
[2] P (Marriages only) 1572–1812. Nottinghamshire Parish Registers, vol. 11, 1907.
[3] P 1560–1653. Edited by Rev. C. H. Wilkie, Canterbury, 1902.
[4] P 1564–1815. Edited by J. J. Howard and H. F. Burke, London, 1891.
[5] Included in the Registers of Ashby (q.v.). [6] P 1561–1881. Edited by T. S. Hill, London, 1884.
[7] P (Marriages only) 1552–1812. Dorset Parish Registers, vol. 2, 1907.
[8] P (Marriages only) 1720–1812. Somersetshire Parish Registers, vol. 8, 1907.
[9] In the press. Yorkshire Parish Register Society.
[10] Included in the Registers of Hampsthwaite (q.v.).
[11] P 1562–1812. Buckinghamshire Parish Register Society, vol 2, 1903.
[12] P (Marriages only) 1587–1812. Nottinghamshire Parish Registers, vol. 1, 1898.
[13] Included in the Registers of Dishley (q.v.).

Parish.	County.	Date of Earliest Entry.	Parish.	County.	Date of Earliest Entry.
Thorpe - - -	York - -	1547	Thurlow, Little -	Suffolk - -	1562
Thorpe - - -	Derby - -	1538	Thurloxton - -	Somerset - -	1558
Thorpe - - -	Norfolk - -	1706	Thurlton - - -	Norfolk - -	1695
Thorpe - - -	Surrey - -	1653	Thurlton - -	Suffolk - -	⁷ —
Thorpe, Abbots -	Norfolk - -	1695	Thurmaston, South -	Leicester -	1719
Thorpe-Achurch -	Northampton -	1670	Thurnby - - -	Leicester - -	1538
Thorpe-Arnold - -	Leicester -	1558	Thurning - -	Huntingdon and	1560
Thorpe-Bassett -	York - -	1656		Northampton.	
Thorpe-by-Ixworth -	Suffolk - -	1718	Thurning - - -	Norfolk - -	1715
Thorpe-by-Newark -	Nottingham -	¹ 1559	Thurnscoe - -	York - -	1619
Thorpe-Constantine -	Stafford - -	1538	Thurrock, Grays -	Essex - -	1674
Thorpe-le-Soken -	Essex - -	1682	Thurrock, Little -	Essex - -	1654
Thorpe, Little -	Norfolk - -	² —	Thurrock, West -	Essex - -	1668
Thorpe-Malsor - -	Northampton -	1683	Thursby - -	Cumberland -	1649
Thorpe-Mandeville -	Northampton -	1575	Thursfield. See New-		
Thorpe-Market - -	Norfolk - -	1538	chapel.		
Thorpe-Morieux -	Suffolk - -	1538	Thursford - -	Norfolk -	1692
Thorpe-next-Haddiscoe	Norfolk - -	1530	Thursley - -	Surrey - -	1613
Thorpe-on-the-Hill -	Lincoln - -	1695	Thurstaston - -	Chester - -	1706
Thorpe, St. Peter -	Lincoln - -	1653	Thurston - -	Suffolk - -	1707
Thorpe-Salvin - -	York - -	1592	Thurton - - -	Norfolk - -	1559
Thorverton - -	Devon - -	1725	Thuxton - -	Norfolk - -	1538
Thrandeston - -	Suffolk - -	1558	Thwaite, All Saints -	Norfolk - -	1562
Thrapston - -	Northampton -	1560	Thwaite, St. Mary -	Norfolk - -	1538
Threckingham - -	Lincoln - -	1572	Thwaite, St. George -	Suffolk - -	1709
Threlkeld - -	Cumberland -	1573	Thwaites - -	Cumberland -	1724
Threxton - -	Norfolk - -	1731	Thwing - - -	York - -	1691
Thribergh - -	York - -	1599	Tibbenham - -	Norfolk - -	1560
Thrigby - - -	Norfolk - -	1539	Tibberton - -	Gloucester -	1659
Thrimby - -	Westmorland -	³ —	Tibberton - -	Worcester -	⁹ 1680
Thriplow - -	Cambridge -	1538	Tibberton - -	Salop - -	1719
Throcking - -	Hertford - -	1612	Tiberton - -	Hereford - -	1672
Throckmorton - -	Worcester -	1546	Tibshelf - -	Derby - -	1626
Throwleigh - -	Devon - -	1653	Ticehurst - -	Sussex - -	1560
Throwley - - -	Kent - -	1557	Tichbourne - -	Hants - -	1667
Thrumpton - -	Nottingham -	⁴ 1679	Tickencote - -	Rutland - -	1574
Thrushelton - -	Devon - -	1654	Tickenhall - -	Derby - -	1627
Thrussington - -	Leicester - -	1660	Tickenham - -	Somerset - -	1538
Thruxton - -	Hants - -	1600	Tickhill - -	York - -	1538
Thruxton - -	Hereford - -	1582	Tidcombe - -	Wilts - -	1639
Thunderley - -	Essex - -	⁵ —	Tidenham - -	Gloucester -	1708
Thundersley - -	Essex - -	1569	Tideswell - - -	Derby - -	1635
Thundridge - -	Hertford - -	1556	Tidmarsh - -	Berks - -	1730
Thurcaston - -	Leicester - -	1561	Tidmington - -	Worcester -	⁹ 1691
Thurgarton - -	Norfolk - -	1538	Tidworth, North -	Wilts - -	1700
Thurgarton - -	Nottingham -	1721	Tidworth, South -	Hants - -	1599
Thurlaston - -	Leicester - -	1588	Tiffield - - -	Northampton -	1559
Thurlbear - -	Somerset - -	⁶ 1700	Tilbrook - -	Bedford - -	1573
Thurlby, near Newark	Lincoln - -	1575	Tilbury, East - -	Essex - -	1627
Thurlby, near Bourne	Lincoln - -	1560	Tilbury-juxta-Clare -	Essex - -	1561
Thurleigh - - -	Bedford - -	1562	Tilbury, West - -	Essex - -	1540
Thurlestone - -	Devon - -	1558	Tilehurst - -	Berks - -	1630
Thurlow, Great - -	Suffolk - -	1636	Tillingham - -	Essex - -	1562

¹ **P** (Marriages only) 1577–1800. Nottinghamshire Parish Registers, vol. 4, 1902.
² Included in the Registers of Billington (q.v.).
³ Included in the Registers of Morland (q.v.).
⁴ **P** (Marriages only) 1680–1812. Nottinghamshire Parish Registers, vol. 7, 1905.
⁵ Included in the Registers of Wimbish (q.v.).
⁶ **P** (Marriages only) 1700–1812. Somersetshire Parish Registers, vol. 7, 1906.
⁷ Included in the Registers of Whitton (q.v.).
⁸ Bishop's Transcripts commence 1612.
⁹ **P** (Marriages only) 1693–1812. Worcestershire Parish Registers, vol. 1, 1901. Bishop's Transcripts commence 1612.

Parish.	County.	Date of Earliest Entry	Parish	County.	Date of Earliest Entry.
Tillington - -	Sussex - -	1572	Tofts, West - -	Norfolk - -	1733
Tilmanstone - -	Kent - -	1558	Tolland - -	Somerset - -	1706
Tilney, All Saints -	Norfolk - -	1538	Tollard-Royal - -	Wilts - -	1688
Tilney, St. Lawrence -	Norfolk -	1653	Toller-Fratrum -	Dorset - -	1558
Tilshead - -	Wilts - -	1650	Toller-Porcorum -	Dorset - -	1654
Tilstock - - -	Salop - -	¹ —	Tollerton -	Nottingham -	⁴1558
Tilston - -	Chester - -	1558	Tollesbury -	Essex - -	1558
Tilsworth - -	Bedford - -	1654	Tolleshunt-d'Arcy -	Essex - -	1560
Tilton-on-the-Hill -	Leicester - -	1610	Tolleshunt-Knights -	Essex - -	1695
Tilty - -	Essex - -	1724	Tolleshunt-Major -	Essex - -	1559
Timberland - -	Lincoln - -	1563	Tolpuddle - -	Dorset - -	1718
Timberscombe - -	Somerset -	1656	Tonbridge - - -	Kent - -	1559
Timsbury - -	Hants - -	1564	Tong - - -	Salop - -	⁵1629
Timsbury - -	Somerset -	1561	Tong - - -	York - -	1550
Timworth - -	Suffolk - -	1565	Tonge - -	Kent - -	1717
Tincleton - -	Dorset - -	1576	Tooting-Graveney -	Surrey - -	1555
Tingewick - -	Buckingham -	1560	Topcliffe - -	York - -	⁶1570
Tingrith - -	Bedford - -	1572	Topcroft - -	Norfolk - -	1556
Tinsley - -	York - -	1715	Toppesfield - -	Essex - -	⁷1559
Tintagel - -	Cornwall -	²1546	Topsham - -	Devon - -	1600
Tintern, Parva -	Monmouth -	1694	Torbrian - -	Devon - -	1564
Tintinhull - -	Somerset -	1680	Torksey - -	Lincoln - -	1654
Tinwell - - -	Rutland - -	1561	Tormarton - -	Gloucester -	⁸1679
Tipton - -	Stafford - -	1513	Tormohun - -	Devon - -	1637
Tirley - - -	Gloucester -	1653	Torpenhow - -	Cumberland -	1651
Tisbury - -	Wilts - -	1563	Torrington, Black -	Devon - -	1604
Tissington - -	Derby - -	1661	Torrington, East -	Lincoln - -	1754
Tisted, East -	Hants - -	1538	Torrington, Great -	Devon - -	1616
Tisted, West -	Hants - -	1538	Torrington, Little -	Devon - -	1672
Titchfield - -	Hants - -	1589	Torrington, West -	Lincoln - -	1721
Titchmarsh - -	Northampton -	1544	Tortington - -	Sussex - -	1560
Titchwell - -	Norfolk - -	1559	Tortworth - -	Gloucester -	⁹1591
Titley - -	Hereford - -	1569	Torver - -	Lancaster - -	1661
Titsey - - -	Surrey - -	1579	Toseland - -	Huntingdon -	1702
Tittleshall - -	Norfolk - -	1538	Tossett (or Tosside) -	York - -	1769
Tiverton - -	Devon - -	1559	Tostock - - -	Suffolk - -	1675
Tivetshall, St. Mary -	Norfolk - -	1672	Totham, Great -	Essex - -	1557
Tivetshall, St. Margaret.	Norfolk - -	1673	Totham, Little -	Essex - -	1558
			Tothill - -	Lincoln - -	1608
Tixall - - -	Stafford - -	1707	Totnes - - -	Devon - -	1557
Tixover - - -	Rutland - -	1754	Tottenham - -	Middlesex -	1558
Tockenham - -	Wilts - -	1653	Tottenhill - -	Norfolk - -	1679
Todbere - - -	Dorset - -	1750	Totteridge - -	Hertford - -	1570
Toddington - -	Bedford - -	1540	Totternhoe - -	Bedford - -	1673
Toddington - -	Gloucester -	1666	Tottington - -	Norfolk - -	1711
Todenham - -	Gloucester -	³1721	Tottington - -	Lancaster - -	1799
Todmorden - • -	Lancaster -	1666	Towcester - -	Northampton -	1561
Todwick - - -	York - -	1577	Towednack - -	Cornwall - -	¹⁰1676
Toft - - - -	Cambridge -	1539	Towersey - -	Buckingham -	1733
Toft, Monk's - -	Norfolk - -	1538	Townstall - -	Devon - -	1653
Toft-next-Newton -	Lincoln - -	1653	Towyn - - -	Merioneth -	1663
Toftrees - - -	Norfolk - -	1763	Toxteth Park - -	Lancaster - -	1775

¹ Included in the Registers of Whitchurch, Salop (*q.v.*).
² **P** (Marriages only) 1588–1812. Cornwall Parish Registers, vol. 2, 1902.
³ **P** (Marriages only) 1721–1812. Gloucestershire Parish Registers, vol. 4, 1898.
⁴ **P** (Marriages only) 1559–1810. Nottinghamshire Parish Registers, vol. 2, 1899.
⁵ **P** 1629–1812. Shropshire Parish Register Society, vol. 4, 1903 (Lichfield Diocese).
⁶ **P** 1654–1888. Edited by W. Smith, London, 1888.
⁷ **P** 1559–1650. Edited by Rev. H. B. Barnes and P. Morant, Topsfield, Mass., U.S.A., 1905.
⁸ **P** (Marriages only) 1600–1812. Gloucestershire Parish Registers, vol. 13, 1908, including West Littleton and Acton Turville.
⁹ **P** (Marriages only) 1620–1812. Gloucestershire Parish Registers, vol. 12, 1906.
¹ **P** (Marriages only) 1676–1812. Cornwall Parish Registers, vol. 3, 1903.

L

Parish.	County.	Date of Earliest Entry.	Parish.	County.	Date of Earliest Entry.
Toynton, All Saints -	Lincoln - -	1716	Trull - - -	Somerset -	⁵ 1670
Toynton, St. Peter -	Lincoln	1742	Trumpington - -	Cambridge -	1671
Toynton, High - -	Lincoln - -	1808	Trunch - -	Norfolk - -	1558
Toynton, Low -	Lincoln	1606	Truro - - -	Cornwall -	1597
Trallong - -	Brecon - -	1752	Trusham - -	Devon - -	1559
Trawsfynydd - -	Merioneth -	1695	Trusley - -	Derby - -	1538
Tredington - -	Gloucester -	1541	Trusthorpe - -	Lincoln - -	1665
Tredington - -	Worcester -	1541	Tryddin - -	Flint - -	1613
Tredunnock - -	Monmouth -	1695	Trysull - -	Stafford -	1572
Treeton - -	York - -	1677	Tuddenham, St. Martin	Suffolk -	1664
Tref-draeth -	Anglesey -	1551	Tuddenham, St. Mary	Suffolk - -	1558
Tref-Eglwys - -	Montgomery -	¹ 1623	Tuddenham, East -	Norfolk - -	1561
Trefgarn, Great -	Pembroke -	1732	Tuddenham, North -	Norfolk - -	1560
Trefilan - -	Cardigan -	1705	Tudeley - -	Kent - -	1663
Trefllys - -	Carnarvon -	1767	Tudy, St. - -	Cornwall -	⁷ 1559
Trefriw - -	Carnarvon -	1713	Tufton - -	Hants - -	⁸ 1716
Tregaion - -	Anglesey -	1708	Tugby - -	Leicester -	1568
Tregare - -	Monmouth -	1751	Tugford - -	Salop - -	1754
Tregaron - -	Cardigan -	1671	Tunstall - -	Kent - -	1538
Tregony - -	Cornwall -	1571	Tunstall - -	Lancaster -	1626
Tregynon - -	Montgomery -	1678	Tunstall - -	Norfolk - -	1557
Trelech-ar-Bettws	Carmarthen -	1663	Tunstall - -	Suffolk -	1539
Trelleck - -	Monmouth -	1763	Tunstall-in-Holderness	York - -	1568
Trelleck-Grange -	Monmouth -	1770	Tunstead - -	Norfolk - -	1678
Tremaen - -	Cardigan -	1763	Tunworth - -	Hants - -	1749
Tremaine - -	Cornwall -	² 1726	Tupholme - -	Lincoln - -	1708
Tremeirchion - -	Flint - -	1601	Turkdean - -	Gloucester -	1572
Treneglos - -	Cornwall -	1686	Turnastone - -	Hereford -	1678
Trent - -	Somerset -	1558	Turnditch - -	Derby - -	1783
Trentham - -	Stafford -	³ 1558	Turnerspuddle -	Dorset - -	1632
Trentishoe - -	Devon - -	1695	Turnworth - -	Dorset - -	1577
Tresmere - -	Cornwall -	1625	Turvey - -	Bedford - -	1629
Treswell - -	Nottingham -	1563	Turville - -	Buckingham -	1582
Tretire - -	Hereford -	1586	Turweston - -	Buckingham -	1695
Trevalga - -	Cornwall -	⁴ 1538	Tutbury - -	Stafford - -	1668
Trevethin - -	Monmouth -	1651	Tuttington - -	Norfolk - -	1544
Trewalchmai - -	Anglesey -	1727	Tuxford - -	Nottingham -	1624
Trewen - -	Cornwall -	1616	Tweedmouth - -	Northumberland -	1711
Treyford - -	Sussex - -	1728	Twerton-on-Avon -	Somerset -	1538
Trimdon - -	Durham - -	1720	Twickenham - -	Middlesex -	⁹ 1538
Trimingham - -	Norfolk - -	1748	Twineham - -	Sussex - -	1716
Trimley, St. Martin -	Suffolk - -	1538	Twining - -	Gloucester -	¹⁰ 1648
Trimley, St. Mary -	Suffolk - -	1654	Twinnel, St. - -	Pembroke -	1729
Tring - -	Hertford - -	1566	Twinstead - -	Essex - -	1567
Troedyraur - -	Cardigan -	1656	Twitchen - -	Devon - -	1715
Troston - -	Suffolk - -	1558	Twycross - -	Leicester -	1585
Trostrey - -	Monmouth -	1723	Twyford - -	Buckingham -	1558
Trottiscliffe - -	Kent - -	1540	Twyford - -	Derby - -	1736
Trotton - -	Sussex - -	1581	Twyford - -	Leicester -	1558
Troutbeck - -	Westmorland -	1572	Twyford - -	Norfolk - -	1558
Trowbridge - -	Wilts - -	1538	Twyford - -	Hants - -	1626
Trowell - -	Nottingham -	⁵ 1568	Twyford Abbey -	Middlesex -	1722
Trowse - - -	Norfolk - -	1695	Twywell - -	Northampton -	1586

¹ **P** 1695–1696. Edited by Sir Thomas Phillipps.
² **P** (Marriages only) 1674–1812. Cornwall Parish Registers, vol. 2, 1902.
³ **P** 1558–1812. Staffordshire Parish Register Society, 1906.
⁴ **P** (Marriages only) 1529–1812. Cornwall Parish Registers, vol. 1, 1900.
⁵ **P** (Marriages only) 1570–1812. Nottinghamshire Parish Registers, vol. 8, 1905.
⁶ **P** (Marriages only) 1671–1812. Somerset Parish Registers, vol. 7, 1906.
⁷ **P** (Marriages only) 1560–1812. Cornwall Parish Registers, vol. 2, 1902.
⁸ **P** (Marriages only) 1754–1812. Hampshire Parish Registers, vol. 1, 1899, and vol. 8, 1906.
⁹ *See* Memorials of Twickenham, by R. S. Cobbett.
¹⁰ **P** (Marriages only) 1674–1812. Gloucestershire Parish Registers, vol. 13, 1908.

Parish.	County.	Date of Earliest Entry.	Parish.	County.	Date of Earliest Entry.
Tydd, St. Giles - -	Cambridge -	1559	Ulpha - - -	Cumberland -	1703
Tydd, St. Mary	Lincoln - -	1541	Ulrome - - -	York - -	1767
Tydweiliog - -	Carnarvon -	1781	Ulting - - -	Essex - -	1723
Tyneham - -	Dorset - -	1581	Ulverstone - -	Lancaster -	[8] 1545
Tynemouth - -	Northumberland	[1] 1607	Underbarrow - -	Westmorland -	1735
Tyr-Abbot. See Llan-			Undy - - -	Monmouth -	1760
dulas-in-Tyr-Abbot.			Unsworth - -	Lancaster -	1730
Tyringham - -	Buckingham -	1629	Upavon - -	Wilts - -	1687
Tysoe - - -	Warwick -	1575	Upchurch - -	Kent - -	1633
Tythby - -	Nottingham -	[2] 1550	Upham - -	Hants - -	1598
Tythegston - -	Glamorgan -	1757	Uphill - - -	Somerset - -	1704
Tytherington -	Gloucester -	1662	Upholland - -	Lancaster -	[9] 1600
Tytherley, East -	Hants - -	1562	Upleadon - -	Gloucester -	1538
Tytherley, West -	Hants - -	1654	Upleatham - -	York - -	1654
Tytherton - -	Wilts - -	[3] —	Uplowman - -	Devon - -	1662
Tywardreath - -	Cornwall -	[4] 1642	Uplyme - - -	Devon - -	1691
			Upminster - -	Essex - -	1543
			Uppingham - -	Rutland -	1571
			Uppington - -	Salop - -	[10] 1650
			Upton - - -	Berks - -	[11] 1588
			Upton - - -	Buckingham -	1538
U.			Upton (or Overchurch)	Chester -	[12] 1600
			Upton - - -	Huntingdon -	1755
			Upton - - -	Lincoln - -	1563
Ubbeston - - -	Suffolk - -	1558	Upton - - -	Norfolk - -	[13] 1558
Ubley - - -	Somerset -	1671	Upton - - -	Northampton -	1594
Uckfield - - -	Sussex - -	1538	Upton - - -	Nottingham -	1660
Udimore - - -	Sussex - -	1558	Upton - - -	Somerset - -	1708
Uffculme - - -	Devon - -	1538	Upton - - -	Pembroke -	[14] —
Uffington - - -	Berks - -	1654	Upton-Bishop -	Hereford - -	[15] 1571
Uffington - - -	Lincoln -	1675	Upton-Cressett -	Salop - -	1755
Uffington - - -	Salop - -	[5] 1578	Upton-Grey - -	Hants - -	1561
Ufford - - -	Northampton -	1570	Upton-Helions -	Devon - -	1678
Ufford - - -	Suffolk - -	1558	Upton-Lovel - -	Wilts - -	1653
Ufton - - -	Warwick -	1709	Upton-Magna -	Salop - -	1563
Ufton-Nervett -	Berks - -	1636	Upton-Noble - -	Somerset - -	1677
Ugborough - -	Devon - -	1538	Upton-Pyne - -	Devon - -	1673
Uggeshall - - -	Suffolk - -	1558	Upton, St. Leonard -	Gloucester -	1646
Ugglebarnby - -	York - -	1732	Upton-Scudamore -	Wilts - -	1654
Ugley (or Oakley) -	Essex - -	1560	Upton-Snodsbury -	Worcester -	1577
Ulceby (Alford) -	Lincoln -	1749	Upton-upon-Severn -	Worcester -	1546
Ulceby - - -	Lincoln - -	1567	Upton-Warren -	Worcester -	1604
Ulcombe - - -	Kent - -	1560	Upton-Waters - -	Salop - -	1563
Uldale - - -	Cumberland -	1642	Upwell - - -	Cambridge and	1650
Uley - - -	Gloucester -	[6] 1668		Norfolk.	
Ulgham - - -	Northumberland	[7] 1602	Upwey - - -	Dorset - -	1654
Ullingswick - -	Hereford -	1561	Upwood - - -	Huntingdon -	1558

[1] **P** 1607–1703. Edited by R. H. Couchman, 1902. **P** (Baptisms only) 1662–1682.
[2] **P** (Marriages only) 1583–1685. Nottinghamshire Parish Registers, vol. 2, 1899.
[3] Included in the Registers of Chippenham (q.v.).
[4] **P** (Marriages only) 1642–1812. Cornwall Parish Registers, vol. 8, 1905.
[5] **P** 1578–1812. Shropshire Parish Register Society, vol. 5, 1904 (Lichfield Diocese).
[6] **P** (Marriages only) 1668–1812. Gloucestershire Parish Registers, vol. 2, 1897.
[7] **P** "North Country Parish Registers," by Robert Blair.
[8] **P** 1545–1812. Edited by Rev. C. W. Bardsley, 1886.
[9] **P** 1600–1735. Lancashire Parish Register Society, vol. 19, 1905.
[10] **P** 1650–1812. Shropshire Parish Register Society, vol. 4, 1903 (Lichfield Diocese).
[11] **P** 1588–1741. Parish Register Society, vol. 8, 1897.
[12] **P** 1600–1812. Parish Register Society, vol. 33, 1900.
[13] **P** (Marriages only) 1558–1812. Norfolk Parish Registers, vol. 1, 1899.
[14] Included in the Registers of Nash (q.v.).
[15] An alphabetical list of all marriages, 1571–1883, in "Records of Upton-Bishop" by Rev. F. T. Havergal.

Parish.	County.	Date of Earliest Entry.	Parish.	County.	Date of Earliest Entry.
Urchfont - -	Wilts - -	[1] 1538	Walcot - -	Lincoln -	1546
Urswick - -	Lancaster -	1608	Walcot - -	Somerset -	1691
Usk - - -	Monmouth -	1742	Walcott - -	Norfolk - -	1558
Usselby - -	Lincoln -	1564	Walden, King's- -	Hertford -	1558
Utterby - -	Lincoln - -	1695	Walden - -	Hertford -	1653
Uttoxeter - -	Stafford -	1596	Waldershare - -	Kent - -	1561
Uxbridge - -	Middlesex -	1538	Waldingfield, Great -	Suffolk -	1539
Uzmaston - -	Pembroke -	1720	Waldingfield, Little -	Suffolk -	1568
			Walditch - -	Dorset -	[4] 1738
			Waldringfield -	Suffolk -	1695
			Waldron - -	Sussex - -	1564
			Wales - -	York - -	1580
			Walesby - -	Lincoln -	1562
V.			Walesby - -	Nottingham -	[5] 1579
			Walford - -	Hereford -	1663
			Walgrave - -	Northampton -	1571
Vange - - -	Essex -	1558	Walkeringham -	Nottingham -	1605
Vaynor - -	Brecon -	1755	Walkern - -	Hertford -	1680
Veep, St. - -	Cornwall -	1538	Walkhampton -	Devon -	1675
Vernham - -	Hants - -	[2] 1598	Walkington -	York - -	1754
Veryan - -	Cornwall -	1683	Wallasey - -	Chester -	[6] 1574
Virginstow - -	Devon -	1730	Wallingford, St. Mary	Berks - -	1638
Vowchurch - -	Hereford -	1642	St. Leonard -	- -	[7] 1711
			Wallington -	Hertford -	1661
			Wallington -	Norfolk -	1570
			Wallop-Nether -	Hants -	1631
			Wallop-Over - -	Hants -	1538
			Wallsend - -	Northumberland	1669
W.			Walmer - -	Kent -	1560
			Walmsgate -	Lincoln -	[8] —
Waberthwaite -	Cumberland -	1695	Walpole, St. Andrew -	Norfolk -	1654
Wacton - -	Hereford -	1663	Walpole, St. Peter -	Norfolk -	1559
Wacton-Magna -	Norfolk -	1560	Walpole - -	Suffolk -	1753
Waddesdon - -	Buckingham -	1538	Walsall - -	Stafford -	[9] 1570
Waddington -	Lincoln -	1675	Walsgrave-on-Sowe -	Warwick -	1538
Waddington -	York - -	1616	Walsham-le-Willows -	Suffolk -	1539
Waddingworth -	Lincoln -	1640	Walsham, North -	Norfolk -	1557
Wadenhoe -	Northampton -	1559	Walsham, South -	Norfolk -	1551
Wadhurst - -	Sussex -	1604	Wylsingham, Great -	Norfolk -	1564
Wadingham -	Lincoln -	1652	Walsingham, Little -	Norfolk -	1558
Wadworth -	York - -	1575	Walsoken - -	Norfolk -	1558
Waghen - -	York - -	1653	Walterstone -	Hereford -	1761
Wainfleet, All Saints -	Lincoln -	[3] 1677	Waltham - -	Kent -	1538
St. Mary -	- -	1611	Waltham - -	Lincoln -	1561
Waithe - -	Lincoln -	1698	Waltham Abbey -	Essex -	1563
Wakefield -	York - -	1613	Waltham, Bishops- -	Hants -	1612
St. John -	York - -	1795	Waltham, Bright- -	Berks -	1558
Wakering, Great	Essex -	1685	Waltham, Cold -	Sussex -	1594
Wakering, Little -	Essex -	1715	Waltham, Great -	Essex -	1703
Wakerley - -	Northampton -	1540	Waltham - -	Berks -	1559
Walberswick -	Suffolk -	1656	Waltham, Little -	Essex -	1540
Walberton - -	Sussex -	1556	Waltham, North -	Hants -	[10] 1654

[1] **P** (Marriages only) 1538–1812. Wiltshire Parish Registers, vol. 4, 1907.

[2] **P** (Marriages only) 1607–1812. Hampshire Parish Registers, vol. 2, 1900.

[3] This Register has been mutilated, apparently to write bills on, as a butcher's bill remains on part of the last leaf.

[4] **P** (Marriages only) 1738–1812. Dorsetshire Parish Registers, vol. 1, 1906.

[5] **P** 1580–1792. Parish Register Society, vol. 12, 1898.

[6] **P** 1574–1600. By Historical Society of Lancashire and Cheshire, vol. 35. *See also* "Historical Gleanings," by E. M. Haver.

[7] Previous to 1711 entered in Registers of St. Mary. [8] Included in the Registers of Burwell (q.v.).

[9] **P** 1570–1649. Edited by F. W. Willmore, Walsall, 1890.

[10] **P** (Marriages only) 1654–1812. Hampshire Parish Registers, vol. 3, 1892.

Parish.	County.	Date of Earliest Entry.	Parish.	County.	Date of Earliest Entry.
Waltham - on - the - Wolds.	Leicester	1565	Warcop	Westmorland	1597
			Warden	Kent	1688
Waltham-Up	Sussex	1790	Warden	Northumberland	1695
Waltham, White	Berks	1563	Warden, Chipping	Northampton	1579
Walthamstow	Essex	1645	Warden, Old	Bedford	1576
Walton	Buckingham	¹1598	Wardington	Oxford	1603
Walton	Cumberland	1684	Wardley	Rutland	1574
Walton	Somerset	1682	Ware	Hertford	1577
Walton	Suffolk	1554	Wareham	Dorset	1762
Walton	York	1619	Warehorne	Kent	1727
Walton-Cardiff	Gloucester	1677	Waresley	Huntingdon	1647
Walton, East	Norfolk	1560	Warfield	Berks	1666
Walton, East	Pembroke	1721	Wargrave	Berks	1538
Walton-in-Gordano	Somerset	1667	Warham, All Saints	Norfolk	1558
Walton-le-Dale	Lancaster	1653	Warham	Norfolk	1565
Walton-le-Soken	Essex	1688	Warkleigh	Devon	1550
Walton-on-the-Hill	Lancaster	²1586	Warkton	Northampton	1558
Walton-on-the-Hill	Surrey	1581	Warkworth	Northampton	⁷—
Walton - on - the - Wolds	Leicester	1566	Warkworth	Northumberland	⁸1677
			Warleggan	Cornwall	⁹1540
Walton-on-Thames	Surrey	³1592	Warley, Great	Essex	1539
Walton-on-Trent	Derby	1639	Warley, Little	Essex	1539
Walton, West	Norfolk	1662	Warlingham	Surrey	1653
Walton, West	Pembroke	1755	Warmfield	York	1652
Walton Wood	Huntingdon	1754	Warmingham	Chester	1538
Walwyn's Castle	Pembroke	1755	Warminghurst	Sussex	1714
Wambrook	Dorset	1653	Warmington	Northampton	1558
Wanborough	Wilts	⁴1582	Warmington	Warwick	1636
Wanborough	Surrey	⁵1561	Warminster	Wilts	1556
Wandsworth	Surrey	⁶1603	Warmsworth	York	1594
Wangford (near Brandon.)	Suffolk	1660	Warmwell	Dorset	1641
			Warmborough, South	Hants	¹⁰1538
Wangford	Suffolk	1678	Warndon	Worcester	1561
Wanlip	Leicester	1561	Warnford	Hants	1541
Wansford	Northampton	1808	Warnham	Sussex	1558
Wanstead	Essex	1640	Warpsgrove	Oxford	¹¹—
Wanstrow	Somerset	1653	Warren	Pembroke	1755
Wantage	Berks	1538	Warrington	Lancaster	1591
Wantisden	Suffolk	1708	Warslow	Stafford	1785
Wapley	Gloucester	1662	Warsop	Nottingham	¹²1539
Wappenbury	Warwick	1753	Warter	York	1669
Wappenham	Northampton	1675	Warthill	York	1689
Wapping	Middlesex	1617	Wartling	Sussex	1538
Warbleton	Sussex	1559	Wartnaby	Leicester	¹³1633
Warblington	Hants	1631	Warton (near Lytham).	Lancaster	¹³
Warborough	Oxford	1538			
Warboys	Huntingdon	1551	Warton	Lancaster	¹⁴1568
Warbstow	Cornwall	1695	Warwick	Cumberland	1681
Warburton	Chester	1611	Warwick, St. Mary	Warwick	¹⁵1651

¹ P 1598–1812. Buckinghamshire Parish Register Society, vol. 1. 1902.
² P 1586–1663. Lancashire Parish Register Society, vol. 5, 1900.
³ Earlier entries but date illegible. ⁴ P 1582–1653. By Sir Thomas Phillipps in " Collections."
⁵ P 1561–1786. Surrey Parish Register Society, vol. 4, 1906.
⁶ P 1603–1787. Edited by J. T. Squire, London, 1889.
⁷ Included in the Registers of Marston St. Lawrence (q.v.).
⁸ P 1677–1812. Newcastle-on-Tyne Society of Antiquaries, 1897.
⁹ P (Marriages only) 1547–1718, and 1682–1812. Cornwall Parish Registers, vols. 4 and 6, 1903–4.
¹⁰ P (Marriages only) 1539–1812. Hampshire Parish Registers, vol. 6, 1904.
¹¹ Included in the Registers of Chalgrave (q.v.). ¹² P Edited by R. J. King, Mansfield, 1884.
¹³ Included in the Registers of Kirkham (q.v.).
¹⁴ P 1568–1669. See Warton Parochial Magazine, October 1883 et seq.
¹⁵ Bishop's Transcripts commence 1611.

Parish.	County.	Date of Earliest Entry.	Parish.	County.	Date of Earliest Entry.
Warwick St. Nicholas	Warwick -	1538	Wednesbury - -	Stafford -	1562
Wasdale, Nether- -	Cumberland -	1711	Wednesfield - -	Stafford - -	1751
Wasdale-Head - . -	Cumberland -	1721	Weedon-Bec - -	Northampton -	1587
Washbourn, Great -	Gloucester -	1567	Weedon Lois - -	Northampton -	1559
Washbourn, Little.			Weeford - - -	Stafford - -	1563
See Alston.			Week - - -	Devon - -	1652
Washbrook - -	Suffolk - -	1559	Week St. Mary -	Cornwall -	1602
Washfield - -	Devon - -	1556	Weeke - - -	Hants - -	1573
Washford-Pyne -	Devon - -	1587	Weekley - - -	Northampton -	1550
Washingborough -	Lincoln -	1564	Weeley - - -	Essex - -	1562
Washington - -	Durham - -	1603	Weethley - -	Warwick -	¹1572
Washington - -	Sussex - -	1558	Weeting - -	Norfolk - -	1558
Wasing - - -	Berks - -	1730	Weighton, Market -	York - -	1653
Wasperton - -	Warwick -	1538	Welborne - -	Norfolk - -	1695
Waterbeach - -	Cambridge -	1653	Welbourn - -	Lincoln -	1561
Waterden - -	Norfolk - -	1730	Welbury - -	York - -	1682
Waterfall - - -	Stafford -	1612	Welby - - -	Lincoln -	1569
Wateringbury -	Kent - -	1705	Welcombe - -	Devon - -	1653
Watermillock - -	Cumberland -	1579	Weldon, Great -	Northampton -	1594
Waterperry - -	Oxford -	1678	Welford - -	Berks - -	⁶1559
Waterstock - -	Oxford -	1580	Welford - - -	Northampton -	1562
Watford - -	Hertford -	1539	Welford - -	Gloucester -	1561
Watford - - -	Northampton -	1565	Welham - - -	Leicester -	1695
Wath - - -	York - -	1565	Well - - -	Lincoln -	1649
Wath-on-Dearne -	York - -	¹1598	Well - - -	York - -	1558
Watlington - -	Norfolk - -	1570	Welland - -	Worcester -	⁷1670
Watlington - -	Oxford - -	1635	Wellesbourne -	Warwick -	1560
Wattisfield - -	Suffolk - -	1540	Wellingborough -	Northampton -	1586
Wattisham - -	Suffolk - -	1538	Wellingham - -	Norfolk -	1765
Watton - - -	Hertford -	1560	Wellingore - -	Lincoln -	1653
Watton - - -	Norfolk - -	1539	Wellington - -	Hereford -	1559
Watton - - -	York - -	1558	Wellington - -	Salop - -	1626
Wavendon - -	Buckingham -	1567	Wellington - -	Somerset -	1683
Waverton - -	Chester - -	1582	Wellow - - -	Hants - -	⁸1570
Wavertree - -	Lancaster -	1794	Wellow - - -	Nottingham -	⁹1703
Waxham - -	Norfolk - -	1763	Wellow - - -	Somerset -	1561
Wayford - -	Somerset -	1704	Wells - - -	Norfolk -	1549
Weald, North -	Essex - -	1557	Wells - -	Somerset -	1608
Weald, South -	Essex - -	²1539	Wells Cathedral -	- -	1664
Weardale, St. John	Durham - -	1788	Welney - -	Norfolk -	1642
Weare - -	Somerset -	1631	Welshampton -	Salop - -	1725
Wear-Gifford - -	Devon - -	1583	Welshpool - -	Montgomery -	1634
Wearmouth, Bishop- -	Durham - -	1567	Welton - - -	Lincoln -	1568
Wearmouth, Monk- -	Durham - -	1768	Welton - -	Northampton -	1578
Weasenham, All Saints	Norfolk -	1568	Welton - - -	York - -	1713
Weasenham, St. Peter	Norfolk -	1581	Welton-in-the-Marsh -	Lincoln -	1558
Weaverham - -	Chester - -	1576	Welton-le-Wold -	Lincoln -	1558
Weaverthorpe -	York - -	1702	Welwick - -	York - -	1650
Weddington - -	Warwick -	³1663	Welwyn - - -	Hertford -	1558
Wedmore - -	Somerset -	⁴1561	Wem - - -	Salop - -	¹⁰1582

¹ P 1598-1779. Yorkshire Parish Register Society, vol. 14, 1902.
² P 1539-1573. Edited by R. Hovenden, London, 1889.
³ P 1663-1812. Parish Register Society, vol. 49, 1904.
⁴ P 1561-1860. Edited by Rev. S. H. A. Hervey, Wells. 3 vols., 1888-90.
⁵ The first Register book is most dilapidated, many of the pages, according to tradition, having been used for covering jam pots, &c. There is also a loose sheet containing some entries belonging to Kinwarton, Great Alne.
⁶ P 1559-1812. Edited by Mrs. H. M. Batson, 1892.
⁷ Bishop's Transcripts commence 1608.
⁸ P Index to Registers, 1570-1887. Edited by C. W. Empson, London, 1889.
⁹ P 1703-1812. Edited by G. W. Marshall, Exeter, 1896. Bishop's Transcripts commence 1626.
¹⁰ P 1583-1675. Shropshire Parish Register Society, vol. 9 (Lichfield Diocese).

Parish.	County.	Date of Earliest Entry.	Parish.	County.	Date of Earliest Entry.
Wembdon - - -	Somerset - -	1672	Westmeston - -	Sussex - -	1587
Wembury - -	Devon - -	1611	Westmill - -	Hertford -	1565
Wembworthy - -	Devon -	1674	Weston - -	Hertford -	1539
Wendlebury - -	Oxford -	1589	Weston - - -	Lincoln -	1678
Wendling - - -	Norfolk -	1539	Weston - -	Norfolk -	1660
Wendens-Ambo -	Essex - -	1540	Weston - - -	Nottingham -	1559
Wenden-Lofts -	Essex -	1674	Weston - -	Somerset -	1538
Wendover - - -	Buckingham -	¹ 1626	Weston - -	Suffolk - -	1538
Wendron - -	Cornwall -	1560	Weston - -	York -	1673
Wendy - - -	Cambridge -	1550	Weston-Bampfylde -	Somerset -	1632
Wenham, Great -	Suffolk -	1648	Weston-Beggard -	Hereford -	1587
Wenham, Little -	Suffolk - -	1558	Weston-Birt - -	Gloucester -	⁶ 1611
Wenhaston - -	Suffolk -	1687	Weston-by-Welland -	Northampton -	⁷ —
Wenlock, Little -	Salop -	1690	Weston, Cold - -	Salop - -	1690
Wenlock, Much -	Salop -	² 1558	Weston-Colville -	Cambridge -	1712
Wenn, St. -	Cornwall -	³ 1678	Weston-Coney -	Suffolk - -	1562
Wennington - -	Essex - -	1654	Weston-Favell -	Northampton -	1540
Wensley - -	York -	1538	Weston-in-Gordano -	Somerset -	1684
Wentloog - - -	Monmouth -	1733	Weston-Market - -	Suffolk - -	1563
Wentnor - -	Salop -	1662	Weston, Old - -	Huntingdon -	1784
Wentworth - -	Cambridge -	1754	Weston-on-Avon -	Gloucester and Warwick.	⁸ 1685
Wentworth - -	York -	1654			
Wenvoe - - -	Glamorgan -	1585	Weston-on-the-Green -	Oxford -	1591
Weobley - - -	Hereford -	1635	Weston-on-Trent -	Derby -	1565
Weonard's, St. -	Hereford -	1624	Weston-on-Trent -	Stafford -	1585
Wereham - -	Norfolk -	1558	Weston-Patrick -	Hants -	1574
Werrington - -	Devon -	1653	Weston, South - -	Oxford -	1558
Westacre - -	Norfolk -	1668	Weston-sub-Edge -	Gloucester -	⁸ 1612
Westbere - -	Kent -	1577	Weston-super-Mare -	Somerset -	1668
Westborough - -	Lincoln -	1567	Weston-Turville -	Buckingham -	1538
Westbourne - -	Sussex -	1550	Weston - under - Ly- ziard.	Stafford -	1701
Westbury - -	Buckingham -	⁴ 1558			
Westbury - - -	Salop -	1637	Weston - under - Pen- yard.	Hereford -	1568
Westbury - -	Somerset -	1713			
Westbury - - -	Wilts -	1556	Weston - under - Wea- therley.	Warwick -	1661
Wesbury-on-Severn -	Gloucester -	1538			
Westbury-on-Trym -	Gloucester -	1559	Weston-Underwood -	Buckingham -	1681
Westcote - -	Gloucester -	1630	Weston-Zoyland -	Somerset -	1558
Westerdale - -	York -	1562	Westoning - -	Bedford -	1560
Westerfield - -	Suffolk -	1538	Westow - -	York -	1560
Westerham - -	Kent - -	⁵ 1559	Westport - -	Wilts -	1661
Westerleigh - -	Gloucester -	1693	Westward - -	Cumberland -	1605
Westfield - -	Norfolk -	1706	Westwell - -	Kent -	1558
Westfield - -	Sussex -	1552	Westwell - -	Oxford -	1602
Westhall - -	Suffolk -	1559	Westwick - -	Norfolk -	1642
Westham - -	Sussex -	1571	Westwood - -	Wilts -	1666
Westhampnet - -	Sussex-	1734	Wetherall - -	Cumberland -	1674
Westhide - -	Hereford -	1660	Wetherby - -	York -	1783
Westhorpe - -	Suffolk -	1538	Wetherden - -	Suffolk -	1538
Westhoughton - -	Lancaster -	1732	Wetheringsett - -	Suffolk -	1556
Westleton - -	Suffolk -	1545	Wethersfield - -	Essex -	1647
Westley - - -	Suffolk -	1565	Wetton - -	Stafford -	1657
Westley-Waterless -	Cambridge -	1557	Wetwang - -	York -	1653

¹ **P** (Marriages only) 1576-1812. Buckinghamshire Parish Registers, vol. 2, 1904.
² **P** 1539-1560. Edited by Rev. C. Hartshorne, Tenby, 1861.
³ **P** (Marriages only) 1678-1812. Cornwall Parish Registers, vol. 11, 1907.
⁴ **P** (Marriages only) 1558-1837. Buckinghamshire Parish Registers, vol. 3, 1907.
⁵ *See* " Parochial History of Westerham," by G. L. Gower.
⁶ **P** (Marriages only) 1596-1812. Gloucestershire Parish Registers, vol. 6, 1900.
⁷ Included in the Registers of Sutton-Bassett (*q.v.*).
⁸ **P** (Marriages only) 1690-1810. Gloucestershire Parish Registers, vol. 4, 1898.
⁹ **P** (Marriages only) 1612-1812. Gloucestershire Parish Registers, vol. 4, 1898.

Parish.	County.	Date of Earliest Entry.	Parish.	County.	Date of Earliest Entry.
Wexham - -	Buckingham -	1606	Whissonsett - -	Norfolk - -	1700
Weybourne - -	Norfolk - -	1727	Whiston - -	Northampton -	1700
Weybread - -	Suffolk -	1687	Whiston - -	York - -	1592
Weybridge - -	Surrey - -	1625	Whitacre-Nether -	Warwick -	1539
Weyhill - -	Hants - -	1564	Whitacre-Over - -	Warwick - -	1653
Weymouth. See Wyke-			Whitbeck - -	Cumberland -	1597
Regis.			Whitbourne - -	Hereford - -	1588
Whaddon - -	Buckingham -	1580	Whitburn - -	Durham - -	⁴1579
Whaddon - -	Cambridge -	1692	Whitby - - -	York - -	1608
Whaddon - -	Gloucester -	¹1674	Whitchurch - -	Buckingham -	1653
Whaddon - -	Wilts - -	1653	Whitchurch - -	Devon - -	1559
Whalley - -	Lancaster -	²1538	Whitchurch - -	Hants - -	⁶1605
Whalton - -	Northumberland	1661	Whitchurch - -	Hereford - -	1675
Whaplode - -	Lincoln - -	1559	Whitchurch - -	Oxford - -	1597
Whaplode-Drove -	Lincoln - -	1713	Whitchurch - -	Salop - -	1633
Wharram-le-Street -	York - -	1538	Whitchurch - -	Somerset - -	1565
Wharram-Percy -	York - -	1554	Whitchurch - -	Warwick -	⁷1561
Whatcote - -	Warwick -	1572	Whitchurch - -	Pembroke -	1752
Whatfield - -	Suffolk -	1558	Whitcombe - -	Dorset - -	1696
Whatley - -	Somerset -	1672	Whitechurch - Canoni-	Dorset - -	1558
Whatlington - -	Sussex - -	1558	corum.		
Whatton - in - the -	Nottingham -	³1538	Whitechapel - -	Lancaster -	⁸ —
Vale.			Whitechurch - -	Pembroke -	1704
Whatton, Long - -	Leicester -	1549	Whitegate - -	Chester - -	1565
Wheatacre - -	Norfolk - -	1558	Whitehaven, St. James	Cumberland -	1753
Wheatacre-Burgh -	Norfolk - -	1538	St. Nicholas - -		1694
Wheatenhurst or Whit-	Gloucester -	1538	Holy Trinity - -	- - -	1715
minster.			Whiteparish - -	Wilts - -	1559
Wheatfield - -	Oxford - -	1721	White-Staunton. See		
Wheathampstead -	Hertford -	1690	Staunton, White.		
Wheathill - -	Salop - -	1573	Whitfield - - -	Kent - -	1585
Wheatley, North -	Nottingham -	1649	Whitfield - - -	Northampton -	1678
Wheatley, South -	Nottingham -	1546	Whitfield - - -	Northumberland	1612
Wheldrake - -	York - -	1603	Whitford - - -	Flint - -	1657
Whelnetham, Great -	Suffolk -	1561	Whitgift - - -	York - -	1562
Whelnetham, Little -	Suffolk -	1557	Whitkirk - - -	York - -	⁹1603
Whelpington, Kirk -	Northumberland	1679	Whitley - - -	Northumberland	1764
Whenby - - -	York - -	1556	Whitley, Lower -	Chester -	1777
Whepstead - -	Suffolk - -	1540	Whitlingham - -	Norfolk - -	¹⁰ —
Wherstead - -	Suffolk - -	1590	Whitmore - -	Stafford -	1558
Wherwell - -	Hants - -	1634	Whitnash - -	Warwick -	1679
Whetstone - -	Leicester - -	1560	Whitney - -	Hereford -	1616
Whicham - -	Cumberland -	1569	Whitsbury - -	Hants and Wilts	1714
Whichford - -	Warwick -	1540	Whitstable - -	Kent - -	1556
Whickham - -	Durham -	⁴1576	Whitstone - -	Cornwall -	1663
Whilton - - -	Northampton -	1570	Whitstone - -	Devon - -	1594
Whimple - -	Devon - -	1653	Whittering - -	Northampton -	1648
Whinbergh - -	Norfolk - -	1703	Whittingham - -	Northumberland	1658
Whippingham - -	Hants - -	1727	Whittington - -	Worcester -	1653
Whipsnade - -	Bedford - -	1682	Whittington - -	Derby - -	1644
Whissendine - -	Rutland - -	1637	Whittington - -	Gloucester -	1539

¹ **P** 1674–1711. Gloucestershire Notes and Queries, vol. 4. **P** (Marriages only) 1620–1812. Gloucestershire Parish Registers, vol. 13, 1908.
² **P** 1538–1601. Lancashire Parish Register Society, vol. 7, 1900.
³ **P** (Marriages only) 1538–1812. Nottinghamshire Parish Registers, vol. 1, 1898.
⁴ **P** (Marriages only) 1579–1812. Durham and Northumberland Parish Register Society, vol. 1, 1898.
⁵ **P** 1579–1812. Durham and Northumberland Parish Register Society, vol. 10, 1904.
⁶ **P** (Marriages only) 1605–1812. Hampshire Parish Registers, vol. 8, 1906.
⁷ **P** (Marriages only) 1562–1812. Warwickshire Parish Registers, vol. 1, 1904.
⁸ Included in the Registers of Kirkham (q.v.).
⁹ **P** 1603–1700. See " Records of the Parish of Whitkirk," by G. M. Platt.
¹⁰ Included in the Registers of Trowse-Newton (q.v.).

Parish.	County.	Date of Earliest Entry.	Parish.	County.	Date of Earliest Entry.
Whittington - -	Lancaster -	[1] 1538	Wickham, West -	Kent - -	1558
Whittington - -	Salop - -	1591	Wickhambreaux -	Kent - -	1623
Whittington - -	Stafford -	1538	Wickhambrook -	Suffolk -	1559
Whittlebury - -	Northampton -	1653	Wickhamford - -	Worcester -	1538
Whittlesey, St. Andrew	Cambridge -	1653	Wickhampton -	Norfolk - -	1561
St. Mary -	- - -	[2] 1559	Wicklewood - -	Norfolk -	1561
Whittlesford - -	Cambridge -	1559	Wickmere - -	Norfolk -	1559
Whitton - - -	Lincoln - -	1546	Wickwar - -	Gloucester -	[7] 1689
Whitton - - -	Suffolk -	1599	Widcombe - -	Somerset -	[8] —
Whitton - - -	Radnor - -	1600	Widdecombe - in - the-	Devon - -	1560
Whittonstall - -	Northumberland	1754	Moor.		
Whitwell - - -	Derby - -	1672	Widdington - -	Essex - -	1666
Whitwell - -	Norfolk -	1559	Widdrington - -	Northumberland	1698
Whitwell - -	Rutland - -	1716	Widford - -	Essex - -	1601
Whitwell (Isle of Wight)	Hants - -	1559	Widford - -	Gloucester -	1751
Whitwick - -	Leicester -	1601	Widford - -	Hertford -	1558
Whitworth - -	Durham - -	1569	Widley - - -	Hants - -	1611
Whitworth - -	Lancaster -	1763	Widmerpool - -	Nottingham -	[9] 1539
Whixall - -	Salop - -	1758	Widworthy - -	Devon - -	1540
Whixley - -	York - -	1568	Wield - - -	Hants - -	1538
Whixoe (or Wixoe) -	Suffolk -	1674	Wigan - - -	Lancaster -	[10] 1580
Whorlton - -	Durham - -	[3] 1626	Wigborough, Great -	Essex - -	[11] 1560
Whorlton-in-Cleveland	York - -	1689	Wigborough, Little -	Essex - -	[12] 1586
Wibsey - - -	York - -	1640	Wiggenhall, St. Ger-	Norfolk - -	1653
Wichenford - -	Worcester -	[4] 1690	mans.		
Wichnor - -	Stafford -	1735	St. Mary Magda-	- - -	1562
Wick - - -	Somerset -	1615	lene.		
Wick - - -	Glamorgan -	1754	St. Mary - the -	- - -	1558
Wick - - -	Gloucester -	1687	Virgin.		
Wick-near-Pershore -	Worcester -	[5] 1695	St. Peter - -	- - -	1695
Wicken - -	Cambridge -	1565	Wigginton - -	Oxford - -	1558
Wicken - - -	Northampton -	1559	Wigginton - -	York - -	1691
Wicken-Bonhunt -	Essex - -	1588	Wiggonholt - -	Sussex - -	1597
Wickenby - -	Lincoln -	1558	Wighill - -	York - -	[13] 1717
Wickersley - -	York - -	1567	Wighton - -	Norfolk -	1660
Wickford - -	Essex - -	1538	Wigmore - -	Hereford -	1572
Wickham. See Welford.			Wigston-Magna -	Leicester -	1572
Wickham - - -	Essex - -	1609	Wigtoft - -	Lincoln -	1638
Wickham - -	Hants - -	1556	Wigton - -	Cumberland -	1613
Wickham, Bishops'.			Wilbarston -	Northampton -	[14] 1746
See Bishops' Wick-			Wilberfoss -	York - -	1618
ham.			Wilbraham, Great -	Cambridge -	1561
Wickham, Child's -	Gloucester -	[6] 1560	Wilbraham, Little -	Cambridge -	1538
Wickham, East - -	Kent - -	1715	Wilburton -	Cambridge -	1739
Wickham, Market -	Suffolk -	1557	Wilby - -	Norfolk -	1541
Wickham-Skeith -	Suffolk -	1557	Wilby - -	Northampton -	1562
Wickham, West -	Cambridge -	1682	Wilby - - -	Suffolk -	1538

[1] **P** 1538–1764. Lancashire Parish Register Society, vol. 3, 1899.
[2] **P** (Marriages only) 1662–1672. Edited by James Coleman, 1883.
[3] **P** "North Country Parish Registers," by Robert Blair.
[4] Bishop's Transcripts commence 1599.
[5] Bishop's Transcripts commence 1608.
[6] **P** (Marriages only) 1560–1812. Gloucestershire Parish Registers, vol. 4, 1898.
[7] **P** (Marriages only) 1689–1812. Gloucestershire Parish Registers, vol. 11, 1905.
[8] Included in the registers of Lynecombe (q.v.).
[9] **P** (Marriages only) 1540–1812. Nottinghamshire Parish Registers, vol. 5, 1903.
[10] **P** 1580–1625. Lancashire Parish Register Society, vol. 4, 1899.
[11] **P** 1560–1812. Edited by Mrs. P. A. F. Stephenson, 1905.
[12] **P** 1586–1812. Edited by Mrs. P. A. F. Stephenson, 1905.
[13] The earlier Registers are said to have been sent to London about 1830 as evidence in a law-suit and are lost.
[14] There are a few tattered paper pages dated 1591.

Parish.	County.	Date of Earliest Entry.	Parish.	County.	Date of Earliest Entry.
Wilcot	Wilts	1564	Wilshampstead	Bedford	1594
Wilcote	Oxford	1755	Wilsthorpe	Lincoln	1754
Wilcrick	Monmouth	1755	Wilton	Norfolk	1634
Wilden	Bedford	1545	Wilton	Somerset	[6] 1558
Wilford	Nottingham	[1] 1621	Wilton	Wilts	1615
Wilksby	Lincoln	1562	Wilton	York	1719
Willand	Devon	1717	Wimbish	Essex	1583
Willen	Buckingham	1666	Wimbledon	Surrey	1538
Willenhall	Stafford	1642	Wimborne, St. Giles	Dorset	1589
Willerby	York	1653	Wimborne-Minster	Dorset	1635
Willersey	Gloucester	[2] 1721	Wimbotsham	Norfolk	1562
Willesborough	Kent	1538	Wimpole	Cambridge	1560
Willesden	Middlesex	1560	Wincanton	Somerset	1636
Willesford	Wilts	1588	Winceby	Lincoln	1579
Willesley	Derby	1677	Winch, East	Norfolk	1678
Willey	Salop	1644	Winch, West	Norfolk	1559
Willey	Warwick	1660	Winchcombe	Gloucester	[7] 1539
Willian	Hertford	1557	Winchelsea	Sussex	1655
Willingale-Spain	Essex	1576	Winchendon, Nether	Buckingham	1563
Willingale-Doe	Essex	1570	Winchendon, Over	Buckingham	1672
Willingdon	Sussex	1560	Winchester, St. Bartholomew Hyde	Hants	1563
Willingham	Cambridge	1559	Cathedral Church		[8] 1599
Willingham by Stowe	Lincoln	1562	St. Cross		1676
Willingham	Suffolk	[3] —	St. John		1595
Willingham	Cambridge	[4] —	St. Lawrence		[9] 1754
Willingham-Cherry	Lancaster	1662	St. Maurice		1575
Willingham, North	Lincoln	1658	St. Michael		[10] 1632
Willingham, South	Lincoln	1711	St. Peter		1595
Willington	Bedford	1676	St. Swithin		[11] 1562
Willington	Derby	1679	St. Thomas		1678
Willisham	Suffolk	1558	Winchfield	Hants	[12] 1659
Williton	Somerset	1792	Wincle	Chester	[13] —
Willoughby	Lincoln	1538	Windermere	Westmorland	1617
Willoughby	Warwick	1625	Windlesham	Surrey	[14] 1677
Willoughby - in - the-Wolds.	Nottingham	[5] 1680	Windrush	Gloucester	1586
Willoughby, Silk	Lincoln	1561	Windsor, New	Berks	1559
Willoughby - Water-less.	Leicester	1559	Windsor, Old	Berks	1754
			Winestead	York	[15] 1578
Willoughton	Lincoln	1599	Winfarthing	Norfolk	1614
Wilmington	Kent	1683	Winford	Somerset	1655
Wilmington	Sussex	1538	Winford-Eagle	Dorset	[16] —
Wilmslow	Chester	1558	Winforton	Hereford	1690
Wilne	Derby	1540	Winfrith-Newburgh	Dorset	1585
Wilsford	Lincoln	1668	Wing	Buckingham	[17] 1546
Wilsford	Wilts	1618	Wing	Rutland	1625

[1] **P** (Marriages only) 1659–1812, Nottinghamshire Parish Registers, vol. 7, 1905.
[2] **P** (Marriages only) 1723–1812. Gloucestershire Parish Registers, vol. 6, 1900.
[3] Included in the Registers of North Cove (q.v.).
[4] Included in the Registers of Carleton (q.v.).
[5] **P** (Marriages only) 1682–1812. Nottinghamshire Parish Registers, vol. 7, 1905.
[6] **P** 1558–1837. Edited by J. H. Spencer, Taunton, 1890.
[7] **P** (Marriages only) 1539–1812. Gloucestershire Parish Registers, vol. 9, 1903.
[8] **P** 1159–1812. Hampshire Parish Registers, vol. 4, 1902.
[9] **P** (Marriages only) 1754–1812. Hampshire Parish Registers, vol. 5, 1903.
[10] **P** (Marriages only) 1632–1812. Hampshire Parish Registers, vol. 5, 1903.
[11] **P** (Marriages only) 1564–1812. Hampshire Parish Registers, vol. 4, 1902.
[12] **P** (Marriages only) 1660–1812. Hampshire Parish Registers, vol. 3, 1902.
[13] Included in the Registers of Prestbury (q.v.).
[14] **P** 1677–1783. Edited by W. Glanville-Richards, London, 1881.
[15] **P** 1578–1811. Yorkshire Parish Register Society, vol. 5, 1900.
[16] Included in the Registers of Troller-Fratrum (q.v.).
[17] **P** (Marriages only) 1546–1812. Buckinghamshire Parish Registers, vol. 3, 1907.

Parish.	County.	Date of Earliest Entry.	Parish.	County.	Date of Earliest Entry.
Wingerworth - -	Derby - -	1539	Winthorpe - -	Lincoln - -	1572
Wingfield -	Suffolk - -	1538	Winthorpe - -	Nottingham -	⁴ 1687
Wingfield, North -	Derby - -	1567	Wintringham - -	York - -	1690
Wingfield, South -	Derby - -	1585	Winwick - -	Huntingdon and	1538
Wingham - -	Kent - -	1568		Northampton.	
Wingrave - -	Buckingham -	1550	Winwick - -	Lancaster -	1563
Winkbourne - -	Nottingham -	1727	Winwick - -	Northampton -	1563
Winkfield - -	Berks - -	1577	Wirksworth - -	Derby - -	1608
Winkfield - -	Wilts - -	1654	Wisbech, St. Peter	Cambridge -	1558
Winkleigh - -	Devon - -	1569	St. Mary	- - -	1557
Winksley - -	York - -	¹ —	Wisborough-Green -	Sussex - -	1560
Winnall - - -	Hants - -	1680	Wishaw - - -	Warwick - -	1688
Winnow, St. - -	Cornwall -	² 1622	Wishford, Great -	Wilts - -	1559
Winscombe - -	Somerset -	1662	Wisley - - -	Surrey - -	1666
Winsford - -	Somerset - -	1660	Wispington - -	Lincoln - -	1662
Winsham - -	Somerset -	1559	Wissett - - -	Suffolk - -	1559
Winslade - •	Hants - -	³ 1723	Wistanstow - -	Salop - -	1687
Winsley - -	Wilts - -	1724	Wistaston - -	Chester -	1572
Winslow - -	Buckingham -	1560	Wiston - - -	Suffolk - -	1538
Winster - - -	Derby - -	1632	Wiston - - -	Sussex - -	1638
Winster - -	Westmorland -	1720	Wiston - - -	Pembroke -	1715
Winston - -	Durham - -	1572	Wistow - - -	Huntingdon -	1629
Winston - -	Suffolk - -	1558	Wistow - - -	Leicester - -	1586
Winstone - -	Gloucester -	1577	Wistow - - -	York - -	1590
Winterbourne - -	Gloucester -	1600	Witcham - - -	Cambridge -	1633
Winterbourne, St.	Dorset - -	1653	Witchampton - -	Dorset - -	1656
Martin.			Witchford - -	Cambridge -	1725
Winterbourne-Abbas -	Dorset - -	1754	Witchingham, Great -	Norfolk - -	1539
Winterbourne - Ander-			Witchingham, Little -	Norfolk - -	1565
stone. See Ander-			Witchling - -	Kent - -	1717
stone, Winterbourne.			Witcombe, Great -	Gloucester -	1749
Winterbourne-Bassett	Wilts - -	1709	Witham - - -	Essex - -	1669
Winterbourne-Came -	Dorset - -	1756	Witham-Friary -	Somerset -	1684
Winterbourne - Clen-	Dorset - -	1684	Witham, North - -	Lincoln - -	1592
stone.			Witham-on-the-Hill -	Lincoln - -	1670
Winterbourne-Dantsey	Wilts - -	1560	Witham, South - -	Lincoln - -	1686
Winterbourne-Earls -	Wilts - -	1557	Withcall - - -	Lincoln - -	1576
Winterbourne-Gunner	Wilts - -	1573	Withcote - - -	Leicester - -	1679
Winterbourne-Hough-	Dorset - -	1558	Witheridge - -	Devon - -	1585
ton.			Witherley - -	Leicester - -	1564
Winterbourne - King-	Dorset - -	1588	Withern - - -	Lincoln - -	1558
ston.			Withernsea - -	York - -	⁵ —
Winterbourne-Monkton	Dorset - -	1756	Withernwick - -	York - -	1653
Winterbourne-Monkton	Wilts - -	1670	Withersdale - -	Suffolk - -	1653
Winterbourne-Steeple-	Dorset - -	1558	Withersfield - -	Suffolk - -	1558
ton.			Witherslack - -	Westmorland -	1670
Winterbourne-Stoke -	Wilts - -	1726	Withiel - - -	Cornwall -	⁶ 1567
Winterbourne - Stick-	Dorset - -	1615	Withiel-Florey -	Somerset -	1696
land.			Withington - -	Gloucester -	1609
Winterbourne - Whit-	Dorset - -	1600	Withington - -	Hereford -	1573
church.			Withington - -	Salop - -	⁷ 1591
Winterbourne-Zelstone	Dorset - -	1548	Withybrook - -	Warwick - -	1653
Winteringham - -	Lincoln - -	1562	Withycombe - -	Somerset -	1669
Winterslow - -	Wilts - -	1598	Withycombe - Raw-	Devon - -	1754
Winterton - -	Lincoln - -	1558	leigh.		
Winterton - -	Norfolk - -	1717	Withyham - -	Sussex - -	1663

¹ Included in the Registers of Ripon (q.v.).
² P (Marriages only) 1622–1812. Cornwall Parish Registers, vol. 10, 1906.
³ P (Marriages only) 1723–1812. Hampshire Parish Registers, vol. 2, 1900.
⁴ P (Marriages only) 1695–1812. Nottinghamshire Parish Registers, vol. 4, 1902.
⁵ Included in the Registers of Hollym (q.v.).
⁶ P (Marriages only) 1568–1812. Cornwall Parish Registers, vol. 6, 1904.
⁷ P 1591–1812. Shropshire Parish Register Society, vol. 5, 1904 (Lichfield Diocese).

Parish.	County.	Date of Earliest Entry.	Parish.	County.	Date of Earliest Entry.
Withypool - -	Somerset -	1613	Wolves-Newton - -	Monmouth -	[10] 1680
Witley - - -	Surrey -	1653	Wolvey - -	Warwick -	1653
Witley, Great -	Worcester -	1538	Wolviston - -	Durham -	1759
Witley, Little -	Worcester -	1680	Wombourne - -	Stafford -	1570
Witnesham - -	Suffolk -	1538	Wombridge - -	Salop -	1721
Witney - - -	Oxford -	1578	Womenswold - -	Kent -	[11] 1574
Witston - - -	Monmouth -	1728	Womersley - -	York -	1564
Wittenham, Little -	Berks -	1538	Wonastow - -	Monmouth -	1674
Wittenham, Long -	Berks -	1557	Wonersh - -	Surrey -	1539
Wittering, East -	Sussex -	1658	Wonston - -	Hants -	[12] 1570
Wittering, West -	Sussex -	1622	Wooburn - -	Buckingham -	1653
Wittersham - -	Kent -	1550	Wood-Dalling -	Norfolk -	1653
Witton - - -	Chester -	1561	Wood-Eaton - -	Oxford -	1539
Witton - - -	Huntingdon -	1633	Wood-Norton -	Norfolk -	1722
Witton (near Norwich)	Norfolk -	[1] 1571	Wood-Rising - -	Norfolk -	1561
Witton - - -	Norfolk -	1721	Woodbastwick -	Norfolk -	[13] 1558
Witton, East - -	York -	1671	Woodborough -	Nottingham -	1547
Witton-Gilbert -	Durham -	1571	Woodborough -	Wilts -	1567
Witton-le-Wear -	Durham -	1558	Woodbridge -	Suffolk -	1545
Witton-Nether -	Northumberland	1696	Woodbury - -	Devon -	1557
Witton, West -	York -	1570	Woodchester -	Gloucester -	1563
Wiveliscombe -	Somerset -	1558	Woodchurch -	Chester -	1572
Wivesfield - -	Sussex -	1559	Woodchurch -	Kent -	1538
Wivenhoe - -	Essex -	1560	Woodcott - -	Hants -	1764
Wiveton - -	Norfolk -	1558	Woodford-Halse -	Northampton -	1619
Wix - - -	Essex -	1686	Woodford - -	Northampton -	1680
Wixford - -	Warwick -	[2] —	Woodford - -	Wilts -	1538
Woburn - -	Bedford -	1558	Woodford - -	Essex -	1638
Woking - -	Surrey -	1653	Woodhall - -	Lincoln -	1562
Wokingham -	Berks and Wilts	1674	Woodham-Ferrers -	Essex -	1558
Wolborough - -	Devon -	1558	Woodham-Mortimer -	Essex -	1664
Woldingham -	Surrey -	[3] 1765	Woodham-Walter -	Essex -	1568
Wolferlow - -	Hereford -	1629	Woodhay, East -	Hants -	[14] 1610
Wolferton - -	Norfolk -	[4] 1653	Woodhay, West -	Berks -	1656
Wolfhamcote -	Warwick -	1558	Woodhead - -	Chester -	1782
Wolford - -	Warwick -	[5] 1654	Woodhorn - -	Northumberland	1605
Wollaton - -	Nottingham -	[6] 1576	Woodhouse - -	Leicester -	1623
Woollaston - -	Northampton -	1663	Woodhurst - -	Huntingdon -	1653
Woollaston - -	Salop -	[7] —	Woodkirk, or West Ardsley.	York -	1652
Wolsingham -	Durham -	1655	Woodland - -	Devon -	1560
Wolstanton -	Stafford -	1628	Woodland - -	Lancaster -	[15] —
Wolston - -	Warwick -	1558	Woodleigh - -	Devon -	1663
Wolterton - -	Norfolk -	1560	Woodmancote -	Hants -	[16] 1762
Wolverhampton -	Stafford -	1603	Woodmancote -	Sussex -	1582
Wolverley - -	Worcester -	1539	Woodmansterne -	Surrey -	1566
Wolverton - -	Warwick -	[8] 1680	Woodnesborough -	Kent -	1561
Wolverton - -	Hants -	[9] 1717			

[1] **P** (Marriages only) 1582–1812. Norfolk Parish Registers, vol. 1, 1899.
[2] Included in the Registers of Exhall (*q.v.*).
[3] **P** 1765–1812. Surrey Parish Register Society, vol. 4, 1906.
[4] **P** (Marriages only) 1653–1812. Norfolk Parish Registers, vol. 2, 1900.
[5] Bishop's Transcripts commence, 1612.
[6] **P** (Marriages only) 1578–1812. Nottinghamshire Parish Registers, vol. 8, 1905.
[7] Included in the Registers of Alberbury (*q.v.*).
[8] Bishop's Transcripts commence 1614.
[9] **P** (Marriages only) 1717–1812. Hampshire Parish Registers, vol. 8, 1906.
[10] One mutilated book only.
[11] **P** 1574–1812. Edited by Rev. C. H. Wilkie, Canterbury, 1898.
[12] **P** (Marriages only) 1570–1812. Hampshire Parish Registers, vol. 9, 1907.
[13] **P** (Marriages only) 1561–1813. Norfolk Parish Registers, vol. 3, 1907.
[14] **P** (Marriages only) 1618–1812. Hampshire Parish Register Society, vol. 9, 1907.
[15] Included in the Registers of Kirkby-Ireleth (*q.v.*).
[16] **P** (Marriages only) 1772–1812. Hampshire Parish Registers, vol. 9, 1907.

Parish.	County.	Date of Earliest Entry.	Parish.	County.	Date of Earliest Entry.
Woodplumpton - -	Lancaster -	[1] 1604	Wootton, North -	Somerset - -	1563
Woodsford - -	Dorset - -	1695	Wootton Rivers -	Wilts - -	1728
Woodstone -	Huntingdon -	1559	Wootton, South -	Norfolk - -	1556
Woodstock - -	Oxford - -	1653	Wootton-Underwood -	Buckingham -	1599
Woodton - -	Norfolk - -	1538	Wootton-Wawen -	Warwick - -	1547
Wookey -	Somerset - -	1565	Worcester, St. Albans-	Worcester -	[7] 1630
Wool - - -	Dorset - -	1736	All Saints - -	- - -	1560
Woolastone -	Gloucester -	1696	St. Andrew -	- - -	[8] 1656
Woolavington -	Somerset - -	1694	St. Clement -	- - -	[9] 1694
Woolbeding -	Sussex - -	1581	St. Helen -	- - -	[10] 1538
Wooler -	Northumberland	1692	St. Martin - -	- - -	[11] 1538
Woolfardisworthy West.	Devon - -	1723	St. Nicholas -	- - -	1563
			St. Oswald's Hos-	- - -	1695
Woolfardisworthy (near Crediton).	Devon - -	1664	pital.		
			St. Peter the Great	- - -	[12] 1686
Woolhampton -	Berks - -	1636	St. Swithin -	- - -	1538
Woolhope -	Hereford -	1558	Cathedral Church	- - -	1693
Wolland -	Dorset - -	1726	Wordwell - -	Suffolk - -	[13] 1581
Woollavington -	Sussex - -	1668	Worfield - -	Salop - -	1562
Woolley -	Huntingdon -	1576	Workington - -	Cumberland -	1663
Woolley - - -	York - -	1651	Worksop - -	Nottingham -	[14] 1558
Woolley -	Somerset - -	1560	Worlaby - -	Lincoln - -	1559
Woolpit - -	Suffolk - -	1558	Worldham, East -	Hants - -	1690
Woolstaston - -	Salop - -	[2] 1601	Worldham, West -	Hants - -	1649
Woolsthorpe -	Lincoln - -	1688	Worle - -	Somerset -	1712
Woolston - -	Berks - -	[3] —	Worlingham -	Suffolk - -	1538
Woolston, Great -	Buckingham -	1538	Worlington - -	Suffolk - -	1719
Woolston, Little -	Buckingham -	1558	Worlington, East -	Devon - -	1725
Woolstone -	Gloucester -	1563	Worlington, West -	Devon - -	1681
Woolvercott - -	Oxford - -	1596	Worlingworth -	Suffolk - -	1558
Woolverstone -	Suffolk - -	1539	Wormbridge -	Hereford -	1753
Woolverston - -	Buckingham -	1599	Wormegay - -	Norfolk - -	1561
Woolverton -	Somerset -	1754	Wormhill - -	Derby - -	1674
Woolwich - -	Kent - -	1669	Wormingford -	Essex - -	1557
Wootton (Isle of Wight).	Hants - -	1760	Worminghall - -	Buckingham -	1538
			Wormington - -	Gloucester -	[15] 1719
Wootton -	Bedford - -	1562	Wormleighton -	Warwick - -	1586
Wootton -	Berks - -	1657	Wormley - -	Hertford - -	1674
Wootton -	Hants - -	[4] 1560	Wormshill - -	Kent - -	1717
Wootton -	Kent - -	1546	Wormsley - -	Hereford -	1595
Wootton -	Lincoln - -	1563	Worplesdon -	Surrey - -	1570
Wootton -	Northampton -	1797	Worsall, High -	York - -	1726
Wootton -	Oxford - -	1564	Worsbrough -	York - -	1559
Wootton-Bassett -	Wilts - -	1591	Worstead - -	Norfolk - -	1558
Wootton-Courtney -	Somerset - -	1558	Worth - -	Kent - -	1720
Wootton-Fitzpaine -	Dorset - -	1678	Worth - -	Sussex - -	1600
Wootton-Glanville -	Dorset - -	1546	Worth-Matravers -	Dorset - -	1762
Wootton-Leek -	Warwick - -	[5] 1581	Wortham - -	Suffolk - -	1538
Wootton, North -	Dorset - -	[6] 1539	Worthen - -	Salop - -	1558
Wootton, North -	Norfolk - -	1654	Worthenbury -	Flint - -	1597

[1] **P** 1604-1613. Chetham Society, vol. 25, New Series.
[2] **P** 1601-1812. Shropshire Parish Register Society, vol. 1 (Hereford Diocese).
[3] Included in the Registers of Uffington (*q.v.*).
[4] **P** (Marriages only) 1560-1812. Hampshire Parish Registers, vol. 1, 1899.
[5] **P** 1685-1742. Edited by Sir Thomas Phillipps.—Index to same by F. A. Crisp.
[6] **P** 1539-1786. Edited by Rev. C. H. Mayo, 1877.
[7] **P** 1630-1812. Parish Register Society, vol. 2, 1896.
[8] Bishop's Transcripts commence 1612. [9] Bishop's Transcripts commence 1609.
[10] **P** 1538-1812. Edited by J. B. Wilson, London, 1900.
[11] Two volumes of marriages are missing, viz.: 1754-1762 and 1762-1776.
[12] **P** 1580-1850. Edited by Rev. S. H. A. Hervey, 1903. [13] Bishop's Transcripts commence 1614.
[14] **P** 1558-1771. Edited by G. W. Marshall, 1894.
[15] **P** (Marriages only) 1719-1812. Gloucestershire Parish Registers, vol. 4, 1898.

Parish.	County.	Date of Earliest Entry.	Parish.	County.	Date of Earliest Entry.
Worthing - -	Norfolk -	1653	Wycombe, West -	Buckingham -	1581
Worthington - -	Leicester -	1759	Wyddial - - -	Hertford - -	1666
Worthy-Headbourn -	Hants - -	1616	Wye - - -	Kent - -	1538
Worthy, King's - -	Hants - -	1538	Wyfordby - -	Leicester - -	1557
Worthy-Martyr's -	Hants - -	1542	Wyham - -	Lincoln - -	1695
Worting - -	Hants - -	[1] 1604	Wyke-Champflower -	Somerset - -	1625
Wortley - -	York - -	1678	Wyke-Regis - -	Dorset - -	1676
Worton-Nether - -	Oxford - -	1562	Wykeham - - -	York - -	1653
Wotton - -	Surrey - -	1596	Wyken - - -	Warwick - -	1600
Wotton-under-Edge -	Gloucester -	1571	Wylye - - -	Wilts - -	1581
Woughton - on - the - Green.	Buckingham -	[2] 1558	Wymering - -	Hants - -	1738
			Wymeswold - -	Leicester -	1560
Wouldham - -	Kent - -	1538	Wymington - -	Bedford - -	1662
Wrabness - -	Essex - -	1650	Wymondham - -	Leicester -	1538
Wragby - -	Lincoln - -	1567	Wymondham - -	Norfolk - -	1614
Wragby - -	York - -	1540	Wymondley, Great -	Hertford -	1561
Wramplingham -	Norfolk - -	1566	Wymondley, Little -	Hertford - -	1650
Wrangle - -	Lincoln -	1653	Wyrardisbury, or Wraysbury.	Buckingham -	1734
Wratting, Great -	Suffolk - -	1593			
Wratting, Little -	Suffolk - -	1555	Wyresdale - - -	Lancaster -	1737
Wratting, West - -	Cambridge -	1579	Wysall - - -	Nottingham -	[7] 1654
Wrawby - -	Lincoln - -	1715	Wythall - - -	Worcester -	[8] 1760
Wraxall - -	Dorset - -	[3] —	Wytham - - -	Berks - -	1559
Wraxall - -	Somerset - -	[4] 1562	Wythburn - - -	Cumberland -	1777
Wraxall, North - -	Wilts - -	1677	Wythop - - -	Cumberland -	1792
Wraxall, South -	Wilts - -	1676	Wyverstone - -	Suffolk - -	1560
Wraysbury. See Wyrardisbury.					
Wreay - - -	Cumberland -	1750			
Wrenbury - -	Chester - -	1684			
Wreningham, Great and Little.	Norfolk - -	1656			
Wrentham - -	Suffolk - -	1602	**Y.**		
Wressell - -	York - -	1724			
Wrestlingworth -	Bedford - -	1578	Yalding - - -	Kent - -	1559
Wretham, East -	Norfolk - -	1748	Yanworth - - -	Gloucester -	1695
Wretton - - -	Norfolk - -	1693	Yapham - - -	York - -	1654
Wrexham - -	Denbigh - -	1618	Yapton - - -	Sussex - -	1539
Wrington - - -	Somerset -	1538	Yarburgh - - -	Lincoln - -	1561
Writhlington - -	Somerset - -	1675	Yarcombe - - -	Devon - -	1551
Writtle - - -	Essex - -	1634	Yardley. See Ardeley.		
Wrockwardine -	Salop - -	[5] 1591	Yardley - - -	Worcester -	1539
Wroot - - -	Lincoln - -	1573	Yardley-Hastings -	Northampton -	1558
Wrotham - -	Kent - -	1558	Yarkhill - - -	Hereford - -	1559
Wroughton - -	Wilts - -	1653	Yarlington - - -	Somerset -	1654
Wroxall - -	Warwick -	[6] 1586	Yarm - - -	York - -	1649
Wroxeter - -	Salop - -	1613	Yarmouth (Isle of Wight).	Hants - -	1614
Wroxham - -	Norfolk - -	1558			
Wroxton - -	Oxford - -	1548	Yarmouth, Great -	Norfolk - -	1558
Wyberton - -	Lincoln - -	1538	Yarnscombe - -	Devon - -	1653
Wybunbury - -	Chester - -	1558	Yarnton - - -	Oxford - -	1569
Wycliffe - - -	York - -	1681	Yarpole - - -	Hereford -	1561
Wycombe - -	Leicester -	1700	Yarwell - - -	Northampton -	1572
Wycombe, High -	Buckingham -	1674			

[1] **P** (Marriages only) 1604–1812. Hampshire Parish Registers, vol. 5, 1903.
[2] **P** 1558–1718. Buckingham Parish Register Society, vol. 5.
[3] Included in the Registers of Rampisham (*q.v.*).
[4] **P** (Marriages only) 1562–1812. Somersetshire Parish Registers, vol. 4, 1902.
[5] **P** 1591–1791. Shropshire Parish Register Society, vol. 8 (Lichfield Diocese).
[6] **P** 1586–1812, in supplement to "Records of Wroxall," by J. W. Ryland, 1903.
[7] **P** (Marriages only) 1654–1812. Nottinghamshire Parish Registers, vol. 7, 1905.
[8] Earlier entries in the Registers of King's Norton (*q.v.*).

Parish.	County.	Date of Earliest Entry.	Parish.	County.	Date of Earliest Entry.
Yate - - - -	Gloucester -	1660	York—continued.		
Yateley - -	Hants - -	[1] 1636	St. Mary, Bishops-hill, Jun.	- - -	1602
Yatesbury - - -	Wilts - -	1706	St. Mary, Castle-gate.	- - -	1604
Yattendon - -	Berks - -	1558			
Yatton - - -	Somerset -	1675	St. Maurice - -	- - -	1647
Yatton-Keynell -	Wilts - -	[2] 1653	St. Michael - le -	- - -	[6] 1565
Yaverland (Isle of Wight).	Hants - -	1632	Belfry.		
Yaxham - - -	Norfolk - -	1686	St. Michael, Spur-rier Gate.	- - -	1598
Yaxley - - -	Huntingdon -	1653	St. Olave, Mary-gate.	- - -	1538
Yaxley - - -	Suffolk - -	1684			
Yazor - - -	Hereford -	1621	St. Sampson - -	- - -	1640
Yealmpton - -	Devon - -	1600	St. Saviour - -	- - -	1567
Yeddingham - -	York - -	1717	Holy Trinity, Goodramgate.	- - -	1573
Yeldham, Great -	Essex - -	1653			
Yeldham, Little -	Essex - -	1564	Holy Trinity, King's Court.	- - -	1616
Yelling - -	Huntingdon -	1583			
Yelvertoft - - -	Northampton -	1573	Holy Trinity, Micklegate.	- - -	[7] 1586
Yelverton - -	Norfolk - -	1559			
Yeovil - - -	Somerset - -	1563	Youlgreave - -	Derby -	1558
Yeovilton - -	Somerset -	[3] 1653	Yoxall - -	Stafford -	1645
Yetminster - - -	Dorset - -	1677	Yoxford - - -	Suffolk -	1559
Yielden - - -	Bedford - -	1653	Yscifiog - -	Flint -	1662
Ynyscynhaiarn -	Carnarvon -	1754	Yspytty-Cynfyn -	Cardigan -	1754
York Minster - -	York - -	[4] 1634	Yspytty-Ivan - -	Denbigh -	1732
All Saints - -	- - -	1577	Yspytty-Ystwyth -	Cardigan -	1781
All Saints, Pave-ment.	- - -	1554	Ystrad - -	Cardigan -	1798
St. Crux - -	- - -	1540	Ystradfellte -	Brecon -	1737
St. Cuthbert -	- - -	1581	Ystradgunlais -	Brecon-	1721
St. Denis - -	- - -	1558	Ystradowen - -	Glamorgan -	1757
St. Helen, Stone-gate.	- - -	1568	Ystradyfodwg -	Glamorgan -	1735
St. John, Mickle-gate.	- - -	1570			
St. Lawrence -	- - -	1606			
St. Margaret, Walmgate.	- - -	1558			
St. Martin, Coney St.	- - -	1557	**Z.**		
St. Martin, Mickle-gate.	- - -	[5] 1539			
St. Mary, Bishops-hill.	- - -	1598	Zeal-Monachorum -	Devon -	1594
			Zennor - -	Cornwall-	[8] 1592

[1] **P** (Marriages only) 1636–1812. Hampshire Parish Registers, vol. 2, 1900.
[2] **P** (Marriages only) 1653–1812. Wiltshire Parish Registers, vol. 1, 1905.
[3] **P** (Marriages only) 1655–1802. Somersetshire Parish Registers, vol. 2, 1899.
[4] **P** 1634–1836. Yorkshire Archæological Society, vols. 1, 2, 3, and 6.
[5] **P** 1539–1653. Edited by E. Bulmer, 1893.
[6] **P** 1565–1778. Yorkshire Parish Register Society, vol. 1, 1899 ; vol. 2, 1901.
[7] **P** 1586–1653. Edited by W. H. F. Bateman, 1893.
[8] **P** (Marriages only) 1617–1812. Cornwall Parish Registers, vol. 9, 1906.